Modern American Literature

Edinburgh Critical Guides to Literature
Series Editors: Martin Halliwell, University of Leicester and Andy Mousley, De Montfort University

Published Titles:
Gothic Literature, Andrew Smith
Canadian Literature, Faye Hammill
Women's Poetry, Jo Gill
Contemporary American Drama, Annette J. Saddik
Shakespeare, Gabriel Egan
Asian American Literature, Bella Adams
Children's Literature, M. O. Grenby
Contemporary British Fiction, Nick Bentley
Renaissance Literature, Siobhan Keenan
Scottish Literature, Gerard Carruthers
Contemporary American Fiction, David Brauner
Contemporary British Drama, David Lane
Medieval Literature 1300–1500, Pamela King
Contemporary Poetry, Nerys Williams
Victorian Literature, David Amigoni
Modern American Literature, Catherine Morley
Modernist Literature, Rachel Potter

Forthcoming Titles in the Series:
Restoration and Eighteenth-Century Literature, Hamish Mathison
Romantic Literature, Serena Baiesi
African American Literature, Jennifer Terry
Postcolonial Literature, Dave Gunning

Modern American Literature

Catherine Morley

For my sisters, Deirdre, Elaine and Rachel, whose support during the writing of this book has been immeasurable.

And for Hilary

Edinburgh University Press Ltd
22 George Square, Edinburgh EH8 9LF

www.euppublishing.com

Typeset in 11.5/13 Ehrhardt
by Servis Filmsetting Ltd, Stockport, Cheshire, and
printed and bound in Great Britain by
CPI Group (UK) Ltd, Croydon, CR0 4YY

A CIP record for this book is available from the British Library

ISBN 978 0 7486 2506 2 (hardback)
ISBN 978 0 7486 2507 9 (paperback)
ISBN 978 0 7486 3072 1 (webready PDF)
ISBN 978 0 7486 6829 8 (epub)
ISBN 978 0 7486 6830 4 (Amazon ebook)

Contents

Series Preface

The study of English literature in the early twenty-first century is host to an exhilarating range of critical approaches, theories and historical perspectives. 'English' ranges from traditional modes of study such as Shakespeare and Romanticism to popular interest in national and area literatures such as the United States, Ireland and the Caribbean. The subject also spans a diverse array of genres from tragedy to cyberpunk, incorporates such hybrid fields of study as Asian American literature, Black British literature, creative writing and literary adaptations, and remains eclectic in its methodology.

Such diversity is cause for both celebration and consternation. English is varied enough to promise enrichment and enjoyment for all kinds of readers and to challenge preconceptions about what the study of literature might involve. But how are readers to navigate their way through such literary and cultural diversity? And how are students to make sense of the various literary categories and periodisations, such as modernism and the Renaissance, or the proliferating theories of literature, from feminism and marxism to queer theory and eco-criticism? The Edinburgh Critical Guides to Literature series reflects the challenges and pluralities of English today, but at the same time it offers readers clear and accessible routes through the texts, contexts, genres, historical periods and debates within the subject.

Martin Halliwell and Andy Mousley

Acknowledgements

Debts accumulated over the course of writing a book can be immense, and that is certainly the case with this book. Firstly, I am extremely grateful to my series editors, Martin Halliwell and Andy Mousley, for their extraordinary patience, and for allowing me to complete other projects when I really ought to have been working on this one. Thanks are also due to the production team at Edinburgh University Press, especially Jackie Jones for her encouragement and kindness throughout the process.

Work on this book began when I was an Academic Fellow in the Cultures of Modernism at Oxford Brookes University. I am grateful to the RCUK for the opportunity to get this book started. My colleagues and friends at Brookes have been fantastic inspirations and sounding boards, especially the incomparably clever Steven Matthews and the ever-enthusiastic Alex Goody. At the University of Leicester, I have benefitted enormously from conversations with my colleagues and students on the Modern Literature MA, especially Nick Everett, Sarah Graham, Emma Parker, Martin Stannard and Victoria Stewart. Thanks too to my superb colleagues in the Centre for American Studies: Linda Benson, Jo Curtis, Guy Barefoot, James Campbell, Elizabeth Clapp, Andrew Johnstone, George Lewis and Alex Wadden. The Centre provides a tremendously positive working environment, which has only made the completion of this project that little bit easier. And I am lucky that one of my series editors, Martin

Halliwell, is not just a colleague at Leicester but a wonderfully supportive friend.

Further afield, I thank all my former BAAS Executive Committee colleagues for their advice and support. I am particularly grateful to Ian Bell for our continuing conversations about Willa Cather and American modernism. For their ongoing support and friendship, I thank Celeste-Marie Bernier, Elleke Boehmer, David Brauner, Anne Marie D'Arcy and Gail Marshall. I've been lucky enough to present papers drawn from my research on various sections of this book at the annual conferences of the Modernist Studies Association, the British Association for American Studies, and the American Literature Association, while I presented some early thoughts at the Rothermere American Institute, University of Oxford. I'm enormously grateful to all the panel organisers, co-speakers and audience members for their wise suggestions.

Finally, I am grateful to my parents, Rhys Sandbrook, Emily and Emer Aherne and my sisters, to whom I dedicate this book, for providing distraction when it was needed and for allowing me to get on with this project when it really mattered.

And above all, I thank my husband, Dominic Sandbrook, for his encouragement, his proofreading skills, his unceasing advice (not all of which I have taken!), and his love – which means everything.

Catherine Morley, University of Leicester

Chronology

Date	Historical events	Literary events
1850		Nathaniel Hawthorne, *The Scarlet Letter*
1851		Herman Melville, *Moby Dick*
1854	Elevator brake demonstrated at Crystal Palace Exhibition	
1855		Walt Whitman, *Leaves of Grass*
1861	American Civil War begins (lasting until 1865)	
1862	Homestead Act	
1865	Reconstruction begins (lasting until 1877)	
1866	First transatlantic telegraph cable	
1867	Invention of the typewriter	
1876	John Wesley Hyatt invents celluloid	Mark Twain, *The Adventures of Tom Sawyer*
1877	Invention of first phonograph record player	

Date	Historical events	Literary events
1879	Invention of first long-burning electric light bulb	
	Development of dry-plate photography	
1880		Henry James, *Washington Square*
		Henry Adams, *Democracy: An American Novel*
1881		Henry James, *The Portrait of a Lady*
1882	Invention of flexible roll film	
1883	Opening of the Brooklyn Bridge	
1884		Henry Adams, *Esther*
1885		Mark Twain, *The Adventures of Huckleberry Finn*
1886	Creation of Coca-Cola	Henry James, *The Princess Casamassima*
	Unveiling of the Statue of Liberty	Henry James, *The Bostonians*
1888	Invention of fixed-focus camera	
	First revolving door	
1890	Completion of the *New York World* Building	
1891	Thomas Edison patents the Kinetoscope	
	Unveiling of first escalator	
1892	Omaha Convention	Charlotte Perkins Gilman, *The Yellow Wallpaper*
1893	Stock Market Crash	
	World's Columbian Exposition, Chicago	

Date	Historical events	Literary events
1895	Booker T. Washington delivers Atlanta Compromise speech	
1896	Plessy v. Ferguson Supreme Court ruling	Sarah Orne Jewett, *The Country of the Pointed Firs*
1897	Klondike Gold Rush begins	Henry James, *What Maisie Knew*
1898	Spanish-American War	
1899		Kate Chopin, *The Awakening* Thorstein Veblen, *The Theory of the Leisure Class*
1900		Theodore Dreiser, *Sister Carrie*
1901	Assassination of President William McKinley	Booker T. Washington, *Up From Slavery*
1902	United Mine Workers Strike Completion of the Flatiron Building in NYC	Ellen Glasgow, *The Battle-Ground* Henry James, *The Wings of the Dove*
1903	Wright Brothers fly first heavier-than-air machine	W. E. B. Du Bois, *The Souls of Black Folk* Gertrude Stein, *Q.E.D.* Henry James, *The Ambassadors*
1904	Opening of New York City subway	Henry James, *The Golden Bowl*
1905	IWW Union ('Wobblies') set up in Chicago W. E. B. Du Bois founds the Niagara Movement Albert Einstein publishes special theory of relativity	Willa Cather, *The Troll Garden* Edith Wharton, *The House of Mirth*
1906	Atlanta Race Riots	
1907	Financial Panic of 1907	Henry Adams, *The Education of Henry Adams* (privately published)

Date	Historical events	Literary events
		Henry James, *The American Scene*
1908	First Model T Ford produced	
1909	NAACP founded by W.E.B. Du Bois and others	Gertrude Stein, *Three Lives*
		William Carlos Williams, *Poems*
1910	Great Migration of African Americans begins	Ezra Pound, *The Spirit of Romance*
1911	Triangle Factory Fire	Edith Wharton, *Ethan Frome*
1912	Founding of *Poetry* magazine	Willa Cather, *Alexander's Bridge*
	Sinking of the Titanic	Theodore Dreiser, *The Financier*
	Woodrow Wilson elected President	James Weldon Johnson, *The Autobiography of an Ex-Colored Man*
1913	New York Armory Show	Willa Cather *O Pioneers!*
	Completion of the Woolworth Building	Ellen Glasgow, *Virginia*
	First English translation of Sigmund Freud, *The Interpretation of Dreams*	Edith Wharton, *The Custom and the Country*
1914	Outbreak of the First World War	Gertrude Stein, *Tender Buttons*
		Theodore Dreiser, *The Titan*
1915	Albert Einstein, *General Theory of Relativity*	T. S. Eliot, 'The Love Song of J. Alfred Prufrock'
	D. W. Griffith, *The Birth of a Nation*	Theodore Dreiser, *The 'Genius'*
	Completion of Equitable Building	Susan Glaspell, *Suppressed Desires*
1916		H. D. *Sea Garden*
		Amy Lowell, *Men, Women, and Ghosts*

Date	Historical events	Literary events
		Susan Glaspell, *Trifles*
1917	United States enters First World War	Ezra Pound, *The Cantos*
	Society of Independent Artists' Exhibition	T. S. Eliot, *Prufrock and Other Observations*
		Edith Wharton, *Summer*
1918	First World War ends	Willa Cather, *My Ántonia*
		Theodore Dreiser, *Free and Other Stories*
		Edith Wharton, *The Marne*
		Henry Adams, *The Education of Henry Adams* (commercial publication)
		James Weldon Johnson, *The Changing Status of Negro Labor*
1919	Prohibition begins	Amy Lowell, *Pictures of the Floating World*
	Founding of the American Communist Party	
	'Red Summer' race riots	
1920	Women in US given the right to vote	F. Scott Fitzgerald, *This Side of Paradise*
	Warren Harding elected President	Eugene O'Neill, *The Emperor Jones*
		Ezra Pound, *Hugh Selwyn Mauberley*
		Edith Wharton, *The Age of Innocence*
		F. Scott Fitzgerald, *Flappers and Philosophers*
		Anzia Yezierska, *Hungry Hearts*
1921	Emergency Quota Immigration Act	John Dos Passos, *Three Soldiers*
		Eugene O'Neill, *Anna Christie*

Date	Historical events	Literary events
1922	Teapot Dome scandal breaks	Willa Cather, *One of Ours* T. S. Eliot, *The Waste Land* Claude McKay, *Harlem Shadows* Eugene O'Neill, *The Hairy Ape* Edith Wharton, *The Glimpses of the Moon*
1923	First issue of *Time* magazine Calvin Coolidge succeeds Harding as President Walt Disney Company founded	Willa Cather, *A Lost Lady* Jean Toomer, *Cane* William Carlos Williams, *Spring and All* Wallace Stevens, *Harmonium* Anzia Yezierska, *Salome of the Tenements*
1924	Johnson-Reed Immigration Act Completion of the Radiator Building	Eugene O'Neill, *Desire Under the Elms* Edith Wharton, *Old New York*
1925	Scopes Trial Coolidge's inauguration is first to be broadcast on radio	Willa Cather, *The Professor's House* Countee Cullen, *Color* John Dos Passos, *Manhattan Transfer* Theodore Dreiser, *An American Tragedy* F. Scott Fitzgerald, *The Great Gatsby* Ernest Hemingway, *In Our Time* Alain Locke, ed., *The New Negro* Gertrude Stein, *The Making of Americans* Anzia Yezierska, *Bread Givers*

Date	Historical events	Literary events
		Ellen Glasgow, *Barren Ground*
1926	Publication of first and only issue of *Fire!!* NBC radio network is launched Sinclair Lewis wins the Pulitzer Prize for *Arrowsmith* (published 1925)	Hart Crane, *White Buildings* William Faulkner, *Soldiers' Pay* Ernest Hemingway, *The Sun Also Rises* Langston Hughes, *The Weary Blues*
1927	Execution of Nicola Sacco and Bartolomeo Vanzetti First transatlantic telephone call (New York-London) Charles Lindbergh makes first solo non-stop transatlantic flight	Willa Cather, *Death Comes for the Archbishop* Countee Cullen, *Copper Sun* Langston Hughes, *Fine Clothes to the Jew*
1928	First regular television programming, New York Mickey Mouse makes sound debut in *Steamboat Willie* Herbert Hoover elected President	Djuna Barnes, *Ryder* and *Ladies Almanack* Nella Larsen, *Quicksand* Claude McKay, *Home to Harlem* (Harmon Gold Award) Eugene O'Neill, *Strange Interlude*
1929	St Valentine's Day Massacre, Chicago Wall Street Crash (24–29 October) Museum of Modern Art opens, New York	Countee Cullen, *The Black Christ and Other Poems* William Faulkner, *The Sound and the Fury* Ellen Glasgow, *They Stooped to Folly: A Comedy of Morals* Ernest Hemingway, *A Farewell to Arms* Nella Larsen, *Passing*

Date	Historical events	Literary events
		Claude McKay, *Banjo*
1930	Chrysler Building is opened	Hart Crane, *The Bridge* John Dos Passos, *The 49th Parallel* (first instalment of *U.S.A.*) William Faulkner, *As I Lay Dying* Twelve Southerners, *I'll Take My Stand: The South and the Agrarian Tradition*
1931	Empire State Building is opened European banking crisis spreads to United States Al Capone sent to prison for tax evasion Scottsboro Boys convicted of rape	William Faulkner, *Sanctuary* Eugene O'Neill, *Mourning Becomes Electra*
1932	Bonus Army protests in Washington, DC American unemployment hits 25% Franklin D. Roosevelt elected President	John Dos Passos, *1919* (second instalment of *U.S.A.*) Ernest Hemingway, *Death in the Afternoon* Langston Hughes, *Dream Keeper*
1933	End of Prohibition Ban on James Joyce's *Ulysses* (1922) lifted Roosevelt launches First New Deal Tennessee Valley Authority created	Ernest Hemingway, *Winner Take Nothing* James Weldon Johnson, *Along this Way* Gertrude Stein, *The Autobiography of Alice B. Toklas* Claude McKay, *Banana Bottom*

Date	Historical events	Literary events
1934	Peak of the Dust Bowl Bonnie and Clyde killed by law officers	Zora Neale Hurston, *Jonah's Gourd Vine* Ezra Pound, *Make it New* Henry Roth, *Call it Sleep*
1935	Harlem Riot Government launches WPA arts projects Establishment of Federal Writers' Project Roosevelt launches Second New Deal	William Faulkner, *Pylon* Ellen Glasgow, *Vein of Iron* Ernest Hemingway, *Green Hills of Africa* Zora Neale Hurston, *Mules and Men* W. E. B. Du Bois, *Black Reconstruction in America*
1936	First costumed comic-book superhero ('The Phantom') Roosevelt re-elected President	Djuna Barnes, *Nightwood* William Faulkner, *Absalom, Absalom!* John Dos Passos, *The Big Money* (final instalment of *U.S.A.*)
1937	Roosevelt tries to 'pack' the Supreme Court Golden Gate Bridge opens, San Francisco Walt Disney's *Snow White and the Seven Dwarfs*	Zora Neale Hurston, *Their Eyes Were Watching God* John Steinbeck, *Of Mice and Men* Richard Wright, 'Blueprint for Negro Writing'
1938	Formation of House Un-American Activities Committee (HUAC) First appearance of Superman Orson Welles's radio broadcast of *War of the Worlds*	William Faulkner, *The Unvanquished* Zora Neale Hurston, *Tell My Horse* Richard Wright, *Uncle Tom's Children*

Date	Historical events	Literary events
1939	New York World's Fair Outbreak of Second World War	William Faulkner, *The Wild Palms* Zora Neale Hurston, *Moses: Man of the Mountain* John Steinbeck, *The Grapes of Wrath*

Introduction: Chicago, 1893

On the first day of May 1893, the World's Columbian Exposition opened to the public on a gigantic 600-acre site in Jackson Park, Chicago. Nobody had ever seen anything like it. From the 'White City' of neoclassical buildings to the hugely popular Ferris wheel, from the replicas of Christopher Columbus's three ships to Frederick Law Olmsted's landscaped layout, it was as though past, present and future had been united in one place. There were carnival rides and log cabins; there were lakes and locomotives; there was a moving walkway and a breech-loaded howitzer. Visitors stared in awe at the world's first fully electric kitchen, which also boasted an automatic dishwasher. Beneath fizzing phosphorescent lamps, they tasted their first Shredded Wheat and Juicy Fruit gum, ate their first hamburgers, listened to Scott Joplin and W. C. Handy, and heard Frederick Jackson Turner outline his famous Frontier thesis. To many of them, it seemed that this was the modern world itself, smouldering with energy and excitement. 'I took in the glories of the Fair with my fingers', the author and activist Helen Keller, who was then just thirteen, wrote later. 'It was a sort of tangible kaleidoscope, this White City of the West.'[1] And for *Harper's*, it was a monument to the accomplishments of a proud nation. 'The genius of the country', the magazine declared, 'has created a work of surpassing grandeur which should not be permitted to pass away without having exerted to the widest extent its enlightening and elevating influences upon the living generation.'[2]

For one visitor, however, the sheer modernity of the Fair was deeply unsettling. In Chicago, wrote the historian and autobiographer Henry Adams, he had 'found matter of study to fill a hundred years, and his education spread over chaos'. Adams had always thought himself a man of learning; now, however, he reeled before the sheer abundance of technological marvels. For the first time, he felt genuinely overwhelmed by the shock of the new:

> Men who knew nothing whatever – who had never run a steam-engine, the simplest of forces – who had never put their hands on a lever – had never touched an electric battery – never talked through a telephone, and had not the shadow of a notion what amount of force was meant by a watt or an *ampere* or an *erg*, or any other term of measurement introduced within a hundred years – had no choice but to sit down on the steps and brood as they had never brooded on the benches of Harvard College, either as student or professor, aghast at what they had said and done in all these years, and still more ashamed of the childlike ignorance and babbling futility of the society that let them say and do it. The historical mind can think only in historical processes, and probably this was the first time since historians existed, that any of them had sat down helpless before a mechanical sequence.[3]

Where, he wondered, would it all lead? Where were the American people heading? The answer, he decided, was that 'they probably knew no more than he did'; they were like lost mariners, tossed hither and thither by the currents of technological change, adrift in a world of chaos.

Henry Adams's reaction to the Chicago exposition is often taken as the supreme example of what we call the 'shock of the new': the unsettling, bewildering experience of modernity itself. And in many ways, this book explores how a generation of American novelists, poets and dramatists found their own ways of addressing the challenges of the modern world. Like Adams, writers as diverse as Ezra Pound, H. D., T. S. Eliot, F. Scott Fitzgerald and Susan Glaspell found themselves confronting a world distorted by the experience of industrialisation, capitalism and urbanism. The plates seemed to be shifting beneath their feet. From Einstein's theory of relativity to Freud's ideas about the unconscious, from Darwin's notion of evolution to Marx's predictions about the coming revolution, bracing, even shocking new ideas were shaking the complacent assumptions of the Victorian era. In an age of dizzying technological change, how could writers and artists possibly hope to capture reality? How could the codes and conventions of realist writing possibly capture the chaos and confusion of the modern world? How could the individual consciousness do justice to the complexity of existence, the play of sensations, the sheer texture of experience? And in an age increasingly defined by the shattering experience of total war, how could the values of the past have any meaning for a generation suffering from a kind of cultural shell shock?

In their responses to these challenges, the writers and artists who flourished between the 1890s and the 1930s produced what we now call modernism. Not all major American writers of the age were experimental modernists; almost all of them, however, were influenced by modernism, or at least addressed some of the same concerns. The word 'modernism' is notoriously slippery; even now, critics argue fiercely about what it means. One very simple definition might be that it simply denotes anything written in the late nineteenth and early twentieth centuries, but of course that does not get us very far. Another might be that it denotes a rejection of the Victorian past and an enthusiasm for a technological future. 'Make it new!', exclaimed Ezra Pound, one of the movement's founding fathers – and yet Pound himself, as we shall see, was profoundly influenced by the legacy of the past. Indeed, far from rejecting their Victorian forebears, many American modernists actively embraced them. And modernism was not the same thing as mere novelty; most modernists spent a surprising amount of time looking over their shoulders, and many were fascinated, even obsessed, with the mythology of the classical world. What united them was partly their self-consciousness about their own art – most modernists went out of their way to draw attention to their own influences, borrowings, allusions and experiments – and their fascination with particular themes. Modernists often wrote about the tension between past and future. They wrote about the confusing experience of life in the city, the bewilderment of diversity, the fragmentation of identity and the excitement of forging a new identity. In the aftermath of the First World War, they often saw society in the throes of disintegration, the old assumptions collapsing like crumbling walls. They often saw language itself as inadequate; they undermined the idea of the steady, reliable individual consciousness; they questioned the nature of rationality itself. At first glance, many of their texts are 'a heap of broken images', to borrow the words of T. S. Eliot's great poem *The Waste Land* (1922). And perhaps this, above all, was the key to modernism. It seemed that everything had been broken; broken by capitalism, by technology, by social change and above all by the war. What they were doing, often tentatively, and fully expecting failure, was putting it together again – only differently.

This book explores one particular kind of modernism: American modernism. That the United States should have been one of the heartlands of literary modernism is hardly surprising. The experience of modernity – the shock of consumerism, industrialisation, immigration and the city – was arguably greater in the United States than anywhere else in the world, largely because its economy was developing so quickly. Only Germany and Britain were serious economic rivals, and both were devastated by the experience of the First World War. But perhaps we should hesitate before embracing the idea of a distinctive American modernism? Once, scholars were keen to divide literary studies into national blocks, with English, American or French literature forming a kind of genre of its own. Today they are much keener to emphasise the links between different literatures; 'transnationalism', breaking down national boundaries and exploring the relations between national literatures and writers, has now become very fashionable. And in many ways modernism is a perfect example of the transnational aesthetic, not least since one of its key themes was exile, reflecting the experience of many modernist writers.[4] Ezra Pound was born in Idaho, did much of his best work in London, moved to Paris, settled in Italy, returned to the United States and then went back to Italy again. F. Scott Fitzgerald left the United States as a young man, lived in Switzerland, Paris and the south of France, and died in Hollywood. Ernest Hemingway was born in Illinois but spent most of the interwar years in France, Spain and the Caribbean. Above all, T. S. Eliot was born in St Louis but worked as a London bank clerk and became a British citizen. Yet even Eliot believed that there was something distinctively American about his work: 'It wouldn't be what it is, and I imagine it wouldn't be so good . . . if I'd been born in England, and it wouldn't be what it is if I'd stayed in America', he told the *Paris Review* in 1959. 'It's a combination of things. But in its sources, in its emotional springs, it comes from America.'[5]

The first chapter of this book explores what *was* distinctively American about American modernism. It begins with a historical and thematic framework, explaining why it makes sense to look for modernism's roots in mid-nineteenth-century American literature, and especially in the writers of the so-called American Renaissance, such as Ralph Waldo Emerson and Walt Whitman. Often studies of modernism focus exclusively on the period after about 1890. What I show here, though, is that American modernists often looked back for inspiration to forebears such as Emerson, whose ideas were to prove tremendously important and influential. After discussing the historical and cultural context, I examine, in turn, the intellectual legacies of Emerson, Whitman, Henry Adams, Henry James and W. E. B. Du Bois, none of whom are typically considered modernists, but all of whom, I believe, left an indelible imprint on American modernism – not least in their emphasis on writing as an act of self-creation, and the writer as the progenitor of a new kind of national identity.

Chapter 2 focuses on the literature of the American city, and specifically New York. The enormous importance of the urban experience in modernist writing is well known; in this chapter, though, I explore New York's dual identity as a palace of dreams and an underworld of nightmares. The introductory section gives some historical context, especially on architecture, skyscrapers, immigration and the 'language' of the city. I then look more closely at the works of John Dos Passos, Anzia Yezierska, Nella Larsen, Edith Wharton, Theodore Dreiser and Hart Crane, showing how each writer grappled with the nature of identity in the urban melting pot. In the third chapter, meanwhile, I look *beyond* the city, showing that far from being polar opposites, regionalist and modernist writing have much in common; indeed, in many ways the regionalist writers produced remarkably good examples of modernism in action. This chapter focuses particularly on the literature of the American South and West, and so I spend some time discussing the legacy of the Civil War, agrarian radicalism and political Populism. In later sections, I explore the works of Willa Cather, Ellen Glasgow and William Faulkner, as well as the poems of the Southern Agrarians: Allen Tate, John Crowe Ransom and Robert Penn Warren. As in Chapter 2, not all of these writers are typically considered as modernists; part of what I am doing in these chapters, therefore, is to broaden the boundaries of modernism, showing how it went well behind the usual handful of canonical authors.

In contrast, the fourth chapter looks at the writers generally known as the 'Lost Generation', who appear in almost every survey of modernist writing, but are nevertheless often misunderstood. In the opening section, I discuss the impact of the First World War on these writers, their relationship with one another, their exile in France, their debt to older precursors such as Gertrude Stein and their attitudes to such issues as consumerism, art and language itself. The chapter then looks more closely at Stein herself, focusing on some of the poems in her early work *Tender Buttons* (1914) and on her gigantic novel *The Making of Americans* (1925), the title of which, of course, is highly suggestive. I then turn to one of the most frequent visitors to Stein's salon, Ernest Hemingway, examining his stripped-down language and his treatment of masculinity in *The Sun Also Rises* (1926), before discussing F. Scott Fitzgerald's *The Great Gatsby* (1925) and Djuna Barnes's *Nightwood* (1936). Chapter 5 returns to the United States, examining the extraordinary cultural melting pot of the Harlem Renaissance. After a brief section exploring the historical and cultural context of black writing in New York in the 1920s, I focus on the poetry of Langston Hughes, Countee Cullen and Claude McKay and the works of Carl Van Vechten, Zora Neale Hurston and Jean Toomer, demonstrating how each, in their different ways, dealt with the issues of race and identity, and showing how the black literary experience in the 1920s and 1930s was a central and indelible element of American modernism.

In the sixth and last chapter, I focus specifically on modernist poetry and drama, exploring the links between Imagism and modernism, the impact of Freud's theories of psychoanalysis, and the depiction of social issues such as inequality and women's rights on the American stage. In particular, I look at a selection of Ezra Pound's *Cantos* and at T. S. Eliot's *The Waste Land* – which stand as perhaps *the* canonical texts of American modernism – as well as H. D.'s Imagist poems and William Carlos Williams's 1920s poems 'The Wanderer', 'This is Just to Say' and 'The Red Wheelbarrow'. I then turn to drama, exploring the complexities of Eugene O'Neill's plays *Anna Christie* (1921), *The Emperor Jones* (1920) and *Mourning Becomes Electra* (1931), as well as Susan Glaspell's *Suppressed Desires* (1915) and *Trifles* (1916).

Finally, the book comes full circle with a conclusion set at the New York World's Fair in 1939 – on the surface, a very different occasion from the World's Columbian Exposition in 1893, but an event that also had some remarkable similarities to it. These two great exhibitions might easily be taken as bookends, marking the advent and decline of American modernism. But there is, I suggest, another way to think about the 1939 World's Fair – one that raises intriguing questions about the rise, fall and persistence of the modernist moment.

In any study such as this, there will inevitably be omissions and this book is no exception: restrictions of space mean that, unfortunately, I have not discussed the work of proletarian and social writers such as Mike Gold and Clifford Odets, or Great Depression writers such as John Steinbeck and Thornton Wilder, or indeed the likes of Wallace Stevens, Henry Roth, James T. Farrell and Erskine Caldwell. I have chosen instead texts that most commonly appear on university courses, influenced by the natural 'fit' of texts into my thematic structure. In some instances, I have examined writers whose impact on American modernism has been undervalued, such as H. D., Djuna Barnes and the Southern Agrarian poets. Of course, there are overlaps between the chapters. Gertrude Stein might well have appeared in Chapter 6, 'Make It New!, Nella Larsen might have been placed in the chapter on the Harlem Renaissance, and Dos Passos could easily have been discussed alongside the Lost Generation. In general, I have tried to achieve a balance across the chapters, and to offer new ways of thinking about specific writers. For instance, my inclusion of Wharton, James and Dreiser is a deliberate attempt to widen the ways in which we usually think about these writers and about American modernism, which did not, after all, emerge from a literary wilderness or a historical vacuum. Thus *Modern American Literature* offers a wider critical appraisal of American modernism, lengthening its temporal framework and expanding its parameters. Each author study draws upon recent critical debates, situates the text within its historical and scholarly context, and offers new close readings of key texts.

The main text of the book is framed by supplementary material designed to assist interpretation. The Chronology provides an overview of modern American literary history, cultural development and the evolving political scene. The Student Resources section includes questions for discussion on each of the authors and a selection of useful electronic resources. The Glossary explains historical, literary and cultural concepts which are central to American modernism, and defines terms that may be unfamiliar to those coming to the subject for the first time.

NOTES

1. Helen Keller, *The Story of My Life* (New York: Cosimo, [1903] 2010), p. 40.
2. 'Columbian Exposition – In the Cairo Street, Midway Plaisance', *Harper's Weekly*, 37 (16 September 1893). For a widely praised and highly readable account of the fair, see Erik Larson, *The Devil in the White City* (New York: Crown, 2003).
3. Henry Adams, *The Education of Henry Adams* (Boston: Houghton Mifflin, 1919), pp. 340–3.
4. For a detailed analysis of transnational American modernism see Catherine Morley and Alex Goody (eds), *American Modernism: Cultural Transactions* (Durham: Cambridge Scholars Press, 2009).
5. Donald Hall, 'T. S. Eliot: The Art of Poetry', *Paris Review*, 1.21 (Spring–Summer 1959), p. 25.

CHAPTER I

The Making of American Modernism

Contemplating the origins of American modernism, we are often presented with the image of swathes of peasant immigrants disembarking a weather-beaten ship at Ellis Island. Alternatively we might picture any one of the New York skyscrapers, iconic structures which have long captivated a collective imagination. Or perhaps we might hear American modernism in the giddy raptures of jazz melodies, tinkling piano keys and furious, jaw-busting trumpets. All of these images are, in some senses, accurate. All capture one or other aspect of the era, critical paradigm and cultural sensibility that have come to be known as American modernism. But each of these images brings with it a set of preconceived ideas which limit our understanding of the depth, complexity, and paradoxes of American modernism.

For a start, each image is bound up with the metropolis – New York in the first instance, but also Chicago and New Orleans with their respective jazz scenes. Each image tells a partial story: American modernism as a result of immigration and multiculturalism; American modernism as contiguous with the development of real estate and the upward ascent of architecture; or American modernism as syncopated with the rhythms of new musical forms and with the smouldering issues of race and segregation. Furthermore each of these versions of American modernism brings us to a different time and place: mass immigration to the United States began in earnest in the latter part of the nineteenth century and gathered pace in the 1900s and 1910s; New York's skyscrapers began to appear from 1910 onwards through to the unveiling of the iconic Chrysler Building in 1930; and the Jazz Age is generally associated with the seven-year stretch from 1919 to 1926. Each of these images, therefore, cements the common view that American modernism was largely a twentieth-century phenomenon. Of course each carries significant resonance and each will be discussed at greater length in the chapters that follow. But to get to the Jazz Age or to the ascent of the skyscrapers, we need a clearer sense of the socio-intellectual background, the context from which modernism emerged. And that means looking further back.

The tried and tested practice of approaching literature in canonical blocks has, quite understandably, long been the critical norm. Breaking timelines into discrete periods and groups is a mainstay in the teaching of literature, bringing writers and thinkers together into easily digested chunks. This book makes no pretence to offer anything different; it is, after all, part of a series of studies which approach literature in this very manner. However, there can be a certain arbitrariness in the assignation of writers to particular paradigms and so-called traditions. The example which springs readily to mind is Laurence Sterne's novel *Tristram Shandy* (1759–69), which in many respects has all the hallmarks of what we now call postmodern fiction. Writers and artists who straddle the cusp of periods can also be tricky to categorise, since their art often couples seemingly incompatible theories and philosophies. One thinks, for instance, of the experimental modernist poet Hart Crane who, in spite of his avant-gardism, bears all the hallmarks of aestheticism and decadence. Edith Wharton and Willa Cather are equally hard to place: both seemingly eschew literary experimentation in favour of a nineteenth-century realist mode, yet each quietly encompasses the paraphernalia of the new century. So in seeking out the origins of American modernism, we need to delve into the immediate period which preceded it: an era which in literary studies has become known as the American Renaissance, lasting from the years before the Civil War to the turn of the twentieth century.

While the dynamism of chaotic changes in American literary culture accelerated in the early part of the twentieth century, not least because they went hand in hand with similar developments in science and technology and the visible rise of consumer capitalism, the mid to late nineteenth century was undoubtedly the cradle of modernism. For instance, celluloid, the crucial component of the American film industry, was invented in 1876 by John Wesley Hyatt. Coca-Cola, the ubiquitous global symbol of American capitalism, was created in Georgia in 1886. George Eastman developed dry plate photography in 1879, flexible roll film in 1882 and the first fixed-focus camera in 1888. In 1846 the Cunard company set up the first transatlantic steamboat line, opening up regular crossings between the United States and Europe. Elisha Otis demonstrated the elevator brake, so crucial to the modern skyscraper, at the Crystal Palace Exhibition in New York City in 1854. And in 1888 and 1891, respectively, the United States saw the first revolving door and escalator – accessible gateways to the modern locations of corporate business and consumerist pleasures. Other nineteenth-century inventions and patents which would play an enormous role in modern American culture include the typewriter (1867), the long-burning electric light bulb (1879), the phonograph record player (1877), the first commercially successful electric streetcar (1834), the Morse American telegraph machine (1837), the hand-held steam iron (1882), the automatic dishwasher (1889), and the first coal-powered steam-driven motorcycle (1867). The development of each of these inventions would bring enormous financial rewards to the United States, copper-fastening its reputation as one of the richest nations in the world and ensuring the nation's global economic and political dominance throughout the century that followed.

By far the most resonant and culturally important American event of the nineteenth century, however, was the Civil War (1861–5). Arguably the first modern war, with its internment camps, trench warfare, mass propaganda and industrialised distribution of weaponry, and with reports of shell shock amongst soldiers on both sides of the conflict, the Civil War helped to create what we now recognise as the modern American nation. Its most tangible outcomes were the destruction of slavery, the restoration of the Union, and the renewed sovereignty of the federal government.[1] The restitution of the Union, the ticket on which Lincoln went to war (rather belying the popular view that he was solely motivated by enthusiasm to abolish the 'peculiar institution' of slavery), greatly strengthened the economic capacity of the United States during and after Reconstruction. In the first instance, it opened up the manpower and resources of the South, bringing thousands of recently emancipated slaves and their manpower to the industrial Northern states. This African American manpower would be crucial to the later war effort and an important factor in the expansion of the railroads throughout the Union, an expansion which facilitated the easy and rapid transportation of rurally produced goods to coastal marketplaces and overseas. And so industrialisation spread throughout the nation and with it the consequential development of new markets, towns and cities as centres for the exchange of goods. Indeed, the Civil War brought about the rise of the business classes in the United States, with the massive profits generated by John D. Rockefeller's oil industry, Andrew Carnegie's steel industry and the excavation of coke from the mines of Henry Clay Frick, which fuelled the Northern rifles throughout the military campaign. These huge funds generated by industry set the Wall Street money machine in motion and helped to create a global system of finance capitalism, symbolised by the merging of the Carnegie Steel Corporation and dozens of smaller companies to form US Steel. The architect of the merger, J. P. Morgan, was the catalyst of a series of further multimillion-dollar mergers in the newly unveiled railroad and shipping industries, as well as electricity and telephone companies. And the National Bank Acts of 1863 and 1864 gave charters to a small number of banks, thereby centrally controlling the production of greenbacks, and centralised the financial hub of the nation to select Northern cities which would prove to be the creative centres of much modern American art and literature.[2]

As well as being the destinations of African American migrants, these cities were the docking places of the millions of immigrants who made the transatlantic passage to the United States in the ante- and post-bellum periods. While some immigrants moved beyond the cities of their arrival to the West, most stayed in the urban hubs at which they had disembarked. New York, in particular, was the metropolitan magnet for immigrants arriving after the war and it expanded exponentially in the latter decades of the nineteenth century. The census of 1890 revealed the population of the city to be 1.4 million people, with approximately half foreign-born. Across the United States the foreign-born population exceeded 9 million people (a remarkable figure, given that the overall population was then just 63 million). In that year alone almost half a million immigrants entered the United States, with almost a quarter arriving from eastern and southern Europe. The immigrants entering American ports were no longer easily assimilated Protestant northern Europeans or Irish Catholics, but Jews, Orthodox Greeks, Italians and Slavs who brought with them their respective customs, beliefs and the idiomatic dialects which would come to characterise the rich tang of the New York cultural scene in the early decades of the twentieth century. The working and living conditions of these immigrants are well known: most came to escape religious persecution and the abject poverty of their homelands only to be confronted by more of the same, albeit in lesser degrees. Writers like Anzia Yezierska and John Dos Passos would later recreate in their modernist texts the conditions faced by such people, blending experimentalism with searing social criticism. Indeed, the migration and immigration facilitated by the success of the Northern states in the Civil War had a profound effect on modern American art and literature. They engendered a fusion of cultures and ethnicities which fed the dazzling polyphony of modernist experimentalism. Immigrants contributed to the labour movement and the socialist-inspired art written by the likes of Mike Gold, John Steinbeck and Clifford Odets. And post-bellum migration liberated African American folk cultures and art forms, providing the catalyst for the New Negro Renaissance.

One of the most crucial nineteenth-century factors in the genesis of American modernism, however, was the rise of print culture and the mechanisms for the rapid distribution of information. In some ways, the growth of the printing industry was a direct result of the Civil War. Chronicles of the war itself, in newspaper reports and editorials, literary and photographic retrospectives, as well as cheap novels created for both Union and Confederate soldiers, were enormously popular. Even President Lincoln's first State of the Union address was transmitted by telegraph, and during the war the westward construction of telegraph lines continued unabated, enabling the distribution of war news from the front lines. And in 1866, a year after the two sides had put down their weapons, the first transatlantic telegraph cable allowed news to travel between the United States and Europe. The post-bellum formation of business trusts and transatlantic trade networks prompted further developments in print and communications technology, which saw an enormous boom in advertising revenue and in newspaper production. In 1850 there had been approximately 260 daily newspapers in the US. Within thirty years this figure had increased fourfold and in 1890 there were almost 1,600 daily editions and by 1900 there were roughly 2,200 daily titles.[3]

Yet a widespread print culture in the nineteenth-century United States long preceded the Civil War, with the early penny presses churning out all sorts of tawdry materials revelling in accounts of criminal activities and perverse sexual behaviour. The American public in the nineteenth century was highly literate, devouring all sorts of highbrow and lowbrow reading materials, including dime-store novels, religious and political pamphlets, magazines, sensational papers and subversive literature. Indeed, the US popular presses throughout the nineteenth century greatly contributed to what is now commonly described as the American Renaissance, with Poe's quasi-erotic tales of melancholia and necrophilia, Melville's sea-questing adventures and Hawthorne's scandalous stories of forbidden lust and its demonic progeny taking their inspiration directly from the trial documents and sensational stories of the era.[4]

Indeed just as the Civil War engendered modern socio-economic America, the writing of the American Renaissance bears within it the seeds of American literary modernism. Ralph Waldo Emerson, Henry David Thoreau, Edgar Allen Poe, Nathaniel Hawthorne, Walt Whitman, Herman Melville and Emily Dickinson produced some of the best-known works of American literature and fiction in the antebellum period, work which is crucially important to our understanding of modern American literature and to our appreciation of the more experimental strands of American modernism. Many canonical works, such as Melville's *Moby Dick* (1851) and Hawthorne's *The Scarlet Letter* (1850), are undeniably modern in their preoccupations and in some of their methods; in many regards, Melville's deliberate experimentation with genre in his magnum opus anticipates the likes of John Dos Passos, William Faulkner and Gertrude Stein. Indeed, in terms of its relationship with its immediate literary precursors, American modernism differs somewhat from its European counterpart. Whereas modernist literature in Britain sought to markedly distance itself from Victorian literary art, its American counterpart was clearly an extension of much antebellum writing.

For instance, the psychological aspects of Hawthorne's writing – his fascination with the wrangling of conscience and the ambiguities of human nature – are clearly evident in the work of Henry James, Edith Wharton, or even in a more overtly experimental writer such as T. S. Eliot. Hawthorne is, in fact, an interesting case in point, his fictions rooted very much in his environment and in the ephemeral presses which would come to fascinate the modernists. In the compilation of all his novels and short stories, Hawthorne looked to what he called 'all sorts of good for nothing books', including crime pamphlets, almanacs and newspapers. To illustrate his philosophical and theological discourses, he borrowed freely from the materials which fed the popular imagination. Indeed, in *Mosses from an Old Manse* (1846), Hawthorne acknowledged the importance of the ephemeral presses:

> It is the Age itself which writes newspapers and almanacs, which therefore have a distinct purpose and meaning . . . Genius effects something permanent, yet still with a similarity of office to that of the more ephemeral writer. A work of genius is but the news paper of a century . . .

And there is no better example than *The House of the Seven Gables* (1851) which employs the presses in the provision of what the Preface calls 'the realities of the moment': the enumeration of up-to-the-minute facts (daguerreotypes, railroads, the invention of the telegraph) and references to mid-century American politics.

All this is basically a question of methodology. The modernists made great claims for their bold ingenuity in deploying the popular presses and integrating newspaper headlines and news stories throughout their fictions. This technique had long been commonplace in American literary fiction; the obvious difference, though, was the perceived end result. For a modernist like Dos Passos, the inclusion of the ephemeral presses was an experimental technique, heavily influenced by James Joyce's 1922 epic *Ulysses*, whereas for Hawthorne it was simply a means toward the achievement of realism. A further paradox, of course, is the perceived intention of the juxtaposition. For Hawthorne and his contemporaries, the fusion of the transient presses with the literary novel was based on democratic principles – the juxtaposition of the common and the elite. For the modernists, by contrast, the inclusion of the snippets from popular culture often served to bamboozle the ordinary reader and add to the perceived 'difficulty' of the modern literary work.

What classic and modern writers had in common, though, was their belief that drawing on the popular presses was an excellent way of using their fiction to make incisive political and cultural observations. So, just as newspaper headlines in Dos Passos's *Manhattan Transfer* (1925) are used to criticise the rise of real estate speculation, Hawthorne's engagement with the transient presses reflects the spirit of gluttonous pilfering which he saw (from his reading) as central to the antebellum social scene. Hawthorne used the stories he found in the penny presses to paint his fellow countrymen and women as driven by a fascination with the vulgarities of the spirit, an abiding sense of greed and an unhealthy interest in the lives of others. Herman Melville's method, too, partook of the spirit of the age. Melville's novels are stuffed with biblical and classical allusions, literary and lexicographical references, prophetic sermonising, encyclopaedic facts and extracts from sensational tracts. Indeed, Charles Olson describes Melville as a 'cutpurse Autolycus . . . [whose] books batten on other books.'[5] Again, however, the writing and the method of composition are designed to be representative of the age, not least in their sheer diffuseness and chaos, which reflect the anarchic nature of the nation of states that was the antebellum Union.

The word 'anarchy' is often used to describe the landscape of both European and American modernism. For scholars such as Walter Kalaidjian and Peter Nicholls, this sense of things falling apart is crucial to understanding the sheer flux of modernity: the massive and variable social shifts of the period including the horror of the First and Second World Wars; the dislocating experience of mass consumerism, immigration and urbanisation; the shock of the end of empire and the beginning of the postcolonial experience; the seismic changes in gender politics that resulted from the transformation of the economy and the increasing liberation of women; and so on. In the United States in particular, where the effects of mass consumerism were most obvious, this anarchic modernity was also the result of technological dynamism, scientific innovation, the rise of cosmopolitanism, the development of a self-consciously progressive metropolitan culture and the emergence of phenomenology, anthropology and sociology, as well as cultural events such as the publication of Einstein's special theory of relativity in 1905 and the translation into English of Freud's *The Interpretation of Dreams* (1913). The newly discovered elasticity of time and the emergence of new social sciences and philosophical discourses would rattle the foundations of individuals' sense of self and shake the pillars of religious belief, adding to the unsettlement caused by the publication of Darwin's *On the Origin of Species* in 1859.

But this kind of cultural anarchy was not unique to American modernity. It was deeply embedded in the socio-cultural landscape; not only were memories of the Civil War still raw (especially in the South), but throughout the nineteenth century the very borders of the nation had been constantly revised, helping to confirm a sense of flux and change. We cannot understand American modernism unless we grasp the importance of this historical framework: a context of upheaval, optimism and expansion, rooted in the experience of the frontier, the shock of civil war and the trauma of occupation, both physical and psychological. And while many commentators and literary critics argue that essentially American modernism grew out of European modernism, the truth is rather different. In reality, American modernism was firmly rooted in the nineteenth century and the antebellum writing of the American Renaissance. William Carlos Williams's minimalist verse, for example, was clearly influenced by Emily Dickinson's compact, elliptical poetry, while his use of American speech rhythms in his longer poems owes much to Walt Whitman. Modernist writers as diverse as Eliot, Pound, Dos Passos, Cather and Stein all drew on Herman Melville's encyclopaedism and his blend of classical intertexts with lofty philosophical discourse, while the psychological complexities of Hawthorne's characters find their way into any number of Jamesian or Wharton-esque heroines.

Over them all, though, is the spirit of Ralph Waldo Emerson. Just as Shakespeare looms over the English canon, Emerson's thought and writings inform much twentieth-century American writing; indeed, it is no exaggeration to say that without Emerson, American writing in general would be unimaginably different. In the next sections of this chapter, therefore, we will examine Emerson's intellectual legacy and discuss the position and importance of other transitional writers such as Whitman, Henry Adams, Henry James and W. E. B. Du Bois, writers at the cusp of modernity, whose impact on more experimental literary innovators was similarly immense.

RALPH WALDO EMERSON

While more likely to be associated with American transcedentalism than American modernism, Ralph Waldo Emerson is nonetheless a crucially important figure for the impetus and development of twentieth-century intellectual thought and culture. Born in Boston in 1803, Emerson wrote dozens of essays and gave hundreds of lectures across the nation, and was best known as the champion of the individual against the pressures of society. Above all, he won lasting fame as the spokesman for transcendentalism, which emphasised the spiritual and the intuitive over the empirical, and contained within its neo-platonic philosophical outlook the germ of many ideas later taken up by modernist artists and thinkers. For instance, the transcendentalist will to recreate spiritual realities symbolically finds its way into the poetry of Stein and Eliot; the notion of the individual's contiguity with the natural world is clear in the writing of Willa Cather or Mark Twain; and certainly the Emersonian notion of transition, the movement between states of being, permeates the writing of any number of modernist literary practitioners. Indeed, the very idea of 'transition' is a foundational tenet of a paradigm which celebrates and seeks to embody flux, instability and fragmentation.

Emerson's writings and essays reveal a mind deeply interested in exploring the condition of instability and movement, the continuous striving of the human intellect. Stasis is never a point at which he seeks to arrive, for stasis means the death of consciousness. His ideas first took root in his 1836 essay 'Nature' and in his subsequent address to the Harvard Phi Beta Kappa Society, later published in 1839 as 'The American Scholar', which Oliver Wendell Holmes described as 'the American intellectual declaration of independence'. Both of these essays are crucial in terms of assessing Emerson's contribution to modern literary culture. In 'The American Scholar', for example, Emerson called for an American literary self-sufficiency and the inauguration of an American literature and intellectual culture distinct from that of European forbears:

> We have listened too long to the courtly muses of Europe. The spirit of the American freeman is already suspected to be timid, imitative, tame . . . We will walk on our own feet; we will work with our own hands; we will speak our own minds.[6]

Emerson reiterated his desire to free the American intellectual landscape in later essays such as 'History' (1841), 'Circles' and 'The Poet' (1844). However, his address to the Divinity College at Harvard in 1838, in which he called for the scholar's liberation from the tyranny of orthodox religious devotion, was sharply criticised and resulted in Emerson's disbarment from speaking at Harvard until after the Civil War. Even so, the Divinity School Address anticipates many of the themes and issues in later essays such as 'Self-Reliance' (1841) and 'Experience' (1844), insisting on the centrality of individual consciousness to the world and the urgency of breaking away from the shackles of empiricism and organised religion. Emerson instructed his audience to 'go it alone', discarding Christian scripture or philosophical treatise, and developing their own individual visions of the self, the surrounding world and the inherent deity (p. 123). It was this emphasis on the *self* which became Emerson's lasting legacy; it was, for example, echoed by Whitman in his epic 'Song of Myself', which is arguably one of the earliest examples of modernist American poetry. Indeed, taking his cue from Emerson's rejection of stasis, Whitman's aim in *Leaves of Grass* was nothing less than the initiation of a poetic tradition which celebrated continual metamorphosis, flux and change, helping to build a society that was open, democratic and free.

What was so shocking about Emerson's 1838 address was its rejection of Christianity and other religious organisations, which he thought obstructed the immediate relationship between the individual and the divine. He viewed religious devotion as enslavement, a pathway to mediocrity which closes the mind rather than emancipates thought, and must be shunned in order to attain a pure, unmediated experience of external realities:

> Let me admonish you, first of all, to go alone; to refuse the good models, even those which are sacred in the imagination of men, and dare to love God without mediator or veil. Friends enough you shall find who will hold up to your emulation Wesleys and Oberlins, Saints and Prophets. Thank God for these good men, but say, 'I also am a man.' Imitation cannot go above its model. (p. 123)

What is immediately apparent from this short excerpt is the faith in the judgement of the self. For Emerson, the individual is the only arbiter of the world and is certainly more important than the institutions which formerly offered interpretative guidance and moral codes. As one of his journal entries from 1840 emphasised, what mattered to Emerson was the 'infinitude of the private man' – a focus on the plenitude of individual consciousness that anticipated the development of psychoanalysis and, in particular, Freud's notion of the layers of human consciousness. We can see this theme in literature, too, from the poetry of Whitman to modernist novels by European writers such as James Joyce and Virginia Woolf, who pioneered a style of writing which mimicked the processes of the mind, and American writers like John Dos Passos and William Faulkner, who tried to map the mental perambulations of thought, the slip-sliding ebb and flow of interior perception. What is also evident, however, is Emerson's belief that some kind of 'veil' or wall, which inhibits direct appreciation and understanding, exists between the individual and the external world. Again, this is a theme taken up by many modernist writers, especially Stein, Pound, Eliot, Hemingway and H. D., who look to strip language of implication, inference and shading, which get in the way of the direct essence of objects and entities.

Emerson's emphasis on the self was undoubtedly influenced by his reading of German philosophical treatises and British Romantic writers such as William Wordsworth, Samuel Taylor Coleridge and Thomas Carlyle, whom he met in the early 1830s after relinquishing his role as a Unitarian minister. The affinities between German idealism and British Romanticism and American transcendentalism have been discussed in numerous studies; the notion of the natural world as the manifestation of the spirit is derived from the work of Immanuel Kant, Johann Fichte and Friedrich Schelling, whom Emerson came to know through Coleridge and Carlyle. Indeed, the derivation of many of these ideas and ontological principles calls into question Emerson's demand for and insistence upon originality and a unique American experience, different to that of Europe.

Nonetheless, the wider point is that Emerson's thinking and his ideas about the individual, society and the nature of perception are remarkably modern (and, indeed, came to be influential upon a large number of late nineteenth- and early twentieth-century thinkers, not least Friedrich Nietzsche, John Dewey, William James, Robert Frost and other modernist writers and artists). One of the most important aspects of Emerson's work, later taken up by William James, is his insistence on transition, the movement between states and selves. Indeed this is precisely one of the more difficult aspects of Emerson's writing, the fact that it is always in a state of becoming and therefore hard to pin down. Certainly, the apparent contradictions throughout Emerson's writings are part of this process of becoming, of moving through the stages of cognitive apprehension. In 'Self-Reliance' (1841), he observes that 'power ceases in the moment of repose; it resides in the moment of transition from a past to a new state, in the shooting to a gulf in the darting to an aim' (p. 190). For Emerson, stasis is equivalent to subjugation of the spirit, and his instructions for self-knowledge, unmediated encounters with the world and with God, are part of this project of renewal and constant movement. And the new state is not the end point but rather part of a wider circle in Emerson's transitive process.

Numerous critics have drawn comparisons between Emerson's style and his philosophy, noting the contiguity between, on the one hand, his emphasis on continual movement and perpetual regeneration, and, on the other, a prose style which seems to mirror the fluctuations in the human mind as it moves from observation, to premise, to hypothesis, to thesis, to refutation, and onward toward a larger issue which is in turn undermined.[7] As Jonathan Levin observes:

> Emerson values processes but not necessarily their end products, which are in any event only instruments of further processes. So long as he keeps faith with these processes, at once cosmic and imaginative, Emerson can identify with the continuously emerging novelty of things.[8]

Indeed, almost all of his essays touch on this issue of the inherent departure within every point of arrival. For instance, 'Circles' opens with the assertion that 'our life is an apprenticeship to the truth that around every circle another can be drawn; that there is no end in nature, but every end is a beginning' (p. 225). Emerson's poet figure 'sees the flowing or metamorphosis'; he recognises that 'within the form of every creature is a force impelling it to ascend into a higher form'. Indeed, the speech of the poet 'flows with the flowing of nature' (p. 270). And in 'Montaigne' (1850), he calls for a philosophy of 'fluxions and mobility' and implores the individual to 'look for the permanent in the mutable and fleeting' (p. 336).

Engaging with this ontological system, many American modernists attempt to integrate the concept of transition into the movement and shape of their language. William James, who was influential in establishing the idea of 'stream of consciousness', writes of the difficulties of settling on a 'substantive conclusion': 'We ought to say a feeling of *and*, a feeling of *if*, and a feeling of *by*, quite as readily as we say a feeling of *blue* or a feeling of *cold*'.[9] Meanwhile, in Henry James's preface to the New York edition of his works, perhaps the first modernist treatise on the novel, James proclaims of *Roderick Hudson* (1875): 'Really, universally, relations stop nowhere'.[10] And in consolidating his vision of modernist poetry, Ezra Pound translates an essay of Jules Romains:

> A being has a centre, or centres in harmony, but a being is not compelled to have limits. He exists a great deal in one place, rather less in others and further on a second being commences before the first has left off . . . Everything over-crosses, coincides, and cohabits . . . A thousand existences are concentric.[11]

For Pound and the James brothers, the rejection of stability and the emphasis upon the point of intersection between moments is crucial, for it is only in the instant of transition that truth is evident. In the moment of rest, Emersonian 'repose', truth wanes. Paradoxically, though, by setting thought and truth in language, by expressing it thus, the writer cannot but undermine it. For Emerson, when truth is put into language – whether in a prose sentence or in the structure of a poem – it is put into repose. It is movement and action that bring truth; but language, by implication, is a prison from which truth cannot escape. The 'Emersonian idealization of action', writes the critic Richard Poirier, 'implicitly disparages the power of words'.[12]

Emerson's sceptical attitude to the 'power of words' was to prove enormously influential. 'Nothing could bother me more', wrote Gertrude Stein in 1936, 'than the way a thing goes dead once it has been said'.[13] 'Language', agreed William James in 'The Stream of Thought', 'works against our perception of truth'.[14] And this raises a further issue which would come to preoccupy the modernists: namely, the social utility (or otherwise) of art. Of course, the question of artistic value or utility is not exclusive to American modernism. But Emerson's notion of the disjunction between action and language left a deep imprint on American arts and letters – not least because it sat awkwardly beside his insistence that Americans needed to build their own literary tradition as a pillar of their democratic New World. So, in 'The Poet' (1844), Emerson describes the poet as a 'Language-maker' and 'liberating god' (p. 276), yet he also writes that 'language is a fossil poetry' and the 'tomb of Muses'. In other words, language is *both* a force of creative generation and the repository of death – a paradox that Emerson himself never quite resolved. And in the decades to come, American literary modernism would come to absorb, challenge and negotiate his rich but contradictory legacy.

WALT WHITMAN

A direct and conscious disciple of Emerson, Walt Whitman was inspired to write as a 'representative American' after attending a lecture in which his mentor prophesied the imminent arrival of an American Homer to capture 'the barbarism and materialism of the times'. Taking up the challenge, Whitman sought to encapsulate Emerson's philosophical creed in the shape of his verse. Indeed, the preface to the first edition of Whitman's magnum opus, *Leaves of Grass* (1855), clearly responds to Emerson's call in 'The Poet' for the literary framing of the United States. The bold statement that 'the United States are essentially the greatest poem' is a reiteration of Emerson's assertion that 'America is a poem in our eyes; its ample geography dazzles the imagination, and it will not wait long for metres' (p. 281). Whitman viewed himself as just the 'genius' that the nation had been waiting for and embarked on a thirty-year project of drafting and redrafting a piece of work which has become synonymous with American individualism and expansionism. His perception of the nation as a poem alerts the reader to his ambitious project of capturing the multiplicity, diversity and democracy of the nation within the parameters of verse form, and thus explains the necessary expansion of and experimentation with such forms. When Whitman asserts 'I am large / I contain multitudes' in 'Song of Myself', he is, of course, speaking of the self, but also invoking the nation, thereby expressing the essential contradiction which lies at the heart of this uniquely American ideology: the national consensus that all are bound together by their distinct individuality.[15] Aware of this tension, inherited from Emerson, Whitman describes the apparent contradiction as a necessary aspect of a multitudinous nation wedded to the democratic ideal. This contradiction is not to be resolved but to be celebrated, as the poem sets out to do.

Whitman's relationship with Emerson has been well documented. Upon the initial publication of *Leaves of Grass*, Emerson wrote to congratulate the poet on his achievement, only to find his letter later republished in the *New York Tribune* on 10 October 1855 and in the appendix pages of the 1856 edition.

> Dear Sir – I am not blind to the worth of the wonderful gift of 'Leaves of Grass.' I find it the most extraordinary piece of wit and wisdom that America has yet contributed. I am very happy in reading it, as great power makes us happy. It meets the demand I am always making . . .
> R.W. Emerson, Concord, Massachusetts, 21 July 1855

Even the cover of the second volume was adorned with an excerpt from the letter, including Emerson's name. Unhappy that his letter had been made public in this manner, Emerson requested the removal of these materials from the third edition of the book, a request ignored by Whitman. And, as the critic Jerome Loving observes, both suffered in the negative reviews of the unexpurgated version of the volume. Whitman's relationship with Emerson is curious. On the one hand, Emerson's praise of the young poet at the beginning of his career offered a protective shield against the tough critical environment he would have faced in the New York presses. The critic Kenneth Price notes that Whitman's inclusion of Emerson's words was 'intend[ed] to deflect harsh criticism by relying on a pure and honored authority'.[16] Yet the recognition of Emerson as an intellectual patron undermined the claims of *Leaves of Grass* to be a work of unalloyed literary and creative independence. Given that Whitman had been moulded by the unashamedly intellectual Emerson, his claims to be a self-made 'rough' were less than convincing. Moreover, it is hard not to see Whitman's exploitation of Emerson's praise as a nakedly commercial promotional tool, and in his 1856 letter to his 'dear Friend and Master', Whitman could not restrain himself from boasting about the number of copies he had sold. Again, this rather undermines his claims to be only interested in the 'making' of poems. But, as already mentioned, Whitman is the supreme poet of contradictions and ambiguities, and these resonate throughout his epic poem of America.

What Whitman took from Emerson's writings was, above all, the spirit of 'becoming'. Just as Emerson lamented the linguistic conceptualisation of an entity or a phenomenon on the grounds that its encapsulation within language effectively shut down its potential to 'be', Whitman turns his verse into an exercise in ceaseless motion, bringing it into being but focusing less on the point of arrival than on the moment of transition. Indeed, we might surmise that the constant amendment and reproduction of the volume is testament to Whitman's belief in the potential of continual metamorphosis. At a more specific level, in Part 6 of 'Song of Myself', the speaker contemplates the nature of grass:

> A child said *What is the grass?* fetching it to me with full hands;
> How could I answer the child? I do not know what it is any
>   more than he.
> I guess it must be the flag of my disposition, out of the hopeful
>   green stuff woven.
> Or I guess it is the handkerchief of the Lord . . .
> Or I guess it is a uniform hieroglyphic
> And it means, Sprouting alike in broad zones and narrow
>   zones,
> Growing among black folks as among white,
> Kanuck, Tuckahoe, Congressman, Cuff, I give them the same,
>   I receive them the same.
> And now it seems to me the beautiful uncut hair of graves . . .
>   (p. 33)

And on it goes, recreating the grass with every statement, but never settling on one definitive meaning. For Whitman, poetry involved a vigorous and direct engagement with his native land, and in this passage he deals with that land directly in terms of the constitutive blades of grass, evoking the land's potential for growth and multiplication, its links to the divine and to the pastoral, its ability to transcend racial and social boundaries (setting the congressman alongside the Native American), and its relationship with the physical corporeality of human life (in terms of its similarity to 'hair' and 'graves'). In its multiple strands, the grass is a 'uniform hieroglyphic', an enigmatic, incomprehensible symbol which will forever puzzle the speaker and quicken with every conjecture.

What is immediately striking, of course, is the centrality of the self. The child's questions facilitate the mental exercise of the self and almost immediately the child gives way to the supreme 'I', for whom the grass constitutes an ever-elusive entity. Here, the 'I' is presented as capable of sympathetic identification with the puzzled child but also with 'black folk', 'Kanuck, Tuckahoe, Congressman' and 'Cuff'. The speaker 'becomes' a whole host of people but never loses sight of the individual self, which is crucial to Whitman's ultimate purpose in merging the individual ego with the democratic collective of the nation. This unification of self and populace enables a discovery of the self; only through the identification with the wider cultural unit can the self know the capabilities and the various dimensions of his personal identity.

The modernist writer and critic Malcolm Cowley was among the first to recognise Whitman's contradictory individualism as his most original contribution to literature, noting the poet's juxtaposition in his introduction to the first edition of *Leaves of Grass* of his 'gross' corporeality with his quasi-mystical abilities. As Cowley notes, Whitman offers himself as subject to his readers as someone who has been 'been granted a vision, the result of which he has realised the potentialities latent in every American and, indeed, he says, in every living person, even "the brutish koboo, called the ordure of humanity"'.[17] This visionary insight connects the poet with every living person, thereby aligning the common (even the base) and the everyday with the mystical and divine.[18] The poetic manifestation of this is evident in the deployment of the colloquial voice and the deliberate rupture of poetic metre throughout the volume. In encapsulating America, Whitman needed a poetic line that would contain the rhythms of American speech, the undulations of the landscape and the diversity of the culture. Thus his varying rhythms, mixed diction, catalogues and *vers libre* are part of his experiment in creating the first successful American epic, a new bible of American democracy, which would celebrate the nation with the poet as the heroic figure at the centre. Truth and beauty are shown to be dependent upon perpetual metamorphosis, precedents (including poetic and intellectual forefathers) are rejected in the assertion of poetic individualism, and the spatial gaps between the subject, object and the reader are at once celebrated and dissolved in a transcendent unity. And needless to say, all of this placed *Leaves of Grass* at the very heart of the nascent American poetic tradition.

On the surface, Whitman's poetic successors were to do precisely as bidden and reject the notion of native influence. (There is, of course, a nice irony here: by following Whitman's advice, they could hardly claim to be entirely devoid of inspiration from others.) Thus, in his 1936 lecture 'Tradition and the Practice of Poetry', T. S. Eliot noted his affinities with British – not American – poets of the 1890s: 'I certainly had more in common with them than with the English poets who survived to my own day – there were no American poets at all.'[19] Similarly, Eliot's mentor and editor, Ezra Pound, also rejected a native influence on his work. Derisively describing Whitman in 1909, Pound observed that 'his crudity is an exceeding great stench but it *is* America'. Yet in the same piece he admitted to an affinity: 'Mentally I am a Walt Whitman who has learned to wear a collar and a dress shirt.'[20] A year later, in the *Lustra* poems of 1913–15, Pound famously declared 'A Pact' between himself and Whitman:

> I make a pact with you, Walt Whitman
> I have detested you long enough.
> . . .
> It was you that broke the new wood,
> Now is a time for carving.[21]

Of course the very notion of 'a pact' recognises an affinity, if only grudgingly. And Pound's acknowledgment of Whitman as the 'pig-headed father', an artisanal figure who 'broke the new wood' of American poetry, alludes to an evident chain of influence, albeit a strained and anxious influence (p. 90). If Whitman is the artisanal lumberjack, then Pound casts himself as the sculptor, carving his art from the raw materials provided by the elder statesman.

In *Patria Mia* (1912–13) Pound recognised the potential for a unique artistic expression borne of an American identity. And as the critic Mark Morrison observes, the influence of Whitman on American modernists might best be defined as a strained and uneasy relationship, with the older poet offering them 'an example of a distinctively modern American voice that could assault the genteel tradition of the later nineteenth century but also generate imitators who were already stultifying and sloppy, by the early twentieth century, and could potentially rob the modernists of their own originality'.[22] While this is undoubtedly true, one could also make the case that modernists like Pound, who struggled with the weight of Whitman upon his shoulders, were, in fact, dealing with the precursor on his own terms. The modernists paid their respects to the ancestor whilst rebelling against him, denying his authority over their poetry in a supreme act of artistic individualism.

Whitman's influence on American modernism, as well as American literature throughout the twentieth century, cannot be overstated. In the middle years of the century, the Beats took up his free verse cadences and his instructive mantra in their poetic enterprises and their exercises in narrative prose. Whitman's 'barbaric yawp' became Ginsberg's 'Howl', his *Starting from Paumanok* (1855) inspired Lawrence Ferlinghetti's *Starting from San Francisco* (1961), and his self-description as 'one of the roughs . . . disorderly, fleshly and sensual' undoubtedly influenced the self-styled image of Jack Kerouac. But Whitman's influence on modernist poetry runs deeper than occasional nods and winks. His revolutionised poetic forms paved the way for an era of poetic experimentation, expanded verse forms, free verse and poetry with an explicit social and political agenda. While many expatriate Americans poets turned their backs on the very notion of native influence, the fact remains that it was Whitman – the American poet par excellence – who did most to define the poetic terms and forms of American modernism.

So, for example, William Carlos Williams's epic *Paterson* (1963) was conceived as a distinctly American celebration and, like *Leaves of Grass*, was viewed by its creator as a fresh and innovative form of American poetry centred on the everyday lives of ordinary people in a real, physical landscape. Indeed, Robert Lowell described *Paterson* as 'Whitman's America, grown pathetic and tragic, brutalized by inequality, disorganized by industrial chaos, and faced with annihilation'.[23] Similarly, Charles Olson's *Maximus Poems* (1953), as an ode to Massachusetts and an exploration of American history, owes much to Whitman's influence on the experimental long poem.[24] In more general terms, Whitman handed American modernism the task of exploding conventional poetic forms to encapsulate the enormity of the self and the nation. Inviting the reader to participate in the production of meaning, he celebrated the city in all its cacophonous and accelerated diversity, and he explored the boundaries and injustices of class and race segregation. It was Walt Whitman, perhaps more than other writer, who gave American modernism the patriotic pride in the national vernacular, the self-importance to equate poetic genius with godliness, and the self-confidence to revel in contradiction.

HENRY ADAMS

Like Whitman, Henry Adams was deeply interested in the American experiment and often confounded by the technological, cultural and social changes he witnessed in the fifty years from the end of the Civil War to the outbreak of the First World War. His seminal book, *The Education of Henry Adams* (1919), though unpublished until after his death, recounts his own and the nation's development from 1838 to 1905.[25] In coupling the self with the nation in this manner, Adams takes his place alongside Whitman in his commitment to both the individual and the democratic collective. However, Adams was not unequivocally impressed by the democratic experiment and saw much to criticise in burgeoning modern America, deploring the widespread and rapid industrialisation of everyday life, which had created a chaotic world in which unity and patterns of progress were no longer perceptible. Adams was sceptical of the very notion of a 'unity of experience' underlying the physical and social worlds. Yet at the same time he was committed to the project of disinterring such a unity. Like Emerson, he was interested in the idea that experience, history and natural phenomena might be connected by an underlying structure of order, perceptible to the individual consciousness. This subjectivist model of history is most evident in *The Education*, which charts Henry Adams's life from both historical and intellectual perspectives. *The Education* uses the self as an apprehending entity, a centre which attempts to make sense of the anarchy of multi-faceted modernity. By placing the individual consciousness at the centre of the 'multiverse', Adams both evokes the frailty of the individual in the face of growing technological industrialisation and shows how the self can be used to manage the disorder of the modern experience. Yet for all the appearance of chronological coherence and historical order, the narrator often admits his inability to make sense of events, his failure to learn lessons from history, his feelings of stupefaction in the face of the 'dynamo', and his ultimate inability to resolve the contradictions of human understanding.

Born into one of the powerful families in the United States, Adams was the heir to a family which included two presidents (John Adams and John Quincy Adams) as well as various diplomatic figures and public intellectuals. During his lifetime he published two novels, *Democracy: An American Novel* (1880) and *Esther* (1884), as well as a number of highly regarded histories and biographies. His patrician inheritance deeply influenced his thinking and writing, inspiring him to juxtapose the life of the mind with the tides of historical process and national change. One of the most striking examples can be found in the 'Chicago (1893)' chapter of *The Education* in which Adams describes a visit to the World's Columbian Exposition, where he 'found matter of study to fill a hundred years, and his education spread over chaos'.[26] Indeed, the 'Exposition itself defied philosophy', and Adams was astonished to find that not even the revered scientists behind the exhibits had any answers:

> Men of science could never understand the naïveté of the historian, who, when he came suddenly on a new power, asked naturally what it was . . . And a score of such questions to which he expected answers and was astonished to get none. (p. 287)

Despite Adams's interest in the Exposition, he could not banish his forebodings about the future direction of the nation and the impact of industrialisation on the consciousness of the American people:

> Chicago asked in 1893 for the first time the question whether the American people knew where they were driving. Adams answered, for one, that he did not know but would try to find out. On reflecting sufficiently deeply . . . he decided that the American people probably knew no more than he did. (p. 287)

What is most striking here is less the perplexity caused by the Exposition than the elision of self and nation. Adams sees himself as a 'representative man', struggling to come to terms with the forces of change. This alignment of the self with the American people is undoubtedly a reflection of the author's inheritance: just as his grandfather and great-grandfather had managed the nation in their political capacities, Adams makes it his duty to attempt to manage the *fin de siècle* American consciousness at a moment of extraordinary technological change. And while it can be difficult to pin down what precisely discomfited Adams, it is clear that he shared with Karl Marx a sense of apprehension about the reification of human consciousness in the age of machinery. Indeed, somewhat ironically given his commitment to the capitalist economic model, Adams read and admired Marx's work, which warned against the inversion of the subject and mechanical object. For Adams the pessimist, any loss of subjectivity to the forces of industry – or the 'dynamo', 'symbol of infinity' as he describes it in *The Education* – is a potential loss of unity (p. 318). But for Adams the optimist, it was the subject that potentially could provide the sense of unity required to make sense of anarchic modernity.

Seven years after he first set out to find the answer to the question of the American future, Adams finds himself in the Gallery of the Machines at the Paris Great Exposition, no more knowledgeable than he had been in Chicago. But while the Chicago experience had ultimately resulted in a renewed optimism and faith in 'American thought as a unity', Paris confounds him:

> In these seven years man had translated himself into a new universe which had no common scale of measurement with the old. He had entered a supersensual world, in which he could measure nothing except by chance collisions of movements imperceptible to his senses . . . (p. 319)

Indeed, after many years' pursuit, 'he found himself lying in the Gallery of the Machines at the Great Exposition of 1900 with his historical neck broken by the sudden irruption of forces totally new' (p. 320). This admission of defeat leads Adams to consider the past, where a semblance of unity was at least perceptible. He casts his mind back to medieval Europe and considers the force of the Virgin Mary as an 'animated dynamo', a unifying cultural power (p. 320). Adams's consideration of the Virgin thus reprises an image from his earlier work *Mont Saint Michel and Chartres: A Study of Thirteenth Century Unity* (1904) which had argued that widespread adoration of the Virgin provided a narrative of cultural order. This clearly stands in stark contrast to the contemporary, mechanistic dynamo which seems capable of producing only chaos. (This contrast between medieval Europe and turn-of-the-century America is even registered in *The Education*'s original subtitle: *A Study of Twentieth Century Multiplicity*.) Adams observes that 'the force of the Virgin was still felt at Lourdes, and seemed to be as potent as X-rays; but in America neither Venus nor Virgin had ever had value as force – at most as sentiment' (p. 321). And what is interesting, of course, about Adams's symbol of unity, the Virgin, is that it takes human form and sets faith in an anthropomorphic power, rather than a mechanistic force. The Virgin is not inherently divine; rather, she is an ordinary woman made precious by the fruit of her womb, by her labour. In focusing on the Virgin, therefore, Adams stresses not her spirituality but her fecundity and sexuality, which represent a kind of primal human energy running through the whole of history. She is the cohesive cultural force which he perceives to be absent in his own American century.

Adams's thoughts on the powers of the Virgin are part of an overarching interest in the feminine, evident even in his first forays into fiction. Both *Democracy* and *Esther* focus on idealistic female protagonists who, not unlike Adams in *The Education*, ultimately fail to make sense of their worlds. In *Democracy*, Madeleine Lee immerses herself in the political hub of Washington society 'to see with her own eyes the action of primary forces; to touch with her own hand the massive machinery of society; to measure with her own mind the capacity of motive power. She was bent upon getting to the heart of the great American mystery of democracy and government'.[27] Madeleine fails in her quest and eventually leaves Washington disillusioned by the machinations of political men intoxicated by the power of greed, money and power. The novel also rehearses the central debate of *The Education*, namely the tension between technological progress as perfection and technological progress as perdition. In this instance, Madeleine takes on the enquiring role of the later Henry Adams, caught in an unresolved dialectic. In *Esther*, meanwhile, the young heroine struggles with her destiny and her rejection of marriage against the backdrop of the sublime Niagara Falls, a site which underlines the connection between the female and divine, yet which, as an emergent newlyweds' destination, also underscores her anxieties regarding her rejection of the social habits which restrict female mobility. Caught between worlds, Esther is not triumphant but rather locked in a state of limbo where she cannot escape the stranglehold of patriarchal values.

In fact, despite the failures of his protagonists, Adams was committed to a particular kind of faith in the feminine. He was by no means a suffragist, but in his quest for an innate order in history he came to emphasise the centrality of womanhood by virtue of genealogy and lineage. His 1876 essay 'Primitive Rights of Women' observed that medieval societies honoured women because property had been intrinsically linked to matrilineal genealogy. While this vision of the past may be perceived as simplistic (and his view of femininity as somewhat limited), Adams sees the inherently masculine entrepreneurialism and scientific rationalism of the late nineteenth century as leading only to war and annihilation. His interest in the feminine and in the female subconscious unites Adams with his friend and correspondent Henry James, whose fictional portraits of upper-middle-class women locked within domestic interiors are less concerned with social manners than with the relationship between the female subject and the world which she inhabits. In short, James, like Adams, is deeply concerned with the means whereby a subject apprehends (or otherwise) the social, cultural and political phenomena which surrounds them. Indeed, both writers use their female protagonists to portray the anarchy of modernity and the futility of efforts to uncover the unity or essence of socio-cultural phenomena. Their writings explore the relations between the individual consciousness and the chaotic modern world and, moreover, the way in which efforts to 'know' the world continually transform the self. Thus, in Adams and James (as in Emerson), the individual self is never static but always in flux as it attempts to make sense of its ever-changing circumstances.

At first glance, Adams seems an unlikely precursor to the moderns. But his influence cannot be overlooked, especially in terms of the autobiographical-historical strain of his writing and his juxtaposition of the supremely modern alongside the medieval and ancient. His nostalgia for an apparent phenomenological unity located in the past was echoed in the moderns' deployment of classical, medieval and Renaissance motifs and structures. His interest in the history and development of the nation, especially when captured in the form of the experimental autobiography, clearly inspired William Carlos Williams's *In the American Grain* (1925) and Gertrude Stein's *Everybody's Autobiography* (1937). Like Stephen Crane and Frank Norris, Adams was determined to search for order in an increasingly anarchic world, which tossed individuals from one experience to the next; like Wharton and James, meanwhile, he was acutely aware of the social limitations placed upon women. And like his literary successors, Adams looked at the world with a degree of excitement yet with a profound sense of dread. As he wrote to his friend and confidante Elizabeth Cameron in 1905:

> The world is now more desperately interesting than it ever was. The disintegration, anxiety, explosions, terrors, are convulsing to anyone who watches our drift. We are sailing over an unknown ocean of torpedoes . . .[28]

At the heart of all this were Adams's visits to the Chicago World Exposition in 1893 and the Paris Exposition of 1900. Chicago gave Adams the realisation that domestic politics was a paternalistic and capitalistic system which created 'monopolies capable of controlling the new energies that America adored' (p. 289). But Paris confounded the historian completely, stripping away his optimism and offering 'a new universe which had no common scale of measurement with the old' (p. 319). And in his transatlantic status, writing in later life from the distance of Europe, Adams anticipated the expatriate Lost Generation, who went to Europe to see the United States more clearly. Just as Hemingway found the motions of grace in the Spanish landscape, old Catholicism and in the ancient art of bullfighting, Adams found the unity he hankered after in medieval

France as well as a perceptible sense 'of measure [and] the allegiance to form . . . which the French mind has always shown . . .'.[29] Meanwhile, his celebration of New York City and his depiction of its anarchic cacophony clearly anticipated that of John Dos Passos, not least since because, like the younger writer, Adams recognised the quintessential American city as a *machine*, with its population cast as mere cogs in the mechanism.

Publicly published in 1918, *The Education* appeared in the same year as modern American classics such as Willa Cather's *My Ántonia*, Carl Sandburg's *Corn Huskers*, Zona Gale's *Birth* and James Weldon Johnson's *The Changing Status of Negro Labor*. In 1907, the year Adams privately published it, Conrad published *The Secret Agent*, J. M. Synge brought out *The Playboy of the Western World* and Picasso exhibited *Les Demoiselles d'Avignon*. Like all of these works, *The Education* experiments with form and language to explore the social and cultural changes of the multiverse. Reviewing *The Education* in 1919, T. S. Eliot described Adams's intellect as like 'the wings of a beautiful but ineffectual conscience beating vainly in a vacuum jar'.[30] Adams would have liked the analogy: its combination of the natural beauty with the paraphernalia of logical science would have appealed to him. But the image connotes much more than a thwarted intellect. It reflects a central conceit of much modern American literature: a figure aware of the 'irregularities in the mental mirror', forever contemplating the futility of his efforts to survive in an increasingly claustrophobic modern world.[31]

HENRY JAMES

In Henry James, Adams had found a lifelong intellectual and spiritual comrade with whom he corresponded throughout his life. Both men were expatriates, writing from European bases about Americans abroad. Moreover, both were keen to understand the workings of the subjective consciousness – and were well aware of the impossibility of ever genuinely doing so. And as John Carlos Rowe has noted, both writers present works which describe and formally embody the struggle to come to terms with radical cultural change at the turn of the twentieth century.[32]

While Adams sought to consolidate a historical consciousness, James was interested in examining the epistemological problems raised at the end of the nineteenth century from an aesthetic point of view. His fictional corpus is more often described as realist than modernist, but scholars have noted the proto-modernist qualities of James's work, not least his thoughts regarding the relationship between the novel and reality as outlined in his various prefaces.[33] Like Adams, James is an intermediary figure, perched upon the bridge between the perceived rationality of the nineteenth century and the relative unpredictability of the twentieth century. Indeed, James acts as a transitional figure in various ways: as a bridge between Old and New Worlds, and as a link between European realism (thanks to the influence of Émile Zola, Gustave Flaubert and Ivan Turgenev upon his work) and an American modernism which focused upon the ambiguities of the individualised self. In their different ways, almost all his major characters, from Christopher Newman to Millie Theale, deal with the clash between cultures and the disconnection between the social codes of the past and the new morals of an emergent modernity.

Not unlike his friend and correspondent, James was of distinctly privileged stock. The son of Henry James Snr, a Swedenborgian-influenced transcendentalist and philosophical writer, and brother to William James, generally regarded as one of the most important American philosophers, who coined the term 'stream of thought', James was nurtured in an intellectual hothouse. One of the most important sibling bonds, however, was that with his younger sister Alice, who spent most of her life as an invalid and died young. Alice is manifestly the inspiration for many of James's doomed heroines, and his relationship with his stricken sister undoubtedly provided him with valuable insights into the female condition. Indeed, one of the most frequently observed aspects of James's *oeuvre* is his sensitive portrayal of female protagonists locked within stifling domestic interiors and social bonds, struggling to express emotions and their subjective identity. From Catherine Sloper and Isabel Archer to Maisie Farange and Maggie Verver, James experimented with the female point of view and plotted the shift from a state of innocence to the understanding brought about by the external world and the machinations of unscrupulous others.

This motif of the shackled female, suffocating within a restrictive domestic space, might serve as a useful analogy for James's fiction more widely. With its close attention to social manners, his work is often thought to have more in common with the nineteenth-century realist novel than with the experimental exuberance of early twentieth-century modern literature. But although James's style owes much to the realist mode, the concerns in his novels and in his theoretical writings are distinctly modern. He was critical of political radicalism, yet devoted two novels to the subject in *The Princess Casamassima* (1886) and *The Bostonians* (1886). He abhorred the new-fangled inventions of the age, such as the telegraph and the typewriter, yet there are frequent references to them throughout his fiction and, of course, he did use them in his day-to-day life. His plots are, for the most part, linear, yet he slowed the novel down, increasingly so in his later phase, to accommodate psychological time, showing the subject's quiet contemplation of external objects and events. So while James's foregrounding of the feminine world is undoubtedly important, perhaps even more influential were his attempts to represent the individual consciousness in all its transformative malleability.

In this context, *Washington Square* (1880), which belongs to James's earlier phase, is absolutely central. Though James later claimed to be disappointed by the book, even omitting it from the *New York Edition* (1905–7), it was his first experiment in the fictional presentation of a developing consciousness. The novel focuses on the relationships between a young woman, her father and her suitor, and its abiding theme is that of control. Catherine Sloper, who desires control over her own life, struggles against an overbearing father who is unashamedly disappointed by a daughter he regards as intellectually stolid and physically 'not scenic'. She becomes infatuated with the dashing Morris Townsend, but it soon becomes clear that the young man's interest lies firmly in acquiring control of the Sloper inheritance. What is more, control is a crucial aspect of James's method throughout the novel, with each tableau tightly plotted to reflect the central theme and to demonstrate the developing self-possession of the heroine. Throughout the story James the narrator remains on the periphery, manipulating the unfolding scenes (and the reader's responses), pulling the strings of his protagonists, and satirising the late nineteenth-century business classes and the social aspects of this genteel world. In this regard, it is Dr Sloper who is the principal target of James's mockery; like Adams, James was distrustful of the rising business and professional classes and unhappily noted the American preoccupation with 'business and busyness' in *The American Scene* (1907). So Sloper views his daughter solely in terms of her value and worth; unable to imagine any other reason for Morris's interest, he reminds her that she will be 'worth' more as a prospective bride having travelled abroad.

Like Isabel Archer and Maggie Verver, Catherine is transformed by the discovery of her own selfhood and inner life. As previously noted, James was increasingly interested in the relationship between the psychological processes of the mind and the world of external realities, a subject which later interested Virginia Woolf and her contemporaries and formed the basis of her essay 'The Art of Fiction' (1927). Paradoxically, the first step in Catherine Sloper's inner development is her attachment to the external reality that is Townsend. As her psychological complexity deepens, Catherine develops an acute sense of self-awareness and imagines herself as an actor in a play but also as an observer watching her own drama: 'She watched herself as she would have watched another person, who was both herself and not herself, had suddenly sprung into being inspiring her with a natural curiosity as to the performance of uninterested functions'.[34] James seems here to be playing metatextual games with the reader, insofar as he presents a young woman within a series of short dramatic scenes contemplating her own existence as both an actor and an observer of the scenes that are her life. By presenting Catherine thus, James assigns a kind of self-awareness to the protagonist which he viewed as essential to the artist. Indeed, in his famous essay 'The Art of Fiction' (1884), James would rebut the idea of learned rules which can be followed in the act of creation. By contrast, he invoked the notion of freedom of experience as a crucial element of the creative process: the creator, he argued, must at all times be alive to experience in order to utilise it in the work of art. Thus Catherine's ability to see herself once removed, as both player and observer, offers a dual perspective as she is at once both inside and outside her own drama and able to activate the shift from servitude to freedom. It is telling, too, that by the end of the novel we meet a Catherine much altered by the experiences life has meted out to her. Refusing a reunion with Morris, she has also denied her father control over her life by withholding the promise not to marry her former suitor. The final image of Catherine with her needlework may depict a woman trapped in a domestic prison-house; equally, it may present a portrait of a lady stitching together a life of her own. Deliberately ambiguous, James presents Catherine as a woman who has accepted her destiny; yet at the same time he reverses the earlier image of her as neglected material, 'a bundle of shawls', and casts her in the role of the self-aware artist pulling the threads across her own canvas.

With *The Portrait of a Lady* (1881), James extended his treatment of the developing psychological identity of a young woman and (in the preface) further developed his theory of fiction. *The Portrait* in some ways offers the inverse of *Washington Square*, depicting a free-spirited young woman who loses her freedom with the acquisition of a large sum of money. Isabel Archer, an impoverished orphan, is taken in by her Aunt Touchett, and the family move to London to care for the tubercular Ralph Touchett. In London Isabel rejects the marriage proposals of Caspar Goodwood, a wealthy American, and the aristocratic Lord Warburton. Upon inheriting a substantial inheritance of £70,000, she travels 'with wind in her sails' to Florence where she is introduced to the seemingly sophisticated Gilbert Osmond, whom she accepts as a husband, becoming stepmother to his daughter Pansy. Shortly into the marriage she realises the sterility of the union and discovers that the mother of her stepdaughter is the scheming Madame Merle, who introduced her to Osmond and engineered the marriage for the sake of her child. Learning of the impending death of her cousin Ralph, Isabel defies her husband's wishes and flees to London to be at her cousin's bedside. After Ralph's death Isabel once again rejects Goodwood and accepts her destiny with Osmond. James's conclusion, as in *Washington Square*, is deliberately equivocal: Isabel faces her destiny and returns to a loveless marriage, but she *chooses* to return because she has learned something of freedom, responsibility and consequence. Gone are the naïve visions of personal freedom which Isabel brought from America, and in their place is an appreciation of the necessary interconnection of subjective freedom and knowledge of external circumstances and realities. Isabel keeps her promise to return to Pansy, accepts responsibility for her past and thereby determines her own future.

In the preface to the novel, James comments directly on his development of Isabel and the technical realisation of this shift in his character's consciousness:

> My dim first move toward 'The Portrait' . . . was exactly my grasp of a single character . . . I saw it in motion and, so to speak, in transit. This amounts to saying that I saw it as bent upon its fate – some fate or other . . . 'Place the centre of the subject in the young woman's consciousness,' I said to myself . . . 'Stick to THAT – for the centre; put the heaviest weight into THAT scale, which will be so largely the scale of her relation to herself.'

In short, James tightens his focus on the individual in isolation, without the trappings of society or social mores. The germ of the novel rests in Isabel's desire for personal freedom and self-determination, and James is most interested in her development as she attains them. He goes on to stress his interest in the character not from some retrospective angle whereupon the point of change can be isolated and described, but in transition. The other furnishings of the novel were built around Isabel, including the other characters through which we have brief perspectives of the protagonist. James recalls that he told himself to 'press least hard, in short, on the consciousness of your heroine's satellites'.[35] Indeed, Isabel's psychological transformation comes not at a moment of interaction but in complete solitude in the early hours of the morning as she sits before the dying embers of her saloon fire. Her 'remembered vision' of 'her husband and Madame Merle unconsciously and familiarly associated' sets off a chain of memories and realisations regarding the state of her marriage, the truth about herself and the necessity of adapting to her circumstances.[36] Isabel realises the importance of keeping her eyes open to the base shabbiness of the world around her, for it is through attention to this world that she will come 'to extract from it some recognition of one's own superiority' (p. 479).

The development of consciousness is fundamental in this chapter; in the preface, James talks of 'positively organising an ado about Isabel Archer' and this essentially is what we have in the fireside chapter, as Isabel moves from thought to thought, and then back again.[37] It would be erroneous to describe this method as 'stream of consciousness', but it is undoubtedly a precursor for the modernist method of filtering a protagonist's contemplations as they come into being. As mentioned, James's brother William wrote extensively on the nature of human consciousness, eventually coming to view it as function and relation rather than an essence. In 'Does Consciousness Exist?' he wrote that 'consciousness connotes a kind of external relation' and, interestingly, Isabel's consciousness is grounded in her realisation of herself in relation to others.[38]

These experiments in consciousness were, perhaps, James's greatest contributions to modernism. Certainly he provided the link between the novel of society and the novel of interiority which was to emerge more regularly in subsequent decades. He championed the autonomy of fiction, a kind of *l'art pour l'art* artistic creed, which would not endear him to detractors such as Theodore Roosevelt, but which would enthuse fellow expatriates such as Eliot and Pound. Eliot left little doubt about his admiration for James, describing him as both 'the most intelligent man of his generation' and as among 'the greatest novelists'.[39] Quite early on, Eliot wrote a review of James's work on Hawthorne, remarking on the two writers' interest in 'the deeper psychology'. And although he later described James as a 'moralist' who 'studied no subtle character, nor any character subtly',[40] he revised this opinion somewhat in the following decade to view James as deeply interested in human consciousness in the moment of moral conflict.[41] Most famously, Eliot described James's method of distilling experience in action (without the knowingness of the author's experience intruding on the protagonist's awakening):

> James's critical genius comes out most tellingly in his mastery over, his baffling escape from, Ideas; a mastery and an escape which are perhaps the last test of a superior intelligence. He had a mind so fine that no idea could violate it.[42]

It was James's 'mastery and escape' in his treatment of a developing consciousness, as well as his 'care and punctiliousness for exact expression', that struck Eliot as particularly 'useful' and 'applicable' 'for our future'.[43] The emphasis on the 'exact expression' reads much like Ezra Pound's Imagist manifesto 'A Few Don'ts'; indeed, Pound too was much enamoured of his fellow expatriate and championed James throughout his career, even including him in his *ABC of Reading* (1934). In August 1918, the *Little Review* brought out a memorial issue devoted to James, of which Pound wrote the bulk, describing the author as 'the greatest writer of our time and of our own particular language'.[44]

What most interested Pound about James, however, was *language* – notably his ability to merge the spoken and written voices. 'Our aim is natural speech', Pound wrote in the essay which followed his piece on James, 'the language as spoken'.[45] He clearly saw himself in the same mould as James, a literary innovator and a technical explorer with a reverence for language.[46] And like the modernists, James was devastated by the outbreak of the First World War and lamented its effects on humanity and its deterioration of language:

> The war has used up words; they have weakened, they have deteriorated like motor car types; they have, like millions of other things, been more overstrained and knocked about and voiced of the happy semblance during the last six months than in all the long ages before, and we are now confronted with the deprecations of all our terms, or, otherwise speaking, with a loss of expression through increase of limpness, that may well make us wonder what ghosts will be left to walk.[47]

Here James speaks of the war in the same tone with which he addressed modern American culture in *The American Scene*, a tone of unmistakable revulsion at mass production and ultimate pessimism for the shape of things to come. The war's assault on language was a subject taken up in earnest not merely by Eliot and Pound, but also by other modernists such as Hemingway, Dos Passos, William Butler Yeats, D. H. Lawrence and Virginia Woolf. For these writers, the war would provide a change in the orientation of the themes, a reinvigoration of sorts. For James, however, the war was the ultimate offensive, and he died in 1916, before its conclusion. A structural innovator of the art of fiction, with a profound reverence for the sculptural qualities of language and a commitment to the depiction of consciousness without the implications of *a priori* experience, James surely deserves the accolade bestowed on him by Gertrude Stein, who called him 'the only nineteenth century writer who being an American felt the method of the twentieth century'.[48]

W. E. B. DU BOIS

One book much admired by James was W. E. B. Du Bois's seminal *The Souls of Black Folk* (1903), which he called the 'only Southern book of any distinction that had been published for many a year'.[49] James had been sent a copy of the work by his brother William, who had taught Du Bois at Harvard and described his protégé's publication as 'a decidedly moving book'.[50] Affinities between Henry James and Du Bois have seldom been explored and, indeed, the pair seem quite at odds with each other: the former a patrician Anglophile apparently appalled by the swathes of immigrants described in *The American Scene* (1907) and the latter an African American activist, committed to the promotion of black equality. Yet, as Ross Posnock has observed, James's questioning of the dividing line between the native and the alien 'articulates a pragmatist pluralism that conceives American identity as radically miscegenated, hybrid against which notions of "American Simplicity" or of authentic Americanism, become quixotic at best, antidemocratic and intolerant at worst'.[51]

This pragmatist pluralism, evident in James's scepticism in *The American Scene* toward the notion of a unified American character in favour of an illegible 'hotch potch' or identity, was shared by Du Bois, who learned from William James to revolt against the shackles of progressive identity and its immutable classifications. In *The Souls of Black Folk* – which should be recognised as a foundational document for American modernism, its essays inspiring a group of writers who would come collectively to form the Harlem

Renaissance, with its defiant rejection of African American subservience and promotion of black culture – Du Bois takes the 'soul' as his central metaphor. His central argument is that to know the soul of one man is to know the soul of an entire race. The soul, which is shared by all, reveals a common bond between individuals. It was on the basis of this common bond that he argued for the abnegation of segregation, the denunciation of racism and equality for African Americans.

Du Bois's description of the 'soul' has much in common with Emerson's notion of the 'Oversoul', that which unites one human being with another, but it was also influenced by the nineteenth-century abolitionist writer and activist Frederick Douglass, who himself drew on Emersonian romanticism in his calls for self-reliance and self-improvement. Throughout his autobiographical writings, Douglass frequently deployed the notion of a shared humanity and appealed to religious ideas of unity and mercy in his call for the emancipation of African Americans. Moreover, Douglass pulled off the same trick as Du Bois in focusing on the individual, the 'I', the self, as a representative of the whole, using his personal story of self-education and liberation to demonstrate the possibilities of freedom for an entire race. Du Bois, too, places himself and his own story at the centre of his work, demonstrating a mind capable of philosophical abstraction and intellectual rigour, as well as revealing a human being subject to emotion and loss, in an effort to make 'visible' the African American soul to a wider, white readership.

Throughout *The Souls of Black Folk*, the term 'soul' is used in different ways: it refers to the non-corporeal aspect of the self, that which is immortal; it refers to the emotional side of the individual, that which is capable of feeling and passion; and, finally, it refers to one's central core, that which makes the individual the man he is. While all of these meanings are important, the one in which Du Bois was undoubtedly most interested was the notion of the soul as an immortal, immaterial aspect of humanity. This definition of the soul appealed to common Christian morality, which, as Douglass had previously demonstrated, allowed the black writer to link black and white Americans in a shared humanity under God. Thus, while Du Bois's book may be eclectic in its generic range (cultural history, folklore and elegy) and subjects (music, education, religion and economics), at its heart is a fierce commitment to a political agenda of social, intellectual and spiritual equality.

Du Bois's method of placing himself, his story and his experiences, at the heart of the book recalls precursors such as Emerson, Douglass and even Whitman. Indeed, it would influence more modern writers such as James Weldon Johnson in *The Autobiography of an Ex-Colored Man* (1912; republished 1927) and Richard Wright in *Native Son* (1940). However, this strategy is also part of the book's deliberate response to a contemporary African American spokesman who had presented himself as a representative African American, namely Booker T. Washington. Founder of the Tuskegee Institute and leader of the so-called 'Men of Tuskegee', Washington was one of the most vocal proponents of African American consent. Speaking at the Atlanta Exposition in 1895, Washington famously made his case for a kind of economic nationalism, claiming that Americans needed to be united in the world of business and commerce for the sake of national prosperity. Yet this unity, he claimed, could stop at economic imperatives: 'In all things purely social we can be as separate as the fingers, yet one as the hand in all things essential to mutual progress'.[52] Needless to say, Washington's programme was palatable to the majority of white Americans (and to many black conservatives), suggesting that the leading spokesman for American Americans was endorsing segregation in education, public services and housing. In education, for example, Washington made the case for a vocational, industrial education provision for African Americans, rather than classical and scientific subjects such as mathematics, the sciences or the humanities, which he viewed as impractical and unnecessary for the living of everyday life. And on the subject of voting, he advised his fellow African Americans to seek the advice of more experienced, white men before casting the ballot. Washington's apparent obsequiousness, naturally, brought him widespread attention and supporters, among them many influential white businessmen and benefactors such as Andrew Carnegie and J. D. Rockefeller, whose financial backing ensured that his message of economic interdependence and social segregation was widely heard.

For Du Bois, Washington's apparently deferential approach

carried too many implications of black inferiority. The Atlanta Exposition, wrote Du Bois, would better be called the 'Atlanta Compromise', and he argued that Washington was essentially asking African Americans to sacrifice political power, the quest for civil rights and the higher, classical education of African American youth, all for the sake of economic stability. For Du Bois, failing to support African Americans in their desire for self-improvement was nothing less than a great betrayal: 'Here is a race transplanted through the criminal foolishness of your forefathers. Whether you like it or not the millions are here to stay, and here they will remain. If you do not uplift them, they will pull you down.'[53] And for Du Bois, it was the simple duty of white America to assist its black brethren. On this latter point, he was particularly critical of Washington's supposed appeasement:

> His doctrine has tended to make the whites, North and South, shift the burden of the Negro problem to the Negro's shoulders and stand aside as critical and rather pessimistic spectators; when in fact the burden belongs to the nation, and the hands of none of us are clean if we bend not our energies to the righting of these great wrongs.[54]

In opposition to Washington's 'Men of Tuskegee' and vocational training as a model for black education, Du Bois came up with the idea of the 'Talented Tenth', a term used to describe the percentage of black individuals who ought to become spokesmen for their community and instigate social change.

In an essay reminiscent of Emerson's 'Representative Men', Du Bois listed a series of black individuals who had promoted improvements in the lot of African Americans, among them the likes of Phillis Wheatley, Lemuel Haynes and Frederick Douglass. To be sure, 'The Talented Tenth' (1903) pitched its argument at a less emotive level than some of the essays in *The Souls of Black Folk*, using empirical data on the professions of African American college graduates to illustrate the empowering and uplifting qualities of a non-vocational education. And in countering the notion of black education as a public burden, Du Bois showed how public wealth had been amassed on the back of black labour. The taxes alone from this wealth, he argued, should be sufficient to cover the cost of a widespread educational programme. Furthermore, he suggested that an educated African American would prove a public benefit, with the cost of this education easily outweighed by benefits reaped by society. This rhetoric of a shared national burden, needless to say, did not appeal to the conservative middle classes. Even the black middle classes feared that this kind of agitation and protest would impede full assimilation. Indeed, Du Bois's eventual involvement with the Niagara Movement (1905) and the National Association for the Advancement of Colored People (1909), as well as his editorship of *The Crisis* magazine, lost him much of the middle-class support which he needed if he wanted to push forward the socio-political aspects of his mission.

On an intellectual level, however, Du Bois had a tremendous impact. Quite apart from his political activities, he became a powerful advocate of key philosophical ideas on the nature of 'blackness'. One of the most enduring of Du Bois's ideas about the psychological ramifications of slavery and institutional racism, for example, was the notion of 'twoness':

> One ever feels his twoness, – an American, a Negro; two souls, two thoughts, two unreconciled strivings; two warring ideals in one dark body, whose dogged strength alone keeps it from being torn asunder.
>
> The history of the American Negro is the history of this strife – this longing to attain self-conscious manhood, to merge his double self into a better and truer self. In this merging he wishes neither of the older selves to be lost. He would not Africanize America, for America has too much to teach the world and Africa. He would not bleach his Negro soul in a flood of white Americanism, for he knows that Negro blood has a message for the world. He simply wishes to make it possible to be both a Negro and an American, without being cursed and spit upon by his fellows, without having the doors of Opportunity closed roughly in his face. (p. 5)

This double consciousness, according to DuBois, allows the African American individual 'no true self-consciousness', but instead forces him to see himself 'through the eyes of others' (p. 5). Thus, the individual is forced to embrace an existing notion of blackness, which precedes his sense of self and the formation of a personal identity. This necessary confrontation with a fully formed version of blackness is potentially detrimental to the development of the individual psyche, and may even inhibit the growth of a personal sense of self. So the black individual is lumbered with a white preconception of black identity, which threatens to blind him to his own, personally formed, sense of identity. An awareness of this externally determined sense of self is the weight of double consciousness with which the subject must battle, and it is this internal war of selves which constitutes the African American identity.

Du Bois's notion of the split psychology of the African American subject is a trope that reappears across a wide range of African American literature, from the poetry of the Harlem Renaissance to more recent novels such as Toni Morrison's *Beloved* (1987) and Percival Everett's *Erasure* (2001). Most famously, perhaps, it informs Ralph Ellison's 1952 novel *Invisible Man*, in which the eponymous narrator tells the reader that white people 'refuse to see [him]'.[55] Ellison's narrator recounts a life in which preconceived notions of what an African American should do and be have come to obscure his actual selfhood to such an extent that he becomes alienated from himself. Even before Ellison, however, the modernist artists involved with Alain Locke's edited book *The New Negro* (1925) took up Du Bois's ideas, not only those regarding the 'twoness' of African American identity, but his sense of the necessity of the classical arts, the need for social action to rehabilitate the race and the necessity of a cultural nationalism that would encompass the dualism at the heart of African American life. Echoing the words of Du Bois two decades earlier, Locke (the first black Rhodes scholar) observed the importance of both Africa and America to the ordinary black American: 'The racialism of the Negro is no limitation or reservation with respect to America; it is only a constructive effort to build the obstructions in the stream of his progress into an efficient dam of social energy and power'.[56] The volume even contained an epilogue by Du Bois himself, tracing the global implications of the New Negro Movement and, in particular, its relationship to colonialism in general, the global leadership role for African Americans and the struggle for freedom in Africa.

What all of the contributors shared, though, was the intoxicating expectation of a second emancipation, brought about by scholarship, literature, music and drama. Angelina Grimke's pithy poem 'The Black Finger' embodies this optimism in its image of the black finger pointing skywards; similarly, the black female object of Anne Spencer's 'Lady Lady' holds God and 'the tongues of flames the ancients knew' in her 'darksome' body. And at the heart of the collective optimism, shared by so many African Americans in the first half of the 1920s, was Du Bois himself. His vision of a divided subjectivity spoke to a people anxious for cultural and social equality, yet reluctant to relinquish an identity shaped by prejudice and discrimination. Later, his vision found its embodiment in the characters of Jean Toomer, Nella Larsen and others, while his commitment to the necessity of a classical education for African Americans helped to encourage a new black activism based in culture and the arts. Du Bois has not always been seen as a modernist. But in his emphasis on the fractured self, his fascination with subjectivity and his passionate political commitment, he deserves as much as anyone to be regarded as one of the fathers of a uniquely American strand of literary modernism.

NOTES

1. For a succinct discussion of the American Civil War, see Hugh Brogan's superb *Penguin History of the United States of America* (London: Penguin, 1985). In the pages that follow, I am greatly indebted to this splendid and mysteriously underrated book.
2. Ibid.
3. See table, 'Number of Daily Newspapers in the US, 1970–1990', in Eric Foner and John A. Garraty (eds), *The Reader's Companion to American History* (New York: Houghton Mifflin, 1991), p. 691.
4. See David Reynolds, *Beneath the American Renaissance: The Subversive Imagination in the Age of Emerson and Melville* (Cambridge, MA: Harvard University Press, 1988).

5. Charles Olson, *Call Me Ishmael* (Baltimore: Johns Hopkins University Press, [1947] 1997), p. 23.
6. R. W. Emerson, 'The American Scholar' (1837), in *Selected Essays*, ed. Larzer Ziff (London: Penguin, 1982), p. 104. All subsequent references to Emerson's essays appear in the text and, unless otherwise specified, refer to this collection.
7. See especially Jonathan Levin's *The Poetics of Transition: Emerson, Pragmatism and American Literary Modernism* (Durham, NC: Duke University Press, 1999). Levin offers a superb reading of this aspect of Emerson's legacy, its direct and indirect influences upon pragmatism and its manifestation in the literary aesthetics of Henry James, Gertrude Stein and Wallace Stevens.
8. Ibid. p. 2.
9. William James, 'The Stream of Thought', in *The Principles of Psychology* (New York: Cosimo, 2007), vol. 1, pp. 245–6.
10. Leon Edel (ed.), *Henry James: Literary Criticism: French Writers, Other European Writiers: The Prefaces to the New York Edition* (New York: Library of America, 1894), p. 1041.
11. Ezra Pound, 'Jules Romains', in *Instigations* (New York: Boni and Liveright, 1920), pp. 69–77.
12. Richard Poirier, *The Renewal of Literature: Emersonian Reflections* (New York: Random House, 1987), p. 50.
13. Gertrude Stein, 'What are Master-Pieces', cited in Barbara Will, *Gertrude Stein, Modernism and the Problem of 'Genius'* (Edinburgh: Edinburgh University Press, 2000), p. 83.
14. William James, 'The Stream of Thought', p. 241.
15. Walt Whitman, 'Song of Myself', in *Leaves of Grass*, ed. Jerome Loving (Oxford: Oxford University Press, [1891–2] 1990), p. 78. Subsequent references will appear in the text and refer to this edition.
16. Kenneth M. Price, *Whitman and Tradition: The Poet in His Century* (New Haven: Yale University Press, 1990), pp. 38–9.
17. Malcolm Cowley, 'Introduction to *Leaves of Grass*' (1959), in Francis Murphy (ed.), *Walt Whitman: A Critical Anthology* (New York: Penguin, 1969), p. 347.
18. Indeed, James Joyce was to do exactly the same in his *Ulysses* (1922) with the marriage of a Homeric epic framework to the

lowly life of an ordinary man. Joyce offers details of Leopold Bloom's diet, his sexuality and even his bowel movements. Yet Bloom is the representative man, a figure of modernity in all his potential and uncertainties. For a critique of Whitman's supposed affinities with the working classes, see Andrew Lawson's superb study, *Walt Whitman and the Class Struggle* (Iowa City: Iowa University Press, 2006).

19. T. S. Eliot, 'Tradition and the Practice of Poetry', in *T. S. Eliot: Essays from the Southern Review*, ed. James Olney (Oxford: Clarendon Press, 1988), p. 14.
20. Ezra Pound, 'What I Feel About Walt Whitman', in *Ezra Pound: Selected Prose, 1909–1965*, ed. William Cookson (London: Faber and Faber, 1973), p. 145.
21. Ezra Pound, 'A Pact', in *Personae*, ed. Lea Baechler and A. Walton Litz (New York: New Directions, 1991), p. 90.
22. Mark Morrison, 'Nationalism and the Modern American Canon', in Walter Kalaidjian (ed.), *The Cambridge Companion to American Modernism* (Cambridge: Cambridge University Press, 2005), pp. 15–16.
23. Robert Lowell on Williams's Platonism, in *The Nation* (19 June 1948), pp. 692–4. Cited in Charles Doyle (ed.), *William Carlos Williams: The Critical Heritage* (London: Routledge and Kegan Paul, 1980), p. 190.
24. Olson's poems were published incrementally from 1953 to 1993.
25. In fact, Adams printed and distributed 300 copies to friends and family in 1907.
26. Henry Adams, *The Education of Henry Adams* (Oxford: Oxford University Press, [1918] 1999), p. 285. All subsequent references will appear in the text.
27. Henry Adams, *Democracy: An American Novel* (New York: Penguin, [1880] 1994), p. 17.
28. Henry Adams, *The Letters of Henry Adams*, ed. J. C. Levenson, Ernest Samuels, Charles Vandersee and Viola Hopkins Winner (Cambridge, MA: Harvard University Press, 1982–8), p. 694.
29. Henry Adams, *Novels, Mont Saint Michel and Chartres, The Education of Henry Adams, Poems* (New York: Library of America, 1984), p. 649.

30. T. S. Eliot, 'A Sceptical Patrician', review of *The Education of Henry Adams: An Autobiography*, in *The Athenaeum* (23 May 1919), pp. 361–2.
31. Henry Adams, *Novels, Mont Saint Michel and Chartres, The Education of Henry Adams, Poems*, p. 695.
32. This is perhaps most evident in *The American Scene* (1907), in which James explores the changes in the American socio-cultural and geographical landscape he encountered on his American tour of 1904–5. He makes a grim forecast for the American future due to the impact of unrestricted immigration, rampant industrialisation, racial unrest and economic materialism on the social fabric of the United States. The writer Colm Tóibín notes that 'James's writings about New York disclose, more than anything, an anger quite unlike any other anger in James, at what has been lost to him, what has been done, in the name of commerce and material progress, to a place he once knew'. See 'Preface', in *The New York Stories of Henry James*, ed. Colm Tóibín (New York: New York Review of Books Classics, 2005), p. x.
33. See, for instance, Michelle H. Phillips's recent article, 'The "Partagé Child" and the Emergence of the Modernist Novel in *What Maisie Knew*', *Henry James Review*, 31.2 (Spring 2010), pp. 95–110.
34. Henry James, *Washington Square* (London: Penguin, [1880] 2007), p. 83.
35. Leon Edel (ed.), *Henry James: Literary Criticism: French Writers, Other European Writiers: The Prefaces to the New York Edition* (New York: Library of America, 1894), p. 1079.
36. Henry James, *The Portrait of a Lady* (London: Penguin, [1881] 2003), p. 484. Subsequent references will appear in the text.
37. Leon Edel (ed.), *Henry James: Literary Criticism: French Writers, Other European Writiers: The Prefaces to the New York Edition* (New York: Library of America, 1894), p. 1077.
38. William James, 'Does Consciousness Exist?' *Essays in Radical Empiricism* (Lincoln: University of Nebraska Press, [1912] 1996), pp. 1–38.
39. T. S. Eliot, 'On Henry James', in F. W. Dupee (ed.), *The Question of Henry James* (New York: Henry Holt, 1948), p. 111.

40. T. S. Eliot, 'American Literature', *Athenaeum* (25 April 1919), p. 236.
41. T. S. Eliot, 'Les lettres anglaises', *La Nouvelle Revue Française*, 28 (1 May 1927), p. 699. Also see Alan Holder's essay 'T. S. Eliot on Henry James', *PMLA*, 79.4 (1964), pp. 490–7.
42. Cited in Holder, 'T. S. Eliot on Henry James', p. 494.
43. T. S. Eliot, 'A Prediction in Regard to Three English Authors', *Vanity Fair*, 21 (February 1924), p. 29.
44. Ezra Pound, 'Henry James', in *Literary Essays of Ezra Pound*, ed. T. S. Eliot (New York: New Directions, 1968), p. 331.
45. Ezra Pound, 'Lionel Johnson', in *Literary Essays of Ezra Pound*, p. 362.
46. See Holder for an excellent analysis of Pound's description of both himself and James as Odysseus-like figures in the literary terrain. Alan Holder, 'The Lesson of the Master: Ezra Pound and Henry James', *American Literature*, 35.1 (1963), pp. 71–9.
47. Cited in Peter Buitenhuis, *The Great War of Words: British, American and Canadian Propaganda and Fiction, 1914–1933* (Vancouver: University of British Columbia Press, 1987), p. 61.
48. Gertrude Stein, *The Autobiography of Alice B. Toklas* (London: Penguin, [1933] 1989), p. 86. See also Stein's portrait of James in *Four in America* (New Haven: Yale University Press, 1947). Eric Haralson discusses the triangulation of Stein, James and Hemingway in '"The other half is the man": The Queer Modern Triangle of Gertrude Stein, Ernest Hemingway and Henry James', in *Henry James and Queer Modernity* (Cambridge: Cambridge University Press, 2003), pp. 173–204.
49. However, as Ross Posnock and Kenneth Warren have observed, Du Bois was actually a native of Massachusetts and a graduate of Harvard, though he had been teaching at Atlanta for a year. See Ross Posnock, 'Affirming the Alien; The Pragmatist Pluralism of *The American Scene*', in Jonathan Freedman (ed.), *The Cambridge Companion to Henry James* (Cambridge: Cambridge University Press, 1998), pp. 224–46.
50. Cited in James Campbell, 'Du Bois and James', *Transactions of the Charles S. Peirce Society*, 28.3 (Summer 1992), p. 579.
51. Ross Posnock, 'Affirming the Alien; The Pragmatist Pluralism of *The American Scene*', p. 232.

52. Address of Booker T. Washington at the opening of the Cotton States and International Exposition at Atlanta (18 September 1895), African American Perspectives: Pamphlets from the Daniel A. P. Murray Collection, 1818–1907; available online at: http://memory.loc.gov/ (accessed 20 January 2012).
53. W. E. B. Du Bois, 'The Talented Tenth' (September 1903); available online at: http://teachingamericanhistory.org/library/index.asp?document=174 (accessed 20 January 2012).
54. W. E. B. Du Bois, 'Of Mr. Booker T. Washington and Others', in *The Souls of Black Folk* (London: Penguin, [1903] 1989), p. 49. Subsequent references will appear in the text.
55. Ralph Ellison, *Invisible Man* (London: Penguin, [1952] 2001), p. 3.
56. Alain Locke, 'The New Negro' (1925), in Alain Locke (ed.), *The New Negro* (New York: Atheneum, 1968), p. 6.

CHAPTER 2

Tales of New York City: The Birth of the Modern Metropolis

The American city has long been synonymous with modernity, and none more so than New York City. As the great sociologist Louis Wirth remarked in 1938, 'the beginning of what is distinctively modern in our civilization is best signalized by the growth of great cities'.[1] To this day the visual image of New York has a global currency; across the world, the glittering pinnacle of the Chrysler Building, the impressive sweep of Brooklyn Bridge and the impassive face of the Statue of Liberty are icons of modernity itself. Much of this can be attributed to the American film industry, which, since its inception, has been drawn to the disjunction between the lower-class drudgery and the giddy splendour of the city. From early films such as J. Stuart Blackton's *The Thieving Hand* (1908), Fatty Arbuckle's *Coney Island* (1917) and Alan Crosland's *The Jazz Singer* (1927), to Martin Scorsese's *Taxi Driver* (1976), John Badham's *Saturday Night Fever* (1977) and Woody Allen's *Manhattan* (1979), as well as more recent pictures such as Scorsese's *Gangs of New York* (2002), Ridley Scott's *American Gangster* (2007) and Matt Reeves's *Cloverfield* (2008), the Manhattan skyline has become a supremely visual symbol of the modern world and its discontents. Meanwhile, television sitcoms such as *Friends* (1994–2004) and *Sex and the City* (1998–2004) wallow in the glitz and the glamour associated with New York, while video games such as *Grand Theft Auto IV* (2008), with its thinly veiled Liberty City, and *Batman: Arkham City* (2011) shift the focus to the city's seedy criminal underbelly. Even the terrorist attacks of 11 September 2001 were a supremely visual spectacle, watched in open-mouthed horror by millions across the world: an assault not just on thousands of innocent, defenceless people, but on the city's iconic skyline and, by implication, on modernity itself, designed for mass television consumption. For what the 9/11 planners recognised and exploited was the flaunting, spectacular nature of the city and of the West's voyeuristic love affair with it. This was a city that loved being watched, a culture fascinated by its modern beauty.

From its very beginnings, New York has always been a city of dreams and a city of nightmares, a place of liberation, wonder, glamour and success and yet also the site of squalor, degradation, poverty and terror. Even when it was first discovered by European settlers in 1524, the future New York was seen as a portent of a possible utopia. Home to a small group of Lenape (Algonquian) Native Americans, it was first visited by a Florentine explorer, Giovanni da Verrazano, who recognised the enormous trade and resource potential of the Lower New York Bay area. A century later, the Dutch founded New York, or New Amsterdam as they called it, capitalising on the potential of the local fur trade with the Lenape population. However, tensions between the Dutch colonists and the natives escalated with the exhaustion of the beaver fur stocks, disputes and misunderstandings over property rights, while the Europeans' introduction of infectious diseases wreaked havoc among the Lenape people. In 1664, during the Anglo-Dutch War, the city was conquered by the English and renamed New York, after the Duke of York, who was granted permission from King Charles II to found a proprietary colony on the land. When a second Anglo-Dutch War confirmed the change of ownership – the Dutch agreeing to exchange the city for the smallest of the Banda Islands in Indonesia – Manhattan began its transformation into the extraordinary economic and cultural melting pot it remains to this day. Yet all was not sweetness and light. Skirmishes with the Native American population and a swathe of epidemics gave the city a distinctly dystopian aspect, a sense of uneasy restlessness which would culminate in the Great Fire of 1776, the innumerable clashes between the Sons of Liberty and the English troops stationed in the city, and the horrific violence of the American Revolution.[2]

By the end of the eighteenth century, however, optimism had regained the upper hand – not least after New York was briefly designated the national capital in 1785. The promise of utopia was perhaps best articulated by Francis Baily in 1796, when he hailed the 'perfect regularity' and geometric order of the new, emergent American cities which were to be the embodiment of scientific rationality and therefore of modernity itself.[3] Baily's vision of the modern American city was rooted in the rectilinear gridiron model which he had first seen in Philadelphia (where it had been installed in 1682) and which was approved for New York City in 1811. The gridiron model was, of course, originally conceived as a convenient means of ordering space, making the city more habitable for its dwellers and enabling more orderly administration. It was also designed to contain the spread of disease (particularly important given the numerous epidemics of the previous century), an idea which developed from Thomas Jefferson's 'checkerboard towns' and his utopian notion of bringing the pleasures of the country into the city.[4] However, the model also enabled the convenient parcelling of land for development and sale. Thus the aesthetic pleasures envisioned by Jefferson increasingly gave way to economically driven urban planning which inevitably led to the expansion of the city. Indeed, the surge in real estate and the industrial development of New York occurred at such a pace that by 1890, the city's population was 1.4 million. (For comparison, at the time of its discovery in 1524, it had been home to approximately 5000 Native Americans.)

By this point, New York was already the largest metropolis in the world and the hub of American enterprise. The nature of its business had subtly changed; originally a mercantile centre, it was becoming a vital industrial and administrative hub. One of the most important economic developments in the city's history was the opening of Erie Canal in 1825, a move which finally realised Verrazano's sense of the trade possibilities of the bay. Erie Canal became the chief port of entry for European immigrants and trade, offering access to the continent's vast interior for the purposes of settlement, export and import. The city's composition also altered hugely with the development of transport networks. New York began to sprawl outwards and lose its identity as a 'walking city' with the introduction of the 'El' transport system in the 1870s, the electric streetcar in the 1880s and the New York City subway in 1904. Other important developments include the opening of Brooklyn Bridge in 1883, the unveiling of the Statue of Liberty in 1886, and the expansion of the city with the addition of new boroughs, Kings, Richmond, Queens and Brooklyn, in 1898 – all of which were widely perceived as symbols of the city's status as the most 'modern' human enterprise in the world.[5]

Accompanying this expansive outward sprawl, the city also made a vertical ascent skywards in the late nineteenth and early twentieth centuries. The age of the American skyscraper was born with the completion of the New York World Building (also known as the Pulitzer Building) in 1890, which was the first building to surpass the 284-foot spire of Trinity Church. The comparison between the church and the skyscraper reflects a wider cultural shift from the unquestioning devotion and obedience demanded by the Catholic Church to the investigative and unsparingly graphic exposés of corruption and degeneracy in the pages of 'scandal sheet' newspapers such as the *New York World*, which was based in the New York World Building. The *New York World* also pioneered the colour supplement, as well as the use of illustrations and advertising, thus inaugurating a wholly new kind of newspaper. As this chapter will discuss, John Dos Passos would exploit the links between the skyscraper and the muckraking penny presses in *Manhattan Transfer* (1925), in which Jimmy Herf walks away from a life as an investigative hack, but finds he is no longer able to access the world within the skyscraper.

Other skyscrapers followed, including the Flatiron Building (1902), the Metropolitan Life Insurance Company Tower (1907), the Woolworth Building (1913) the Equitable Building (1915), the American Radiator Building (1924), the Western Union Building (1930), the Chrysler Building (1930) and the Empire State Building (1931). The skyscraper, of course, was an architectural leap forward, representing a new, modern method of design and construction with the use of glass and steel illuminated by electric light. Decoratively too, the skyscraper embraced the art deco eclecticism of modern art; one need only glance at the glittering, symmetrical arches of the Chrysler spire or the neo Beaux Arts styling of the Flatiron Building. Moreover, the skyscraper encapsulated New York's business ethic in its thrusting upward ascent, its delight in competition and dominance. Tellingly, most of the new buildings were developed to provide office space for the new or expanding American businesses of corporate banking, advertising and insurance. Here too, therefore, the aesthetic pleasures of the city were closely tied to its business imperatives; it was no accident that the modernist architectural landmarks developed hand in hand with the economic explosion within the city. American modernism, in other words, was no less an economically driven shift than it was a cultural phenomenon.

The expansion of the city was not only geographical and architectural but, of course, numerical in terms of the explosion in the number of city dwellers. Some 27 million immigrants entered New York between 1880 and 1930. Even before this, though, the United States had been a prime destination for European immigrants seeking a better way of life. From 1845 to 1852, for instance, during the years of the Irish Potato Famine, over a million people crossed the Atlantic. By 1850 the Irish represented a quarter of New York's population. Other national groups migrating to the United States during this time included Germans, French, Italians and Scandinavians, but this wave of immigration reached a peak in the 1850s, curtailed by the American Civil War, which brought further demographic changes. From 1880 immigration resumed in earnest, with the arrival of Jewish immigrants from Eastern Europe and Russia who sought to escape grinding poverty and religious persecution. Not all immigrants entering through New York settled in the city, but many did. In 1890 the city's population stood at 1.5 million; a decade later the figure had leapt to 3.5 million, representing a growth of 126.8 per cent. By 1930 New York was home to just under 7 million people.[6]

The incongruity of the glittering skyscraper set alongside the immigrant ghetto struck a chord with many writers, juxtaposing the dream and the nightmare, the utopian and dystopian. To some, the fact that the very rich could coexist in close proximity with the very poor was a symbol of democracy; to others, it served to highlight the social injustices of the city. New York brought the lower and the upper classes into closer proximity than ever before seen in the United States. Anzia Yezierska directly addresses this issue in her coming-of-age novel *Bread Givers* (1925), which frequently mentions genuine New York millionaires such as John D. Rockefeller and J. P. Morgan in a story of grinding poverty and degradation. As the heroine, young Sara Smolinsky, dreams of a better life, the electric light of the skyscraper both taunts and impels her on her quest for social and intellectual self-improvement. Though contextually very different to Yezierska's novel, Nella Larsen's *Passing* (1929) also illuminates the coexistence of wealth and poverty, using the skyscraper as a central metaphor for the rise and fall of the outsider, the transgressive African American woman. Dos Passos, too, uses his fiction to demonstrate the brute force of modernity, setting newly arrived immigrants alongside real estate prospectors to demonstrate how the very wealthy are dependent upon the sweat and blood of the very poor for their wealth and glamour.

The net result of the massive glut of immigration was a profound reappraisal of American identity. With many immigrant groups trapped in their ghettos, progressive notions that new immigrants would adapt and assimilate to the codes of Anglo-Saxon gentility and adopt the lingua franca were often not realised. And large enclaves of immigrant communities, whose values and ambitions could be at odds with those of the nation, often caused consternation among the Anglo-American intelligentsia. It is true that for some intellectuals such as Randolph Bourne and Horace Kallen, immigrant communities embodied a cultural pluralism that was true to the original ideals of the nation. For most, though, naturalisation was an impossibility and the influx of immigrants represented a threat to national 'purity'. So in his polemic *America: A Family Matter* (1922), Charles G. Gould argued that immigrants can never be 'Americanised' because such qualities could not be taught but 'must come to us from the mother's milk, the baby's lisping questions, and grow with our nerves and thews and sinews until they become part and parcel of our very being'.[7] This was the background for reforms such as the Emergency Quota Act of 1921, which limited national immigration to the 1910 quotas, and the Johnson-Reed Immigration Act of 1924 which brought quotas back to the 1890 limit. The effect was to lower the number of people entering the city, but by this stage the immigrant stamp was deep indeed. Indeed, the surge in immigration was one of the key factors in cementing New York's reputation as a centre of modernism; as Werner Sollers has observed, 'ethnicization and modernization go hand in hand'.[8]

As the critic Raymond Williams has remarked, the figure of the immigrant is an important link between the development of aesthetic modernism and the growth of the metropolis:

> The most important general element of the innovations in [modernist] form is the fact of immigration to the metropolis, and it cannot too often be emphasized how many of the major innovators were, in this precise sense, immigrants. At the level of theme, this underlies, in an obvious way, the elements of strangeness and distance, indeed of alienation, which so regularly form part of the repertory.[9]

For Williams, immigration drew attention to the phenomenon of language itself, with second languages (i.e. not English) often being described by nativist contemporaries as slippery, unreliable or artificial. And as Peter Brooker has remarked, the fractured discourses and linguistic experiments which characterise much modernist literature are clearly rooted in the specific socio-cultural phenomenon of immigration.[10] Thus countless modernist writers juxtapose a range of different languages with English, hoping to defamiliarise the reader from the language he takes for granted, and also to make authentic the experience of a complex and strange modernity. T. S. Eliot's *The Waste Land* (1922) is a case in point, with its 'unreal city' punctuated by received, cockney and Elizabethan English, as well as untranslated German and Sanskrit. Often English itself is altered in an attempt to show the modernist artist's perception of language as arbitrary and shifting, but also to offer a lived experience of language: that is, language as mediated by the new modern consciousness. So in *Manhattan Transfer*, Ed Thatcher's conversation with a German father shortly after his wife has given birth requires a second glance before the reader understands that the 'poy' to which the immigrant refers is actually a 'boy', his new baby son. And Dreiser's *Sister Carrie* (1900) quite deliberately plays with linguistic registers to effect a dissonance which acts as both an illumination on and an indictment of modern American life.

In his seminal essay 'The Metropolis and Mental Life' (1903), Georg Simmel identified the plight of the modern city dweller as the maintenance of one's individuality in the face of the overwhelmingly assimilative powers of society. For Simmel, the metropolis engenders a new human psychology which has adapted to the multitudinous and violent stimuli of city life:

> They have in common a purely matter-of-fact attitude in the treatment of persons and things in which a formal justice is often combined with an unrelenting hardness . . . The metropolis [as] the seat of the money economy . . . is concerned only with what is common to all, i.e. with the exchange value which reduces all quality and individuality to a purely quantitative level.[11]

Certainly, the levelling effect of the city is an abiding theme in both modern and modernist American literature, a theme taken up by many of the writers in this thematically driven chapter which begins with Dos Passos, who borrows from the Marxist ideological lexicon for his portrayal of individuals transformed into pieces of machinery or into organic matter which is pulped down by the machine that is the city. Larsen, too, depicts the city as a ravenous beast which consumes its human inhabitants; and Wharton draws attention to both the conspicuous consumption which characterises the New York elite and the consumption of women within the city's entrenched social hierarchies. Lily Bart may occupy the opposite end of the social spectrum to Sara Smolinsky, but she is no less a victim of the forces of the city, which seek to chisel her identity into an acceptable femininity, thereby stripping her identity of its idiosyncrasies and basic humanity – and reducing her to her quantitative value. This chapter's beginning with Dos Passos and working chronologically backwards toward Dreiser and Wharton is a considered strategy, deliberately designed to foreground the experimental features of canonical modernist writers and then explore how earlier writers had been working towards these techniques in their work.

As we have seen, some writers have always seen New York as a potentially liberating site, a place where fortunes can be amassed and dreams can be realised. For others, it has always been a lonely space which undermines selfhood and gnaws away at the individual's humanity. And for the modernist artist the metropolis is a space which facilitates anonymity, enabling the observer, the *flâneur*, to move undetected through the crowds, quietly feeding his imagination. The city is an unfinished canvas, a work of art in perpetual progress, reshaped and reconfigured in every new architectural addition and in every new personal rendition. It is the quirky, futuristic city depicted in Joseph Stella's *New York Interpreted* (1920–2) and, simultaneously, the claustrophobically lonely space of Edward Hopper's *Room in New York* (1932). As Brooker points out, New York was a 'found object', not dissimilar from Marcel Duchamp's signed urinal, a found object that had been designated as a work of art and submitted to the Independent Artists' Exhibition in 1917. Indeed, New York was officially put on the map as a work of art in 1913 with Duchamp's inauguration of New York Dada and the New York Armory Show's exhibition of works by John Marin, Joseph Stella and others, depicting aspects of the city (such as skyscrapers, the Brooklyn Bridge, Coney Island and the Port) in Cubist, cubo-realist, or Futurist terms.[12] And from the moment of its discovery to the present-day reconstruction of Ground Zero, New York has been endlessly designed and redesigned, imagined and re-imagined, both as utopia and dystopia. Each reconfiguration makes the city anew: a space up for grabs; a space to be refashioned, reinterpreted and redrawn; a metropolis which continues to bewitch, dazzle and perplex, at once city of dreams and landscape of nightmares.

JOHN DOS PASSOS

One writer greatly interested in the fusion of the visual arts with literary fiction was John Dos Passos, whose best-known novel, *Manhattan Transfer*, works to elide the visual, the aural and the literary arts in order to depict the interrelationship and interconnectivity between the various disciplines of modernity. Though often neglected in modernist literary studies, Dos Passos was one of the more experimental writers of the so-called Lost Generation (see Chapter 4) and was greatly admired by his fellow exiles Ernest Hemingway, Gertrude Stein and F. Scott Fitzgerald.

Though he was an established writer and reviewer from 1916 onwards, the publication of *Manhattan Transfer* in 1925 lifted Dos Passos into the pantheon of American literary modernism. Sinclair Lewis's review of the novel for the *Saturday Review of Literature* described the book as 'the first novel to catch Manhattan' which marked 'the dawn of a whole new school of writing', before concluding that *Manhattan Transfer* was 'more important in every way than anything by Gertrude Stein or Marcel Proust, or even the great white boar Mr. Joyce's *Ulysses*'.[13] D. H. Lawrence called it 'the best modern book about New York' he had ever read and praised its

> endless series of glimpses of people in the vast scuffle of Manhattan Island, as they turn up again and again, in a confusion that has no obvious rhythm, but wherein at last we recognise the systole-diastole of success and failure, the end being all failure

It was, Lawrence wrote, 'a very complete film . . . of the vast loose gang of strivers and winners and losers which seems to be the very pep of New York'.[14] Other early reviewers, too, fell back on similarly visual terms, describing the book as 'expressionistic', 'impressionistic', 'cubist narrative', 'super-naturalistic', 'neo-realistic', 'architectonic', 'panoramic', 'kaleidoscopic', 'fragmented' and 'cinemascopic'. And of course this was no accident: Dos Passos, who was also a talented and committed painter, actively aspired to incorporate the tenets of Cubism into his literary narrative.

In 1920, after a holiday hiking along the Mediterranean coast, Dos Passos returned to the United States to begin work on *Manhattan Transfer*. Upon settling into an apartment in Greenwich Village, he wrote to a French friend that New York was:

> magnificent . . . a city of cavedwellers, with a frightful, brutal ugliness about it, full of thunderous voices of metal grinding on metal and of an eternal sound of wheels which turn, turn on heavy stones. People swarm meekly like ants . . . crushed by the disdainful and pitiless things around them.[15]

In this very visceral language, which evokes the tangible realities of the city, Dos Passos captured the city that would emerge in his novel. For Dos Passos, the metropolis was a vast incalculable machine in the face of which the individual was helpless. The novel is concerned, both formally and thematically, with the individual's relationship to the system, the relationship of the part to the whole (the whole being the city and its culture, the parts being the protagonists Ellen, Jimmy, Emile, Bud, Congo and so on). In *Manhattan Transfer*, as indeed in the city itself, there is no organic centre that might bind the various parts together. The parts jostle against each other as their narratives unfold, but there is no overarching plot that neatly links the entire cast of characters. Thus, Bud Korpenning's initial remark upon disembarking the ferry at New York harbour – 'I want to find my way to the centre of things' – is doomed from the outset.[16]

This lack of a central, unifying plot mechanism led some early critics to perceive only the representation of chaos and degeneration in the novel – which, to an extent, is perfectly understandable. At its core, the novel is concerned with the dissolution of the human, the organic and the holistic. But it is also the story of the construction of a powerful machine, with the structure of the novel reflecting the culture of the city. For Dos Passos, *form itself* – the constant motion, the to-ing and fro-ing of the narrative in a dynamic swirl of characters – is the message. Indeed, the novel could be described as a machine composed of the various parts of New York City, from the countless immigrant voices to the skyscrapers, trains, subways, songs and newspaper clippings. The novel contains all the paraphernalia of the modern city, all the cogs required to maintain the functioning of an urban system, and Dos Passos shows how these components, both human and mechanical, sometimes jar, depicting the mowing down of women and children (not to mention Gus O'Neil) by automobiles near the opening of the novel.

In considering the novel itself as a machine it is useful to return to one of the visual comparisons evoked by so many early reviews of the novel: the notion of *Manhattan Transfer* as 'cinemascopic'. Dos Passos was very influenced in his early writing career by D. W. Griffith, who had directed the controversial film *The Birth of a Nation* (1915).[17] Though now largely considered disreputable because of its racial content, the film popularised a cross-cutting style of editing to switch between past and present. And Griffith's influence on Dos Passos was absolutely crucial. The filmmaker's editorial techniques, which he had learned from the Russian Constructivist director Sergei Eisenstein, his sudden, unexpected jump-cuts, his use of the United States as a ready-made film set and his insistence upon the importance of message over plot are clearly at work throughout *Manhattan Transfer*. Dos Passos picks up the techniques engaged by Griffith and applies them to his prose: montage editing, jump cuts across time, crane shots and close-up shots, dolly shots in which the reader moves along several narrative tracks at once, and perhaps above all, the integration of factual, documentary history with fiction.

Chapter 2, 'Metropolis', offers an excellent example of these techniques in action. The opening epigraph sets the theme, juxtaposing the ancient brick-built cities of Nineveh and Babylon with the new modern city of steel, glass and concrete. The modern city, teeming with people and their stories, ascends into the clouds much like the epigraph which hovers above the chapters containing the lives and stories of the city's inhabitants. The narrative shifts to Ed Thatcher's story, evoking the new father's loneliness and desire to make 'big money'. To characterise Ed's struggles with his commercial goals and his desire to provide for his new family, Dos Passos inserts sections of newspaper stories into the narrative montage, thereby also illustrating the effects of the press and the manner in which it infiltrates Ed's consciousness. Thus the text cuts into a heading from the journal:

> MORTON SIGNS THE GREATER NEW YORK BILL COMPLETES THE ACT MAKING NEW YORK WORLD'S SECOND METROPOLIS (p. 23)

Within moments Ed dreamily envisages his firm offering him a junior partnership and flicks his coat tails in a theatrical bow (perhaps foreshadowing his daughter's career as a performer). The sudden rupture in the narrative with the newspaper headline is designed to illustrate the means whereby the city impinges upon and alters human consciousness. When Ed pokes his head out of the apartment window in the next section, the word 'metropolis' permeates his narrative. Thus his story is overthrown in favour of the clamour and noise of the city: the El train, the hoof beats, the bell, the crowds, the fire engine. The impersonality and life-threatening nature of the city is compounded by the uncontrollable fire which eats its way up the six-story tenement block, burning to death a pregnant Italian immigrant trapped within. At the end of the section, the bereft and lonely father and husband takes us back to the lonely father that was Ed Thatcher at the beginning of the chapter. The next fragment of the montage depicts a property developer, Mr Perry, surveying a stretch of parched land and chancing upon the skull of a dead ram amongst the sun-scorched grass. The skull, of course, is a reminder of the incinerated woman of the previous scene and the entire montage compounds the idea of the subjugation of the human by the mechanistic and economic imperatives of the metropolis.

Amid the swirl of voices and fragments of stories, two characters, Jimmy Herf and Ellen Thatcher, are given backgrounds and articulated emotional lives. As critics such as Linda Wagner-Martin and Barry Maine have noted, each character represents a different response to the city as a symbol of the corrupted ideal of American success. Beneath the apparent discontinuity of the novel Jimmy and Ellen are connected by the extended imagery of prostitution, the colour green and the firebug. Both characters are determined from their initial appearances in the novel. Ellen is born to an ineffectual father and a mentally unstable mother whose initial response to her baby is that the child is an imposter, a changeling (a description which follows Ellen through life as she assumes a variety of new guises and new names). Rejected by her mother, Ellen learns to entertain her father through her dancing, her charm and her grace, all of which she will exploit later in life as a dancer and actress and as the editor of a high-society fashion magazine. Jimmy, meanwhile, first appears in the novel as a child returning to the United States aboard a liner, having been abroad with his mother. As the liner edges toward the city, the boy catches his first glimpse of the Statue of Liberty, frantically waves an American flag and exults in the Fourth of July celebrations on deck. As phrases from 'Yankee Doodle Dandy' wander through his child's mind, Dos Passos deliberately aligns Herf with a kind of immigrant optimism – an idealism which is dashed and broken as the novel progresses.

Ellen's career trajectory and her various amorous relationships reflect the degree to which she is dehumanised by her idea of success in the city. She first marries an actor, John Oglethorpe, who secures her connections within the theatre world, allowing her to rise from a mere chorus girl to a principal actress in Broadway musicals by exploiting her looks and charm. When she abandons Oglethorpe she dallies with a succession of progressively more prosperous men, one of whom describes her as 'no better than a common prostitute' (p. 209). And when she finally does fall in love, it is with Stan Emery who, in one of the novel's many fatal fires, immolates himself whilst in a drunken stupor. Finding herself pregnant with Stan's child, she enters a marriage of convenience with Jimmy, who devotes himself to her and the child despite the baby's paternity. Stan Emery's death solidifies in Ellen the steely mechanical hardness that she has nurtured in her ambition to succeed within the city. Dos Passos charts this loss of humanity through a series of images of machines, buzz-saws and motion; she is described as 'an intricate machine of sawtooth steel whitebright bluebright copperbright', her voice like a 'flexible sharp metalsaw' (p. 208). In her quest for success, Ellen has become alienated from herself, stripped of any authentic and individual selfhood, and pulled into the whirl, into the vortex of the amoral city.

Like Ellen, Jimmy must choose between his career and the maintenance of his individuality. When he witnesses a fight between bootleggers over a shipment of liquor, he finds himself planning how to sell the story to the newspaper's Sunday supplement. Instead of writing honest reportage, he finds himself locked within a swirl of clichés and formulaic sentences, and chides himself for being 'a parasite on the drama of life' (p. 292). Perhaps recalling John Oglethorpe's damning words – 'How do you like being a paid prostitute of the public press?' (p. 288) – Jimmy resolves to find a menial job which would be better that becoming 'a goddam travelling dictograph . . . You get so you don't have any private life, you're just an automatic writing machine' (p. 309). However, even when he resigns his job, Jimmy finds it hard to disengage, to separate himself from the machine, to give up the American dream of self-made success. He imagines a newspaper story of his failure as a surreal parody of glib journalistic phrases: 'Deported: James Herf young newspaper man of 190 West 12th Street recently lost his twenties. Appearing before Judge Merivale they were remanded to Ellis Island for deportation as undesirable aliens' (p. 317). The reference to the undesirable aliens brings us back to our first encounter with Jimmy on the liner, where he waved his flag and looked down on the immigrants who had been separated from the other passengers.

From the very beginning of the novel, Jimmy is identified with a fundamental questioning of American values in an age of materialism. By the end, he struggles to reclaim the idealism of those old words which have become imprinted upon the skyscrapers of the city:

> Pursuit of happiness, unalienable pursuit . . . right to life and liberty and . . . A black moonless night; Jimmy Herf is walking alone up South Street . . . All these April nights combing the streets alone a skyscraper has obsessed him, a grooved building jutting up with unaccountable bright windows falling onto him out of the scudding sky. Typewriters rain continual nickelplated confetti in his ears . . . And he walks round blocks and blocks and still no door. (p. 327)

In pursuing happiness Jimmy must reject the city and extricate himself from the machine. And so he does. He walks out of Manhattan without money, without transport. As he walks, he passes a horse and wagon loaded with flowers, suggesting, perhaps, that in fleeing the so-called 'City of Destruction', Jimmy will regain something of the organic wholeness of his humanity.

ANZIA YEZIERSKA

Though less formally experimental in her writing than Dos Passos, Anzia Yezierska deals with many of the same ideas in her novels and short stories, which track the lives of young Jewish immigrants working to extricate themselves from the shackles of gender, ethnicity and poverty. Criticised in her lifetime for a prose which was unapologetically melodramatic, unrestrained, sentimental and thin in terms of characterisation, Yezierska was also praised for her powerful portrayals of ghetto life, her personal tenacity and drive to succeed as a writer, and her success in highlighting the plight of immigrant women on New York's Lower East Side, an area of some twenty blocks south of Houston Street and east of Broadway. In 1919 one of her first pieces, 'The Fat of the Land', was selected as the best short story of the year, a literary breakthrough that won her a contract for a collection of short stories for Houghton Mifflin.[18] The story, the unhappy tale of Hanneh Breineh, tracks the rags-to-riches tale of a tenement family from Delancey Street to a brownstone on Eighty-Fourth Street, where the heroine, a Jewish mother to fully assimilated and hugely successful children, laments her isolation and loneliness within the family. Accustomed to the comforts but not the sociability of wealth, Hanneh is unable to stay. Nor is she able to return to the ghetto.

However, it was the 1925 novel *Bread Givers* which sealed Yezierska's reputation as a writer devoted to uncovering the complexities of immigrant life in the United States. The novel, the story of Sara Smolinsky's rise from the crowded tenement blocks of Jewish New York and her concurrent loss of familial loyalty, appeared in an auspicious year for American literary fiction, with the publication of Fitzgerald's *The Great Gatsby*, Hemingway's *In Our Time*, Dreiser's *An American Tragedy*, Stein's *The Making of Americans*, Alain Locke's *The New Negro* and Sinclair Lewis's Pulitzer Prize winning *Arrowsmith*, amongst many others. Yezierska's novel undoubtedly attracted less publicity. But it nevertheless touched on the same themes and issues which preoccupied her fellow modernists, namely the sacrifice of one's individuality for the sake of American success, the alienating capacity of the American city and the social impact of the emergent 'New Woman', as well as the modernist interest in authenticity.

In this latter regard, the novel is particularly ambiguous, straddling the uneasy division between fictional melodrama and autobiography. Although all of Yezierska's stories are autobiographical to some extent, she never had much respect for the boundaries between fact and fiction; indeed, much of her autobiography, *Red Ribbon on a White Horse* (1950), was probably invented. Yezierska seized on the accident of her missing birth certificate to play fast and free with the details of her date and place of birth, changing her name (as did the rest of her family) to the more Anglo-friendly Mayer upon arrival in the United States before changing it back to Yezierska when she began writing, and throughout her life she deliberately misrepresented much of her personal history.[19]

This wilful fabrication of a life history mimics the ambitions of all her immigrant heroines: the desire to become someone American, to banish the original self in the attempt to assimilate with a mainstream American identity, to escape predetermined identities, whether gendered, ethnic or otherwise. In a way, Yezierska's manipulation of the details of her life was a kind of self-invention, allowing her to 'make for herself a person in America' not unlike Smolinsky, Hanneh Breineh or Shenah Pessah of the early short story 'Wings' (1920).[20] However, the transformation to an American selfhood is never the straightforward reconstitution of one identity as another. Her stories recall what has been lost in overthrowing one's ancestry and, again, this mirrors her own story: in an article for *Cosmopolitan* magazine, 'This is What $10,000 Did To Me', for example, Yezierska admitted that a Hollywood deal turned her into a 'tortured soul', unhappy, alone and alienated from her people.[21]

Yezierska's ambiguous authenticity extended to the content of her fiction: notable examples are her resolute determination to use real Jewish names (for instance, Shprintzeh Gittel in *Bread Givers* or Motkeh Pelz in 'Wings'), the insertion of Yiddish, German and Russian phrases throughout ('Oi wei' and 'Blut und Eisen' recur frequently throughout *Bread Givers*), and her deployment of an English which is syntactically altered to reproduce the inflections of an immigrant speaking in a second language. Moreover, her fiction documents the very real conditions endured by the Lower East Side's 135,000 Jews, from the constant threat of eviction to the dank apartments which often housed families of ten or more. These cramped experiences are reflected in *Bread Givers'* preoccupation with space. Sara Smolinsky's life can, in fact, be mapped out by the gradually more expansive spaces she comes to occupy, from the cluttered tenement room she shares with her family, to the street, the ghetto, the suburban space of the college, the city and, finally, the corridor in which she agrees to take her antagonistic father back into her life. Sara's quest for an uncluttered room of her own is a part of a wider American tradition of conquering geographical space in order to make a new American identity. What is more, the upward ascent of New York City (the vertical rise of the skyscraper) mirrors Sara's success. But the acquisition of space is also part of a feminist agenda, enabling the female subject to be educated, to think and to write. So Yezierska emphasises the small, enclosed, private spaces of feminist discourse rather than the public, architectural spaces associated with American success.[22]

Sara's journey begins in the crowded slums of Hester Street, where there is no room for personal expression or neat American maxims on cleanliness: 'The school teacher's rule, "A place for everything and everything in its place" was no good for us because there weren't enough places' (p. 10). Defying her 'Old World' father, who insists on claiming the largest room in the apartment for himself and his religious books, Sara rents a room of her own, a filthy 'dark hole' which at least has 'a door I could shut'. From this room Sara moves to a suburban setting, forsaking the cityscape as she attends college among 'quiet streets, shaded with green'. She tries out a number of different rooms in an attempt to fit in with her teachers and fellow students, but all of her choices seem inauthentic and ill-fitting, perhaps because she is trying to force herself into an alien space. It is only after completing her college course that Sara finds a room which mirrors her newfound independence and status:

> I had selected a sunny, airy room, the kind of a room I had always wanted . . . No carpet on the floor. No pictures on the wall. Nothing but a clean, airy emptiness . . . I celebrated it

> alone with myself. I celebrated it in my room, my first clean, empty room . . . I had achieved that marvelous thing, 'a place for everything and everything in its place'. (p. 267)

With the acquisition of the new apartment, far removed from the cluttered room on Hester Street in which the novel opens, Sara not only conquers geographical space but finds a room which is testimony to her own sense of selfhood and her personal achievement.

This strong sense of selfhood is evident from the very outset of the novel. The narrative voice is characterised by an insistence upon an individualistic 'I'. For instance, in struggling with the family detritus in the kitchen on Hester Street, the narrating 'I' battles heroically against the smothering rags, tables, chairs and unclean windows. For Yezierska the 'I' is a site of uncertainty. Traditionally the 'I' is associated with a unified, coherent, male selfhood and manacled to the autobiographical genre. In *Bread Givers*, however, the 'I' is the nexus where the 'real' and the 'imagined' collide, thus opening up a new narrative space between the autobiographical and the fictional. This new narrative space ideally fits Yezierska's hitherto untapped subject, the immigrant woman in an early twentieth-century urban environment. And this space, between the autobiographical and the fictional, allows the female subject (and indeed the writer herself) to move in to and out of 'controlling' generic structures. Not only is the invention of this new literary space a deeply political act of self-expression and self-definition, therefore, it also allows Yezierska to play with the boundaries of genre in exploring both the liminality and the 'in between-ness' of her subject, a woman *outside* both Jewish and American patriarchal cultures yet also caught *between* them. The final scene of the novel, in which Sara stands in the corridor deciding her father's fate, is a physical spatial representation of this bind, as indeed is Hannah Breinah's final position on the street between the ghetto and the genteel apartment. And while this 'in-between' space can be liberating, allowing the subject to move between worlds and identities without being contained by either, it can also be a site of limbo, a no-man's land in which the subject is locked until she decides which way to turn.

While undoubtedly linked to a feminist tradition, Yezierska's deceptively simple novel is also immersed in the debates about ethnicity which permeated early twentieth-century American culture. For many readers, Yezierska's writing actively encourages the assimilation of Yiddish culture into the United States. Her own primary aim in her early life, and indeed the aim of most of her characters, was to become a 'real' American:

> Then came a light – a great revelation! I saw America – a big idea – a deathless hope – a world still in the making. I saw that it was the glory of America that it was not yet finished. And I, the last comer, had her share to give, small or great, to the making of America, like those Pilgrims who came in the *Mayflower*.[23]

However, Yezierska's work is often critical of the processes of Americanisation and assimilation, as exemplified in the subtitle to *Bread Givers*: *The Struggle Between a Father of the Old World and a Daughter of the New*. The relationship between first- and second-generation American Jews is presented as an ordeal, a tortured emotional process for both parties. As the critic Ron Ebest convincingly argues, Yezierska's overwrought style and frequent use of anti-Semitic stereotypes (for instance, the selfish scholarly father as personified in Reb Smolinsky) are best understood as the products of the context in which she wrote. Yezierska's stories appeared in periodicals which ran nativist, anti-immigrant articles and ongoing debates on the so-called 'Jewish Question', and Ebest observes that 'Yezierska's stories engaged this debate in the space it was already occupying . . . Thus the stories may be understood as arguments, offered by one of the Jews under discussion, and interjected into an ongoing, often ugly, frequently nativist, many voiced debate.'[24] So while Sara may celebrate the success embodied in her empty female space, her freedom is compromised by her willingness to accept her misogynistic father back into her life after she finds him hawking matches in the ghetto: 'I felt the shadow still there, over me. It wasn't just my father, but the generations who made my father whose weight was still upon me' (p. 297). Sara's independence from the 'Old World' is an unrealised dream, and her bleak honesty at the very end of the novel denies the reader the closure or the happy ending one expects of the rags-to-riches story. In a way, therefore, the conclusion depicts a subject in an indeterminate state of limbo. Stuck out in the corridor between rooms, Sara is caught between worlds, and like Henneh Breineh, learns that she cannot fit into either.

NELLA LARSEN

In her two acclaimed novels *Quicksand* (1928) and *Passing* (1929), the African American writer Nella Larsen addressed many of the issues Yezierska had raised. Both novels focus on women caught between worlds due to their gender and ethnicity, both focus on the female consciousness, and both use the architectural spaces of New York City to map the destinies of their protagonists. *Quicksand*, a deeply personal and autobiographical novel, established Larsen as a writer interested in using different cultural spaces to chart the lives of ethnically ambiguous women; Larsen uses her protagonist, Helga Crane, who travels between Chicago, the American South, Copenhagen and New York, to explore the intersection of race, space and gender. Helga, who like Larsen is of Danish and West Indian ancestry, is forced to confront the conditions of patriarchy in European and American society, the commodification of women by modern, consumer-based culture, and the bleaching of black identity and culture by the uplift programmes pioneered by Booker T. Washington and deplored by the likes of W. E. B. Du Bois. Indeed, Du Bois rated the novel very highly, describing it as:

> fine, thoughtful and courageous . . . the best piece of fiction that Negro America has produced since the heyday of Chesnutt, and stands easily with Jessie Fauset's *There is Confusion*, in its subtle comprehension of the curious cross currents that swirl about the black American.[25]

Alain Locke, who by the latter half of the 1920s had become the official spokesman for the Harlem Renaissance (which is discussed at length in Chapter 5), similarly admired the novel as 'a social document of importance . . . a living, moving, picture of a type not often in the foreground of Negro fiction'.[26] Both reviewers' emphasis on 'currents' and 'movement' is entirely appropriate. At every point in the book, from the Langston Hughes epigraph to Helga's wish to extricate herself from the Southern 'bog' she occupies with the Reverend Pleasant Green at the novel's conclusion, Larsen emphasises the character's journey or quest, using her external migration as a structural device for Helga's emotional and intellectual development.

Helga's restless striving takes her to New York, to Harlem, during the height of the district's cultural awakening. Initially the city is a daunting, imposing and unfriendly place:

> She felt its aggressive unfriendliness. Even the great buildings, the flying cabs, and the swirling crowds seemed manifestations of purposed malevolence. . . . New York seemed more appalling, more scornful, in some inexplicable way even more terrible and uncaring than Chicago. Threatening almost. Ugly.[27]

But Harlem, 'teeming black Harlem, welcomed her and lulled her into . . . contentment' (p. 46). In the 1920s, Harlem certainly was teeming, attracting record numbers of African American residents. In 1920, central Harlem was 32 per cent black and 67 per cent white. By 1930, however, the black proportion had more than doubled, with the annual census revealing that over 70 per cent of the population were African American, and just 23 per cent of the inhabitants being white.[28] And while Helga comes to reject Harlem, spurning the activists and intellectuals who try to shape and prescribe her identity, the allure of the area never dwindles for Clare Kendry Bellow, one of the central figures in Larsen's second novel, *Passing*. Clare, a pale-skinned African American who has rejected her racial heritage to pass as white, encounters an old friend on the rooftop of the Drayton Hotel in Chicago and thereafter becomes obsessed with Irene Redfield's home, lifestyle and social circle in middle-class, black Harlem. While *Quicksand* is more interested in the potential and limitations of transition between places and cultures, *Passing* is firmly rooted in New York, which is described by Clare's husband, Jack, as 'the city of the future'.[29]

Despite the novel's opening in Chicago, it is the glamour and the vibrancy of Manhattan and Harlem which dominate the lives of both women. Not unlike Harlem, industrial Chicago in the 1920s was also home to swathes of black migrants. Indeed it is the hometown of both women, but *Passing* is more concerned with the cosmopolitanism of the Harlem Renaissance and the complexities of black middle-class affluence. As in *Manhattan Transfer* and *Bread Givers*, the modern city is characterised by its mechanistic nature, its architecture and its crowds, all of which are signalled in the opening section of the novel. After a pedestrian has been knocked over by a car, a vast crowd converges, the heat and the congestion of which almost cause Irene to pass out. She therefore ascends to the open-air rooftop of a 'whites only' hotel where a chance encounter reintroduces a childhood friend. The city is presented, therefore, as modern, cacophonous and dangerous. Not only does the metropolis threaten the lives of its inhabitants but it risks the revelation of their secrets. At another moment, Irene needs to retouch her cosmetics and compose her face as the heat and smog of the city have caused her make-up to run and thereby reveal her 'real' identity – for Irene, like her recently rediscovered friend, has been passing for a white woman.

When the narrative moves to New York City, the novel shifts into a subtle critique of early twentieth-century consumption. Just as Helga Crane sought out beautiful things, artworks and fine clothing, Irene and Clare are frequently seen shopping and set against a dazzling cornucopia of gowns and jewels. The novel is peppered with place and street names, references to designer shops, nightclubs and dancehalls, both in Harlem and in downtown Manhattan, where the women do their shopping. And when Irene worries that her husband may be conducting an affair with Clare, her first inclination is for a spot of retail therapy: she goes shopping for flowers. At the time, of course, the United States was riding the wave of post-war affluence which would sink in the Wall Street Crash of 1929, and Larsen neatly shows how a particular class of African Americans participated in this material culture. Throughout the novel, conspicuous consumption is presented as the antithesis of Irene's charitable uplift work for the Negro Welfare League (NWL) and her choice of shopping venues is testimony to her enslavement to white middle-class values. And while

Larsen's work is never overtly political, she is here presenting a curious complex which characterised 1920s Harlem and many of its artists and activists, namely the commitment to ending black poverty and white racism while relying upon middle-class money and the affluence generated by leisure.

The cumulative effect of these references is to offer a subtle critique of consumption, not only in terms of class and aesthetics, but with regard to the cultural objectification of women. In *Quicksand* the younger Helga Crane resists the institution of marriage, turning down multiple proposals from 'eligible' bachelors whom she sees as attempting to buy her. In *Passing*, both Irene and Clare have entered willingly into marriages, both of them apparently loveless (or at least sexless in Irene's case), and while Irene believes hers to be a marriage of equals, Clare is more than aware that she has sold something of herself by entering into marriage with a white racist bigot who is unaware of her black heritage. Indeed, Clare's relationship with men is always something of a power struggle. Her story begins with her struggles with an abusive father and culminates in a showdown with her husband when he confronts her about her secret history. The relationship with Jack is especially pernicious, grounded in fear on Clare's part (for instance, fear that her secret would be revealed in the colouring of her child) and in disrespectful malevolence on the side of her husband, who refers to her as 'Nig'. The reference to 'Nig' is a clear allusion to Harriet Wilson's *Our Nig* (1859), the autobiographical story of a woman born to a black father and a white mother. However, the power struggle works both ways, for while Clare has bartered herself for a life of luxury and security, she has also fooled a man who believes himself impervious to the tricks of a race he despises. Thus Clare holds the power to shatter his masculine certainty, his identity and his happy family – and indeed she is often presented as something of a sorceress, even a witch, thanks to her power to beguile the men around her. For instance, she awakens a gentleness in Brian Redfield which is absent in his interactions with his wife, her beauty entrances those at the NWL dance including notables such as Hugh Wentworth (who is clearly a fictional version of Carl Van Vechten, author of the controversial 1926 novel *Nigger Heaven*), and she entrances every waiter with whom she comes into contact.

The power struggle between the sexes is not the only tension in the story, for the novel is primarily a meditation on the relationship of the two women. When they meet on the rooftop of the Drayton, each watches the other, Clare rather covetously and Irene guardedly. These initial reactions extend through the remainder of the novel, with Clare coveting Irene's lifestyle and friendships and Irene warily trying to keep Clare, a reminder of her forgotten Chicago childhood, at arm's length. Both women are passing when they meet, though curiously it is Irene who condemns her friend for the act, seemingly unperturbed by her own selective passing.

Despite Irene's admonitions of Clare, she betrays a possible attraction to her friend, kissing her shoulder, marvelling at her loveliness and staring at her as they sit before Irene's dressing-table mirror. The dressing room scene is crucial for understanding the relationship between the women, for while we might read it as freighted with a latent eroticism, a suppressed sexual desire, it is also possible to read the scene as portraying Irene's desire for her suppressed black identity (as embodied by Clare). For although Irene is living openly as an African American woman, she has suppressed something of herself in her attachment to the white middle-class values which govern her existence. So while Clare's greed for Irene's Harlem life is open and evident throughout the novel, it is Irene's desire for the blackness within Clare which is really hidden. Both women 'pass', but Clare does so openly and Irene does so clandestinely. And as Clare and Irene sit before the dressing-table mirror and stare at each other's reflections, their desire (sexual or otherwise) overlaps and the women come to mirror each other. In this way, Larsen offers a clever and subtle dissection of 1920s Harlem – a Harlem dominated, as Helga Crane puts it, by a class of African Americans who 'like the despised people of the white race . . . preferred Pavlova to Florence Mills, John McCormack to Gordon Taylor, Walter Hampden to Paul Robeson' (p. 51).[30]

While *Passing* is clearly concerned with racial passing, the creation of an illusory identity, it is also preoccupied with the matter of creating fictions and by the processes of storytelling, reading and inscrutability. This is best encapsulated by the reference to the white envelope Irene receives early in the narrative. The envelope is described as having something sly and furtive about it, perhaps holding a secret within. The pale envelope, with its beautiful but illegible black script which betrays the sender, is undoubtedly a reference to Clare herself, whose true identity is revealed (to Irene at least) by her pool-black eyes. One might also read the envelope as a metaphor for the novel itself, a slight and seemingly straightforward entity which hides its thematic weight beneath illusions of simplicity. What the novel presents, like the envelope containing Clare's letter, is a story within a story. We are given Clare's story through Irene. Indeed, all the reader knows of Clare is supplied by Irene, and this in turn is filtered through the voice of the narrator, creating the modernist effect of *mise en abyme*.

Clare herself remains something of a ghost, at the periphery of Irene's soirées and, of course, dead by the end of the novel, having been apparently pushed to her death through the upper floor window of a high-rise New York apartment (a descent which both mirrors and inverts Irene's ascent to the rooftop of the Drayton at the beginning of the novel). However, this is also a novel about the *suppression* of stories, with the events surrounding Clare's death occupying a central place. It is unclear, for instance, who killed Clare. Irene? Bellew? Clare herself? Earlier, Irene withholds the story of her downtown encounter with Bellew from her friend, thereby leaving Clare unprepared for her unmasking. She also withholds the story of her encounter with Clare from her father, while the little stories Clare tells in the company of Gertrude and Irene are withheld from the reader, obscured by Irene as she tells her own version of events. The obfuscation of Clare's stories takes the reader back to the letter. We see Irene holding Clare's allegedly illegible words in her hands – words she eventually discards from the back of a moving train. In a way, we might read Irene's discarding of the shredded letter as a metaphor for her abandoned black identity. Or we might see it as a deeply buried narrative clue, suggesting the identity of the person who ultimately holds the fate of Clare Kendry in her hands.

EDITH WHARTON

Though rarely included in studies of American literary modernism, Edith Wharton, too, examines a society at the crossroads between the Gilded Age and modernity. Her work examines the consequences of being caught between worlds, both at macro- and micro-textual level. The heroine of her most famous novel, *The House of Mirth* (1905), Lily Bart, must come to terms with the incongruity of her values and mores in an emergent social world of affluence and leisure. She must also accept her inability to fit into either the world of the leisure class to which she aspires or the world of industrial working women into which she is forced. At one level, therefore, the novel satirises the new classes of New York high society, those without the moral code and decorum that Wharton sees as part and parcel of the legacy of inherited wealth.[31]

While Wharton's writing is steeped in naturalism and devoid of the experimental pyrotechnics of high-modernist innovators such as Dos Passos, Pound or Stein, many commentators have viewed her novels as either modernist or presaging modernism. Candace Waid and Claire Colquitt, for example, portray Wharton as 'a radical experimentalist *malgré lui*' and argue that 'she anticipated many of the defining elements of the radical modernism'.[32] And while she certainly had reservations about the modernists' rejection of the recent past, she was deeply affected by the work of Woolf, Joyce, Eliot, Proust and especially Faulkner. Martin Halliwell makes the case that Wharton aspires to the proto-modernism of Tolstoy and Flaubert 'by interweaving realistic physical descriptions with a subtle symbolic rendering of the emotional and moral complexities of characters'.[33] Carol Singley, meanwhile, describes *The House of Mirth* as modernist on the basis that it subverts genres by blending realism with sentimentalism, and indeed many recent critics have claimed Wharton's meditation on issues of gender, class, fractured identities and art distinguish her as a modernist.[34] Certainly Wharton shared with modernists such as Yeats, Lawrence and Pound the idea that the First World War, in which she served as a nurse, was an inevitability: 'The only consoling thought is that the beastly horror had to be gone through, for some mysterious cosmic reason of ripening and rotting, and the heads on whom that rotten German civilisation are falling are bound to get cracked'.[35] And her experiences in the war, her writing about it and her eventual émigré status strengthen the case for her modernist credentials.

The idea of Wharton as a reluctant modernist is a compelling one, not least because it reflects the emotions experienced by many of her characters, from Newland Archer in *The Age of Innocence* (1920) to the gauche American belles of *The Buccaneers* (1938) as they face a new world of altered moral values. On the one hand, such characters cling to the certainty and comfort of the past, but on the other they recognise the need to adapt to the changing modern world. In *The House of Mirth* this transformed world and its new values are embodied in the altered architecture of the city itself. The novel is saturated in distaste for the disreputable morals and vulgarity of the nouveaux riches classes, which are often exhibited in the houses they have built. So Ned Van Alstyne offers Lawrence Seldon a tour of 'that versatile thoroughfare', Fifth Avenue:

> That Greiner House, now – a typical rung on the social ladder! The man who built it came from a *milieu* where all the dishes are put on the table at once. His façade is a complete architectural meal; if he had omitted a style his friends might have thought the money had given out . . . Mrs Bry thinks her house a copy of the *Trianon*; in America every marble house with gilt furniture is thought to be a copy of the *Trianon* . . . Now for the Trenors, you remember, he chose the Corinthian: exuberant, but based on the best precedent. The Trenor house is one of his best things – doesn't look like a banqueting hall turned inside out.[36]

Van Alsteyne astutely notes the competitiveness, the awed aping of European fashions and the rather crude mixing of architectural styles which had characterised the houses of the rich in New York for the previous twenty years. As Louis Auchincloss observed, William H. Vanderbilt spent $2 million of his $90 million inheritance on his New York 'Triple Palace', 'a great hodge-podge of styles', while Alexander Stewart's 'Marble House' on Fifth Avenue was a mixture of French, Greek and Renaissance, with fifty-five rooms of 'stupendous opulence', wall-to-wall Carrara marble and a picture gallery. Such properties were funded by the enormous prosperity of the 1880s and 1890s, founded on steel, railroads, real estate, banking, clothing industries, department stores and other luxury goods industries.[37]

While Wharton belonged to this wealthy world – as does Lily, whose smoking, dancing and gambling perplex her respectable Aunt Peniston – she deplored the creation of a class of millionaires whose lack of lineage bespoke a lack of social responsibility, and she recognised the novelistic potential in pitching Old and New New York against each other. Just a few years earlier Thorstein Veblen had addressed this very issue in his *Theory of the Leisure Class* (1899), which identified conspicuous consumption and leisure as 'evidence of pecuniary strength' and consequently 'evidence of social worth'. For the gentleman of leisure, his opulence must be demonstrated through the 'giving of valuable presents and expensive feasts and entertainments'.[38] Wharton's Augustus Trenor embodies this class of gentlemen, from his dazzling properties (both in New York and fashionable Bellomont), to his routine assistance of a series of needy women, from the scheming Carry Fisher to the naively grateful Lily. Trenor offers Lily what she assumes to be a simple Wall Street investment 'tip', which he has gathered from the up-and-coming millionaire Mr Rosedale. Lily's acceptance of the gift places her in a precarious position, paving the way for the eventual confrontation with Trenor. He demands repayment 'not in kind' and makes her the subject of spiralling gossip and innuendo, which results in her eventual ostracism from her social circle and disinheritance by her aunt (p. 116).

Lily's situation reflects the status of women in the leisure class, for her duty is to adorn, beautify and display the wealth of the male benefactor. Again, Veblen had already penetrated to the heart of the matter:

> It grates painfully on our nerves to contemplate the necessity of any wellbred woman's earning a living by useful work. It is not 'woman's sphere.' Her sphere is within the household, which she should 'beautify,' and of which she should be the chief 'ornament.' . . . By virtue of its descent from a patriarchal past, our social system makes it the woman's function in an especial degree to put in evidence her household's ability to pay.[39]

Nowhere is this more in evidence than in Mr Rosedale's marriage proposal:

> I wanted money, and I've got more of it than I know how to invest; and now the money doesn't seem to be of any account unless I can spend it on the right woman. That's what I want to do with it: I want my wife to make all the other women feel small. I'd never grudge a dollar that was spent on that . . . What I want is a woman who'll hold her head higher the more diamonds I put on it. (p. 140)

For Rosedale, Lily's intrinsic value is of no concern or interest. Indeed, as with the beautiful women of *Passing*, Lily's social value is viewed entirely in her decorative appeal and the amount of money she is 'worth'. At the very beginning of the novel, in her encounter with Selden at Grand Central Station, the reader is offered a vision of Lily through the eyes of her male companion, who has 'a confused sense that she must have cost a great deal to make, that a great deal of dull and ugly people must, in some mysterious way, have been sacrificed to make her' (p. 7). Even Lily herself is aware that her monetary value is dependent upon the spectacle of her beauty and takes measures to preserve and enhance it. Yet she is also aware that she is 'the victim of the civilization which had produced her' (p. 8) and it is the development of Lily's social consciousness regarding the fate of women which is one of the more modern aspects of the novel.

Lily's moment of epiphany comes after her dramatic encounter with Trenor, when she seems 'a stranger to herself, or rather there were two selves in her, the one she had always known, and a new abhorrent being to which it found itself chained' (p. 117). Lily finally comes to realise the inability of separating some unsullied aspect of her being from the debauched ugliness of the moneyed class to which she is tied. This realisation brings together a series of recurrent motifs of insects or bluebottles which run throughout the novel, alluding to the parasite which is dependent upon others for its pickings, and sets Lily, not unsympathetically, alongside other women such as Mrs Haffen (the charwoman who sells Selden's incriminating letters to Bertha Dorset) and the much derided divorcée Carry Fisher to illustrate the ultimate expendability of all leisured women, and their enslavement to the rich elite.

The emphasis on Lily's aesthetic beauty and its availability for purchase is reflected in a number of references to the reproduced copies of visual art throughout the novel, from Aunt Peniston's copy of *The Dying Gladiator* to the Cenci portrait which adorns the bronze box on her beadwork table. The most important instance of Wharton's use of the visual arts, however, is undoubtedly the *tableaux vivants* scene, in which the group recreates scenes from great artworks. As the narrator informs us:

> *Tableaux vivants* depend for their effect not only on the happy disposal of lights and the delusive interposition of layers of gauze, but on a corresponding adjustment of the mental vision . . . they may give magic glimpses of the boundary world between fact and imagination.

We can read the method described here as self-reflexive ekphrasis; after all, this is the trick of Wharton's novel itself, to draw the reader's attention to the uncertain line between reality and fiction. Lily herself is alerted to this process when she is forced to confront the bleak reality of her situation beneath the intoxicating veneer of her apparently luxurious lifestyle. Her 'epiphany', we learn, brings about an 'adjustment in her mental vision' (p. 105). Returning to the scene itself, Lily recreates a picture entitled *Mrs Lloyd* by the English portraitist Joshua Reynolds. The picture shows a diaphanously clad young woman, Miss Joanna Leigh, carving the name of the man she wishes to marry into the bough of a tree:

> She had shown her artistic intelligence in selecting a type so like her own that she could embody the person represented without ceasing to be herself . . . The noble buoyancy of her attitude, its suggestion of soaring grace, revealed the touch of poetry that Selden had always felt in her presence . . . He seemed to see before him the real Lily Bart, divested of the trivialities of her little world, and catching for a moment a note of the eternal harmony of which her beauty was a part. (p. 106)

Selden reads his desires into the picture Lily presents, as he also does in the novel's opening and closing portraits of her. But Lily's presentation of herself is more complex than Selden's reading. She presents herself as a 'copy' of a lady, signalling her self-consciousness about the situation into which the modern world has pushed her in its prizing of her beauty alone. The latter part of the novel represents her struggle to recover her original integrity: hence her rejection of the various marriage proposals and her determination to pay off her debts.

While ekphrasis is by no means a uniquely modernist technique, it had a special significance for many modernists. By definition it implies a copy of an original artwork: something which lacks the integrity of the original. Modernist artists were alert to modernity's capacity for mass reproduction and were keen to recapture the 'essence' of objects and identities, from Pound's imagist subway crowd to Woolf's unhappy Mrs Dalloway. In doing so, the narrative ekphrasis (or the *tableau vivant*) stops narrative time and allows the reader and the viewers within the text to learn something of the character performing the scene. Wharton's deployment of the ekphratic *tableau* reveals her thoroughly modern sensibility, which recognises both the shaping of women into passive objects of spectacle and the emerging will within women to negate the male gaze and chisel out their own fates and identities. And the *tableau* may also reveal something of Edith Wharton's desire to carve out an identity for herself as both parodist of and participant in the modern complexities of New York society.

THEODORE DREISER

Theodore Dreiser's *Sister Carrie* (1900) is undoubtedly one of the most important twentieth-century novels of urban growth and decay. Like *Passing*, the book straddles two cities, Chicago and New York, and recounts the fortunes of a young Wisconsin migrant, Carrie Meeber, and her sometime companion, George Hurstwood. Dreiser has generally been described as the antithesis of the modernist writer. He was simply not interested in formal issues and his writing style, though interesting for the opprobrium it drew from many critics, is almost invariably described as naturalistic. An early critic proclaimed him 'one of the unafflicted: a modern without the doctrine of modernism'.[40] And when Dreiser surveyed the completed draft of *Sister Carrie*, he declared: 'It is not intended as a piece of literary craftsmanship, but as a picture of conditions done as simply and effectively as the English language will permit.'[41]

The themes of the novel, however, are indisputably modern and have much in common with those of the radically modernist John Dos Passos and the reluctant modernist Edith Wharton. As the novel follows the ascent of Carrie Meeber, it addresses questions of gender and equality, luxury and materialism, the alienation of the individual, the glamour and squalid reality of the American metropolis, and the nature of success. In many ways, Carrie's experiences of city life are closely based on Dreiser's own adventures. He too was a migrant from a rural background, moving through a series of American cities in an attempt to find literary and economic success. In his autobiography, Dreiser describes his initial intoxication with the glamour of Chicago (which we also see in Carrie's first encounter with the city) and the subsequent disillusionment, born of his rejection from various positions and his downtrodden wandering along the city's thoroughfares. The opening chapters of *Sister Carrie* reiterate this pattern, as our dejected heroine finds only disappointment in her search for employment in Chicago's downtown streets. The story, however, mirrors almost directly the experience of Dreiser's sister, Emma, who had been supported in Chicago by an architect but found herself attracted to the manager of a well-known bar. By the time she discovered he was married, she was sufficiently overawed by the man to agree to elope with him to Toronto, where he confessed to her that he had stolen a sum of money from his employers.

This method of drawing from direct experience and merging factual accounts with fictional stories is Dreiser's literary *modus operandi*, derived from his training as a reporter on, among many other publications, the St Louis *Globe-Democrat*, *The Republic*, *The Cosmopolitan*, *The Delineator* and later *The American Spectator*, and from his literary mentor, Balzac.[42] Described by Émile Zola as the 'father of the naturalist novel', Balzac's works contextualise and explain human behaviour in terms of the lived environment and therefore emphasise the contours of the city, domestic interiors and social behaviour.[43] Under such influences, there is a documentary quality to Dreiser's writing which many early reviewers and critics found rather trying. Arnold Bennett, for instance, wrote in 1930 that 'Dreiser simply does not know how to write, never did know, never wanted to know'.[44] Alfred Kazin remarked that 'Dreiser makes painful reading' and even the author's fiercest champion, H. L. Mencken, wondered 'if Dreiser gets anything properly describable as pleasure out of this dogged accumulation of threadbare, undistinguished, uninspiring nouns, adjectives, verbs, adverbs, pronouns, participles, and conjunctions'.[45]

Some critics, however, have seen Dreiser's cataloguing of information as reflecting the rampant materialism of modern America, a literary counterpart to the tawdry world described within the novels.[46] Certainly the lengthy descriptions of New York and Chicago, which in their sheer volume represent the overwhelming density of both cities, seem to bear this out. Dreiser believed it was his duty as a writer not only to provide a social record of what was changing in American life but also to document a particular world before it disappeared completely – a sense of duty he shared with many modern writers, including regionalists such as Willa Cather and William Faulkner. For instance, in locating the apartment block of Carrie's fellow New York chorus girl, Lola Osborne, on Nineteenth Street and Fourth Avenue, he describes the building in terms of what it was and how it has changed: 'a block now wholly given to office buildings'.[47] In an early chapter, 'What Poverty Threatened', Dreiser gives a lengthy overview of Chicago in 1889, offering details on the swelling population, up-and-coming businesses, transportation networks, sewage mechanisms and poverty-stricken underclass. Later in the novel, meanwhile, the reader is offered a similar potted history of New York City.

As already explained, the turn of the twentieth century was a time of enormous economic and demographic growth in the cities of the United States, and Dreiser was keen to explore the individual and sociological consequences of all these changes. When Carrie Meeber first makes her way through the streets of the metropolis, she is a wide-eyed innocent, optimistic about her prospects and eager to experience the joys and material comforts of city life: 'A flame of envy lighted in her heart. She realised in a dim way how much the city held – wealth, fashion, ease – every adornment for women, and she longed for dress and beauty with a whole heart' (p. 21). Keen to get to know the layout of the city, Carrie is disappointed when her taciturn brother-in-law points her toward the 'manufacturing houses along Franklin Street' (p. 11) rather than the theatre district or the department stores she longs to visit. And on her various walks through the 'giant magnet' that is the city, she is alternately charmed and disillusioned by the scenes around her. This alternation of aspects is one of the reader's first insights into Dreiser's style, which offers two or more opposing viewpoints, presenting a rounded perspective on an issue or an event. Thus, the reader is shown the beauty of the city as well as its ugliness; and the personal experiences of the protagonist are counterbalanced by the objective overview of the narrator.

On a wider narrative level, if Chicago is the city of Carrie's impoverished youth, New York is the site of her mature success. And for the novel's other major character, George Hurstwood, Chicago is the site of an affluent existence, while New York brings destitution and homelessness:

> Whatever a man like Hurstwood could be in Chicago, it is very evident that he would be but an inconspicuous drop in an ocean like New York . . . In other words, Hurstwood was nothing. (p. 269)

His New York experiences form a counterpart to Carrie's early scenes, emphasising the gulf between the city's rich and poor:

> The entire metropolitan centre possessed a high and mighty air calculated to overawe and abash the common applicant, and make the gulf between poverty and success seem both wide and deep. (p. 15)

Carrie is made all too aware of her shabby clothes and pinched features, which inhibit her entry to the fancy department stores and make the chance of a job in such an establishment a foolish dream. However, through her association with the travelling salesman Charlie Drouet, she does move out of poverty, away from the sweatshop future which seemed inevitable, away from her sister's dreary apartment and into a comfortable flat and a lifestyle characterised by shopping, theatre visits and restaurants.

The juxtaposition of Carrie's ascent with Hurstwood's decline is deliberately devised to illuminate the proximity of poverty and affluence in the modern metropolis. Within the space of a chapter or so Carrie is elevated from a bedraggled waif to a kept young lady, and by the end of the novel she is a star with her name in lights, while her former lover shivers in the gutter. The propinquity of wealth and poverty in the modern city was a subject about which Dreiser was passionate (indeed, it is the most overwhelmingly important theme in the novel), and which he covered in much of his journalism, prompting him to join the Communist Party in the 1940s. In a portentous Chicago scene, Carrie, Drouet and Hurstwood leave the theatre, oblivious to the homeless man imploring them for help:

> 'Say, mister,' said a voice at Hurstwood's side, 'would you mind giving me the price of a bed?' . . .
>
> 'Honest to God, mister, I'm without a place to sleep.' . . .
>
> Drouet was the first to see. He handed over a dime with an upwelling feeling of pity in his heart. Hurstwood scarcely noticed the incident. Carrie quickly forgot. (p. 129)

The homeless man is a foreshadowing of Hurstwood in New York, awaiting Carrie outside the theatre door and begging for help. Though terrified by his ragged appearance, Carrie is more upset by the depth to which her former lover has fallen; later, of his 'death she was not even aware' (p. 459). Dreiser uses both scenes to illustrate the obliviousness of urban society to the poor and dispossessed, a subject about which he had written for *Demorest's* a year before.

While Carrie is aware of poverty and indeed has first-hand experience of it, she quickly forgets it and moves onwards and upwards. Here, the author demonstrates the effect of urban life upon human nature and interpersonal relationships. Carrie's indifference toward the poor typifies a greater indifference toward human beings and society more generally. She has a restless and acquisitive heart, moving from Columbia City to Chicago to Montreal to New York, but like many self-made people, she is apt to lose interest as soon as she has attained the object of her desire. Upon leaving Wisconsin, little reference is made to the family Carrie has left behind; when she leaves Minnie and Hanson, she does not return to offer help when she is flush with success; when Drouet discovers her love affair, she argues that he has done little or nothing for her; and in New York she leaves Hurstwood when it is clear that he cannot recreate the successful persona she encountered in Chicago. In fact, Carrie is not unlike Elaine Thatcher in *Manhattan Transfer*: like Elaine, she changes her name many times, takes up a career as an actress and, arguably, prostitutes herself for material gain. Alienated from her family and her community, she is also somewhat alienated from herself, unaware of her true identity and cut off from a close circle of friends or family. It is telling that after her New York successes 'there was no one she knew well enough' (p. 404) to show the newspaper clippings detailing her achievements, and she ends her days in her rocking-chair dreaming of 'such happiness as [she] may never feel' (p. 460). The isolation of the individual and the breakdown of family and community (Hurstwood, like Carrie, is divorced from his family) are, for Dreiser, the inevitable consequences of modernity.

Carrie's career as an actress, and especially her appearance as Laura in Augustin Daly's melodramatic play *Under the Gaslight*, brings to mind Lily Bart's *tableau vivant*, wherein narrative time is halted to enable the spectator to learn something of the inner personality of the character before him. The moment also allows the performer to reveal something of her true self. Swept away by Carrie's performance, both Drouet and Hurstwood are deeply moved, each perceiving a vulnerability in need of protection and attributing an inner grace to her winsome demeanour. The reader, of course, is struck by Carrie's adaptability: her ability to transform herself under new circumstances and fool those around her, and perhaps even to fool herself. Buoyed by Drouet's encouragement, she turns her nervous first-scene performance into a powerful display of moral rectitude in the final act. Her relative ease betrays the adaptive nature that has been developing across the novel. And while at the end of the book Carrie is the figure much observed, through much of the novel she plays the part of the observer, alert to the habits and gestures of other women, practising poses in front of the mirror and imitating the gait and swagger of the well-heeled. Her performance, though devastatingly disarming to both Drouet and Hurstwood, reveals an inner hollowness in Carrie herself. She can inhabit the part of Laura because she is happy to sacrifice her sense of self, her own personality and her own history. Her sheer ease in moving from one identity to another, from Carrie Meeber to Carrie Madenda to Carrie Wheeler and so on, coupled with her effortlessness in transforming from factory girl to lady of leisure to Broadway star, makes her the perfect symbol of what Dreiser regarded as the vices of modernity. For as he saw it, urban modernity was creating a new kind of human nature: ruthless and hollow, endlessly adapting itself to a world in which only the fittest survived.

HART CRANE

Writing to a friend in the late 1920s, Hart Crane described his epic poem *The Bridge* (1930) as 'a mystical synthesis of "America"'.[48] No description better suits this eight-book condensation of the history of the nation. *The Bridge* takes as its central metaphor New York City's Brooklyn Bridge, which Crane overlooked from his apartment at 110 Columbia Heights. Indeed, the address Crane occupied was the very one which Washington Roebling, the architect of the structure, inhabited when overseeing the construction of the bridge, and his book uses the bridge's connective identity to build an epic of modern consciousness of the kind pioneered by James Joyce and T. S. Eliot in *A Portrait of the Artist as a Young Man* (1916) and *The Waste Land* (1922) respectively. However, while certainly a condensation of the history of the United States, *The Bridge* is also a working-through of the act of construction, in terms of the production of the poem itself. The central metaphor of the bridge is the 'arc synoptic' of this process, enacting and rehearsing its own theme of creation, with the bridge symbolising the poet's intellectual and spiritual journey toward the realisation of the poem.[49] The vibrancy and ever-evolving nature of New York City complements this sense of an evolving imagination and the construction of a mythic edifice, be it the poem or the bridge. In a city that was endlessly creating itself anew both architecturally and demographically, artists were faced with the challenge of encompassing this dizzying progression through ever more ambitious means. And for Crane, the man-made nature of New York provided the essence of *The Bridge*.

We have seen how writers like Dreiser and Wharton integrated the social and cultural history of the metropolis and depicted its impact on the lives and behaviour of city dwellers, while Larsen and Yezierska focused on the figure of the migrant 'outsider' as she struggles to make a life for herself in the city. Crane, however, is most usefully considered alongside John Dos Passos. Both deal with the complexity of the city at a social and political level, but they also altered their art as a means of 'matching' it to the kaleidoscopic and mechanistic contours of the city. Both quite deliberately created 'difficult' texts, designed to confuse and confound the reader, in an effort to portray the effects of urban modernity. In *Manhattan Transfer*, the reader is faced with a cubistic piece of writing which attempts to offer a multi-angled perspective of the city. Crane's literary methods are no less complex, and many readers of his early work found it disconcertingly recondite, irrational and opaque. Indeed, Harriet Monroe, the founder and editor of *Poetry* magazine from 1912 to 1936, hesitated to publish 'At Melville's Tomb' (1926) until the poem's obscurities had been cleared up. Crane's reply to Monroe provides a theory of poetry, in which he describes 'the logic of metaphor' and the liberties a poet may take with figurative language:

> The [logic of metaphor's] paradox, of course, is that its apparent illogic operates so logically in conjunction with its context in the poem as to establish its claim to another logic, quite independent of the original definition of the word or phrase or image thus employed. It implies (this *inflection* of language) a previous or prepared receptivity on the part of the reader.[50]

What Crane was interested in were the associative meanings of words rather than their logical or literal significance, so that his poetry could map the workings of thought extension and consciousness.[51]

Indeed, what Crane was keenest to achieve in his poetry was the truth of the imagination. The organic fluidity of the imagination, both within the poet and the reader, is the key to Crane's method and is evident throughout a number of sections in *The Bridge*. For instance, towards the end of 'The River' in Section II, Crane presents an illogical metaphor:

> The River lifts itself from its long bed,
> Poised wholly on its dream, a mustard glow
> Tortured with history, its one will – flow! (p. 21)

Crane's critics would argue that the metaphor breaks down because a river cannot lift itself to poise on a dream. However, Crane always insisted that his seemingly illogical metaphors engendered a new state of consciousness and cohered to the 'truth of the imagination'. The punning 'wholly' suggests the proximity of the divine while the 'mustard glow' evokes the image of a haloed entity, thus further accentuating the necessary dispensation of rationality and submission to the inexplicable force of the imagination. Though tortured by the burden of the past, the will of the river, indeed its dream, is to flow forward, to thrust into the future and break into the higher state of consciousness which is promised in the consecutive section of the poem, 'The Dance'. This desire to achieve a mythic state of consciousness is, as we can see from this short reading, a microcosmic example of both the overall goal and the method of *The Bridge*. The poem sets out to deliver us from one state of being to another, from one side of the bridge to the other, where we will have achieved the truth of the imagination in the composition of the poem, symbolised as the attainment of Atlantis.

This notion of the river as 'tortured with history' is crucial to the poem as a whole, which, in attempting to chart the poet's movement from darkness to the light of creativity, synthesises the discovery and history of the United States from Columbus to modernity. Section I, 'Ave Maria', begins with Columbus and his struggle to record and relate the truth of his American Cathay. Thus the theme of the poem is signalled from the beginning: the voyager's quest to bring enlightenment and truth through language. The second section of *The Bridge*, 'Powhatan's Daughter', offers a departure from the awakened imagination to an exploration of the possibilities and limitations of the flesh. Moving across the continent and back in time to the early seventeenth century, the poet concludes that the body alone cannot sustain the imagination. 'Cutty Sark' concludes the first half of *The Bridge* and shifts across time into the present as the poet crosses the bridge and presents his imaginative vision of the glorious old days of the clipper ships. The epigraph to the section, too, is worthy of comment. Taken from Melville's poem 'The Temeraire', it laments the lost oak beams of the old English ship. Crane takes this further throughout this section, noting how the organic 'oaken' ship has given way to steel and iron, which imprison the imagination.

'Cape Hatteras' launches the second half of the poem, immediately suggesting the correspondence of poetic creation and cosmic creation in its rehearsal of the birth of the Appalachians; concurrent with this is the construction of the bridge, signalling the poet's attempted architecture of words. Section V, 'Three Songs', explores the possibility of love in the modern world, each song being addressed to a different type of woman: Eve, Mary Magdalene and the Virgin Mary; 'Quaker Hill' returns the reader to the cosmic journey of the poet. Section VII, 'The Tunnel', set in the early twentieth century, transports the poet to his ultimate destination through the hellish underworld that is the subway which, like the river, will rise up and merge with the vaulting bridge to deliver him to his destiny. Section VIII, 'Atlantis', returns to the point of the poem's departure in 'Ave Maria'. Spanning time, the bridge links the poet's Atlantis with Columbus's dream vision of an American Cathay. Purported to be the origin of language, Atlantis (and by implication America/Cathay) gives the poet the linguistic power at last to realise the timeless truth of the imagination.[52]

As well as the weight of the American past, the ghosts of a number of nineteenth-century precursors haunt *The Bridge*, as the poet seeks instruction in articulating the spirit of the continent. Perhaps unsurprisingly, given their emphasis on the revelatory nature of individual consciousness and the centrality of the poet in uncovering higher Platonic truths, Emerson, Melville, Dickinson, Poe and Whitman are all present throughout. Dickinson's elliptical dashes, which simultaneously hint at the divine and drive the poem forward, punctuate the early half of 'The River' and 'Cutty Sark'. Typically macabre, Poe appears as a disembodied head in 'The Tunnel', a hellish underworld section in which the poet makes the final leap from the bodily world of sensation to the world of the intellect, prior to his arrival at Atlantis. Emerson's faith in the poet as interlocutor between the world of men and the transcendental world of the spirit, as outlined in Chapter 1, is evident in Crane's perception of the poet's quasi-messianic quest. But, of all Crane's nineteenth-century ancestors, it is the spirit of Whitman in 'Cape Hatteras' and the rough bard's emphasis on movement and 'becoming' which truly dominate the poem. Though Crane is not an exponent of Whitman's free verse structure or prose-lines (he writes for the most part in iambs and often in iambic pentameter), he takes from Whitman, and by inference from Emerson, a faith in the poet as a recorder of the truth, and shares with him the quest of creating an epic of the nation.[53] For Crane's poet, Whitman is the Bridge which will take him from the 'glacial sierras . . . back to earth' (p. 45):

> Our Meistersinger, thou set breath in steel;
> And it was thou on the boldest heel
> Stood up and flung the span on even wing
> Of that great Bridge, our Myth, whereof I sing! (p. 46)

A spiritual brother with whom the poet moves hand-in-hand 'onward without halt' beneath 'the rainbow's arch' (p. 47), Whitman is himself the bridge between death and life, between the natural and the intellectual, the body and the imagination. With the resurrected Whitman at his side, the poet may go on to record his Atlantis.

In the spirit of Crane, it is surely fitting to conclude by returning to the beginning. 'To Brooklyn Bridge', the prelude to the poem, sets *The Bridge* firmly in modern New York City, offering the opening image of a seagull rising from the Hudson, leaving 'the chained bay waters' in its flight of 'Liberty' (p. 1). The image of the soaring bird 'building high' in flight, its trajectory an 'inviolate curve' which evokes the shape of the bridge, serves as an inspiration to the poet as he begins his own architectural climb, constructing a poem which will deliver him to the truth of the imagination. The mounting heights of the seagull are quickly juxtaposed with the falling elevators which drop the 'multitudes' of the city from their clerical jobs of 'figures to be filed away' into cinemas and subways. The freedom of the bird and the enslavement of the multitudes represent the alternate pillars of the bridge, and it is the duty of the poet to construct the edifice which will allow him to move from one side to the other. In a futile bid for freedom, one of the multitudes, 'a bedlamite', leaps to his death from the bridge – an image that brings to mind Bud Korpenning's suicide in *Manhattan Transfer*. The reference to the 'bedlamite' is important, referring to the famous London psychiatric asylum Bethlem Hospital, and thereby suggesting the insanity of modern New York City, a theme we have already encountered in Dos Passos, Larsen and Yezierska. The sacrifice of the bedlamite sustains the city; thereafter the cables of the bridge 'breathe', 'Down Wall, from girder into street noon leaks', and a new day dawns. Through death comes a kind of rebirth; the city, yet again, creates itself anew. For all their mechanical destructiveness, the architectural contours of the modern metropolis are also life-giving and will deliver the poet to the eternal truth he seeks. The bridge in its 'curveship [will] lend a myth to God' (p. 2) and provide the poet with his symbolic and formal pathway to the truth of the imagination. And so, as so often, we are left with New York as a vision of utopia.

NOTES

1. Louis Wirth, 'Urbanism as a Way of Life', *American Journal of Sociology*', 44.1 (July 1938), p. 1.
2. I have drawn from various sources for this brief history of New York, including: the 'New York City Timeline' at http://www.gothamcenter.org/features/timeline/ (accessed 20 January 2012); David Reynolds, *America: Empire of Liberty*

(London: Penguin, 2009), pp. 3–25; and especially Edwin G. Burrows and Mike Wallace, *Gotham: A History of New York City to 1898* (Oxford: Oxford University Press, 1998).

3. See John W. Reps, *The Making of Urban America: A History of City Planning in the United States* (Princeton: Princeton University Press, 1965), p. 294.
4. John W. Reps, 'Jefferson's Checkerboard Towns', *Journal of the Society of Architectural Historians*, 20.3 (October 1961), p. 108.
5. I have relied for the account of these developments on Peter Brooker, *New York Fictions: Modernity, Postmodernism, The New Modern* (London and New York: Pearson, 1996), pp. 27–79.
6. See Campbell Gibson, 'Population of the 100 Largest Cities and Other Urban Places in the United States: 1790–1990' (June 1998): http://www.census.gov/population/www/documentation/twps0027/twps0027.html (accessed 20 January 2012).
7. Cited in Walter Benn Michaels, *Our America: Nativism, Modernism and Pluralism* (Durham, NC: Duke University Press, 1995), p. 8.
8. Werner Sollers, *Beyond Ethnicity: Consent and Descent in American Culture* (New York: Oxford University Press, 1986), p. 246.
9. Raymond Williams, 'The Metropolis and the Emergence of Modernism', in Peter Brooker (ed.), *Modernism/Postmodernism* (London: Longman, 1992), p. 91.
10. Peter Brooker, *New York Fictions: Modernity, Postmodernism, The New Modern*, p. 11.
11. Georg Simmel, 'The Metropolis and Mental Life' (1903), in Vassiliki Kolocotroni, Jane Goldman and Olga Taxidou (eds), *Modernism: An Anthology of Sources and Documents* (Edinburgh: Edinburgh University Press, 1998), p. 53.
12. Peter Brooker, *New York Fictions: Modernity, Postmodernism, The New Modern*, pp. 46–7.
13. Cited in Virginia Spencer Carr, *Dos Passos: A Life* (Evanston: Northwestern University Press, 2004), p. 215.
14. Ibid. p. 215.

15. Letter to Mme Championière, cited in Townsend Ludington's *John Dos Passos* (New York: Dutton, 1980), pp. 200–1.
16. John Dos Passos, *Manhattan Transfer* (New York: Penguin, [1925] 2000), p. 16. All subsequent references will appear in the text.
17. For an extended discussion of the filmic aspects of *Manhattan Transfer* and the mechanisation of the individual see Lisa Nanney, *John Dos Passos Revisited* (London: Twayne, 1998), pp. 152–69.
18. The collection was published in 1920 under the title *Hungry Hearts*.
19. See Blanche H. Gelfant's 'Introduction' to Anzia Yezierska, *Hungry Hearts* (London: Penguin, 1997), pp. vii–xxxvi.
20. Anzia Yezierska, *Bread Givers* (New York: Persea, [1925] 2003), p. 78. All subsequent references will appear in the text.
21. See Gelfant, 'Introduction' to Yezierska, *Hungry Hearts*, p. vii.
22. Interestingly, Woolf's *A Room of One's Own* did not appear until 1929.
23. Anzia Yezierska, 'America and I', in *Children of Loneliness: Stories of Immigrant Life in America* (New York: Funk and Wagnalls, 1923), p. 50.
24. Ron Ebest, 'Anzia Yezierska and the Popular Debate over the Jews', *Melus*, 25.1 (2000), p. 106.
25. W. E. B. Du Bois, 'Two Novels', *The Crisis*, 35 (June 1928), p. 202.
26. Alain Locke, '1928: A Retrospective Review', *Opportunity*, 7 (January 1929), pp. 8–9.
27. Nella Larsen, *Quicksand* (London: Penguin, [1928] 2002), p. 43. Subsequent references will appear in the text.
28. See Andrew Beveridge, 'Harlem's Shifting Population' (August 2008): http://www.gothamgazette.com/article//20080827/255/2635 (accessed 20 January 2012).
29. Nella Larsen, *Passing* (London: Penguin, [1929] 2002), p. 41. Subsequent references will appear in the text.
30. For a full biography of each of these people see Thadious Davis's excellent text notes to the 2002 edition of Larsen's *Quicksand*, pp. 144–5, n. 5.

31. See Wharton's letter to Dr Morgan Dix, in which she notes: 'Social conditions as they are just now in our new world, where the sudden possession of money has come without inherited obligations . . .'. From *The Letters of Edith Wharton*, ed. R. W. B. Lewis and Nancy Lewis (New York: Charles Scribner's Sons, 1988), p. 99.
32. Candace Waid and Clare Colquitt, 'Toward a Modernist Aesthetic: The Literary Legacy of Edith Wharton', in Paul Lamb and G. R. Thompson (eds), *A Companion to American Fiction, 1865–1914* (Oxford: Blackwell, 2005), p. 547.
33. Martin Halliwell, *Transatlantic Modernism: Moral Dilemmas in Modernist Fiction* (Edinburgh: Edinburgh University Press, 2006), p. 45.
34. Carol J. Singley, *Edith Wharton: Matters of Mind and Spirit* (Cambridge: Cambridge University Press, 1998), p. 84.
35. Hermione Lee, 'An American in Paris', *Guardian Review* (20 January 2007), p. 6.
36. Edith Wharton, *The House of Mirth*, ed. Elizabeth Ammons (New York: Norton Critical Editions, [1905] 1990), pp. 126–7. Subsequent references will appear in the text.
37. Louis Auchincloss cited in Hermione Lee, *Edith Wharton* (London: Chatto and Windus, 2007), p. 45.
38. Thorstein Veblen, 'Conspicuous Leisure and Conspicuous Consumption', in Edith Wharton, *The House of Mirth*, ed. Elizabeth Ammons (New York: Norton Critical Editions, [1905] 1990), pp. 268, 263.
39. Ibid. p. 270.
40. Dorothy Dudley, *Forgotten Frontiers: Dreiser and the Land of the Free* (New York: Harrison Smith, 1932), p. 3. Dudley's comment anticipates contemporary scholarship which has turned to plural, non-doctrinal modernisms. See, for instance, Peter Nicholls, *Modernisms* (London: Macmillan, 1995), and Steven Matthews, *Modernism* (London: Arnold, 2004).
41. Cited in F. O. Matthiessen, *Theodore Dreiser* (London: Methuen, 1951), p. 60. Indeed, Dreiser's thoughts on experimentalism are evident in a review of Ford Madox Ford's *The Good Soldier* (1915): 'Of far more importance is it that, once begun it should go forward in a more or less direct line, or at

least that it should retain one's uninterrupted interest. This is not the case in this book. The interlacings, the cross references, the re-re-references to all sorts of things which subsequently are told somewhere in full, irritate one to the point of laying down the book.' See Theodore Dreiser, 'The Saddest Story', *New Republic*, 3 (12 June 1915), p. 155.

42. Interestingly, even within his journalism he was able to merge the factual with the fictional. As a feature writer for the *Globe-Democrat*, he wrote a series of real and imaginary interviews, the latter containing invented characters with 'interesting philosophies'. See Matthiessen, *Theodore Dreiser*, p. 28.
43. Graham Robb, *Balzac: A Biography* (New York: Norton, 1994), p. 421.
44. Michael Lydon, 'Justice to Theodore Dreiser: On the Greatness of a Writer Who Critics Have Long Treated with Either Scorn or Condescension', *The Atlantic* (9 August 1993), p. 98.
45. Alfred Kazin, *The Stature of Theodore Dreiser* (Evanston: Indiana University Press, 1955), p. 3. For Mencken's extended comments see Edmund Wilson (ed.), *The Shock of Recognition* (Garden City, NY: Doubleday, 1943), p. 1169.
46. See Saul Bellow, 'Dreiser and the Triumph of Art', *Commentary*, 11 (May 1951), pp. 502–3.
47. Theodore Dreiser, *Sister Carrie*, ed. Lee Clark Mitchell (Oxford: Oxford University Press, [1900] 1991), p. 361. Subsequent references will appear in the text.
48. Letter to Gorham Munson (1923), from *The Letters of Hart Crane, 1916–1932*, ed. Brom Weber (Berkeley: University of California Press, 1965), p. 124.
49. Hart Crane, *The Bridge* (New York: Liveright, [1930] 1992), p. 72. All subsequent references will be made in the text.
50. Letter to Harriet Monroe, from *The Letters of Hart Crane, 1916–1932*, p. 330.
51. This is very close to the method of European modernists such as Joyce and Woolf. In Woolf's *Mrs Dalloway* (1925), for instance, Clarissa's opening of windows in her London home opens the doors of perception and releases her past, bringing the character and the reader into the whirl of her conscious-

ness and memories through a series of associative links. This method is even more complex in Joyce's *A Portrait of the Artist as a Young Man* (and later *Ulysses*), where the sounds of childhood release a series of seemingly illogical associations.

52. For a brief overview of the various sections of the poem see 'An Introduction by Waldo Frank' to Hart Crane's *The Bridge* (New York: Liveright, [1930] 1992), pp. xvii–xxxvi. For a more detailed section-by-section breakdown of the poem see Richard P. Sugg's *Hart Crane's The Bridge: A Description of its Life* (Tuscaloosa: University of Alabama Press, 1976).
53. Herbert A. Leibowitz, *Hart Crane: An Introduction to the Poetry* (New York: Columbia University, 1968), pp. 220–56.

CHAPTER 3

Regional American Modernism

On the face of it, the combination of modernism and regionalism can seem a contradiction in terms. After all, modernism is synonymous with the international avant-garde, stylistic experimentalism and formal innovation, whereas regionalism brings with it connotations of nostalgia, parochialism and literary realism. For a long time, literary regionalism was tied up with the term 'writing of local color', a somewhat dismissive expression which allowed critics such as F. O. Matthiessen to relegate writers like Sarah Orne Jewett to the ranks of the second division, where she languished as a supposedly minor American writer. Whatever one's thoughts on Jewett (and recent critics have done much to rescue her from the literary scrapheap and revive her reputation), the negative connotations of sentimentality, folk wisdom, localism and resistance to wider national forces continue to be associated with much regional writing.[1]

In some cases, of course, these associations were not unfair. Much nineteenth-century regional writing was indeed saturated with a mawkish nostalgia for lost innocence, lovingly describing the recent past with a documentary realism that bordered on the obsessive. Thomas Nelson Page and Joel Chandler Harris offer clear examples of this kind of fiction, with their emphasis on the domestic rituals of the homestead and the kinship bonds of regional communities. As early as 1937, the critic James Gray wryly remarked of regional writing:

> The militantly American doctrine called regionalism, which has tended in recent years to make a local prejudice something vaguely resembling a religion, would probably hold that the heavenly Muse does herself over, with protean variability, each time she crosses a state line . . . The costume assigned to the Minnesota Muse, in the regionalist's handbook, is a decent, though shabby, Mother Hubbard. She sings exclusively of ruined wheat harvests and sings of them with a strong Swedish accent.[2]

Amusing as Gray's article was, though, it obscured the complexity of much regional writing, as well as overlooking the very specific historical circumstances which contributed to the growth of literature concerned with regional cultures. And inevitably, all such caricatures or misunderstandings of regionalism fail to grasp its subtle connections with modernist writing. It is quite simply a mistake to think of regionalism and modernism as polar opposites. They grew out of identical historical circumstances and were often animated by remarkably similar thematic and ideological concerns. And nothing bears this out better than the work of writers such as Willa Cather and Ellen Glasgow, whose work straddles the geographical divide between them. Neither card-carrying modernists nor stereotypical regionalists, they are valuable reminders that all literary labels are ultimately slippery and artificial.

Regional writing blossomed in the latter part of the nineteenth century. Mark Twain, for instance, is often described as a regionalist, thanks to the emphasis on the particular (and peculiar) institutions of the South and the rendition of Southern dialect, pronunciation and speech patterns in his most famous work, *The Adventures of Tom Sawyer* (1876) and *The Adventures of Huckleberry Finn* (1885). Other notable regional writers of the day include the previously mentioned Jewett, who was primarily associated with the Maine forests of New England, Francis Bret Harte and Bayard Taylor, whose works were set in California, and Midwesterners such as James Whitcomb Riley and Edward Eggleston. The reasons behind the development of this particular kind of literature are manifold: on an aesthetic level, many writers felt suffocated by the sweeping 'American' narratives of New England, which seemed to neglect the lives of citizens in other states and regions; and on a social and political level, the Civil War (as discussed in Chapter 1) had left a profound impact on the very idea of a unified national identity. On the surface, the Civil War had united the nation. In many ways, though, the experience of war, and the Reconstruction (1865–77) which followed it, actually accentuated regional differences. Once a prosperous plantation region which in the nineteenth century had provided more the half the world's cotton, much of the South was now in ruins, its institutions broken, its communities devastated. Southern farmers found themselves without the vast supplies of livestock that had formerly helped them compete with the more mechanised farmsteads of the North. And many of the urban centres of the South, including Atlanta, Georgia, and New Orleans, Louisiana, were severely damaged and their populations depleted. The cost of the Confederate war effort had been enormously high, with a consequential neglect of state infrastructure and the decimation of transportation networks. Furthermore, the abolition of slavery, through which the South had also lost its most lucrative economic asset, as well as the inflation of the Confederate dollar, meant that the South was forced to rebuild its economy from scratch.

The cost of rebuilding the South forced many states to increase the property tax rate, which exacerbated the poverty of the region and contributed to the widespread feeling that Reconstruction was little more than an attempt by wealthy Northern industrialists to push through costly programmes at the expense of the beleaguered region. In short, the South became gradually more and more disenfranchised during the era of Reconstruction. And, in fact, the entire programme of Reconstruction was considered by many contemporary thinkers, including black spokesmen such as W. E. B. Du Bois and Booker T. Washington, to have been a complete failure.[3] Writing in *Black Reconstruction in America* (1935), Du Bois observed that 'the slave went free; stood a brief moment in the sun; then moved back again toward slavery'.[4] Indeed, even at a cultural and literary level, the impact of the Civil War and Reconstruction upon the South cannot be overestimated, taking the region from a strong and vibrant self-sufficiency to a demoralising and debilitating poverty. For many Southerners,

Reconstruction left a sour taste of disappointment which solidified rather than dissolved their sense of a separate regional identity.[5]

In the Midwest and across the Great Plains a different set of historical circumstances prevailed. From the late 1870s to the mid-1880s, thousands of settlers, largely of Scandinavian, German, Polish and Hungarian stock, rushed to occupy Nebraska, central and western Kansas and the Missouri Plateau. The 1862 Homestead Act, signed into law by Abraham Lincoln, gave applicants freehold titles to undeveloped land west of the Mississippi River, and with the benefit of Eastern mortgage investment capital, towns sprung into being and farms flourished. The harsh winter of 1886, however, killed huge numbers of livestock and the following years of severe drought meant the failure of successive harvests. Homesteaders found themselves lumbered with crippling mortgages from East Coast lending banks as well as the annual taxes they had approved in the good times to pay for the infrastructure of new towns and cities. These continued hardships, combined with fluctuations in the value of the dollar and an eye toward the comparative successes of the Eastern seaboard states in industry, finance and urbanisation, led many Midwesterners to believe there was something of a conspiracy against the American farmer. To give expression to their grievances, they established the Farmers Alliance, which lobbied Congress, advised on marketing, purchasing and modern machinery, and eventually sought redress in politics.

Made up of small groups of cooperatives and independent farmers, the Alliance set up conventions and conferences throughout the late 1880s and eventually gave birth to the People's Party, which aspired to contest elections at a national level to bring the plight of the nation's wheat and cotton farmers to the attention of all Americans. In a bid to forge new political ground, General James Weaver was nominated as the Populist candidate for President of the United States at the Omaha Convention in 1892. What became known as the Omaha Platform neatly summarised the farmers' grievances:

> We meet in the midst of a nation brought to the verge of moral, political, and material ruin. Corruption dominates the

> ballot box, the legislatures, the Congress . . . The newspapers are largely subsidized or muzzled; public opinion silenced; business prostrated; our homes covered with mortgages; labour impoverished and the land concentrating in the hands of the capitalists . . . The fruits of the toil of millions are boldly stolen to build up colossal fortunes for a few, unprecedented in the history of mankind.[6]

Of course Weaver lost the election, and the demands of the Agrarian Alliance went largely ignored. But the financial panic of 1893, caused by overexpansion in the banking sector and a subsequent squeeze on debtors, brought the Populists increased public support and an affiliation with the Democratic Party. Indeed, by the 1896 presidential election, the Populist agenda had become so firmly entrenched in political discourse that the Democrats embraced many of its themes, nominating the passionate Nebraska Presbyterian William Jennings Bryan, who made no secret of his rural values and his enthusiasm for the Populist cause. Despite his success in the West and in the South, Bryan never won the White House, and the People's Party disappeared completely, effectively fusing with the Democratic Party. But although the party vanished from sight, it left a considerable legacy. Many rural voters felt deeply betrayed; paradoxically, their estrangement only deepened their sense of regional identity. The American farmer, they believed, had been left behind, cheated and abandoned by a society run for the benefit of Wall Street speculators and East Coast millionaires. These would be powerful themes in the politics of the early twentieth century; but they were powerful themes, too, in the literature of the day.[7]

Literary regionalism was deeply informed by the bitter legacy of the Civil War and the rise and fall of Populism. Willa Cather, for example, was an ardent supporter of Bryan despite his anti-suffrage stance, and worked Populist concerns such as the relentless poverty faced by the Midwestern farmer, the distrust of the railroads and the harsh face of capitalism into early novels such as *O Pioneers!* (1913), *My Ántonia* (1918) and *A Lost Lady* (1923). Similarly, William Faulkner, who was an enthusiastic admirer of Mark Twain, charted the decline of wealthy Southern families and the rise of agrarian violence in *The Sound and the Fury* (1929) and *Absalom, Absalom!* (1936). And yet as both these examples demonstrate, regionalism was not entirely backward-looking. It was concerned not just with the past but also with the present; and like more cosmopolitan authors such as Hemingway and Fitzgerald, regionalists were often keen to explore the impact of the past *upon* the present rather merely indulging a sentimental yearning for days of yore. In fact, in many regionalist novels, the past is a place of unspeakable crimes, bequeathing a trauma that simmers beneath the surface of the present, threatening to erupt from beneath the facade of propriety and to destroy the lives of the principal characters. It is true that some regionalist writers follow the example of T. S. Eliot and show the past offering succour from the ills of the present, and many writers of the South and Midwest were clearly kicking against the encroaching and homogenising tendencies of urbanisation. Yet it would be erroneous to argue that all regionalist writers were inherently anti-urban or opposed to modernisation. Ellen Glasgow's *Barren Ground* (1925), for instance, demonstrates the regenerative possibilities of innovative farming techniques, and she was far from alone in showing the tremendous benefits that cities, technology and mass communications had brought to the regional community.

The other common charge against regionalist writing is that it encouraged a supposedly inward-looking anti-immigrant nativism. This is perhaps not altogether surprising given the People's Party's rather negative views on cheap immigrant labour, which was often brought in to deal with strike action. However, many so-called regionalists, especially Willa Cather, embraced the figure of the immigrant and made him or her the centrepiece of their fictions. Indeed, on numerous occasions in the years before the First World War, Cather championed the immigrant's individuality against the forces of assimilation and Americanisation. Asked about the importance of immigrant communities in her work in an interview for the *New York Times Book Review* in 1924, she remarked:

> They have come here to live in the sense that they lived in the Old World, and if they were let alone their lives might turn into the beautiful ways of their homeland. But they are not let

> alone. Social workers, missionaries – call them what you will – go after them, hound them, pursue them and devote their days and nights toward the great task of turning them into stupid replicas of smug American citizens. This passion for Americanizing everything and everybody is a deadly disease with us.[8]

The key term here is 'Americanizing', which Cather clearly sees as a baleful process that threatens to iron out the idiosyncrasies of immigrant and, by implication, regional cultures. After all, Cather's prairie fictions are populated by Germans, Scandinavians and Czechs. Indeed, what are often regarded as Cather's mythic pastoral visions of American identity at the beginning of the twentieth century can also be viewed as narratives of dislocation and social isolation. Just like any experimental avant-garde writer, in fact, Cather was keen to explore the hypocrisies and inequalities beneath the surface of modern American society.

In the South, perhaps the most influential regionalist group was that originally known as the Fugitives, which later evolved into the Southern Agrarians. The group, which included writers such as John Crowe Ransom, Allen Tate and Robert Penn Warren, were mostly affiliated with Vanderbilt University and began meeting informally in Nashville from about 1915 to discuss poetry, philosophy and the social value of literature. They took their name from their magazine, *The Fugitive*, which was first published in 1922 and ran for three issues until 1925. As John Duvall argues, the magazine was effectively a response to H. L. Mencken's dismissal of all Southern literature in his essay 'The Sahara of the Bozart' (1917). 'You will not find a single Southern poet above the rank of neighborhood rhymster', Mencken had written contemptuously, adding that, with the exception of James Branch Cabell, 'you will not find a single prose writer who can actually write'. Little wonder, then, that the future Agrarians were so keen to prove him wrong.[9]

The first issue of *The Fugitive* outlined the group's desire to break with the Southern romanticism of the past, as well as with the urban, consumer-driven culture more commonly associated with the East Coast. They were, wrote Tate, 'an intensive and historical group as opposed to the eclectic and cosmopolitan groups that flourished in the East'.[10] And indeed, they saw themselves as exiles from the world around them, detached from both the Southern regional world in which they had grown up, and the wider socio-cultural landscape of the United States. Yet while the Fugitives distanced themselves from a particular Southern past, their Southern-ness was precisely what defined and united them. It was no coincidence, for example, that it took the Scopes Trial of 1925 to bring them together again after a brief separation – precisely because the trial, in which a high school biology teacher was prosecuted for teaching evolution, was widely perceived as an attack on the South by the forces of urban, secular modernity. Foremost among the region's critics was, once again, H. L. Mencken, who told the readers of the *Baltimore Sun* that it was inhabited by 'yokels', 'hill-billies', 'yaps' and 'morons', and mocked the prosecution lawyer – none other than William Jennings Bryan – for spouting 'theological bilge'.[11] Moved to defend their birthplace, Tate, Ransom and others reconvened to form the Southern Agrarians, the label under which they are best known. Antipathetic to the forces of industrialisation and modernity, they looked to the rural and the pastoral as the spiritual wellsprings of American literary and philosophical thought, and promoted a traditionalist approach to literature and an organic approach to everyday life. Their ideas were best captured in their manifesto *I'll Take My Stand: The South and the Agrarian Tradition* (1930), which 'support[ed] a Southern way of life against what might be called the American prevailing way . . . Agrarian *versus* Industrial' and reaffirmed the necessity of a society 'in which agriculture is the leading vocation, whether for wealth, for pleasure, or for prestige'.[12]

Three writers emerged as the most important of the group, Tate, Ransom and Penn Warren, the last-named going on to win the Pulitzer Prize for his novel *All the King's Men* (1946) and subsequent prizes for his poetry in 1958 and 1979. Each produced works which clearly withstand the accusations of parochialism and sentimentality, although Tate's most famous poem, 'Ode to the Confederate Dead' (1929), an elegiac lament for the dead Southern soldiers of the Civil War, is nothing if not sentimental. The lasting legacy of the Southern Agrarians, however, lies not so much in the principles outlined in the preface to *I'll Take My Stand* as in their contributions to the shape of American literary criticism in the mid-twentieth century.[13] Ransom published *The New Criticism* in 1941, and it is from this volume that New Criticism took its name. This new kind of literary criticism, not unlike Russian formalism, emphasised close reading of the text with scant (if any) attention to contextual or biographical details. The interrelationship between structure and meaning was crucial to the New Critics, and structural devices such as poetic scansion, prose plotting and characterisation were viewed as central to the revelation of theme. What the New Critics sought in literary art was precisely what they deemed to be missing from contemporary American life: a regard for and faith in tradition and wholeness, venerating the organic as the antithesis of a fractured and uncontainable modernity, hurtling toward an unrecognisable future.

For all the Agrarians' respect for tradition, however, much of their work is recognisably modern. Tate in particular is often regarded as the 'modernist' of the group, not least since he responded positively to Eliot's *The Waste Land* (1922), which Ransom had publicly dismissed. And, indeed, the influence of both Eliot and Hart Crane can be seen in Tate's poetry, freer forms alternating with more traditional poetic patterns. Warren, too, is recognisably a modern writer, and indeed in later life he admitted that his obsession with the Cold War had come to trump his purely regionalist concerns. But the truth of the matter is surely that *all* regionalists are the products of modernity. Though ostensibly resistant to the structures and philosophies of literary modernism, the regionalists' antipathy toward the modern (whether it be modern warfare, mass industrialisation or technology's alienation of a basic humanity) meant they were articulating precisely the same themes favoured by many leading modernists. So, for example, the regionalists' search for a lost poetic harmony in the forms of the past is little different to the quests of Eliot or H. D. (Hilda Doolittle), who deployed Hellenic verse structures and a raft of classical imagery as a means of structuring a chaotic modernity and as an antithesis to the ephemeral nature of much modern writing. Even Cather, who embraced and encouraged the regionalist tag, engaged with some of the more innovative strands of literary modernism and called for a de-cluttering of the modern novel in her seminal essay 'The Novel Démeublé' (1922). And few critics today would deny the modernist impulses and influences which run throughout the work of Faulkner.

Still, for the regional modernist, the importance of the local and the small scale cannot be elided or minimised. For each of the writers discussed in this chapter, the customs of the county, town or region are integral to the text. In some instances, these customs are manifold and diverse – which means they are not completely unlike the complex cultures explored in much modern urban literature. In others, regional cultures can seem monocultural and static. But in all cases, the writer is attempting to awaken the reader to a fresh perception of reality and to offer a new understanding of a particular place or regional identity – a literary aspiration that is both deeply traditional and undeniably modernist.

WILLA CATHER

It is no secret that Willa Cather is consistently characterised as a regional writer. Indeed, as the critic Guy Reynolds has observed, Cather was conscious of her reputation and willingly embraced it. The irony is that although it was the 'regionalist' tag which first brought Cather national success, it has also come to stifle her literary reputation. But the caricature of Cather as a nostalgic Nebraskan regionalist completely misses her deep immersion in a broader and more invigorating national and international culture.[14] Several scholars have explored her literary influences, both American and European, her taste in the visual and the culinary arts, and her deployment of Greek and Latin epic conventions and allusions in even the earliest of her fictions. Yet the assumption of parochialism persists.[15] One of the reasons for this, of course, is the success of Cather's earlier fiction, namely *O Pioneers!* (1913) and *My Ántonia* (1918), which were deeply rooted in her Nebraska settings. Another is her fascination with the processes of memory and recovery, her lifelong interest in origin, purity and identity. However, even in these early novels Cather's world is much wider than the prairie. Certainly the prairie location and context are vitally important, and Cather's poetic descriptions of the landscapes her protagonists inhabit were a crucial ingredient in her novels' success. However, the world she presents in these earlier books is distinctly modern and multicultural, teeming with immigrant voices in all their discordant polyphony. The problem, therefore, is less the regionalist label, and more the nostalgic undertones and cultural homogeneity that regionalism is perceived to represent – a caricatured homogeneity which actually flattens out the richness and diversity of the region and which is perceived as the antithesis of industrialisation, cosmopolitanism and modernism.

The European allusions, intertexts and influences in Cather's work are well known, from classical writers such as Homer, Euripedes and Virgil to French and Russian novelists such as Balzac, Flaubert and Tolstoy. Her writing occupies a transitional zone between cultures, situated 'on the divide' between Old and New Worlds, between the regional world and the terrain of international modernity. But she does not straddle this 'divide' comfortably. There is in Cather's work a profound sense of loss, a desire to rekindle cultures that are at the brink of extinction or on the threshold of assimilation: one thinks, for instance, of the cliff dwellers in *The Professor's House* (1925) or the Southwestern Indian communities in her novel *Death Comes for the Archbishop* (1927). And as Guy Reynolds and others have pointed out, the preservation of these distinct cultures against the wider forces of Americanisation suggests a writer deeply attuned to the political and ideological concerns of the day. Moreover, given the concerns of many regionalist writers in the early twentieth century, it suggests a writer who, despite the apparent simplicity of her approach, was deeply suspicious of the project of Americanisation and the idea of a 'naturalised inheritance'.

During Cather's lifetime, one of her most sympathetic reviewers was the anti-war intellectual and sometime writer for *The Dial* Randolph Bourne. In his review of *My Ántonia* in 1918, Bourne described Cather as belonging to the international group of modernist writers – an oddly curious ascription, when one considers that this is one of the books that supposedly situates Cather most firmly in the prairies. However, a closer look at Bourne's writing shows that he saw the idea of 'region', indeed even of 'nation', in distinctly cosmopolitan terms. For Bourne, the term 'trans-national America' referred to 'a federation of cultures', 'a cosmopolitan federation of national colonies, of foreign cultures' with 'an intellectual internationalism . . . [interested in] different cultural expressions'. He envisaged the United States as a nation of immigrants who could 'retain that distinctiveness of their native cultures' and hence be 'more valuable and interesting to each other for being different', a nation of 'cosmopolitan interchange . . . in spite of the war and all its national exclusiveness'.[16] And Cather, too, clearly shared his approach. For Cather, the very notion of Americanisation and even the doctrine of the melting pot embodied precisely the cultural and racial homogeneity she most abhorred. And while elegiac in tone, her novels were less a lament for some stable American or regional identity than a *repudiation* of a fixed, Americanised identity, which, she believed, threatened to eradicate diverse cultures such as that of the cliff-top dwellers. Indeed, in her 1938 essay 'On *The Professor's House*', Cather admitted that she deliberately engaged with French and Spanish forms to present an antithesis to the stifling conformity of St Peter's American house: 'In my book I tried to make Professor St. Peter's house rather over-crowded and stuffy with new things; American proprieties, clothes, furs, petty ambitions, quivering jealousies – until one got rather stifled'.[17] Thus the world of St Peter and his daughters is less the protected and vulnerable space identified by critics such as Walter Benn Michaels than a space which threatens to infect, commodify and eradicate immigrant and indigenous cultures.[18] And far from being inward-looking and parochial, Cather's methodology reveals a writer attuned to the wider dangers of cultural conformity.

More than any other Cather novel, it is *My Ántonia* that demonstrates her sense of lost innocence and the perils of industrial mechanisation and modern values. The book opens with an 'Introduction' in which an unnamed narrator shares a train journey with Jim Burden, the pair reminiscing about their shared childhood in the prairie landscape. Jim reveals his renewed friendship with a lost childhood friend, Ántonia Shimerda, the daughter of Czech immigrants, and the narrator then discloses Jim's unhappy adult life. Uprooted from Nebraska, Jim works in New York as a legal counsel for a great Western railway, and is unhappily married to a woman who 'play[s] the patroness to a group of young poets and painters of advanced ideas and mediocre ability'.[19] It is hard to miss Cather's dig at New York's modern salon culture, or indeed her portrayal of the railroad as somehow degrading. Later in the novel, Ántonia is even betrayed by a railroad man who abandons her with an illegitimate child. The motif of the journey in which the narrator returns to the place of his childhood, from which a story then unravels is borrowed from French and Russian novelists (thereby linking her story of the American Midwest with the Old World) and gives the entire novel a retrospective feel, which helps to explain the perception of sentimentality which dogs Cather's work. The double journey, the physical journey and the narrative journey into the past, however, is linked to another journey: Jim's seemingly 'interminable' childhood train journey 'across the Midland plain of North America' (p. 3) from Virginia to Nebraska following the death of his parents. These journeys reflect a sense of longing for something which has been lost, whether it is innocence, youth, loved ones or memories, all of which are tied indelibly to the Nebraskan landscape which is so crucial to Jim Burden's narrative. Yet there is also, in these journeys, a sense of renewal and revitalisation. In a way, each brings him closer to Ántonia and the radiance and life-giving powers he associates with her and, by implication, with the landscape she inhabits; she is both divine Muse and, in later life, supreme earth mother, boasting some ten or eleven children. Of course, the overarching journey brings about the story itself, and therein lies one of the crucial paradoxes of this seemingly simple novel: creation, renewal and regeneration come precisely from what has been lost or is on the verge of extinction.

Cather's use of Virgil compounds this thematic paradox. The novel's haunting Virgilian epigraph, '*Optima dies . . . prima fugit*' ('the best days are the first to flee') is manifestly a lament for lost youth and the lost days of pioneering America, the vanished pastoral idyll Jim associates with his childhood and with Ántonia. The epigraph foreshadows Jim's later immersion in Virgil as a student at the University of Nebraska and his resolution, '*Primus ego in patriam mecum . . . deducam Musas*', to 'be the first, if I live to bring the Muse into my country' (p. 264). His method of doing so, and by inference Cather's own method, is to turn his memories of the ordinary immigrant figures and the physical landscape of his regional past into an American pastoral, which culminates in the novel's mythic image of the plough encased on the horizon within the red disc of the sun. Indeed, on his first day at his grandparents' homestead farm, we see the young Jim take possession of the landscape:

> As I looked about me I felt that the grass was the country, as the water is the sea. The red of the grass made all the great prairie the colour of wine-stains, of certain seaweeds when they are first washed up. And there was so much motion in it; the whole country seemed, somehow, to be running . . . I felt the motion in the landscape; in the fresh, easy-blowing morning wind, and in the earth itself, as if the shaggy grass were a sort of loose hide, and underneath it herds of wild buffalo were galloping, galloping . . . (pp. 15–16)

Jim's recollection of his first childhood impressions of the landscape have an Emersonian quality: not merely does he insist on the totality of the natural world but he emphasises the movement and flux which underlie it. Certainly, his observation of the 'queer little red bugs' which 'moved in red squadrons' (p. 18) recalls Thoreau's observation of the red ants which marshalled themselves in militaristic rows outside his Walden hut. These intertextual allusions not only anchor the novel in a classic tradition but also reinforce the importance of preserving memories. After all, these recollections are Jim's memories of the past, and by retrieving them, he is salvaging their inhabitants from complete extinction in the brave new American world.

For a more complex demonstration of Cather's desire to salvage the past, the obvious candidate is *The Professor's House*, a novel of memory, loss and disillusionment. Though the story does not deal with immigrants, at least not in the same way as *O Pioneers!* and *My Ántonia*, the physical composition of the novel, with its gap in the middle, a gap where one culture is framed by another, demonstrates precisely the kind of cultural harmony and coexistence advocated by Bourne. And though the novel deals with the Native American past of the Blue Mesa rather than a regional past of immigrant histories, it formally and allusively occupies a transatlantic imaginary world, integrating the literary, historical and mythological classics with the endangered history of the Mesa and the American story of capitalist inventiveness and frontier expansion.

The novel is deeply concerned with possession and the problems of a burgeoning capitalist economy, and thus it is essentially a story about the disconnection between aesthetics and economics.[20] The novel centres on Godfrey St Peter's refusal to move to a new and improved family home, favouring the comforts of his old attic for his academic work; it documents the transformation of the university into a business enterprise; and it charts St Peter's growing unease with his family's accumulation of wealth on the back of his dead student Tom Outland's inventions. Furthermore St Peter is struck by the similarities between Tom's activities on the Mesa and the acts of the first Spanish colonisers, seeing both as a kind of scramble for the artefacts of an ancient and dead civilisation. In formally presenting this kind of appropriation and the protagonist's uneasiness with it, Cather's insertion of Tom's narrative into the world of the professor is one of the most startling dislocations in her writing, a sign of her experimentalism, but also a technique devised to project the professor's profound sense of dislocation.

This thematic uneasiness with American culture is formally entangled with European art: in a later essay on the novel, Cather remarked that its structure came from early French and Spanish novels' interpolation of a 'novella' into a 'roman'. Above all, she said, the form was like the Dutch paintings she had seen in Paris, in which a warmly furnished living room or kitchen would have an open square window looking out onto the masts of ships or stretch of grey sky.[21] And needless to say, the novel teems with references to Virgil, Lucretius, Julius Caesar (with a reference to Mark Antony in the context of material gain and plunder), Plutarch and Euripides, as well as countless references to archaeological expeditions. Yet at the same time it is firmly grounded in the expansive American capitalism that forms the context for the Professor's musings. What is most interesting about many of these classical references, however, is the way in which Cather uses them and deliberately chooses them to illuminate her theme of possession and commodification. She thus creates a complex web linking the ancient world with the New World and with the older Native American world, which privileges no culture over another but emphasises the affinities between the regional and the national, the local and the global, and the trans-temporal worlds of Tom's past and the Professor's present.

A clear example of this mixture of old and new comes in the fifth chapter of the novel's first section, which uses the image of the Parthenon frieze to describe the Professor's head in a rubber bathing cap as he swims in Lake Michigan: 'his head looked sheathed and small and intensely alive, like the heads of the warriors on the Parthenon frieze in their tight archaic helmets'.[22] The comparison foreshadows the novel's wider theme of possession, insofar as the Parthenon sculptures (the so-called Elgin Marbles) are one of the most famous examples of the plundering of the ancient world. Indeed, Cather anticipates this reference to the friezes twice in the first chapter of the novel. First, Kathleen compares her father's head to that of a statue: 'it was more like a statue's head than a man's' (p. 5). In the second instance, Augusta's dressmaking dolls are described as 'her archaic forms', being headless torsos like many ancient statues, and Augusta herself refers to one as 'the bust' which can also be read as a work of sculpture confined to the head and upper body. Early in the novel, St Peter resists Augusta's attempt to repossess her attic forms, implying that they are a necessary accompaniment for his work into the Spanish plunderers of North America. Thus, in this single extended metaphor, Cather implies a transcultural history and weaves a complex web of literary connections, underpinning her theme of the increasingly capitalist and consumerist nature of American culture in the twentieth century.

ELLEN GLASGOW

While Willa Cather's stories of hardy pioneers and disillusioned professors cling to the values and ideals of the past, her Southern counterpart, Ellen Glasgow, is deeply critical of the past. Glasgow's novels and short stories depict a culture tarnished by a sentimental commitment to an idealised past. Like the Southern Agrarian writers, Glasgow sought to move away from a particular type of Southern romantic literature which portrayed the pre-Civil War South as a chivalric and bounteous region, and which painted the Confederate war effort as a doomed but knightly effort to preserve a passing way of life. She saw Southern culture as the preserve of 'sanctified fallacies', arrant pomposity and sanctimonious cruelty, and perceived her role as a debunker of the myths of the South, especially the myth of Southern white womanhood. Writing in *A Certain Measure* (1943) she observed:

> I was, in my humble place and way, beginning a solitary revolt against the formal, the false and affected, the sentimental, and the pretentious, in Southern writing. I had no guide. I was, so far as I was then aware, alone in my rejection of a prescribed and moribund convention of letters. But I felt, 'Life is not like this.' I thought, 'Why must novels be false to experience?'[23]

Her words suggest her commitment to the rejection of illusion, whether in Southern culture but or in writing itself. Glasgow's writing, like Cather's, is often deceptively simple, lacking the experimental pyrotechnics or painstaking technical virtuosity of her fellow innovators, but it is nonetheless highly stylised.[24] She too deploys the conventions of the classics (for instance, alluding to the story of Jason and Medea in *Barren Ground*), reveals a strong sense of irony throughout all her writing, and, influenced by Freud and especially Jung, offers psychological portraits of her protagonists.[25]

Unlike Cather, however, Glasgow rejected association with the school of local colour, which she saw as synonymous with a certain 'gentility of letters' and a 'sentimental elegiac tone'. Instead, she embraced a realism rooted in her own experiences as a genteel Southern woman, as well as in the lives of the struggling white lower classes, and often included sympathetic portraits of newly emancipated African American Southerners. Her commitment to a narrative realism brings to mind the likes of Theodore Dreiser and Edith Wharton (see Chapter 2) and is rooted in the same general philosophy of literature which guided writers such as Pound or Faulkner, with the text seen as a means of getting at the innate truth of an object without the encumbrance of artifice or verbosity. It was also clearly a rejection of the elaborate romanticism of her predecessors, which, she thought, had inhibited truth and illumination. And just as the self-consciously 'difficult' experimentalists sought to encapsulate and reflect modernity, Glasgow's aim, throughout all of her writing, was to capture the emergence of the modern South and the articulation of a new Southern sensibility.

For Glasgow, this new Southern sensibility was embodied by the emergent Southern woman, who would bring about the cultural and economic regeneration of the South through her fortitude, sacrifice and forbearance. Glasgow dismissed the stereotype of the virginal and physically delicate white aristocrat, as satirised in novels like *Virginia* (1913). Instead, she preferred to emphasise strong women linked to the soil and committed to a course of personal and communal redemption, for example in her novels *Barren Ground* (1925) and *Vein of Iron* (1935). Her commitment to the development of a new kind of Southern womanhood in her writing was undoubtedly born out of her own experiences, both as a sickly child observing the gender roles taken up by her parents, and as a adult woman who enjoyed intense friendships with Thomas Hardy and Hugh Walpole, as well as numerous courtships and a long affair with a married man. She identified in her own life a gulf between social expectations of women and their repressed, inner, emotional and intellectual lives, and in *They Stooped to Folly: A Comedy of Morals* (1929) she satirises these expectations in the words of Virginius Littlepage:

> If only women had been satisfied to remain protected, how much pleasanter the world, even the changing modern world, might be to-day! If only they had been satisfied to wait in patience, not to seek after happiness! For it seemed to him, while his mood, if not his heart, froze into resentment, that there could be nothing nobler in women than the beauty of long waiting and wifely forbearance . . . the true feminine character had never flowered more perfectly than in the sheltered garden of the Southern tradition.[26]

Glasgow herself had little time for the 'sheltered garden'. As she admitted, she readily equated the torpor of the South in the aftermath of the Civil War with the inertia of patient white Southern women, who were supposed to embody the region's virtues:

> The Victorian era, above all, is one of waiting, as hell is an eternity of waiting.
>
> Women waiting for the first word of love from their lovers.
>
> Women waiting with all the inherited belief of the omnipotence of love, for the birth of their sons. Women waiting during the civil war, for news of their sons and husbands. Women waiting beside the beds of the sick and dying – waiting – waiting –.
>
> As a result I think it almost impossible to overestimate the part that religion, in one form or another, has played in the lives of Southern women. Nothing else could have made them accept with meekness the wing of the chicken and the double standard of morals.[27]

Determined to avoid a lifetime of waiting and dependence upon men, resolute in her determination to avoid repeating such stories and histories, Glasgow created characters with a 'vein of iron' (89): characters of such steel and grit to be truly transformative.

Chief among her heroines is Dorinda Oakley of *Barren Ground.* Dorinda has much in common with Cather's first strong female protagonist, Alexandra Bergson of *O Pioneers!* Both struggle against circumstance, do battle with an inhospitable terrain and deliberately harden their emotional core, denying themselves love and sexual fulfilment in their quest to subjugate the soil and transform their worlds. Just as Bergson's story of transforming a battered landscape is a parable of female sacrifice, so is the tale of Oakley, who comes to believe that her transformation of the barren Southern soil, though born out of a life without happiness, has, nonetheless, been a good life. Though stoical and rooted in her later years, Dorinda is first shown at the age of twenty, standing at the window of Pedlar's store, giving the impression of 'arrested flight, as if she were running toward life' as the 'bare, starved desolate . . . country closed in around her'.[28] This compelling image subtly encapsulates Dorinda's story: a hopeful young woman who loves and is betrayed by Jason Greylock, she flees to New York City bearing an illegitimate child and returns to the South following the loss of her unborn child and the death of her father, a man defeated by the land which his daughter will conquer and return to fertility. Dorinda's enclosure by the frame of Pedlar's window hints at her future as Nathan Pedlar's wife in a sexless, though affectionate, marriage of convenience. And the notion of the land encroaching upon her is a nod to her future emotional (and physical) self-sacrifice to the soil, which will come to thrive upon her barren existence.

Dorinda's abandonment of her romantic idealism and hopes for a more exciting life means that in many ways she follows a similar trajectory to her mother, Eudora, who as a young woman had planned to marry a missionary and move to the Congo: 'all the time her mother had dreamed of coral strands and palm trees' (142). After the death of her fiancé, Eudora remains trapped in Pedlar's Mill in a passionless but happy marriage to an ineffectual man, suffocated by the dirt and poverty. As Dorinda explains to Dr. Burch:

> Poor Mother, the farm has eaten away her life. It caught her when she was young, and she was never able to get free. . . .I sometimes think she hates it, but I know it would kill her to leave it. It is like a bad heart. You may suffer from it, but it is your life and it would kill you to lose it. . . . If I had the money, I'd go back and start a dairy farm there. (188)

While Dorinda recognises her mother's devotion to the farm and to her family (especially her feckless son Rufus) as a kind of captivity, she also elects for this lifestyle. In her earlier years she has no choice in the matter, being compelled to work at Pedlar's store and hand over her earnings for the maintenance of the farm and the support of her brothers. Even when she returns with dairy foodstuffs from the store, the women go without so that the men can devour the produce. Like the ungrateful son who consumes his mother's portions of the family milk and butter, the land eats away at Eudora and gives nothing back. Dorinda, on the other hand, seeks some kind of retribution, both for the wasted life of her mother and for the toil it devours, and for what she herself has put it into the land. 'Old Farm,' she remarks, 'must be made to pay.' (190)

The focus on Eudora's dedication to her family and homestead is part of a chain of instances throughout the novel which link womanhood and motherhood to the Southern landscape, thereby engaging with romantic clichés of the South while simultaneously subverting them. Initially, Dorinda is presented in bleak wintertime, eager to escape the 'immutable and everlasting . . . poverty of the soil' (p. 10). But after Jason Greylock arouses her interest, the threatening tyranny of the broomsedge is radically altered, 'shot through with romance'. As critics have recognised, 'the land acts as canvas and mirror for Dorinda's newly awakened sexuality, providing her with a sense of agency': her sexual initiation comes with the sowing of springtime and her expected marriage during the harvest time of autumn.[29] Thus the landscape, for Dorinda, becomes a site of potential transformation, but not before she rejects it as the site of thwarted desire. Pedlar's Mill teems with instances of a downtrodden motherhood, from the broken Eudora, who perjures herself to save her wastrel son, to the ailing Emily Rose, and from the childless Geneva Ellgood to the wilfully chaste Dorinda. But Jason and Geneva's marriage wrenches Dorinda from the landscape, sending her reeling to New York, where she miscarries her unborn child – a wrenching example of the same theme. Indeed, the weakness of motherhood is portrayed very early in the novel, in the playtime scenario invented by her daughter, Minnie May, described by Dorinda as a 'born mother':

> Now Mrs. Brown has lost her little girl, and she is going to Mrs. Smiths to look for her. And Mrs. Brown found that her little girl had been run over in the road and killed in the middle of the road . . . So she decided that all she could do for her was to have a handsome funeral and spend the ten dollars she's saved from her chicken money. (p. 19)

The child's game foreshadows Dorinda's miscarriage, which strikes when she steps from a sidewalk curb and is hit by a car. But the story hints at a deeper meaning: the inability of mothers to save or help their children with the limited resources allocated them.

Reflecting Glasgow's scorn for 'moonlight and magnolia' nostalgia, this portrait of motherhood deliberately dismantles nineteenth-century ideas of a nurturing Southern femininity.

Dorinda resists this version of femininity from very early on in the novel. She fails to see the similarities between herself and her mother and, indeed, avoids them completely, choosing to spend the money she has saved for a cow on a blue dress in order to please Jason Greylock, thereby placing herself before the family. Jason's betrayal and her subsequent miscarriage stifle her romantic proclivities and crystallise her growing desire for economic success, born out of the subjugation of the soil which would otherwise bury her. Even as she watches Mrs Faraday nurse her infant, Dorinda divulges her desire to start a dairy farm. This intimate, feminine scene is purposefully complicated by the language of business and science, with Dorinda adamantly resisting Mrs Faraday's talk of marriage and children. And while critics have often observed a repressed femininity in Dorinda's learning of the new science of agriculture, her return to Old Farm and her sacrifice of sensual love, an alternative view is that Dorinda's salvaging of the family farm, her acquisition of Five Oaks (Greylock land) and her clever marketing of Southern rural produce (using the pine, a symbol of the South, to brand her butter) actually symbolises the way in which female labour has always supported and nurtured the region – again, strengthening the link between Dorinda and her long-suffering mother. The difference, of course, is that Dorinda's use of Northern modern technologies facilitates her productive nurturing of the hitherto barren region.

Early in the novel, Dorinda dismisses the male discussions about farming as 'impersonal', preferring to focus on the private workings of her own mind and heart. But as the novel progresses, these 'impersonal' discussions wind their way into Dorinda's psychological landscape and meld with the language of fertility and reproduction. Near the conclusion of the novel, Dorinda surveys her property:

> Yes, the land would stay by her. Her eyes wandered from far horizon to horizon. Again she felt the quickening of that sympathy which was deeper than all other emotions of her

> heart . . . the living communion with the earth under her feet. (p. 408)

In this way, Glasgow's emerging modern South is inextricably tied to an emergent modern femininity; a femininity which, in the struggle for survival, both preserves the boundaries of region and looks beyond the local; a femininity which maintains old-fashioned notions of female sacrifice, but on entirely new terms; a femininity that is tied to the seasons and soil, yet which has conquered the workings of nature. Glasgow's new South, in other words, is engendered in a distinctly modern femininity of fortitude.

WILLIAM FAULKNER

In the second section of William Faulkner's *The Sound and the Fury* (1929), which takes its title from Shakespeare's *Macbeth*, Quentin Compson twists the hands from the face of a wristwatch given to him by his father. This symbolic act represents the manipulation of time, which occurs throughout Faulkner's technically challenging novel. Chronological time breaks down completely, and the reader is shuttled forwards and backwards through the thoughts and memories of a series of characters, notably the Compson brothers, Benjy, Quentin and Jason, and latterly their African American servant Dilsey Gibson. In temporally mapping the novel, we can detect four important timeframes: the period around 1900 when the four Compson children, the brothers and their sister Caddy, are very young; 1910, with Quentin's suicide and Caddy's ill-fated marriage; 1913, when Benjy is sterilised having frightened a schoolgirl he mistakes for his absent sister; and 1928, the novel's present, in which Caddy's nineteen-year-old daughter, Miss Quentin, hatches her escape from the family home with a man from a nearby visiting carnival.

Quentin's removal of the hands from the watch is a moment heavy with significance; perhaps even more than Benjy, it is Quentin whose grip on temporal reality is most skewed. Critics and readers often find Benjy's narrative the most complex and confusing section of the novel, and while the youngest brother's narrative is undoubtedly challenging, Quentin's lost grip on time is perhaps the most startling. Benjy's cognitive and linguistic disabilities clearly hinder his grasp of contemporary reality; for him, the past lives and breathes within the present. The past *is* the present in Benjy's interior world, which is why the narrative slips from 1928 to the early 1900s without the debilitating sense of loss or self-consciousness which the reader encounters in Quentin's narrative. In Benjy's section the shift in the temporal setting is accompanied by a switch to italics in the typeface, or induced by particular images (for instance, the word 'caddie' called by the golfers in the adjacent plot of land sets Benjy off into the past and his life with Caddy), or evident from the change in his African American companion: Versh and T. P. in the past, but Luster in the present.

By contrast, the temporal slippages in Quentin's narrative are more disquieting, filtered as they are through what initially seems the lucid and rational mind of a Harvard undergraduate. Indeed, Quentin's narrative, set in the past and being about the past, opens with a deliberate and considered meditation on the nature of time:

> When the shadow of the sash appeared on the curtains it was between seven and eight o'clock and then I was in time again, hearing the watch. It was Grandfather's and when Father gave it to me he said, Quentin, I give you the mausoleum of all hope and desire . . . I give it to you not that you may remember time but that you may forget it now and then for a moment and not spend all your breath trying to conquer it.[30]

In fact, the rather pompous and ponderous words of Jason Compson III are some of the most important in the entire novel. Reflecting the tomb-like nature of marked clock time, these words haunt Quentin's narrative and torture his consciousness in the hours before his death, as he struggles with his memories of his sister's sexual awakening and his own imminent suicide. And whereas Benjy is seemingly untroubled by the overlapping of time, Quentin is haunted by the past and unable to reconcile it with the present – which is why he elects to lie down in the mausoleum of time altogether. In short, he is unable to conquer time, and it is precisely his struggle to come to terms with this failure which creates the fitful, analeptic narrative of a mind consciously hurtling toward disintegration.

This representation of the difficulties in apprehending the processes of time is not, of course, unique to Quentin Compson. Both James Joyce's Stephen Dedalus in *A Portrait of the Artist as a Young Man* (1916) and Virginia Woolf's tragic Septimus Warren Smith in *Mrs Dalloway* (1925) struggle to make sense of the past as it wheedles its way into the present. Perhaps most famously, Marcel Proust's seven-volume novel *A la recherche du temps perdu* (*In Search of Lost Time*, 1909–22) explores the notion of involuntary memory. The tension between the rigidity of measured time and the spontaneous fluidity of experienced time is a primary modernist concern, impelled by Bergsonian ideas about the spatial representation of successive and deterministic time as a fallacy which neglects the mobility and incomplete nature of time as experienced by the individual. The impulse to measure time, to 'conquer it', as Jason Compson puts it, is instantly to kill it, compartmentalise and forget it. Thus, the modernist impulse to reveal the truth of time is to offer incomplete glimpses of moments past and present without the false unity of linearity or moments of consecutive experience. And so Quentin Compson's fragmented and broken interior narrative, as well as that of his younger brother, are clear examples of Faulkner's modernist preoccupations with the nature of time, memory and consciousness. Indeed, Quentin's suicide, his leap into the Charles River, is not unlike Septimus Smith's leap to his death: both, in their psychological unravelling, trying and failing to find an equilibrium in the streams of time.

The novel's preoccupation with time is, of course, also a regional matter. The story charts the decline of the South through the fortunes of the Compsons, whose land is eventually eroded to a thin plot and whose control over their African American servants becomes increasingly feeble. For Faulkner, the decline of the South was a frequent concern, and the imaginary Yoknapatawpha County (based on his home county of Lafayette), in which *The Sound and the Fury* is set, is part of this impulse to create a mythical South. In his later novel *Go Down, Moses* (1942), the narrator describes the ledgers of the McCaslin plantation, which record the

> slow trickle of molasses and meal and meat, of shoes and straw hats and overalls, of plowlines and collars and heelbolts and clevises, which returned each year as cotton . . . that chronicle which was a whole land in miniature, which multiplied and compounded as the entire South.[31]

Faulkner's own writing, with its portrayal of fields, farms, small business holdings and family fortunes, can be seen as a 'whole land in miniature'. Indeed, the desire of various characters to return to the past is a marker of a wider regional impulse to reinvent a Southern past. For Faulkner, identity, whether personal or cultural, is indelibly marked by history. And just as all his characters are haunted by their pasts, so too is the South of his fictions:

> 'Don't you see?' [McCaslin] cried. 'Don't you see? This whole land, the whole South, is cursed, and all of us who derive from it, whom it ever suckled, white and black both, lie under that curse?' (p. 266)

However, not unlike the Fugitive writers, Faulkner had no desire to contribute to the development of the metropolitan 'New South', or to embrace the kind of business ethic we see in Jason Compson IV, the most dislikeable of the Compson brothers, and neither was he interested in recapturing the pomp and grandeur of the Old South. His goal seems to have been merely to show how the economic and historical circumstances of the past had transformed the South since the Civil War, and at bottom, his personal history of the South is a story of defeat, loss and fatality. Take, for instance, this passage from *Intruder in the Dust* (1948):

> For every Southern boy fourteen years old, not only once but whenever he wants it, there is the instant when it's still not two o'clock on that July afternoon in 1863, the brigades in position behind the rail fence, the guns are laid and ready in the woods, and the furled flags are already loosened to break out and Pickett himself with his long oiled ringlets and his hat in one hand probably and his sword in the other looking up

> the hill waiting for Longstreet to give the word and it's all in the balance, it hasn't happed yet.[32]

The desire to return to the moment before catastrophe for the white American South represents a wider regional desire to recapture a lost radiance and the innocence that comes from the ignorance of failure. But such moments when 'it's all in the balance' are only possible for fourteen-year-old boys, and it is the stark, cold reality of past defeat that contaminates and determines the present of Faulkner's dark South.

For Faulkner's supreme symbol of the Southern past, we should turn to Caddy Compson, the absent heart at the centre of *The Sound and the Fury*. Caddy exists only in the novel's past, as a child and later as a promiscuous teenager. Each of the Compson brothers, in one way or another, is obsessed by her purity and her dignity, entangled as it is with the reputation and fortunes of the family. Indeed, Faulkner readily admitted that the central scene of the novel, its driving force, comes when young Caddy climbs a pear tree outside the family home to spy through a window at her dead grandmother. While Caddy is up the tree, each of her brothers gazes upon her muddy drawers; and each, as we learn through their different narratives, emotionally responds to her soiled undergarments in different ways. Jason is disgusted by the sight; Quentin worries for her dignity; and Benjy looks on in wonder. Faulkner explained that he had 'used the tools which seemed to me the proper tools to try to tell, try to draw the picture of Caddy', and each brother's narrative, in its regressions and preoccupations, represents an attempt to somehow portray and 'possess' Caddy.[33]

Benjy, for instance, shares a bed with Caddy until the age of thirteen and howls when she is separated from him. Unable to recognise her as a detached entity from himself, he reacts strongly to her loss of virginity and recognises it instantly, feeling himself defiled and somehow altered:

> Caddy came to the door and stood there . . . I went towards her, crying, and she shrank against the wall and I saw her eyes and I cried louder and pulled at her dress. Her eyes ran.
>
> *Versh said, Your name Benjamin now.* (p. 56)

As the switch to italics denotes, Caddy's lost virginity sends Benjy reeling into the past to retell his change in name from Maury to Benjamin. His personal story, his identity, even, is intimately bound up with the wider tale of the Compsons. Similarly, Quentin, who spends much of his narrative trying to restore a lost immigrant girl whom he addresses as 'sister' to her family in Boston, finds himself locked into past memories of his sister. For Quentin, Caddy's promiscuity and subsequent pregnancy stir thoughts of incest, which, paradoxically, he feels will somehow protect her from punishment and preserve her integrity. These past thoughts of incestuous relations with Caddy bleed into the present when Quentin is accused of molesting the young Italian girl and ordered to pay a six-dollar fine to her family. And Jason, too, is preoccupied by his absent sister, whose legacy is embodied by her teenage daughter's seductive sexuality, which he spends most of his time attempting to control. Like Caddy, Miss Quentin eventually escapes the clutches of the Compson men. Yet Caddy Compson's imprint upon each of her brothers is indelible, like the dark muddy stain on her white drawers, or the stain of the South's bloody history upon the region's present.

Faulkner's commitment to the South, with its peculiar history and institutions, was real and undeniable. Yet he was nevertheless one of the most important American modernists of his generation. As a young man he was hugely influenced by French symbolism and modelled his own poetry on that of Stéphane Mallarmé and Paul Verlaine. Like Ernest Hemingway and F. Scott Fitzgerald, he took the mandatory trip to Paris, albeit with less success than his contemporaries, returning to Mississippi after just a few months. Nonetheless, in France he encountered Gertrude Stein and Ezra Pound, from whom he learned the economy of language, and, for a time, he befriended Hemingway and Fitzgerald. The biggest modernist influence upon his work, though, was undoubtedly Joyce's *Ulysses* (1922), from which he learned the art of the interior monologue, the stream of consciousness, the collapse of linear time and the importance of preserving voice and dialect, as we see most convincingly in the voice of Dilsey. In the character of Stephen Dedalus, meanwhile, he found a model for an intellectual young hero simultaneously repelled by and yet drawn back to his homeland. Like Stephen, Quentin Compson is a solipsistic young man, preoccupied by his role in life, by the arbitrary nature of language, and by the fleeting yet circular nature of time. For both Stephen and Quentin, history is 'the nightmare from which [they] are trying to awake'.[34]

Moreover, both men are haunted by guilt. Stephen believes himself to be responsible for the death of his mother, while Quentin holds himself culpable for the banishment of his sister. And just as Joyce (via Stephen) believed himself to be awakening the 'conscience of his race', so Faulkner sees himself as attempting to 'know' (much like the Compson boys with their sister) the South as a region. For both, however, language seems an insufficient vehicle to explore the dense history and emotional tiers of the region. Stephen Dedalus can only '*forge* the conscience' of his race, the linguistic tools at his disposal rendering the truth of that native conscience at best ambiguous.[35] And in *The Sound and the Fury*, Faulkner's narrators attempt to tell the same story four times – and each time fail. In Benjy's narrative, for example, language lets him down when he attempts to communicate with the passing schoolgirls:

> They looked at me, walking fast, with their heads turned. I tried to say, but they went on, and I went along the fence, trying to say, and they went faster. Then they were running and I came to the corner of the fence and I couldn't go any further, and I held to the fence, looking after them and trying to say. (p. 42)

Similarly, Quentin's language disintegrates completely as his narrative comes to a close, losing all sensible grammar and meaning before 'the last note sounded' (p. 151). And words fail Jason, who moves in circles around the sentence 'Once a bitch always a bitch' (p. 224) when considering his inability to control his niece or come to terms with his sister. Even Dilsey, whose rich, colloquial and biblical intonations make the final chapter of the novel the most readable, is tempted to give up on language in approaching the history of the Compsons. Softly weeping, she makes 'no sound' but the sad refrain, 'I've seed de first and en de last' (p. 252). But the failure of words to express the ambiguous history of the South is best encapsulated by the final paragraph of the novel. As Luster drives left instead of right around the square in which 'the Confederate soldier gazed with empty eyes beneath his marble hand into wind and weather', Benjy roars in 'astonishment . . . horror; shock; agony eyeless; tongueless; just sound' (p. 271). In this final stunning image, sound, history and sterility come together to provide a portrait of a region beyond the compass of words.

FUGITIVES AND SOUTHERN AGRARIANS: ALLEN TATE, JOHN CROWE RANSOM AND ROBERT PENN WARREN

Allen Tate's most celebrated poem, 'Ode to the Confederate Dead' (1929), presents a speaker standing at a cemetery gate, surveying the military rows of headstones which mark the Southern dead who had fallen during the Civil War. While ostensibly a lament for a generation of lost soldiers, the poem is in fact a cry against the solipsism engendered by modernity. Heavily influenced by T. S. Eliot's *The Waste Land* (1922) and 'The Love Song of J. Alfred Prufrock' (1917), the 'Ode' enacts a battle, pitting the supposed heroism of the past against the alienation and self-absorption of the present. In his essay 'Narcissus as Narcissus' (1938), Tate summed up the poem as the story of a man stopping at the gate of a Confederate graveyard on a late autumn afternoon, paralysed by his realisation of the inevitability of mortality and the ultimate purposelessness of his life. The similarities between this figure and Eliot's ineffectual Prufrock are self-evident, culminating in the startling image of the blind crab (Eliot's 'pair of ragged claws scuttling at the floors of silent seas') which symbolises what Tate describes as the 'locked-in ego', the isolation of the stymied modern man who is unable to look beyond his own mortality or to feel the joy of a greater heroism.[36]

In a letter to Tate, his friend Hart Crane once described the man at the cemetery gates as locked within a 'fragmentary cosmos', an image Tate himself adopted when discussing the 'Ode'.[37] And indeed, in the loose iambic shape of this first section of the poem (which Tate described in classical terms as the 'strophe'), with its varying line lengths and glut of arresting images, the fragmentary cosmos is made manifest; from the whirring wind to the 'splayed leaves' and from the desolate plots to the 'uncomfortable angels', the bluster of autumn captures the chaotic melancholy of the unnamed man's emotions and his abiding sense of impotence in the face of being turned, like the soldiers and the staring angel, 'to stone'.[38] Indeed the man himself exemplifies what Tate refers to as 'the modern squirrel cage of our sensibility', his selfhood locked within a closed and unseeing shell.[39]

The pathetic fallacy in the whirring movement of the wind and the leaves dramatically enacts a battle within the consciousness of the man at the gates as he struggles to recognise the 'active faith' or heroism of the Confederate soldiers.[40] Also, the shift into the second strophe (or antistrophe) of the poem, which begins immediately after the first refrain, formally enacts the struggle, with the intervening refrain documenting the flux of the leaves, which symbolise the man's inner turmoil. The heroism embodied by the dead as a commitment to a wider, social ideal seems impossible in the desolate modernity embodied by the figure kept outside the cemetery gates. Those 'who have waited by the wall' (p. 20) are the exemplars of this mythical heroism, who like the pre-Socratic philosophers Zeno and Parmenides possessed a heroic vision and believed in higher truths beyond the realm of individual perception, making for a stark contrast with the solipsism embodied by the subject at the gates.[41] These figures recognise the 'unimportant shrift of death' (p. 20), unlike the trembling modern man. Unable to make the imaginative leap from neurotic selfhood to heroic sacrifice, he is unable to see the wind-swept leaves, which symbolise the sacrament of death but also the promise of new life, as anything other than their immediate physical manifestation, 'seeing only leaves / Flying, plunge and expire' (p. 21). The inclusion of names connected with the Civil War alongside those of the ancients, not least that of 'Stonewall' Jackson, takes the poem from the Southern context and connects it to a wider heroic cosmos. Again the subject is unable to turn his 'eyes to the immoderate past' and see 'heroic virtues': he is cast as a blind Lear howling at the wind, 'cursing only the leaves crying / Like an old man in a storm' (p. 21). Modern man is a 'frozen' mummy, preserved within yet also smothered by time. And he is the toothless 'hound bitch', a once vital participant in the knightly hunt, who now 'hears the wind only' in the 'musty cellar' of his isolated consciousness (p. 21).

The final section of the poem, the 'epode', in which the man takes his leave of the cemetery, gathers the opposing themes of the first two sections and dramatises the victory of modern solipsism over heroism. The image of the jaguar leaping to devour his own image in the jungle pool evokes the myth of Narcissus and the ultimate tragic fate of the modernist mind unable to personify the 'active faith' of the past. The poem concludes with the image of Time, the 'gentle serpent' that 'riots with his tongue' (p. 23) which, as Tate points out in his essay, complements the earlier image of the screeching owl. The emphasis on voice or sound in these images – the rioting tongue and the screech – projects a final violent struggle between the atrophied silence of the toothless hound and the smothered mummy and the chivalric past. The concluding rhyme scheme, with 'wall' and 'all' enclosing the serpent in the mulberry 'bush' rioting through the 'hush' (p. 23), formally reflects the means whereby the mythic past (symbolised by the snake) is locked within the cemetery walls, since it is unviable in secular modernity. Alternatively, these lines might suggest the means whereby the modern man, while unable to realise the heroism of the past, keeps his glimpses of that past locked within the coffin of his mortal body. On this point the poem is deliberately ambiguous: as Tate conceded, his poem offers no 'practical solutions' and does not even answer the questions he poses in the epode.[42]

This lack of finality, of course, reflects the central drama of the poem, the struggle between solipsism and active faith, and maintains the impression of a chaotic uncertainty which runs through the poem's evasive metre and slippery rhyme scheme. While the scheme is mostly iambic with varying three, four and six stressed lines, it is hard to get a purchase on the rhythm. Similarly, the reader grasps at the complex rhyme scheme rather as the man at the gate grasps uncertainly at the past. And the caesurae and seemingly incomplete strophes (for instance, the unpunctuated refrain at the end of the first section) dramatise the halted and hindered apprehension of the individual at the gates. Finally, in its altered representation of the 'ode' and its elusive form, Tate's 'Ode to the

Confederate Dead' demonstrates the way in which in the classical poetic forms of the past elude the modern poet, who remains locked outside the gates of heroic tradition, trapped in his unseeing consciousness, doomed like Narcissus to tumble into the bewitching abyss of selfhood.

John Crowe Ransom's poem 'Antique Harvesters' (1927), which looks to an older, more traditional South as a place of cultural unity and individual wholeness, echoes similar themes. Perhaps even more than Tate or Penn Warren, Ransom saw the past as a preferred alternative to the fragmentation and anonymity of the present. Most of his poetic output, which was deliberately restrained, deals with ineffectual personae: modern individuals unable to recapture their lost innocence; individuals struggling to attain the 'unity of being' sought by the man at the gates in Tate's 'Ode'. Warren observes in Ransom's poetry a consistent interest in the 'dissociation of sensibility', his work presenting 'intimate little psychological cruxes' upon which the poem itself often offers a commentary.[43] Certainly 'Antique Harvesters' matches this description. A poet figure observes the scene of an early autumn harvest, where 'dry, grey' and 'spare' men assemble to gather the corn.[44] The older men who have known the land as plentiful and who remember the Civil War are dismissed by the younger men who want none of their memories 'rehearsed in sable' (p. 83). But central to the scene is the figure of the poet, who is simultaneously detached from and within the group. Stepping forth, he entreats the younger men not to forsake the soil to which they are the heirs, but to recapture the mythical past of the land with reference to the hunt, 'the Lady' (a curiously Catholic incarnation of the Old South), and, in an image which evokes a classical past, the bronze bounty of the harvest – as so often with Tate, the ideals of the classical world appearing as a corrective to the ills of modernity. Ultimately, the poet reminds the young men, all of life depends upon the will and the vitality of God.

While the agrarian substance of the poem is undeniable, it is the figure of the poet at the centre of the scene that really commands our attention. It is through this poetic consciousness that the tension between the values of the older men and those of their young counterparts is dramatised. It is the poet who offers the 'psychological crux', who enacts the dialectic at the heart of the poem. The poet, after all, might well be regarded as the 'scornful beholder' who asks why 'one spot [of land] has special yield?' (p. 83). In many ways, then, the debate between the two sets of men reflects the poet's private debate, a clash between the allure of the modern and the solidity of the traditional, between the promise of the emergent New South and the apparently defeated Old South, and between the tangible realities of the present and the imagined myths of the past. Not for nothing does the poem open with some consciously concretising scene-setting on the left banks of the Mississippi and the Ohio rivers, '*Of the Mississippi the bank sinister, and of the Ohio the bank sinister*' (p. 83), which is followed by three stanzas which continue the concretising strand by outlining the situation: the men gathering their harvest and the attempt to regale the younger gatherers with the history of the area. In the fourth stanza the poem shifts in tone and in setting, moving into the past with the description of the hunters, those 'archetypes of chivalry', in pursuit of the 'lovely ritualist', the self-sacrificing fox (p. 83). The next stanzas maintain the emphasis on the past with the image of 'the Lady' and the bare-armed 'dainty youths beneath their 'bronze burdens' (p. 84), but take on an exhortative tone, the poet imploring remembrance of and allegiance to the past, before culminating in what Vivienne Koch describes as 'a note of invocation and prayer'.[45] The shape of the poem, therefore, dramatises the poet's struggle between reason and sensibility, between that which is observed and that which is imagined. Similarly, his divided consciousness is shown in the oscillation between the individual 'I' and the collective 'we' and distancing 'their', as he comes to identify with but then break away from the group over the course of the first three stanzas.

Indeed, what first impresses itself upon the reader is not the idealisation of the South but the fractured subjectivity of the speaker at the heart of the poem, as he attempts to attain a unity of being through active mythmaking. Still, there is no doubt that the poem is firmly rooted in a particular vision of the South. Ransom's commitment to the agrarian South was, after all, evident in his non-poetic writing, not least his essay 'Reconstructed but Unregenerate' in *I'll Take My Stand*, in which he defended the 'village South and the rural South' and 'conservative Southern tradition' against the dehumanising new 'slavery' of industrialism. For Ransom, only a small-scale subsistence lifestyle could provide aesthetic wholeness and the rituals of religious life:

> [The Southern man] identifies himself with a spot of ground, and this carries a good deal of meaning; it defines itself for him as nature. He would till it not too hurriedly and not too mechanically to observe in it the contingency and the infinitude of nature; and so his life acquires its philosophical and even its cosmic consciousness . . . industrialism . . . means the dehumanisation of his life.[46]

These ideas appear in abundance throughout 'Antique Harvesters', which in its iambic rhythms, regular rhyme scheme and elegant sestets embodies a formal traditionalism that mirrors the idealised world presented in the verse. The poem merges the tangible, natural world with the abstract cosmos of memory, myth and the divine. The outsider poet, in the third stanza of the poem, merges with the group with the use of the collective 'we' (p. 83) and divulges the old men's stories of the heroic past ingrained within the 'spot of ground' they harvest. 'Echoes from the horn' signals the re-emergence of the Southern past and the start of the hunt. The reference to the fox as a 'lovely ritualist' (p. 83) encapsulates Ransom's vision of the past as the site of leisure and aristocratic refinement and prepares for the arrival of 'the Lady' (p. 84). The Lady is the South. She transcends time and, like the Virgin Mother, commands the adoration that 'bends the knees' (p. 84). Worship will yield revelation 'by an autumn tone / As by a grey, as by a green' (p. 84), in the hues of old age, military prowess (grey being the colour of the Confederate uniform) and youth. Urged to cast off the temptations of forsaking the South, the young men are reminded, in suitably biblical language, that the earth abideth upon the will of God just as the heirs to the South remain at the mercy of the Lady. And while seemingly at odds with the Fugitive critique of a nineteenth-century nostalgia for the Old South, Ransom's faith in the past shifts beyond sentimental wallowing to offer a curiously modern insight into the angst-ridden

Southern poetic consciousness and the comforting processes of mythmaking.

Robert Penn Warren's early poetic work offers similar meditations on the natural world of the South, likening nature to religious experience and mindful of the permanence of the land. 'Kentucky Mountain Farm', which he began writing upon leaving Vanderbilt University for California in 1925, offers an immediately local setting for a more expansive meditation on the self, the natural world, death and the transience of human existence.[47] Here Warren's self, not unlike Ransom's poet figure or Tate's man at the cemetery gate, struggles with an Emersonian desire to realise a world beyond the immediate and a fear of what might be found by submitting to a world other than that which is known and visible. The first section of the poem, 'The Rebuke of the Rocks', marks the coming of spring with the 'hungry equinox' which 'disturbs the sod, the rabbit [and] the lank fox' (p. 319). Yet this is no triumphal springtime arrival. Rather, spring is rendered through the eyes of the weary, cynical rocks which scoff at the enslavement of the woodland plants and creatures to the eternal reproductive cycles of nature. Superior in their vantage point and in their perceived immutability, the rocks advise the creatures of the forest and humankind to cease their cyclical permutation and embrace the 'sweet sterility of stone' (p. 319). The influence of the opening section of Eliot's *The Waste Land*, with its exhausted announcement that 'April is the cruellest month, breeding / Lilacs out of the dead land, mixing / Memory and desire, stirring / Dull roots with spring rain' is strikingly apparent, and we also see the spectre of Eliot in the later image of death by drowning.[48] And the ability of spring to stir the natural world and enliven the intellectual imagination of the self is one of the central themes of 'Kentucky Mountain Farm' – although it is also worth noting that in the chiding of the rocks, the poem entertains the dialectically opposite idea that the natural world keeps humanity locked within a ceaseless prison sentence of birth, death and rebirth.

The poem's second section, 'At the Hour of the Breaking of the Rocks', shows nature's retribution in the breaking of the rocks upon the 'wrack' that is the winter frost:

The rocks are stricken and the frost has torn
Away their ridged fundaments at last
So that the fractured atoms now are borne
Down shifting waters to the tall, profound
Shadow of the absolute deeps,
Wherein the spirit moves and never sleeps. (p. 320)

The proud rocks are shattered and absorbed into the wider stream of nature, and swept into the natural waters of ceaseless time, where they will encounter the animating spirit of the natural world. Within the 'shifting waters' the 'fractured atoms' are carried toward a deeper understanding of the individual self, presented with a selfhood which is unified with nature and dependent upon it for survival. The waters of nature are thus presented as ambiguous, both renewing and appropriating life, but gushing ever forward in an ongoing motion of regeneration, expiration and revelation.

'History Among the Rocks', the third section of the poem, takes the reader further into the indiscriminate workings of nature with a sustained contemplation of extinction. The 'many ways to die' (p. 320) are presented as delicious temptations, from the invitation to lay one's 'drowsy head' on the snow to drowning 'with hair afloat in waters that gently bend' (p. 321). The reference to the sycamore tree grounds the contemplation in the immediate context of the natural world, but also performs a temporal trick in evoking the ancient Egyptians, who regarded the holy sycamore as being set on the threshold of life and death. Thus the immediate reflections on life, death and the tides of the natural world are linked to an ancient and eternal rumination. The 'other way' to die returns to the reader to the particularly Southern context:

In these autumn orchards once young men lay dead—
Gray coats, blue coats. Young men on the mountainside
Clambered, fought. Heels muddied in the rock spring. (p. 321)

The 'autumn orchards' mark the seasonal distance travelled from the first section of the poem; we have moved from springtime to autumn. The 'rocky spring' takes us back to the cynical, sterile rocks which here are shown as having yielded to nature, becoming one with the water of the spring. The extended metaphor of the duplicitous waters recurs in the encumbered heels of the dead men in their Confederate and Yankee colours, who lie beneath an orchard which each year produces a new harvest. Indeed, the soldiers are not unlike the falling apple in the final line of the section, 'falling in the quiet night' (p. 321), surrendering to a greater truth. This brief and fleeting meditation on the war links the Southern landscape to the eternal workings of time, thereby mythologising the terrain and testifying, as in the works of both Tate and Ransom, to its capacity for endurance and rebirth.

The final section of the poem, 'The Return', resumes this thematic strand in its two twelve-line stanzas. Just as the soldiers return for each autumn harvest, so the sycamore's 'timeless gold / Broad leaf released' to 'the water's depth below' gives rise to 'a richer leaf' (p. 321). The poem switches tone and focus in the second of these stanzas, moving from the joyous certainty of rebirth to doubt and estrangement, shifting from the natural world to a personal scene of familial rupture. This final stanza marks a return to the fear of death, which characterised the first section of the poem. The contemplating mind at the centre of the poem here imagines the reality of annihilation whereby 'a buried world is lost / In the water's riffle or the wind's flaw' (p. 322).

Gone are the still, welcoming waters of the previous stanza, replaced by a threatening choppy surface. The last four lines of the poem shift firmly from the natural to the personal, the realities of cyclical nature being brought to bear on human relationships:

> How his own image, perfect and deep
> And small within loved eyes, had been forgot,
> Her face being turned, or when those eyes were shut
> Past light in the fond accident of sleep. (p. 322)

The pathos in this altered relationship is palpable, evoking a returning son whose childlike perfection in the eyes of a mother is no longer remembered. And the final line concludes the dialectical struggle, the speaker's failure to submit to a greater truth than the 'fractured atom' of individual selfhood, and reveals his final deduction that the natural cycles of life bring neither renewal nor perpetuity, but separation and oblivion.

NOTES

1. F. O. Mathiessen, *Sarah Orne Jewett* (Boston: Houghton Mifflin, 1929). And see, for instance, Sarah W. Sherman, *Sarah Orne Jewett, an American Persephone* (Hanover, NH: University Press of New England, 1989); and Judith Fetterley, '"Not in the Least American": Nineteenth-Century Literary Regionalism', *College English*, 56.8 (December 1994), pp. 877–95.
2. Cited in Tremain McDowell, 'Regionalism in American Literature', *Minnesota History: A Quarterly Journal*, 20.0 (June 1939), p. 105.
3. See, for instance, Eric Foner, *Reconstruction: America's Unfinished Revolution: People and Politics After the Civil War, 1863–1877* (New York: Harper Perennial, 1990) and Michael W. Fitzgerald, *Splendid Failure: Postwar Reconstruction and the American South* (Chicago: Ivan R. Dee, 2007). An excellent resource for students and teachers is Richard Gray's and Owen Robinson's edited collection, *A Companion to the Literature and Culture of the American South* (Oxford: Blackwell, 2004).
4. W. E. B. Du Bois, *Black Reconstruction in America, 1860–1880*, ed. David Levering Lewis (New York: The Free Press, [1935] 1992), p. 30.
5. For this brief synthesis of the American South after the Civil War, I am indebted to the following sources: Hugh Brogan, *The Penguin History of the United States of America* (London: Penguin, 1985) and Edward L. Ayers, *Southern Crossing: A History of the American South, 1877–1906* (New York: Oxford University Press, 1996).
6. Cited in George Brown Tindall, *A Populist Reader: Selections from the Works of American Populist Readers* (New York: Harper and Row, 1966), pp. 90–6.
7. Again, I am indebted to Brogan; Andrew R. L. Cayton, 'The Anti-Region: Place and Identity in the History of the

American Midwest', in Andrew R. L. Cayton and Susan E. Gray (eds), *The American Midwest: Essays on Regional History* (Bloomington: Indiana University Press, 2001), pp. 140–59.

8. See Rose C. Field, 'Restlessness Such as Ours Does Not Make for Beauty', *New York Times Book Review* (21 December 1924), p. 11.
9. Cited in John Duvall, 'Regionalism in American Modernism', in Walter Kalaidjian (ed.), *The Cambridge Companion to American Modernism* (Cambridge: Cambridge University Press, 2005), p. 253.
10. Allen Tate, *Memoirs and Opinions, 1926–1974* (Athens, OH: Ohio University Press, 1975), p. 33.
11. Cited in William Manchester, *Sage of Baltimore: The Life and Riotous Times of H. L. Mencken* (New York: Andrew Melrose, 1952), pp. 143–5.
12. Susan V. Donaldson's introduction to Twelve Southerners, *I'll Take My Stand: The South and the Agrarian Tradition* (Baton Rouge: Louisiana State University Press, [1930] 2006), p. xli.
13. For an insightful and provocative insight into the impact of the Southern Agrarians/New Critics on American literary criticism see Florence Dore's essay 'The Modernism of Southern Literature', which makes the case that many Southern-born African American writers were written out of the canon of Southern literature by the core contributors to *I'll Take My Stand*. Florence Dore, 'The Modernism of Southern Literature', in Peter Stonely and Cindy Weinstein (eds), *A Concise Companion to American Fiction, 1900–1950* (Oxford: Blackwell, 2008), pp. 228–52.
14. Most notable amongst her contemporary critics were Granville Hicks and Lionel Trilling, who lamented the perceived nostalgia and celebration of rural values within her work. See: Granville Hicks, 'The Case Against Willa Cather', *English Journal* (November 1933), in James Schroeter (ed.), *Willa Cather and Her Critics* (Ithaca: Cornell University Press, 1967), pp. 139–47; Lionel Trilling, 'Willa Cather', *New Republic*, 90 (1937), in Schroeter (ed.), *Willa Cather and Her Critics*, pp. 148–55.

15. Guy Reynolds argues persuasively against the negative and parochial connotations associated with Cather's regionalism, describing her representation of lost communities not as a retreat into the past but as 'a form of regionalist commitment (and recommitment) to the American spaces where a "beloved community" once existed'. Furthermore, Reynolds observes that Cather weaves a progressive agenda derived from Populism into her characters' lives and stories. See Guy Reynolds, 'Willa Cather as Progressive', in Marilee Lindemann (ed.), *The Cambridge Companion to Willa Cather* (Cambridge: Cambridge University Press, 2005), p. 21.
16. Randolph Bourne, 'Trans-national America' (1916), in Paul Lauter (general ed.), Richard Yarborough, Jackson R. Bryer et al. (eds), *The Heath Anthology of American Literature* (New York: Houghton Mifflin, 2006), pp. 1637–48.
17. Willa Cather, 'On *The Professor's House*' (1938), in *Willa Cather on Writing* (New York: Bison Books, 1988), p. 31.
18. For an interpretation of Cather as writer with nativist proclivities see Walter Benn Michaels's *Our America: Nativism, Modernism and Pluralism* (Durham, NC: Duke University Press, 1995).
19. Willa Cather, *My Ántonia* (London: Virago, [1918] 2003), p. ii. All subsequent references will be made in the text.
20. For a compelling study of the classical allusions and economic tensions throughout *The Professor's House* see Sean Lake and Theresa Levy, 'Preserving and Commodifying the Past: Allusions to the Classical World in *The Professor's House*', *Willa Cather Review* (Spring 2007), pp. 15–20.
21. Willa Cather, 'On *The Professor's House*', p. 31.
22. Willa Cather, *The Professor's House* (London: Virago, [1925] 2003), p. 57. All future references will be made in the text.
23. Ellen Glasgow, *A Certain Measure: An Interpretation of the Prose Fiction* (New York: Harcourt Brace, 1943), p. 8.
24. In many regards, Glasgow resembles Virginia Woolf and refers to her own enterprise as a writer focused on the emancipation of a female consciousness in the same terms as Woolf: 'If I have missed any of the external rewards of success, I have never lost the outward peace and the inward compensation that comes

from doing the work one wishes to do in the solitary way in which one wishes to do it . . . I wanted "a room of my own," and it was granted me' (Glasgow, *A Certain Measure*, p. 178).

25. For extended readings of Glasgow's use of the classical tradition in *Barren Ground* see: Blair Rouse, *Ellen Glasgow* (New Haven: Twayne, 1962), pp. 86–96; Julius Rowan Raper, 'Ellen Glasgow', in Richard Gray and Owen Robinson (eds), *A Companion to the Literature and Culture of the American South* (Oxford: Blackwell, 2004), pp. 403–19.
26. Ellen Glasgow, *She Stooped to Folly: A Comedy of Morals* (New York: Literary Guild, 1929), p. 333.
27. Cited in Linda W. Wagner's *Ellen Glasgow: Beyond Convention* (Austin: University of Texas Press, 1982), p. 4.
28. Ellen Glasgow, *Barren Ground* (New York: Hill and Wang, [1925] 1957), p. 3. All subsequent references will appear in the text.
29. Tanya Ann Kennedy, 'The Secret Properties of Southern Regionalism: Gender and Agrarianism in Glasgow's *Barren Ground*', *Southern Literary Journal*, 38.2 (Spring 2006), p. 49.
30. William Faulkner, *The Sound and the Fury* (London: Vintage, [1929] 1995), p. 63. All subsequent references will appear in the text.
31. William Faulkner, *Go Down, Moses* (New York: Vintage, [1940] 1990), p. 280. Subsequent references will appear in the text.
32. William Faulkner, *Intruder in the Dust* (London: Penguin, [1948] 1964), pp. 187–8.
33. See Jean Stein, 'William Faulkner: Interview with Jean Stein van den Heuvel' (1956), reprinted in William Faulkner, *The Sound and the Fury*, ed. David Minter (New York: Norton, 1987), p. 240.
34. James Joyce, *Ulysses* (London: Penguin, [1922] 1992), p. 42.
35. James Joyce, *A Portrait of the Artist as a Young Man* (London: Penguin, [1916] 1965), p. 276.
36. Allen Tate, 'Narcissus as Narcissus' (1938), in *Reason in Madness: Critical Essays* (New York: G. P. Putnam, 1941), pp. 132–51.
37. Ibid. pp. 139, 140.

38. Allen Tate, 'Ode to the Confederate Dead', in *Poems, 1922–1947* (New York: Charles Scribner's Sons, 1948), pp. 19–23. All subsequent references will appear in the text.
39. Allen Tate, *The Man of Letters in the Modern World: Selected Essays, 1928–1955* (Oklahoma City: Meridian Books, 1955), p. 335.
40. Allen Tate, 'Narcissus as Narcissus', p. 140.
41. For a stunning reading of the heroic vision provided by Parmenides and Zeno and the links between Tate's leaves and those in Homer's *Iliad* see Lillian Feder's 'Allen Tate's Use of Classical Literature', *Centennial Review*, 4 (Winter 1960), pp. 89–114. Tate regarded this essay as the best piece of scholarly work written on his poetry.
42. Allen Tate, 'Narcissus as Narcissus', p. 142.
43. Robert Penn Warren, 'John Crowe Ransom: A Study in Irony', *Virginia Quarterly Review*, 11 (January 1935), p. 109.
44. John Crowe Ransom, 'Antique Harvesters' (1927), in *Selected Poems* (London: Carcanet, [1945] 1991), p. 83. All subsequent references will appear in the text.
45. Vivienne Koch, 'The Achievement of John Crowe Ransom', in *John Crowe Ransom: Critical Essays and a Bibliography*, ed. Thomas Daniel Young (Baton Rouge: Louisiana State University Press, 1968), p. 136.
46. John Crowe Ransom, 'Reconstructed but Unregenerate', in Twelve Southerners, *I'll Take My Stand: The South and the Agrarian Tradition* (Baton Rouge: Louisiana State University Press, [1930] 2006), p. 20, p. 15, p. 23 and pp. 19–20.
47. For the purposes of this discussion, I will be referring to the shorter, edited version of 'Kentucky Mountain Farm' which can be found in *Selected Poems, 1923–1975* (London: Secker and Warburg, 1976), pp. 319–22. All subsequent references will be made in the text.
48. T. S. Eliot, *The Waste Land* (London: Faber and Faber, [1922] 1972), p. 23.

CHAPTER 4

Home Thoughts from Abroad: The Lost Generation

The most acclaimed and popular exponents of American literary modernism are undoubtedly those now known as 'the Lost Generation', a group of writers whose work is synonymous with the decadent flavour of the 1920s. Many had first-hand experience of the First World War, in one capacity or another. Some had been part of the Norton-Harjes Ambulance Corps in Paris, while others went into combat service after the United States entered the war. Their experiences naturally differed: while John Dos Passos and Ernest Hemingway saw the full horrors of the war when working in the ambulance corps, E. E. Cummings was imprisoned in France in 1917 and F. Scott Fitzgerald's war took him no further than his training base in Alabama. For all of them, however, the war was a transcendent and unifying experience, an episode of unparalleled excitement, adventure and horror, a carnival of death. Indeed, Fitzgerald clearly regarded his inability to participate as a missed opportunity, viewing the war as a great romantic experience from which he had been excluded. More typical, perhaps, was the revulsion of Ezra Pound, expressed in his poem 'Hugh Selwyn Mauberley' (1920): 'There died a myriad . . . For an old bitch gone in the teeth / For a botched civilization'.[1]

But it was not only in its themes – death, suffering, the futility of idealism and the 'botched' nature of civilisation – that the war left a deep imprint on the Lost Generation. Participation in the war effort necessarily meant exile, which was central to the experience of this group of writers. Dos Passos, Hemingway, the Fitzgeralds and Cummings were joined in European exile by Gertrude Stein, Edith Wharton, William Carlos Williams, Wallace Stevens, Archibald MacLeish, Djuna Barnes, Mina Loy, Langston Hughes and Sherwood Anderson, all of whom left the United States in the late 1910s or early 1920s, eventually forming a collective group on the left bank of the Seine in Montparnasse. Some had left to participate in the war effort, others to find new values and new art forms which they felt were absent in the United States, and others still sought liberation from the stultifying sexual, racial and moral codes of American society. But it was the desire to find and make something *new* in the literary arts which united these writers as a 'generation'. They saw Europe as a uniquely rich cultural and historical landscape – certainly richer than the supposedly bland modernity of the United States – and believed, like T. S. Eliot and Ezra Pound, that only in the Old World could they nurture their experimental artistic tendencies. As the literary critic Malcolm Cowley, one of the finest early chroniclers of the Lost Generation, put it:

> It was lost, first of all, because it was uprooted, schooled away and wrenched away from its attachment to any region or tradition. It was lost because its training had prepared it for another world than existed after the war . . . It was lost because it tried to live in exile. It was lost because it accepted no other guides to conduct and because it had formed a false picture of society and the writer's place in it. The generation belonged to a period of transition from values already fixed to values that had to be created.[2]

Many of these writers shared this sense of themselves as a generation in transition; as Gertrude Stein allegedly remarked to Hemingway, 'you are all of you a lost generation'.[3] These were writers who did not necessarily have the bedrock of traditional Victorian values or Protestant progressive impulses against which earlier modernists had pitched their art. Born into a period of dynamic social, political and moral flux, they sought in their lifestyles and in their writing to find new means of exploring the frontiers of consciousness. Indeed, one obvious reason they travelled abroad was because they believed they could then see America and Americans *more clearly* with geographical distance. This gave their writing a slightly different tone to that of their immediate predecessors, who had recoiled from the United States as devoid of inspiration. Indeed, among the older writers, perhaps only Gertrude Stein took pride in her American nationality, never identifying herself as an expatriate; it was no coincidence, therefore, that of all the older writers, she came closest to the themes and flavour of the Lost Generation experiments. For Stein, the United States was the progenitor of modernism and the heart of modernity. Indeed, Stein claimed that the new modernist art forms, such as Cubism, were genuinely *American*, because they were the expression of modern history, which is precisely how she defined the United States.

Whatever we think of Stein's fiercely patriotic, even parochial interpretation of modernism's early history, it says a great deal about the impulses behind her writing and the values of visitors to her literary salon at 27 rue de Fleurus. Her salon was the point of entry to the European avant-garde for many young American writers and artists, including Hemingway, Fitzgerald and Barnes, all of whom came under her influence at some point. Indeed, she regarded Fitzgerald as the most promising writer of his generation, complimenting him on his ability to 'write naturally in sentences' and on his creation of 'the modern world much like Thackeray did in his *Pendennis* and *Vanity Fair*'.[4] For Stein, it was Fitzgerald's ability to conjure modern American history that marked him out from his contemporaries as a true innovator. And although she had developed her modernist voice outside the United States, she never lost her fascination with 'America' itself, celebrating her native land as the neo-Emersonian epitome of transition and movement:

> Think of anything, of cowboys, of movies, of detective stories, of anybody who goes anywhere or stays at home and is an American and you will realise that it is something strictly American to conceive a space that is filled with moving, a space of time that is filled always filled with moving.[5]

Of course this idea of *movement* recurs repeatedly throughout the literature of the Lost Generation, whether it is migration across the United States, as seen in Fitzgerald's novel *The Great Gatsby* (1925), or the nomadic tribe of wandering Americans making their way from Paris to Pamplona, in Hemingway's *The Sun Also Rises* (1926). But what emerges from each of these texts, as well as from Stein's own works, is the transitional nature of American identity itself.

Many of the Lost Generation are hailed for works which encapsulate an American consciousness and the effects of a specific historical era on the nation's sense of self. Fitzgerald, for one, went out of his way to cultivate this reputation, wanting to be a chronicler of his age as well as the voice of his generation.[6] This desire to speak on behalf of the nation from a distance is, of course, derived from an earlier modernist innovator, James Joyce, whose alter ego, Stephen Dedalus, finding himself in self-imposed exile at the end of *A Portrait of the Artist as a Young Man* (1916), decides 'in the smithy of my soul to forge the uncreated conscience of my race'.[7] Like Dedalus, the Lost Generation simultaneously rejected the nation and yet were intent on evoking it. For all their contempt for the bland modernity of the United States, they were nevertheless eager to redeem it, not least through language, which many felt had been tainted by the rhetoric of the war.

When President Warren Harding led a delegation to Arlington National Cemetery to bury the Unknown Soldier in 1921, he claimed that the soldier's 'sacrifice, and that of the millions dead, shall not be in vain'.[8] Many, however, scoffed at these words. In 'Hugh Selwyn Mauberley', Pound had already anticipated similar sentiments: 'Died some, pro patria / non "dolce" non "et décor" . . . believing in old men's lies, then unbelieving'.[9] Thorstein Veblen lamented 'the rant and bounce of Red Cross patriotism',[10] while Archibald MacLeish, writing in 1926, lamented an ambassador's words at a ceremony for the war dead at a cemetery in which his brother was buried: 'Oh, not the loss of the accomplished thing! Not dumb farewells . . .'.[11] And for writers who had taken part in the war, one of its tragic legacies was the gulf between the carnage and the pieties surrounding it, which is well captured by Hemingway's *A Farewell to Arms* (1929):

> I was always embarrassed by the words sacred, glorious, and sacrifice and the expression in vain. We had heard them, sometimes standing in the rain almost out of earshot, so that only the shouted words came through, and had read them, on proclamations that were slapped out by billposters over other proclamations, now for a long time, and I had seen nothing sacred, and the things that were glorious had no glory and the sacrifices were like the stockyards at Chicago if nothing was done with the meat except to bury it.[12]

For the Lost Generation, language was in dire need of purgation – and this helps to explain why, in the 1920s, many writers preferred to cultivate a stripped-down, colloquial style which, on the surface at least, seemed to lack deep emotion. In *Death in the Afternoon* (1932), for example, Hemingway describes learning 'to put down what really happened in action; what the actual things were which produced the emotion that you experienced . . . the real thing, the sequence of motion and fact which made the emotion'.[13] In other words, social reality is only important insofar as it affects the consciousness through which it is filtered. As Chip Rhodes observes: 'language imitates the social process by which a subject comes to feel a certain relation to his/her historical circumstances'.[14]

The 1920s, Fitzgerald once remarked, were an 'age of miracles, it was an age of art, it was an age of excess and it was an age of satire'.[15] He was not exaggerating. By the dawn of the decade, the United States had become the most potent industrialised nation in the world, overtaking Britain and Germany. Its cities were booming; from Los Angeles and Seattle to Minneapolis and Detroit, American capitalism was forging a new urban culture. City-dwellers now outnumbered their rural counterparts, but wherever they lived, Americans were part of an emerging technological culture.[16] Telephones had become commonplace; as early as 1915, there was one radio for every ten people; in 1926 the establishment of two gigantic nationwide radio networks marked the peak of the radio age; and three years later, radio sales hit a record 5 million. From *Time* (1923) and *The New Yorker* (1923) to 'talkies' and dance bands, a new kind of urban popular culture, rooted in mass consumerism, was sweeping the nation, often buttressed by advertising for products such as cars, vacuum cleaners and record players. Not for nothing was this known as the Jazz Age, for from about 1917 onwards, jazz had become an increasingly popular phenomenon, spreading beyond its heartlands in New Orleans and Chicago, and shocking older moral guardians. 'The word "jazz" in its progress toward respectability, has meant first sex, then dancing, then music', remarked Fitzgerald. 'It is associated with a state of nervous stimulation, not unlike that of the big cities between the lines of war.'[17] But even more than a Jazz Age, this was an age of the automobile. By 1925 a Ford Model T was rolling off the assembly line every ten seconds and by 1929 there were approximately 26.5 million Model T Fords on the American roads. Indeed, motoring and advertising became two of the most important industries of the era, with General Motors alone spending over $20 million in advertising during the 1920s. With so many voices clamouring for attention, from radio stars and jazz singers to car advertisers and magazine columnists, it was no wonder that contemporary writers – as, for example, in *Manhattan Transfer* (1925) – were almost overwhelmed by the sheer polyphony of an age of apparent capitalist abundance.

This abundance was not, however, universally shared. In 1928, shortly before the Wall Street Crash and the ensuing Great Depression, President Herbert Hoover proclaimed that 'we in America today are nearer to the final triumph over poverty than ever before in the history of the land'. But this was to prove a cruel illusion. For some 40 million Americans, a third of the population, which included single-parent families, the rural poor, the forgotten elderly and disenfranchised African Americans, the buoyant promise of laissez-faire capitalism often seemed a hollow sham. And for the tens of millions of Americans marooned at the bottom, daily life was less a whirlwind of jazz music and mass consumerism than a struggle against destitution, damp, dirt and disease. What was more, many people were shocked rather than invigorated by the changes of the day. Moral and religious values were in flux: traditional religious orthodoxies had been badly shaken by Darwin and his successors, whose ideas seemed to undermine the foundations of Christian faith. Terrified by the Russian Revolution and the militancy of the American labour unions, many middle-class conservatives believed that communism was on the march, while others were horrified by the advance of the so-called New Woman, which seemed to pose a threat to traditional notions of female separateness and subordination. Perhaps above all, the increasing popularity of Freudianism seemed to challenge the idea of the unitary personality or self; perhaps not even the all-American hero, it seemed, was in control of his own consciousness. Little wonder, then, that so many people felt they were living in an era of unparalleled flux and fragmentation. In 1893 the philosopher William James had predicted the emergence of the 'multiverse'; now, thirty years on, his forecast seemed to have become a dizzying reality.[18]

Almost a century on, what is most striking about the culture of the 1920s is this distinctly recognisable flavour of fragmentation and discontinuity. Consciousness itself seemed up for grabs, and at a time of enormous economic dislocation, national soul-searching and fascination with the workings of the mind, it was no accident that many writers worked with an almost demonic nervous energy, their prose sparkling with a rare intensity as they strove to capture the sheer rawness of lived experience. The point of writing, said Hemingway, was to get at 'the real thing', a sentiment his contemporaries universally shared. This was not a question of narrative realism; what he and his peers sought was rather to show how emotional and imaginative reality is shaped by broad historical forces. Hence the plethora of antipathetic heroes and heroines, who are often radically altered by their relationship with the mechanised luxuries of modernity, stripped of their faith and traditions, and left rudderless and bereft. Often these characters are profoundly cynical, which is why Daisy Fay Buchanan's laughter sounds like money, or why the permanently gloomy Jake Barnes is suddenly enlivened by a bullfight. Tellingly, they are also often big drinkers. This was the era of Prohibition: between 1919 and 1933, the sale, manufacture and transportation of alcohol were strictly illegal. Prohibition was an attempt to turn back the clock to the vanished moral values of an imagined golden age; it was also a complete failure. For the rich and cosmopolitan, flouting the law became a badge of status and sophistication; for the exiled Lost Generation, meanwhile, Prohibition became a symbol of everything they despised about the modern United States, a country they associated with pious, ignorant reformers who were determined to crush human pleasure and high culture. And of course Prohibition also helped to drive up crime, encouraging the development of an underworld of racketeers and bootleggers, most famously the Chicago gangster Al Capone.

Crime itself was becoming a central theme of the era; not for nothing is Jay Gatsby, formerly a war veteran, a self-made millionaire who owes his fortune to bootlegging. And Fitzgerald's attitude to Gatsby – both fascinated and repelled – reflects the Lost Generation's wider attitude to the new modernity, which is nicely epitomised by Dick Diver's relationship with the brittle and broken Nicole in his novel *Tender is the Night* (1934). Mesmerised by her exterior beauty, Dick is horrified by the inner hollowness engendered by a world of money, excess and moral bankruptcy. But although Fitzgerald specialised in depicting hollow characters, nobody could accuse his prose itself of being hollow. Time and again in Lost Generation writing, the intensity, complexity and variety of the prose reflects the giddy raptures of the decade, from the swinging cadences of the Charleston and the upward ascent of the glittering skyscraper to the underground pleasures of the speakeasy and the whispered delights of bootlegged liquor. And in their different ways, Fitzgerald's colloquial yet precise style, Hemingway's stripped-down, muscular prose and the complex linguistic experiments of Stein and Barnes are all attempts to find a new kind of literary expression, capturing the way in which social, economic and technological change affected the consciousness of the individual.

For many readers, the style of the era is best encapsulated in the lives and lifestyles of the writers themselves. Fitzgerald and his wife, the first flapper, Zelda Sayre, are often seen as poster children for the glamour and the despair of the era, thanks to their roller-coaster lifestyle of high excess and insanity. For others, it is the adventures of Hemingway and his various wives which best capture the atmosphere of this unique group of writers. But the legacy of the Lost Generation is more than a set of intriguing biographies. As critics such as Martin Halliwell have observed, it was the Lost Generation that truly *internationalised* American modernism.[19] And as Dos Passos wrote in his foreword to a poem by Blaise Cendrars:

> [We were] part of the creative tidal wave that spread over the world from the Paris of before the last European war. Under various tags – futurism, cubism, vorticism, modernism – most of the best work in the arts in our time has been the direct product of this explosion, that had an influence in its sphere comparable with that of the October revolution in social organisation and politics and the Einstein formula in physics. Cendrars and Apollinaire, poets, were on the first cubist barricades with the group that included Picasso, Modigliani, Marinetti, Chagall; that profoundly influenced Maiakovsky, Meyerhold, Eisenstein; whose ideas corom [sic] through Joyce, Gertrude Stein, T. S. Eliot (first published in Wyndham Lewis's *Blast*). The music of Stravinsky and Prokofiev and Diaghilev's Ballet hail from this same Paris already in the disintegration of victory, as do the windows of Saks Fifth Avenue, skyscraper furniture, the Lenin Memorial in Moscow, the paintings of Diego Rivera in Mexico City and the newritz styles of advertising in American magazines.[20]

What Dos Passos recognised was that the Lost Generation's art had been profoundly shaped by its encounters with France, Britain, Italy and Russia, among others. Though distinctly American, their work was also part of a gigantic international cultural shift, and though their themes and methods were clearly rooted in American contexts, the Lost Generation nevertheless were part of a genuinely *global* artistic vanguard, perhaps the first that has ever existed. Behind the frivolity of endless parties, all-day lunches and wanton consumption, what strikes the reader most is the abiding sense of disillusionment, the emptiness and lost plenitude which each writer vainly seeks to represent and recapture. Yet for all their disappointments and disenchantments, there is beneath it all a profound faith in the power of words to bring redemption and transcendence. And beneath all the cynicism and criticism there is also, as we shall see, a profound affection for the lost promise of America.

GERTRUDE STEIN

Although the work of her numerous protégés is better known and more beloved than her own literary endeavours, the writing of Gertrude Stein is of utmost importance to American literary modernism. Indeed, Stein is one of the most important American modernists, her ideas about art and literary style influencing an entire generation. Her writing is notoriously difficult and during her lifetime was openly dismissed by a variety of critics and by her brother Leo Stein, an art collector with whom she lived in Paris. Yet it distils in purest form many of the conventions of literary modernism as practised by her salon visitors. For instance, her commitment to the relationship between visual and literary art is clearly evident in Dos Passos's Cubist narratives; her faith in simple, unadorned words to recreate the world strongly influenced Hemingway's famous technique; and the patterns of her words and interest in etymology are undoubtedly the inspiration behind the textures of William Carlos Williams's poetry.

For Sherwood Anderson, Stein was able to recreate life in words:

> One works with words and one would like words that have a taste on the lips, that have a perfume to the nostrils, rattling words one can throw into a box and shake, making a sharp jingling sound, words that when seen on the printed page, have a distinct arresting effect upon the eye, words that when they jump out from under the pen may feel with the fingers as one might caress the cheeks of his beloved.
>
> And what I think is that these books of Gertrude Stein's do in a very real sense recreate life in words.[21]

Her writing, for Anderson, removed the gap between language and the real world to evoke the object, emotion or sensation described, moving beyond the state of 'representation' to 'be'. And yet for another critic, James Thurber, Stein's work was little more than nonsense:

> Anyone who reads at all diversely during these bizarre nineteen twenties cannot escape the conclusion that a number of

> crazy men and women are writing stuff which remarkably passes for important composition among certain persons who should know better. Stuart P. Sherman, however, refused to be numbered among those who stand in awe and admiration of the most eminent of the idiots, Gertrude Stein. He reviews her *Geography and Plays* in the Aug. 11 issue of the *Literary Review* of the *New York Evening Post* and arrives at the conclusion that it is a marvellous and painstaking achievement in setting down approximately 80,000 words which mean nothing at all.[22]

Amusing as this is, there is a good case that Thurber was missing the point. Stein was not interested in the 'meaning' of words; what she was interested in was the relationship between the object and the linguistic signifier, seeking some way of sealing the distance between the 'thing' and the 'word'. What was more, she wanted to interrogate and play with the relationship between a given object and the word used to describe it.

Stein's literary project is in many ways a philosophical one, and it is therefore unsurprising that she was tutored at Radcliffe College by William James, whose work on the philosophy of psychology was to guide her through many of her literary endeavours.[23] As mentioned in Chapter 1, in his essay 'The Stream of Thought', James had observed that language often works against the individual's perception of truth. Like Stein, he thought that language actually blurs our apprehension of the object: 'What, after all, is so natural as to assume that one object, [be] called by one name?' Language applied in this way, he suggested, inhibits the individual's experience of a given object; it necessarily ties the object to one thing and cuts it off from a myriad of others with which, in the mind of the apprehending individual, it might otherwise be associated. 'We name our thoughts simply, each after its thing, as if each knew its own thing and nothing else', he added. 'What each dimly knows is clearly the thing it is named for, with dimly perhaps a thousand other things. It ought to be named after all of them, but it never is.'[24]

Stein took up this idea in her lecture 'Poetry and Grammar' (1934): 'Do you always have the same kind of feeling in relation to the sounds as the words come out of you or do you not' [sic].[25] And we see this enacted in the 'portraits' of objects, food and rooms she produced in her early work *Tender Buttons* (1914). For instance, in the portrait 'A PIECE OF COFFEE.' our usual understanding of the word 'coffee' is deliberately undermined:

> More of double.
> A place in no new table.
> A single image is not splendor. Dirty is yellow. A sign of more in not mentioned. A piece of coffee is not a detainer. The resemblance to yellow is dirtier and distincter. The clean mixture is whiter and not coal color, never more coal color than altogether.[26]

Obviously, this is not what one expects from a description of coffee. But of course, the reader's expectations are dashed from the outset with the unconventional combination of 'coffee' and 'a piece'. The noun 'coffee' is disturbed by the application of the pre-modifying 'piece', which is more commonly used to describe a solid rather than a liquid object. Of course, one is then pushed to reconsider the assumption regarding the necessarily liquid nature of coffee, as well as one's assumptions about why certain linguistic phrases are used and not others; Stein is implicitly asking the reader to consider why it is not acceptable to have 'a piece of coffee' rather than the more commonly used 'cup of coffee'. The use of the word 'piece' performs a double function in its deployment, as the reader is forced to use the word as a verb (rather than as a noun) and 'piece' the portrait together, much like we would do if looking at a Cubist Picasso portrait. This grammatical form, the gerund, a verb which functions as a noun, was much favoured by Stein.

'More of double' is, if anything, even more perplexing, thanks to the lack of any noun at all. More of double what? Again, the reader's expectations are confounded; the 'more' may refer to the coffee; the double may also refer to coffee. Together, perhaps, these words draw our attention to the actual letters which constitute the word 'coffee': the double 'f', followed by a further (more) double in the 'ee'. Yet the second line in the portrait, 'A place in no new table', takes the reader in another direction, with the clear reference to a coffee table, and the 'piece' referring to a place or section of the table. The following line offers a clear insight into Stein's point: the 'single image' or singular understanding of coffee does not offer the reader any new understanding and is, for the writer, defunct. A multiple appreciation, however, can yield much pleasure and is more in tune with the way individuals perceive objects.

Stein's dislike of the 'single image' in this instance can be linked to her disregard for proper nouns which, she feels, deaden the object to which they refer. The naming of an item is an act of conquering, which delimits perception. Again, this can be traced to James's notion that certain aspects of language work against the individual's apprehension of the truth. Stein tells us that 'a noun is a name of anything' and asks, with characteristic lack of punctuation, 'why after a thing is named write about it'. In fact, the entire project of *Tender Buttons* is to get rid of nouns, which 'must go' in order for 'anything that was everything was to go on meaning something'. Hence the seeming lack of correspondence between the named object in a portrait such as 'MILDRED'S UMBRELLA.' and the text of the linguistic sketch which follows.[27]

What a portrait such as 'EATING.' demonstrates, however, is that the words which truly interest Stein are verbs, adverbs, prepositions and conjunctions, the parts of language which move and progress to new states. 'Verbs', she tells us, 'can change to look like themselves or to look like something else, they are, so to speak on the move and adverbs move with them', whereas prepositions, in their representation of 'nothing', are something one 'can be continuously using and everlastingly enjoying'.[28] Her emphasis on motion within language is very similar to James's distrust of the 'substantive conclusions' in the linguistic 'stream of thought'. The substantive conclusions in language refer to the names or signifiers of objects, which create a hierarchy within language. This hierarchy subordinates important elements of language such as Stein's prepositions and conjunctions, which have the power to alter the static nature of nouns. Thus, according to James, 'we ought to say a feeling of *and*, a feeling of *if*, and a feeling of *by*, quite as readily as we say a feeling of *blue* or a feeling of *cold*'.[29]

What emerges from all this is an insistence on the necessary democratisation of language, and Stein applied this thoroughly American 'democratising method' on a larger scale to her most ambitious and certainly most capacious work, *The Making of Americans* (1925). Stein, never one to hide or underestimate her sense of her own genius, declared this work as 'the beginning, really the beginning of modern writing'.[30] Quite apart from her works' merits, or perhaps lack of them, there is at least some chronological truth to this. In 1903, the canonised giants of modernism were either in college or at high school, and James Joyce had not even set sail for Trieste. Written between 1903 and 1911 though not published until the 1920s, *The Making of Americans* chronicles the lives of two immigrant families, the Herslands and the Dehnings, and their union through the marriage of Julia Dehning to Alfred Hersland. In some ways the book recalls the nineteenth-century historical novel, but the narrator's frequent metafictional asides add a modernist dimension, often articulating Stein's quest to find a language commensurate with the scale of her ambitions:

> I will go on writing, and not for myself and for any other one but because it is a thing I certainly can be earnestly doing with sometimes excited feeling and sometimes happy feeling and sometimes longing feeling and sometimes almost indifferent feeling and always with a little dubious feeling.[31]

For Stein, however, what really made the story modern was the subject matter: the birth and development of a new civilisation. The story opens with a firm assertion of American identity:

> It has always seemed to me a rare privilege, this, of being an American, a real American, one whose tradition it has taken scarcely sixty years to create. We need only realise our parents, remember our grandparents and know ourselves and our history is complete.
>
> The old people in a new world, the new people made out of the old, that is the story that I mean to tell, for that is what really is and what I really know. (p. 3)

Here, the narrator states the novel's intention from the outset: to unravel what it means to be an American. She also places the story of immigration at the centre of the text and, as we have seen with *Tender Buttons*, illuminates the central concern with *process*, with the 'making' of Americans. Again, Stein revels in the multiplicity of language (indeed the book is teeming with carefully nuanced repetitions and rearrangements of phrases and verbal clauses) and the 'making of Americans' is twofold. The making of Americans, meaning what Americans make and produce (money, architecture or art, for instance) is one of the subjects of the text; the other is *the process of making Americans*, the experiences and interactions which produce American identities. Stein's use of the present participle throughout the text, alongside her repetitive use of gerunds such as 'making' in the novel's title, roots the historical story of a family's progress in the continuous present. Thus what the novel presents is Stein's earliest version of the principles seen in *Tender Buttons*: an experiment with grammar to make objects and identities fresh and new, to portray the originality of American identity. This idiosyncratic use of grammar is also an attempt to stage her writing in the absolute moment, while nevertheless engaging with the past that produces the here and now.

The Making of Americans also stages a struggle with a patriarchal figure, which in many ways recalls the relationship between American modernists and their literary progenitors and educational mentors: one thinks of Stein's relationship with James, for example, or even Hemingway's fractious relationship with Stein herself. In the 'Alfred Hersland and Julia Dehning' section, the reader is presented with a scene in which a man 'does something' and is later made a 'paralytic' when reminded of his act by one of his children (p. 491). The act of telling represents a conscious act of rebellion by the child against the possibly incestuous paternal figure. Critics have speculated about the nature of the act, but Stein keeps its exact nature hidden.[32] It remains a secreted or repressed history, which nonetheless has a profound influence both on the paralysed man and on the child who kicks against the father. Stein does not excise but incorporates the father, a representative of the past, into her history of the making of Americans, again exemplifying the interconnectivity between past, present and future. This highly charged struggle between a father and his progeny is also rehearsed at the beginning of the novel in a strange tableau in which 'an angry man dragged his father along the ground through his own orchard'. Yet even this scene, we learn, repeats a previous historical moment in which the old man had dragged his own father through the same orchard; '"Stop !" cried the groaning old man at last, " Stop ! I did not drag my father beyond this tree"' (p. 3).[33] The narrative repetition is yet another manifestation of the grammatical and linguistic repetition so common in this text, as well as a return to Stein's ideas about the living past which shapes the present. After all, she considered it 'the business of Art' to live in 'the complete and actual present'.[34]

For Stein, the business of living in the present was a uniquely American enterprise – everybody else, presumably, living in the past – and the privilege of being an American to which she refers at the beginning of *The Making of Americans* was something she did not take lightly, despite her exile in Paris. Her work shows a persistent interest in America and American modernity, from the films and personality of Charlie Chaplin to the life of Susan B. Anthony and her fondness for 'The Trail of the Lonesome Pine'. She read the *Herald Tribune* rather than the French newspapers, idolised General Ulysses S. Grant, and was deeply interested in the lives of the American doughboys caught up in the carnage of the Great War. Despite her exile, she had a profound faith in the American idiom and believed that it was the voice of the avant-garde and the language of modernity. Like Barnes, Hemingway and Fitzgerald, she needed to get away from America in order to see it more clearly and to write about it. As she explained her émigré status: 'America is my country and Paris is my home town'.[35] She may have developed the voice of her modernism in Europe, but her modernism is profoundly American in its pursuit of a language adequate to express the constant newness, movement and multiplicity of objects, events and individuals. Genius or 'most eminent of the idiots' overseas (as Thurber described her), Stein is undoubtedly one of the most important American modernists and mother of the Lost Generation.

ERNEST HEMINGWAY

Ernest Hemingway was one of the most frequent callers at Gertrude Stein's salon and learned a great deal from his mentor. She encouraged him to give up his journalism and concentrate on his literary efforts, she taught him a colloquial style full of repeated words and prepositional phrases which he deployed in much of his early fiction, and she instilled in him the necessity of appreciating 'the abstract relationship of words'. Though Stein advised Hemingway to discontinue his work for newspapers, advising that journalism would train him to see only words and never 'things', which would be to the detriment of his authorial aspirations, it was Hemingway's work as a reporter which consolidated his most lasting literary legacy, his style. From his first job as a reporter for the *Kansas City Star* before the First World War, Hemingway worked consistently for a series of newspapers, both as an overseas correspondent and staff reporter. In *Death in the Afternoon* (1932), he recalled:

> I was trying to write then and I found the greatest difficulty . . . was to put down what really happened in action; what the actual things were that produced the emotions you experienced.[36]

Dispatched to the Near East in September 1922 for the closing days of the Greco-Turkish War and to Lausanne in November for the peace conference which followed, Hemingway learned the art of what Malcolm Cowley calls 'cabelese': 'an exercise in omitting everything that can be taken for granted . . . in which every word had to do the work of six or seven'.[37] These journalistic assignments, as well, of course, as his earlier experiences as an ambulance driver in France and Italy, not only shaped his style, but provided him with many of the topics which were to preoccupy him throughout his career. The war provided Hemingway with the portraits of heroism, battered, bruised yet stoical, which would inform the characterisation of Jake Barnes, Frederic Henry and Robert Jordan, among others. But it was also through interviews with the likes of Georges Clemenceau, David Lloyd George and Benito Mussolini that Hemingway nurtured his ideas about the nature of language and the way in which abstract generalisations missed the truth of the lived experience of warfare.

Hemingway's journalism cultivated his sense of the necessary weight of words so that they might adequately convey the sensation of the event, experience or emotion described. His aim, ultimately, was to write the 'truest sentence', which would elicit a particular and enduring emotional reaction within the reader. Writing of his literary apprenticeship in Paris, he recalled his efforts to capture

> the real thing, the sequence of motion and fact which made the emotion and which would be as valid in a year or ten years or, with luck and if you stated it purely enough, always, was beyond me and I was working very hard to get it.[38]

The key words here are 'the real thing' and 'purely': there is a purity in Hemingway's writing which has become his signature feature and which is linked to the reader's ability to sense the situation at hand. The emphasis on sensation is twofold: the reader's senses must be stimulated, but the lives described within the text are themselves driven by a lust for sensation, passion and feeling. For Hemingway, the concreteness and immediacy of the senses were to be trusted above the abstractions of the mind, and he resolved to place them at the centre of his writing. We might well regard his technique and vision as a response to the emotional numbness which resulted from the war. And certainly there is often a clear sense of the emotional (and physical) numbness which has overpowered a generation. The 'purity' Hemingway sought was also socially based, representing an escape from the tawdriness of contemporary existence, the apparent decadence of the age, the cheapness of lives, the availability of sex, and the fascination with money. Indeed, the young Hemingway was repulsed by Fitzgerald's fixation upon money and his letters to Dos Passos reveal a relationship which became strained partly because of disagreements about unpaid debts.[39] But 'purity' in literary terms also refers to a writing style which lacks excessive verbiage, figurative language, symbolism and emotive language. For Hemingway, each word had to perform the work of six or seven words, delivering the maximum effect with the minimum means. Language had to deliver an intense emotional experience under immense pressure.

The works which most successfully deliver on Hemingway's promise are *In Our Time* (1925) and *The Sun Also Rises*, published in 1926, which is undoubtedly his most popular novel.[40] For several years, Hemingway had attended the festival of San Fermín in Pamplona, with its seven days of bullfighting, revelry and religious celebration. The festival is the climactic event of *The Sun Also Rises*, which tells the story of a group of friends in Paris who spend their days and nights in an endless pursuit of sensory pleasures. Among them is the taciturn hero, Jake Barnes, an American reporter who has been afflicted both physically and emotionally by his experiences in the war. The novel is arguably the best portrait of a lost generation, a group so disillusioned by history and enervated by existence itself that they lack purpose, direction and the bonds of loyalty which might otherwise hold a group of expatriate friends together. For one of the group, Bill Gorton, this aimlessness derives from their self-imposed exile:

> You're an expatriate. You've lost touch with the soil. You get precious. Fake European standards have ruined you. You drink yourself to death. You become obsessed by sex. You spend all your time talking, not working. You are an expatriate, see? You hang around cafés. (p. 100)

Although Hemingway wrote the first draft of the novel in just five weeks, he spent five months in extensive revision and editing. Sales were disappointing, despite wide and generally favourable reviews. Though John Dos Passos and Allen Tate disliked the book, Edmund Wilson declared it the best novel of the Lost Generation.[41] In the *New York Herald Tribune*, Conrad Aiken commended the dialogue while Bruce Barton remarked that Hemingway wrote as if 'he had fashioned the art of writing himself'.[42] H. L. Mencken, too, praised the tautness of the writing, and Cowley observes that the novel 'soon became a handbook of conduct for the new generation . . . many of the younger writers had begun to walk, talk and shadowbox like Hemingway, when they weren't flourishing capes in front of an imaginary bull'.[43] The

Stein-inspired epigraph at the beginning of the novel consolidated the author's reputation as the voice of his generation; ironically, though, Hemingway protested to his publisher, Maxwell Perkins, that he had included it simply to play against Stein's 'bombast' and her 'assumption of prophetic roles':

> The point of the book to me was that the earth abideth forever – having a great deal of fondness and admiration for the earth and not a hell of a lot for my generation and caring little about Vanities. I only hesitated at the start to cut the writing of a better writer [Stein] – but it seems necessary. I didn't mean the book to be a hollow or bitter satire but a damn tragedy with the earth abiding forever as the hero.[44]

Again, what is striking is his emphasis on the tangible and the concrete, with the earth – rather than the attitudes of a generation – at the heart of the writer's sense of his novel. By excising over 40,000 words from the original manuscript Hemingway removed the various interior monologues which would have fleshed out his characters' inner worlds, which he thought explained the failure of some critics to understand the point, purpose and economy of the novel.

Set in the immediate aftermath of the Great War, *The Sun Also Rises* depicts a series of characters struggling with the war's effects upon their innate sense of self, their values and their physical being. In essence, they are united by their war wounds, which affect how they view the world and how they behave. Jake's wartime service has left him impotent and as he associates sexual pleasure with the fullness of life, he regards himself as an incomplete man. He seeks to develop his sensory experiences in other ways, most clearly through his affection for bullfighting. Similarly, the object of Jake's affections, Brett Ashley, a VAD and former nurse at the Ospedale Maggiore, is so deeply affected by her experiences and by Jake's afflictions that she promiscuously indulges in affair after affair as a means of sensory fulfilment. This sense of the importance of the war as a uniting force is evident when she announces Count Mippipolulous as 'one of us' who 'remembers everything that has happened' after he has stripped to show the wound left by an arrow which pierced his body (p. 53). However, 'one of us' excludes the likes of Robert Cohn, the first character we meet in the novel, who is witheringly described by Jake as someone nobody remembers from Princeton. Cohn is never accepted by the group and never learns to play by its rules. He is a perpetual outsider, unlike Pedro Romero, the young matador who, in his passion for his sport and his unaffected behaviour, is immediately welcomed as one of the circle.

Those that are welcomed, therefore, are not only war veterans but those who have learned to live life 'all the way up' (p. 9), those who know the value of life because they have come so close to death. This emphasis on the sensuous is reflected in the way each character is described: Brett has 'curves like the hull of a racing yacht' (p. 19), while Romero's bullfighting style is 'always straight and pure and natural in line'. Indeed, as Jake reminds us, Romero 'had the old thing . . . the holding of his purity of line through a maximum of exposure' (pp. 145–6). The emphasis on clean lines, unembellished curves and purity of technique is, of course, exactly what Hemingway sought in his writing. The descriptions are pithy but utterly compelling, transcending narrative time and space to elicit a visceral reaction. Using the simplest language, Hemingway places the object directly before the reader who, in turn, is moved to consider the sensuousness of a woman shaped like a yacht or the gentle curve in the spine of a matador artfully evading his eventual prey. Thus content, theme and technique merge in the purest yet most evocative of sentences.

While the impact of the war is undoubtedly a predominant theme in the novel, one of its repercussions, the altered nature of heroism and masculinity, is also clearly an important issue for Hemingway. Critics have noted that there are two heroes in the novel: the public hero, Romero, and the hidden hero, Jake Barnes.[45] By dint of his profession, Romero is a public figure, a hero who publicly performs acts of daring and skill, and a man who can physically perform as Brett's lover. It is no coincidence that Jake admires bullfighters and their ability to live life 'all the way up'. Cut off from the role he most desires, that of Brett's lover, Jake is forced into the role of the silent, stoical hero who must exercise a strong willpower to bear his emasculation and overriding sense of hopelessness. Not unlike the steers in the corral who receive the bulls and stop them from fighting, Jake calms the group as they tussle for Brett's affections – but he is nevertheless wounded by them. As Cohn observes: 'It's no life being a steer' (p. 123). Indeed, Jake is the glue which holds the group together, the human link in all the relationships: he is Brett's support and confidant, he is a friend to Robert Cohn, he listens to Harvey Stone and he manages to calm the drunken Mike. He is the link between the Americans and the Spaniards and the only character we see who seems to engage with the French.

While Jake's love for Brett is beyond doubt, it is in the company of men that he is at his most relaxed. This is most evident in his affectionate and tactile dealings with Montoya and in the novel's pastoral fishing scene, in which Jake accompanies Bill Gorton to the hills of Burguete en route to Pamplona. As they return to the physical, natural world, a serenity falls upon the male companions, who immerse themselves in the water and later bask semi-naked in the sunshine. This homosocial scene is laden with subliminal references to male virility, perhaps suggesting that through activities such as fishing and bullfighting, Jake can regain something of his lost masculinity:

> In the white water at the foot of the dam it was deep. As I baited up, a trout shot up out of the white water into the falls and was carried down. Before I could finish baiting, another trout jumped at the falls, making the same lovely arc . . . (p. 104)

In a sequence rich with references to upward movement and vitality, the slippery fish shooting upwards from the white plume of the water hints at the natural radiance which Jake believes has been stolen from him. Furthermore, the natural, European world facilitates male camaraderie in a way that seems impossible in the American city. As Bill explains: 'Listen. You're a hell of a good guy, and I'm fonder of you than anybody on earth. I couldn't tell you that in New York. It'd mean I was a faggot . . . Sex explains it all' (p. 101). Indeed, sex is at the root of Jake's unhappiness. But his temporary serenity and masculine happiness are shattered with the arrival of a letter from Mike announcing his and Brett's imminent arrival in Pamplona. In the company of men, Jake is able to live life fully; when Brett appears, however, the picture radically changes.

The portrait of Brett Ashley is, perhaps, one of the most interesting features of the novel. Likened to Homer's Circe, a sorceress with the ability to transform men into swine, Brett controls the behaviour of the men who, literally and figuratively, dance around her. An embodiment of the 'New Woman' in her independence, confidence and relative domestic freedom, Brett is presented from her very first appearance as expressing sexual confusion and disarray. She arrives at the *bal musette*, curvaceous but with a boyish haircut, in the company of a group of young homosexual men who offend Jake with their effeminacy and gregariousness. She is loving and generous to Jake, yet she is also promiscuous and flighty and readily informs him of her sexual liaisons and opportunities with a variety of men. In many ways, therefore, she is a perfect representative of the sexual and moral ambiguities associated with the New Woman who had emerged in the late nineteenth century as a supremely unsettling figure.

Hemingway was drawn to strong and in some ways sexually ambiguous women in his personal life. He admired 'tomboyish' qualities in his four wives, including Hadley's hiking and skiing, Pauline's riding and shooting, Martha's hunting and Mary's skill as a deep-sea fisherwoman. In Paris he was surrounded by an extensive community of sexually experimental lesbian artists and writers, including Stein and her lover Alice B. Toklas, H. D. and Djuna Barnes, all of whom challenged his ideas and writing, yet encouraged and nurtured his talents. Indeed, he was somewhat fearful of Stein, breaking their friendship when she described him as 'yellow', not least because he was worried that he would become known as one of her disciples.[46] Brett elicits a similar kind of reaction in Jake, who worries that he will come to resemble the 'steer-like' Cohn, feels hurt by her flaunting behaviour, yet also nurtures a great affection for her.

But Brett is a sexual conundrum. While in Paris she appears the quintessential, self-possessed modern woman, but she is positively undone in rural, traditional Spain. Out of place with her short hair and fashionable clothing, she attracts stares from the locals, is refused entry at the chapel in San Fermín for failing to cover her head, and loses her control in her infatuation with Pedro Romero, who wants her to become a more 'traditional' woman by growing out her hair. The relationship with Romero renders Brett vulnerable but it also demonstrates her power. Her seduction of the young bullfighter causes Jake to sacrifice his deepest held principles. By facilitating the relationship, Jake breaks his bond with his fellow aficionado Montoya to whom he had vowed to protect Romero. Just as Brett repeatedly betrays Jake with her licentious conduct, so he betrays the innkeeper – but what is more, he betrays his own sense of conduct and code of behaviour. By stepping aside, Jake, the steer, allows Brett, the bull, to conquer the matador. His appearance in Madrid at her summons in the final, necessarily anticlimactic, section of the novel reflects his enduring enslavement to her and is proof of the repetitive cycle of their feckless lives. For Jake and Brett, scarred by war, severed by exile and perplexed by modernity, life brings with it no ultimate climax, only yearning and disillusionment.

F. SCOTT FITZGERALD

Born in St Paul, Minnesota, in 1896 and educated at Princeton, from which he never graduated, F. Scott Fitzgerald was not merely the author of numerous well-received short stories, screenplays and novels, but one of the first genuine literary celebrities. Influenced by European ideas and culture despite his brief stay in Paris, Fitzgerald's stories often appeared in such fashionable periodicals as the *Smart Set*, *Vanity Fair* and the *Saturday Evening Post*, chronicling the mood and the manners of the time; these were later collected in *Flappers and Philosophers* (1920) and *Tales of the Jazz Age* (1922). His first novel, *This Side of Paradise* (1920), made him instantly famous and shortly after its publication he married the beautiful and glamorous Zelda Sayre. Together they embarked on a course of high-living, big-spending and party-going, becoming representative figures of the Jazz Age. They were regularly thrown out of five-star hotels and caused a scandal by dancing on tables, cartwheeling in the streets and jumping into the fountain in Washington Square in New York. But it could not last.

By the early 1930s Zelda was suffering from a mental breakdown and Scott was feeling the effects of their increasingly violent lives; his novel *Tender is the Night* (1934) reflects, through the story of the American psychiatrist Dick Diver and his schizophrenic wife Nicole, his sense of impending disaster. With its Riviera setting and cast of predominantly idle, wealthy expatriates, it was not well received in a nation afflicted by the Great Depression, and Fitzgerald's own 'crack-up' accelerated as Zelda failed to recover. By 1936 the title of his book *The Crack-Up* drew an explicit parallel between his own disintegrating life and the plight of his nation. By the end of the decade Fitzgerald had become a Hollywood hack, and in 1940, sunk in alcoholism, he died of a massive heart attack.

It was Fitzgerald's best-loved book, *The Great Gatsby*, which confirmed his place in the pantheon of American writers. More than perhaps any other book of the century, it has the reputation of being a 'Great American Novel', not least because the themes of self-invention, material success and hollow glamour cut to the heart of the American Dream. Curiously, though, *The Great Gatsby* attracted remarkably little praise when it was first published on 10 April 1925. 'F. Scott Fitzgerald's Latest a Dud', declared the *New York World*, while the *New York Evening World*'s reviewer concluded: 'We are quite convinced after reading *The Great Gatsby* that Mr Fitzgerald is not one of the great American writers of today'.[47] Even the British critic L. P. Hartley, himself a fine novelist, considered the book 'a piece of mere naughtiness', remarking that:

> Mr. Scott Fitzgerald deserves a good shaking. Here is an unmistakeable talent unashamed of making itself a motley to the view. *The Great Gatsby* is an absurd story, whether considered as romance, melodrama, or plain record of New York high life . . . [Fitzgerald's] imagination is febrile and his emotion over strained . . .[48]

It was only after Fitzgerald's death, in 1940, that the critical tide began to turn, with the novel's reputation, like the eponymous Gatsby, undergoing a kind of rebirth.

Among many important essays in reviving the novel's reputation was Arthur Mizener's piece 'F. Scott Fitzgerald 1896–1940: The Poet of Borrowed Time', published in 1946. Mizener not only thought that Fitzgerald's impressionistic method was reminiscent of Joseph Conrad, he considered the novel 'a kind of tragic pastoral', setting up a powerful contrast between the sophisticated, corrupt urban East and the virtuous simplicity of the rural West.[49] Even more significant, though, was William Troy's essay for *Accent* magazine, 'Scott Fitzgerald – The Authority of Failure', which had been published twelve months earlier. Troy was the first critic to make the case that Fitzgerald was deeply influenced by T. S. Eliot – who had himself praised *The Great Gatsby* as 'the first step that American fiction has taken since Henry James'.[50] As Troy saw it, the novel successfully achieved Eliot's 'objective correlative', a term the poet had coined to describe how a combination of words or situations are used to elicit an emotional experience within the reader. And for Troy, the book properly belonged in the company of Eliot's *The Waste Land* (1922), since it was not just telling an *American* story but embracing a universal mythology:

> The legendary Jay Gatsby [is] one of the few truly mythological creations in our recent literature – for what is mythology but this same process of projected wish-fulfilment carried out on a larger scale by the whole consciousness of a race? Indeed, before we are quite through with him, Gatsby becomes much more than a mere exorcizing of whatever false elements of the American dream Fitzgerald felt within himself: he becomes a vast symbol of America itself, dedicated to 'the service of a vast, vulgar and meretricious beauty'.[51]

Thanks partly to Mizener and Troy, the reputation of *The Great Gatsby* now underwent a dramatic transformation. Like Gatsby himself, the novel found itself lifted from the ranks of the mediocre to the level of greatness, becoming a myth in its own right. There is, of course, a lovely irony in this. The novel turns on the re-invention of the self, but it is also an exploration of the possibilities and perils of illusion and self-delusion. It revels in the gaudy gorgeousness of the Jazz Age, yet it simultaneously reveals the rot beneath the myths of decadent indulgence. And if *Gatsby* is, as

Troy suggests, 'a mythological creation', it is also a supreme exercise in demythologising, in tearing down the dreams and promises with which modern American capitalism veils its own hypocrisies.

The Great Gatsby is a recollection of events that took place in the summer of 1922. Jay Gatsby, who apparently began life as Jimmy Gatz, has enjoyed an extraordinary ascent from farm boy to student to fisherman, from first mate for the rich benefactor Dan Cody to the rich and decorated ex-major Jay Gatsby. He believes that money will win back his lost love, Daisy Buchanan, although he has obtained his money by shady means (probably bootlegging). When the novel begins, all of this has already happened; we enter the story *in medias res* alongside Nick Carraway, Daisy's cousin and Gatsby's neighbour, and we watch as the characters' lives become increasingly entangled. From the beginning there are a number of parallels between Nick and Gatsby: both, it seems, desire success, both are educated and both are former soldiers (though the revelation of Gatsby's lies casts doubt on the veracity of his military service). But soon Nick realises that the world he desires is founded upon ambiguities and insincerity. Jay's stories are false and those that swirl around him are laden with error and rumour. Many characters, such as Jay, Daisy, Tom, Myrtle, lead either disingenuous or adulterous lives, and Jordan, the woman Nick believes he loves, is a cheat and a liar. And in their cynicism, their vacuity and their selfishness – as in their glamour and their vast wealth – all these characters are compelling symbols of American society in the Jazz Age.

As William Troy pointed out, the shadow looming unmistakeably over Fitzgerald's novel is that of Eliot's *The Waste Land*, which had been published just three years earlier and is perhaps the most monumental and influential example of post-war modernist cynicism.[52] Traces of the poem are littered throughout the text: there are references to valleys of ashes and wasteland heaps; Daisy is a kind of belladonna; Nick refers to Gatsby's quest for Daisy as the 'following of a grail'; and the novel is full of images of 'all-seeing' characters.[53] For Fitzgerald, as for Eliot, the character of the 'seer' is absolutely critical. In *The Waste Land*, Tiresias is an androgynous figure who sees past, present and future, allowing him to narrate for the reader. In *Gatsby*, meanwhile, an owl-eyed man regularly pops up uttering truths: for instance, he appears in the library at the party, and is one of the few mourners at Gatsby's funeral. In *Gatsby*, though, the seer is updated to fit into a 1920s setting: instead of Tiresias, therefore, we have the oculist Dr Eckleberg, hovering like a spectre (through his billboards) over the modern metropolis: a wasteland, a valley of ashes.

What made *The Waste Land* so influential was its role in disinterring, dismantling and reinventing the myths underpinning Western civilisation. Here too, *Gatsby* follows suit, although in this case the myths are strongly flavoured with the heady atmosphere of American society in the Jazz Age. Perhaps above all, the novel actively exposes the corruption beneath the myth of success embedded in American culture (the so-called American Dream) at the time. A great self-mythologiser himself, Fitzgerald explores the means whereby an individual or a nation invents its own history, its own identity and selfhood, and deliberately integrates such processes into the narrative itself. So Jay Gatsby, to take an obvious example, is wreathed in myth and mystery. Although the title character, he is absent for much of the first part of the novel, playing the part of the mystery man, until he introduces himself at one of his own parties: 'I'm Gatsby' (p. 49) – a line fraught with ambiguity. But the most explicit reference to his mythic status comes from Nick: 'Jay Gatsby of West Egg, Long Island, sprang from his Platonic conception of himself. He was a son of God' (p. 95). There is, of course, a contradiction here: on the one hand Gatsby is the self-made man, yet on the other he is 'a son of God'. The ambiguity compounds the mystery. And indeed the ambiguity of his origins is insisted upon throughout: even Tom Buchanan calls him 'Mr. Nobody from Nowhere' (p. 123), and while Nick discovers a great deal about the title character, it is never easy to tell fact from fiction, or to dispel the swirl of apocryphal stories that circulate around him.

All of this talk of myths and mystery is underpinned by a series of religious references. For instance, Gatsby himself perceives his love of Daisy as a quasi-religious quest: he describes his wait outside the Buchanan house as 'a sacred vigil'. Meanwhile, Nick describes Gatsby's romantic obsession as 'the following of a grail' (p. 142) and makes repeated references to Gatsby's supernatural power for transforming the ordinary into the glittering and the gorgeous: for instance, the moon is described as having been produced 'like the supper, no doubt, out of a caterer's basket' (p. 44). Even the natural world is at the behest of Gatsby's money. A series of biblical connotations and allusions to Gatsby as a Christ-figure are also implicit throughout: obviously, Gatsby's liquor-producing abilities at the party are reminiscent of the wedding feast at Cana, where Christ transformed water into wine; it is only after the last supper, after midnight, that Gatsby appears; the murder near the end of the novel occurs at three o'clock; and three days later, Gatsby's father appears on the scene to resurrect his son's identity as James Gatz. There is also, of course, Gatsby's uncanny ability to appear and disappear; he is frequently described by Nick as luminous and glowing; and when he first comes to see Daisy at Nick's house he performs minor miracles throughout the day in preparation for her visit, and then appears dressed in the celestial colours of white, gold and silver.

The novel also contains numerous references to Gatsby's place in the American past, most notably in the references to the Declaration of Independence on the opening page and in the final paragraphs, in which Carraway evokes the Dutch sailors who, on seeing America for the first time, shared Gatsby's wonder and innocence at the opportunities offered by the New World. As the critic J. F. Callahan points out, October is not only the month that Daisy and Gatsby shared their love, it was also the month in which Columbus discovered the Americas. Thus Gatsby's attempt to recapture the emotions of October can easily be seen as a part of a wider cultural desire to recapture the lost innocence of the past.[54] On top of that, when Gatsby is set in a purely American context, there are obvious parallels with legendary fictional heroes such as James Fenimore Cooper's Natty Bumppo or Mark Twain's Huckleberry Finn, who are the embodiments of characteristics seen as vital to the American sense of self, from personal freedom and self-reliance to individualism and self-invention. Gatsby, as the critic Richard Chase has argued, clearly belongs in this tradition: 'although he is treated with more irony than they . . . he shares their ideal of innocence, escape and the purely personal code of conduct'. And as Chase observes:

> if [the novel] is a myth about America, then it is about America's failure to live up to its stated ideals and to its past of frontier and pioneer. While Natty and Huck had a frontier or a territory to which they could escape, Gatsby has nowhere; significantly in the novel he moves from West to East, reversing the pattern of the pioneer and the settler, and thereby indicating that the dream of individual freedom from institutions and settlements is over.[55]

Since Gatsby is a *failed* frontiersman, his role is to deflate the myths of nationhood, prosperity and individualism. And this, of course, is a classic modernist tactic: for Eliot and Joyce, the whole point of engaging with myths was to show their flaws and failings, to expose their vacuity, to strip down their hollowness, to reveal the nothingness behind the facades.

In many ways *Gatsby* is a novel of double vision. It not only offers a dual perspective through the character-narrator, it offers a vision of two islands (East and West Egg) and two societies (gritty Manhattan and glamorous Long Island), the world of the rich alongside the valley of ashes. Seeing is, as already explained, a key theme of the book, from the presiding figure of Dr Eckleberg to the recurring character of Owl Eyes. Beyond this there is the double vision of the author, namely Fitzgerald's ability, as Malcolm Cowley observes, to hold and suspend a series of opposed ideas before the reader: the simultaneous promise and demise of the American dream, a sense of possibility and limitation, profundity and meaninglessness.[56] Nick Carraway is crucial to this double vision. Both inside and outside the story, both character and observer, Nick reveals he is 'simultaneously enchanted and repelled by the inexhaustible variety of life' (p. 37). Such ambiguity is, for Fitzgerald, the natural state of twentieth-century American life, suggesting a lack of ideals, beliefs, values and goals. It engenders a sense of nervous uneasiness or restlessness, which Nick attributes to the fact of his recent return from the war but which seems to affect every character in the novel. So Tom and Daisy drift from place to place, while Jordan's movements are described as restless, as are those of Gatsby himself, who, Nick observes, was 'never quite still' (p. 63).

When setting out to write the novel Fitzgerald had reread Conrad's preface to *The Nigger of the 'Narcissus'*, which outlines the necessity of placing the objects of the story vividly before the reader to create a truly rounded narrative world.[57] It is not surprising, then, that there is a precision and freshness to the novel's language, an emphasis on colour, shape and the animacy of objects, which develops the narrative tension and embodies the restlessness at the heart of the novel. What is also revealing, however, is the novel's awareness of its own condition as a work of artifice. For one thing, the novel is quite clearly a series of set-piece scenes, which in their presentation make the reader aware of a self-conscious author arranging his work into patterns. Second, Fitzgerald's chosen themes directly draw attention to his work as a piece of fiction: this is above all a story of *creation*. Gatsby creates a fictional persona for himself, while Fitzgerald creates a fictional character called Gatsby who, even within that fictional world, is a fabrication. This is especially clear in Chapter 3 when the owl-eyed man claims to be moved by Gatsby's capacity for realism, likening him to the dramatist David Belasco. This, of course, is not a testimony to Gatsby's 'realness' as Belasco is the creator of a *fictional* realism. The reality he presents is in fact an artifice, a fiction.

Third, this self-consciousness manifests itself around the 'swirls and eddies' of stories that make up the text (p. 43). Obviously, there are all the stories that surround Gatsby but the theme of storytelling is also enacted in the structure of the text: Jay tells his story, Nick's whole narrative is a story, Jordan tells stories about Jay and about Daisy's past, Myrtle wants to tell her story, and Daisy too has a story to tell. Finally, there are moments of acute meta-textuality, when Nick draws specific attention to the fact that he is telling a story: in Chapter 3, for example, he draws attention to the physical act of his writing. This self-consciousness in the text, combined with its themes and narrative, can readily be seen as an act of profound cynicism on the part of the author, rendering everything, the whole narrative and the whole world of Jay and Nick and Daisy, impermanent, transient and fake. Nothing better suggests the boredom, disappointment and faithlessness at the heart of the glittering Jazz Age than the fact that its most iconic text, one of the most acclaimed novels in American history, draws attention to its own status as a figment of the imagination, a story of lies that is itself a calculated, self-conscious fiction.

DJUNA BARNES

Ambiguous sexualities, complex modernities and exiled Americans all feature in Djuna Barnes's dark and strange novel *Nightwood* (1936). The story chronicles the effect of an enigmatic young American woman, Robin Vote, on three characters: Baron Felix Volkbein, Nora Flood and Jenny Petherbridge.[58] The events and lives of all characters are overseen by the bizarre, Tiresias-like figure (not unlike the owl-eyed seer in *The Great Gatsby*) of Dr Matthew Mighty-Grain-of-Salt-Dante O'Connor, an unlicensed, cross-dressing Irish-American gynaecologist. Robin, the Baronin after she marries von Volkbein, is the mute heart of the novel. She inspires the story but is barely present in it (even when we first meet her she is unconscious), settling into the lives of the various characters only to disappear once they have come to love her. Indeed, it is her absence which ties together the various strands of the narrative, implying, perhaps, that at the heart of the modernist novel is a cultural, spiritual and emotional void.

Certainly Barnes was critical of many of the classifying discourses of literary modernism, which she felt inhibited rather than facilitated freedom of expression. In *Nightwood* she is unequivocal in her sense of the degeneracy of modernity; there is nothing redemptive in this novel. The reunion of the lovers in the final chapter, 'The Possessed', is highly ambiguous and disturbing in its depiction of bestiality. And in what even now is a deeply shocking image, even the child Robin bears the Baron is palsied and physically defective, a symbol of the author's sense of the hopelessness of future generations. Robin's effect on those around her is not unlike that of Lady Brett Ashley: arresting in her appearance (though boyish rather than curvaceous), sexually ambiguous and psychologically vulnerable, she reduces individuals to quaking, shivering wrecks as they struggle with their unrequited love for her. And just as Brett's discarded lovers in *The Sun Also Rises* talk through their heartbreak with the central figure of Jake Barnes, Felix and Nora discuss their emotional travails with Dr O'Connor, who, unlike the silent and chivalrous Barnes, is loquacious and garrulous and seems to have no clear code of honour guiding him through his tawdry life of thievery and fakery. Indeed, O'Connor uses the talking cure sessions he holds with Felix and Nora as much to reveal his own hidden desires and lamentations as to assist his friends.

Nightwood is undoubtedly Barnes's masterpiece. Lauded by T. S. Eliot for its beautiful phrasing and brilliance of wit and style, and compared by Edwin Muir to Joyce for its powerful style and rich, exact and vivid imagery, the novel anticipates the work of Samuel Beckett in its depiction of lonely, homeless individuals who speak to each other in monotonous non sequiturs. The book was the last novel Barnes ever wrote and many critics have commented that it represents the last gasp of a modernist art form which has exhausted itself.[59] In this regard, the comparison to Beckett is apposite for he, too, has been described as one of the last modernists, and there is a sense of imminent collapse both formally and at the level of characterisation throughout his writing.

In her early career, however, Barnes was indefatigable. A star reporter for *McCall's* magazine when she arrived in Paris in 1921 to research a story on expatriate writers, she had already written for almost every New York newspaper on a range of popular and polemical topics. Katherine Biers observes that Barnes inhabited 'a varied repertoire of roles for her public . . . from flamboyant female "stunt journalist" and investigative reporter in the tradition of Nellie Bly to straightforward chronicler of local color and notable events around the city' (p. 239).[60] Famously, in 1914 she agreed to be forcibly fed in order to report for the *New York World Magazine* on the shocking abuses endured by hunger-striking suffragists, deliberately exposing and embracing the fetishised image of the strong feminist body strapped down and forced to consume against her will. Ever provocative, she later interviewed James Joyce for *Vanity Fair* and while deeply in awe of the 'most significant figure in literature today', she admitted in a later piece, 'Vagaries Malicieux' (1922), to missing part of their conversation after losing concentration when he was speaking.[61] The influence of Joyce is clear in *Nightwood*, from its uncompromising portrayal of sexuality to the frequently bawdy tones in the monologues of

O'Connor. Certainly, the doctor's ramblings tend toward a Molly Bloom-like stream of consciousness, both in their often unpunctuated fluidity and in their content. While Joyce's sleepy Molly dreams as she sits on her chamber pot, lamenting all that is lost of her girlhood hopes and lovers, O'Connor, ostensibly speaking to Nora, tells of his dream to have a 'high soprano' voice and 'deep corn curls to my bum, with a womb as big as the king's kettle, and a bosom as high as the bowsprit of a fishing schooner'.[62] And just as Molly's unbounded sexuality shocked early readers (and outraged the American censors until 1933), O'Connor's transvestism bewildered and titillated much of Barnes's readership. Indeed, Eliot, her publisher at Faber and Faber, felt forced to tone down much of the language and sexual content before the book was released.

The emphasis on sexual identity is, perhaps, one of the most modern aspects of the novel and certainly surpasses anything that Barnes's American expatriate contemporaries were doing in their writing. Uncompromisingly and unsentimentally, she focuses her story on the love between two women. While hints of the homosocial bonds of men are clearly discernible in the work of Hemingway and Fitzgerald and even in the more conservative Willa Cather, the portrayal of lesbian love was almost unheard of until the publication of Radclyffe Hall's *The Well of Loneliness* in 1928. However the text does not present a muted or tortured representation of forbidden love, nor does it celebrate the supposed sexual liberation of the bohemian milieu. Indeed, there remains a question mark about Barnes's own attitudes and politics, and throughout her life she strove to be ambiguous. Despite her long, often passionate and somewhat hopeless relationship with Thelma Wood and a series of same-sex relationships, she denied that she was a lesbian, referred to homosexual men as 'pansies', and toward the end of her life reported that she had not wanted to 'make a lot of little lesbians'.[63]

These personal statements and her failure to take a strong position on sexual identity in the novel seem to indicate another direction in Barnes's work, a strong refutation of all sexual and gender identity categories. As Susana S. Martin astutely notes, Barnes was happy to discuss her affairs with women but disliked the thought of being categorised. In a 1936 letter to Ottoline Morrell, Barnes wrote, 'I am not offended in the least to be thought a lesbian – it's simply that I'm very reticent about my personal life'.[64] For Barnes, being labelled a 'lesbian' enters the individual in question into a particular cultural discourse over which she has no control. Resisting such categorisation, Barnes presents *Nightwood* as what Jane Marcus calls 'a book of communal resistances of underworld outsiders to domination'.[65] And as another critic, Diane Chisholm, puts it, the book is a statement of 'defiance of [the] rationalization and *embourgeoisement*' of sexual identity which she attributed in large part to Freudian theories of sexual deviancy and which she had observed in recent literary treatments of sexual outsiders.[66]

This resistance is evident in a particular passage from 'Go Down, Matthew' in which the Doctor, never once using the word 'lesbian' but preferring Krafft-Ebbing's term 'invert', argues with Nora about the nature and identity of same-sex sexuality:

> What is this love we have for the invert, boy or girl? It was they who were spoken of in every romance that we ever read. The girl lost, what is she but the Prince found? . . . And the pretty lad who is a girl, what but the prince-princess in point lace – neither one and half the other, the painting on the fan! We were impaled in our childhood upon them as they rode through our primers, the sweetest lie of all, not come to be in boy or girl, for in the girl it is the prince, and in the boy it is the girl that makes a prince a prince – and not a man. (p. 136)

As voluble as ever, the Doctor resists the implementation of sexual categories through rhetorical indirection. He refuses to accept (perhaps necessarily given his unlicensed status) his power to name and categorise, denying the practically minded Nora the diagnostic answers she seeks. In this regard, Barnes resists one of the dominant discourses of 1920s American culture, namely Freudianism and its implicit categories; and many critics argue that O'Connor is a satirical version of the psychologist and the fictional doctor's ramblings are an inversion of the so-called talking cure. Indeed, by way of the Doctor's failure to pathologise sexual identity, Barnes denies the Freudian notion of same-sex desire as an illness or aberration caused by trauma.

This negotiation of identity politics is also evident in the character of the Jewish Baron, Felix Volkbein, whose story opens the novel. The reader is given a long account of Felix's birth to Hedvig Volkbein, 'a Viennese woman of great strength and military beauty' (p. 1), who dies upon delivery of her child. We learn that Guido Volkbein, the Baron's father, died six months before the birth of his son, and was 'a Jew of Italian descent [who] had been both a gourmet and a dandy, never appearing in public without the ribbon of some quite unknown distinction tinging his buttonhole with a faint thread' (p. 1). Immediately, Barnes sets up a vague indeterminacy in her portrait of Guido: he is both a gourmet and a dandy; his ribbon is of 'unknown distinction' and attached to his jacket by a 'faint thread'. This strategy of vagueness extends to the history of his baronial title and his racial identity. Like O'Connor, Guido constructs for himself a genealogy and a past based on fakery: the family portraits are posed by 'intrepid and ancient actors', he adopts 'the sign of the cross', and he swaps his national identity for that of an Austrian (p. 3). For Guido, the Jewish history he seeks to escape is one of a subjugation and degradation made manifest in 'the ordinance of 1468 . . . demanding that, with a rope about its neck, Guido's race should run in the Corso for the amusement of the Christian populace' (p. 2). And so he steps outside history and creates a new identity and a new life for himself and his descendants. Felix inherits this unstable sense of identity and stands outside the discourse of history with no parents, no accurate records of his past and two portraits. Felix's lack of history renders him a 'wandering Jew' who seems to be everywhere but from nowhere (p. 7). Exiled and without a firm identity, he clings 'to his title to dazzle his own estrangement' (p. 11) and bows down to anybody who might be somebody in the hope that 'the great past might mend a little . . . if he succumbed and gave homage'.

Unlike the Doctor, therefore, the partially blind Felix, though drawn to the 'odd' world of the 'circus and the theatre', 'sham salons' drenched in a 'splendid and reeking falsification', seeks solidity and a home (p. 11), and takes no pleasure in his peripatetic nature or his indeterminate identity. Mairéad Hanrahan notes that 'the Barnesian Jew suffers from so total a lack of identity, so unredeemable a confusion that any attempt to redeem his condition only aggravates it'.[67] So when Felix attempts to solidify his identity by marrying Robin, their union only worsens his unstable sense of identity and culminates in the freakish family he forms with his disabled son and the circus performer Frau Mann. Through Felix, Barnes demonstrates the impossibility of stable identity. Constantly undermining permanent categorisation, she presents the figures of the Jew and the lesbian (and the queer transvestite O'Connor) as supreme exiles, lost beyond the controlling forces of identity politics.

NOTES

1. Ezra Pound, *Hugh Selwyn Mauberley* (Sussex: BiblioLife, [1920] 2009), p. 13.
2. Malcolm Cowley, *Exile's Return: A Literary Odyssey of the 1920s* (New York: Viking, 1956), p. 9.
3. She later denied the statement and after it became a cliché Hemingway tried to have it removed from *The Sun Also Rises* (1926). He reveals the origins of the term in *A Moveable Feast* (1964).
4. Cited in Matthew J. Bruccoli, *Some Sort of Epic Grandeur: The Life of F. Scott Fitzgerald* (London: Hodder and Stoughton, 1981), p. 236.
5. Gertrude Stein, 'The Gradual Making of *The Making of Americans*' (1935), in *Selected Writings*, ed. Carl Van Vechten (New York: Random House, 1946), p. 226.
6. See Bruccoli, *Some Sort of Epic Grandeur*, p. 75.
7. James Joyce, *A Portrait of the Artist as a Young Man* (London: Penguin, [1916] 1965), p. 276.
8. 'Mr Harding's War on War', *Pittsburgh Press* (12 November 1921), p. 6.
9. Pound, *Hugh Selwyn Mauberley*, p. 12.
10. Thorstein Veblen, 'Dementia Praecox', from *The Freeman* (21 June 1922), cited in Loren Baritz, *The Culture of the Twenties* (London: Macmillan, 1970), p. 33.
11. Archibald MacLeish, 'Two Poems from the War' in *Collected Poems, 1917–1982* (New York: Houghton Mifflin, 1990), p. 40.

12. Ernest Hemingway, *A Farewell to Arms* (London: Arrow, [1929] 2004), p. 165.
13. Ernest Hemingway, *Death in the Afternoon* (London: Vintage, [1932] 2000), p. 2.
14. Chip Rhodes, *Structures of the Jazz Age: Mass Culture, Progressive Education and Racial Disclosures in American Modernism* (London: Verso, 1998), p. 47.
15. F. Scott Fitzgerald, 'Echoes of the Jazz Age', in *The Crack-Up: With Other Pieces and Stories* (Harmondsworth: Penguin, 1965), p. 10.
16. See the 1921 US Census report: http://www2.census.gov/prod2/statcomp/documents/1921-02.pdf (accessed 22 January 2012).
17. F. Scott Fitzgerald, *The Crack-Up*, ed. Edmund Wilson (New York: New Directions, 1956), p. 16.
18. For many of the details of this account of the 1920s I have been reliant upon the following excellent studies: Edward D. Berkowitz, *Mass Appeal: The Formative Age of the Movies, Radio and T.V.* (Cambridge: Cambridge University Press, 2010); Hugh Brogan, *The Penguin History of the United States of America* (London: Penguin, 1985); Susan Currell, *American Culture in the 1920s* (Edinburgh: Edinburgh University Press, 2009); David Reynolds, *America: Empire of Liberty* (London: Penguin, 2009); Thomas Streissguth, *The Roaring Twenties* (New York: Infobase Publishing, 2007).
19. See Martin Halliwell, 'The Modernist Atlantic: New York, Chicago, and Europe', in Peter Brooker, Andrzej Gasiorek, Deborah Longworth and Andrew Thacker (eds), *The Oxford Handbook of Modernisms* (Oxford: Oxford University Press, 2010), pp. 725–39; Martin Halliwell, 'Tourists or Exiles? American Modernists in Paris in the 1920s and 1950s', *Nottingham French Studies*, 44.3 (Autumn 2005), pp. 54–86.
20. John Dos Passos, cited in Virginia Spencer Carr, *Dos Passos: A Life* (New York: Northwestern University Press, 2004), p. 273.
21. Sherwood Anderson, 'Preface' to *Geography and Plays* (1922), reproduced as 'The Work of Gertrude Stein', in Richard

Kostelanetz (ed.), *Gertrude Stein Advanced: An Anthology of Criticism* (London: McFarland, 1990), p. 2.

22. James Thurber, *Collecting Himself: James Thurber On Writers and Writing, Humor and Himself*, ed. Michael J. Rosen (London: Harper Collins, 1989), p. 32.
23. For an excellent and authoritative study of Stein's debts to James see: Ronald B. Levinson, 'Gertrude Stein, William James, and Grammar', *American Journal of Psychology*, 54.1 (January 1941), pp. 124–8.
24. William James, 'The Stream of Thought', in *The Principles of Psychology* (New York: Cosimo, 2007), vol. 1, p. 236, p. 241.
25. Gertrude Stein, 'Poetry and Grammar', in *Look at Me Now and Here I Am: Writings and Lectures, 1909–45*, ed. Patricia Meyerowitz (London: Penguin, 1971), p. 125.
26. Gertrude Stein, *Tender Buttons* (Mineola: Dover Publications, [1914] 1997), p. 5.
27. Gertrude Stein, 'Poetry and Grammar', p. 125, p. 145.
28. Ibid. p. 127.
29. James, 'The Stream of Thought', pp. 245–6.
30. Gertrude Stein, *The Autobiography of Alice B. Toklas* (London: Penguin, [1933] 2001), p. 233.
31. Gertrude Stein, *The Making of Americans* (Normal: Dalkey Archive Press, [1925] 1995), p. 708. Subsequent references will appear in the text.
32. Lisa Ruddick reads the section as a scene of 'patricidal rage' in *Reading Gertrude Stein: Body, Text, Gnosis* (Ithaca: Cornell University Press, 1991), p. 58.
33. Furthermore, G. F. Mitrano observes that this scene is a reworked epigraph from Aristotle's *Nichomachean Ethics* via Montaigne, which Stein uses at the beginning of her novel to undermine the foundational Oedipal narrative. See G. F. Mitrano, *Gertrude Stein: Woman Without Qualities* (Aldershot: Ashgate, 2005), p. 33.
34. Gertrude Stein, 'Plays', in *Look at Me Now and Here I Am: Writings and Lectures 1909–45*, p. 66.
35. Gertrude Stein, 'An American and France', in *Lectures in America* (New York: Beacon Press, 1985), p. 61.
36. Ernest Hemingway, *Death in the Afternoon*, pp. 1–2.

37. Malcolm Cowley, *A Second Flowering: Works and Days of the Lost Generation* (London: Andre Deutsch, 1973), p. 49.
38. Ernest Hemingway, *Death in the Afternoon*, p. 2.
39. See *Ernest Hemingway: Selected Letters, 1917–1961*, ed. Carlos Baker (London: Granada, 1981), p. 446, pp. 463–5.
40. The novel was published in the UK as *Fiesta* and in the US as *The Sun Also Rises.* The edition I am using is: Ernest Hemingway, *Fiesta: The Sun Also Rises* (London: Arrow, [1926] 2004). All subsequent references will appear in the text.
41. See *Ernest Hemingway: Selected Letters, 1917–1961*, p. 239, p. 240.
42. Cited in James Mellow, *Hemingway: A Life without Consequences* (Boston: Houghton Mifflin, 1992), pp. 334–6.
43. Cowley, *A Second Flowering*, p. 71.
44. See *Ernest Hemingway: Selected Letters, 1917–1961*, p. 229.
45. See Linda Wagner-Martin (ed.), *Ernest Hemingway's The Sun Also Rises: A Casebook* (New York: Oxford University Press, 2002) and Linda Wagner-Martin (ed.), *New Essays on The Sun Also Rises* (New York: Cambridge University Press, 1990).
46. See Carlos Baker, *Hemingway: The Writer as Artist* (Princeton: Princeton University Press, 1972).
47. Cited in Jackson R. Bryer, *F. Scott Fitzgerald: The Critical Reception* (New York: Butt Franklin, 1978), p. 195, p. 196.
48. L. P. Hartley, 'New Fiction', *Saturday Review* (20 February 1926), pp. 234–5.
49. Arthur Mizener, 'F. Scott Fitzgerald 1896–1940: The Poet of Borrowed Time' (1946), reprinted in Alfred Kazin (ed.), *F. Scott Fitzgerald: The Man and His Work* (New York: World Publishing, 1962), pp. 23–4.
50. See 'Three Letters About *The Great Gatsby*', in F. Scott Fitzgerald, *The Crack-Up*, ed. Edmund Wilson (New York: New Directions, 1993), p. 310.
51. William Troy, 'Scott Fitzgerald – The Authority of Failure' (1945), in Arthur Mizener (ed.), *F. Scott Fitzgerald* (Englewood Cliffs: Prentice Hall, 1963), pp. 20–4.
52. For an excellent study of Fitzgerald's debts to Eliot see Letha Audhuy's '*The Waste Land*: Myth and Symbols in *The Great Gatsby*', in Harold Bloom (ed.), *Modern Critical Interpretations*

of The Great Gatsby (New York: Chelsea House, 1986), pp. 43–58.

53. F. Scott Fitzgerald, *The Great Gatsby* (London: Penguin, [1925] 1990), p. 142. Subsequent references will appear in the text.
54. See John F. Callahan, *The Illusions of a Nation: Myth and History in the Novels of F. Scott Fitzgerald* (Urbana: University of Illinois Press, 1972).
55. Richard Chase, *The American Novel and its Traditions* (New York: Doubleday, 1957), p. 165.
56. See Malcolm Cowley, 'Third Act and Epilogue', *New Yorker* (30 June 1945). Available online at: http://fitzgerald.narod.ru/critics-eng/cowley-3act.html (accessed 22 January 2012).
57. F. Scott Fitzgerald, 'Introduction to the Great Gatsby', in Ernest Lockridge (ed.), *Twentieth Century Interpretations of The Great Gatsby* (Englewood Cliffs: Prentice Hall, 1968), p. 109.
58. See Lynn DeVore for an excellent background analysis of Robin Vote, Felix and Nora. Through extensive detective work, DeVore identifies Robin as Baroness Elsa von Freytag-Loringhoven, whom Barnes first met in 1918. Felix is identified as the Canadian writer Felix Paul Greve. See Lynn DeVore, 'The Backgrounds of *Nightwood*: Robin, Felix, and Nora', *Journal of Modern Literature*, 10.1 (March 1983), pp. 71–90.
59. See, for instance, Charles Baxter's 'A Self-Consuming Light: *Nightwood* and the Crisis of Modernism', *Journal of Modern Literature*, 3.5 (July 1974), pp. 1175–87.
60. Katherine Biers, 'Djuna Barnes Makes a Specialty of Crime: Violence and the Visual in Her Early Journalism', in Ann L. Ardis and Leslie W. Lewis (eds), *Women's Experience of Modernity, 1875–1945* (Baltimore: Johns Hopkins University Press, 2003), p. 239.
61. See Phillip Herring, 'Djuna Barnes Remembers James Joyce', *James Joyce Quarterly*, 30.1 (Fall 1992), pp. 113–17.
62. Djuna Barnes, *Nightwood* (New York: New Directions, [1936] 1961), p. 91. All subsequent references will appear in the text.
63. For an excellent account of Barnes's relationship with Wood

see Philip Herring's 'Djuna Barnes and Thelma Wood: The Vengeance of *Nightwood*', *Journal of Modern Literature*, 18.1 (Winter 1992), pp. 5–18. On Barnes's comments regarding sexuality see Susana S. Martins, 'Gender Trouble and Lesbian Desire in Djuna Barnes's *Nightwood*', *Frontiers: A Journal of Women's Studies*, 20.3 (1999), p. 109.

64. Cited in Mary Lynn Broe (ed.), *Silence and Power: A Reevaluation of Djuna Barnes* (Carbondale: Southern Illinois University Press, 1991), p. 53.
65. Jane Marcus, 'Laughing at Leviticus: *Nightwood* as Woman's Circus Epic', in Broe (ed.), *Silence and Power*, p. 221.
66. Diane Chisholm, 'Obscene Modernism: ErosNoir and the Profane Illumination of Djuna Barnes', *American Literature*, 69.1 (1997), p. 195.
67. Mairéad Hanrahan, 'Djuna Barnes's *Nightwood*: The Cruci-Fiction of the Jew', *Paragraph: A Journal of Modern Critical Theory*, 24.1 (March 2001), p. 32.

CHAPTER 5

'When Harlem Was in Vogue': African American Modernism

In the 1920s, few places in the United States carried more glamour and allure than Harlem. As the writer Langston Hughes remarked in his autobiography *The Big Sea* (1940), this was the era 'when Harlem was in vogue': the so-called Harlem Renaissance, when one little corner of Manhattan became suffused with the heady expectations of the African Americans who migrated northwards in the late 1910s and early 1920s.[1] As the neighbourhood's fame rose, so white Americans, too, were drawn to the city's jazz-suffused nightspots, to dance the Charleston at clubs like Small's Paradise, Connie's Inn and the Cotton Club, or to watch shows like *Shuffle Along* (1921) and *Runnin' Wild* (1923). Indeed, for Hughes, it was the success of such shows that launched the so-called renaissance. As he saw it, this was an era defined by the literary, visual and performing arts, rather than by any of the political events of the day. 'Certainly', he wrote, 'it was the musical revue, *Shuffle Along*, that gave a scintillating send-off to that Negro vogue in Manhattan, which reached its peak just before the crash of 1929, the crash that sent Negroes, white folks, and all rolling down the hill toward the Works Progress Administration.'[2]

In fact, cultural commentators and literary critics have never managed to agree on a precise chronology for the Harlem Renaissance. Emily Bernard, for example, sees it as peaking between 1924 and 1929, and uses Charles S. Johnson's party at the Civic Club as the starting point, pointing out that it was at this event that the foundations for Alain Locke's edited volume, *The New Negro* (1925), were laid. By contrast, George Hutchinson stretches the era from 1918 to 1937, arguing that more cultural works were published in the 1930s than the 1920s, while David Levering Lewis persuasively makes the case that it ended in 1935, taking the Harlem riot of that year as an end point.[3] What seems clear, though, is that the seeds were sown in about 1919, when the Red Summer race riots, prompted by white working-class anger towards returning African American military veterans, and the influx of African Americans from the former slave states, were instrumental to the birth of the New Negro, which in turn fed into the development of the Harlem Renaissance. Writing in May 1919 in *The Crisis*, W. E. B. Du Bois seized on the moment:

> We return from the slavery of uniform which the world's madness demanded us to don to the freedom of civil garb. We stand again to look America squarely in the face and call a spade a spade. We sing: This country of ours, despite all its better souls have done and dreamed, is yet a shameful land.
>
> It *lynches* . . .
> It *disfranchises* . . .
> It encourages *ignorance* . . .
> It *steals* from us . . .
> It *insults* us . . .
> We *return*.
> We *return from fighting*.
> We *return fighting*.[4]

Du Bois's essay advocated and stirred a racial pride, embracing a New Negro identity, which would enable African Americans to work towards racial, social and political equality. Later, he even claimed not to 'care a damn for any art' other than that which did the work of racial uplift.[5]

For the black sociologist and civil rights activist Charles S. Johnson and others, the figure of the New Negro was absolutely crucial for black art. Indeed, Johnson equated his literary and editorial work on *The Book of American Negro Poetry* (1922) with his work for the National Association for the Advancement of Colored People (NAACP):

> The status of the Negro in the United States is more a question of national mental attitude toward the race than of actual conditions. And nothing will do more to change that mental attitude than a demonstration of intellectual parity by the Negro through the productions of literature and art.[6]

This faith in the redemptive power of literature was shared by Alain Locke, whose seminal *The New Negro* is commonly regarded as the handbook for the Harlem Renaissance. And in the introductory essay to the volume, entitled 'The New Negro', Locke claimed that art (especially the kind of works contained within the volume) provided new models of identity for the African American community, ushering in 'a new dynamic phase' and a 'spiritual emancipation'.[7]

Johnson's and Locke's belief in the liberating powers of the literary arts was very much at odds with the more militant politics of the day, epitomised by Marcus Garvey and Chandler Owen. As leader of the United Negro Improvement Association, a staunch Black Nationalist and proponent of Pan-Africanism, Marcus Garvey advocated a complete black exodus from the United States and a return to Africa. Meanwhile Owen, popularly known in Harlem as 'Lenin' to his comrade A. Philip Randolph's 'Trotsky', was a member of the Socialist Party of America and co-founder of *The Messenger*, a literary and political journal which described its mission as rising above the 'cringing demagogy' of the times and surpassing 'the cheap peanut politics' of the past. 'Patriotism', it declared, 'has no appeal to us'.[8] This disdain for patriotism was what separated the likes of Garvey and Owen from Johnson, Locke and Du Bois, who felt that there was a place for the black community in mainstream democratic American life.

Though by no means deferential in the manner of Booker T. Washington (indeed, as noted in Chapter 1, Du Bois presented an antithetical model of racial advancement to that of the Tuskegee leader), all three were sympathetic to the notion of racial harmony within the existent system. So in 'The New Negro',

Locke condemned 'quixotic radicalisms' (p. 11), equated 'Negro objectives' with the 'ideals of American institutions and democracy' (p. 10), and saw the success of the New Negro experiment as 'the fullest sharing of American culture and institutions' (p. 12). Similarly Johnson, who had worked as a consular diplomat in Venezuela and Nicaragua, was reticent about criticising white American social models and government structures, and had been instrumental in buoying African American support for Woodrow Wilson's presidential campaign in 1912 and subsequent bid to take the United States into the First World War. As the critic Jonathan W. Gray observes, the faith of Johnson and Locke in the American capitalist model clearly informed the selection of authors who feature in *The Book of American Negro Poetry* and *The New Negro*. Both, writes Gray, 'neutralize voices in the black community that might contest their assertions about the relationships between art and democracy' by deliberately excluding them from their respective anthologies.[9] In short, both attempted to present a model for racial equality and a black modernism which would be palatable to the white elite and the black masses.

The tension between radicalism and assimilation had, of course, been at the heart of American race relations for the previous twenty years, embodied in the relationship between Washington and Du Bois and their respective 'Men of Tuskegee' and Niagara movements. Even Du Bois was perceived as too moderate by younger Harlem Renaissance writers and thinkers such as Claude McKay and Le Roi Jones, who demanded 'pure' black forms of expression, often suffused with anger at a history of injustice. But in *The New Negro*, Locke, a firm follower of Du Bois, was keen to present an optimistic, forward-looking outlook. This vision is carefully outlined in his title essay, which pits the 'New Negro', a black invention, against the 'Old Negro', a decidedly white creation, described by Locke as 'more of a myth than a man' (p. 3). And while Locke's anthology is often regarded as the handbook for the Harlem Renaissance, it was itself a product of a much wider political context. Even the term 'New Negro' was not invented by Locke or his contributors, but had been used since the latter part of the nineteenth century to depict black identity during and after Reconstruction. Indeed, Du Bois and the Niagara Movement had articulated a clear New Negro ideology in their 1905 Declaration of Principles.[10]

Locke, however, used the term to describe a 'new psychology', a 'new spirit . . . awake in the masses' (p. 3), which he traced to the great migration out of the South, the associated issue of adjustment and the development of class structures amongst the transplanted population (pp. 5–6). As Locke put it:

> The day of 'aunties,' 'uncles' and 'mammies' is equally gone. Uncle Tom and Sambo have passed on, and even the 'Colonel' and 'George' play barnstorm roles from which they escape with relief once the public spotlight is off. The popular melodrama has played itself out, and it is time to scrap the fictions, garret the bogeys and settle down to a realistic facing of facts. (p. 5)

These facts included not only migration but an educated black population – Du Bois was a graduate of Harvard; Locke was the first black Rhodes scholar; and Johnson went on to be professor at New York University and Fisk University – ready to mobilise the masses into programmes of self-reliance, political leadership and cultural and economic prosperity.

The critic George Hutchinson has noted the importance of early twentieth-century American intellectual culture to the New Negro Movement, detailing the influence of philosophical pragmatism, cultural nationalism, New York print culture, literary regionalism, Robert Park's sociological theory of the race relations cycle and Franz Boas's anthropological ideas. In the politically charged summer of 1919, all these things helped to mould the New Negro Movement into the artistic phenomenon that was the Harlem Renaissance. For example, Zora Neale Hurston, one of the key female contributors to *The New Negro*, had worked with Franz Boas at Barnard College, and her ethnographic research clearly informs novels like *Jonah's Gourd Vine* (1934) and *Mules and Men* (1935), as well as 'Spunk' (1925), her contribution to Locke's collection. The novelist and poet Jean Toomer had corresponded with Sherwood Anderson and Waldo Frank about the development of a regional black American literature, while Charles Johnson, editor of *Opportunity: A Journal of Negro Life*, had studied directly under Robert Park. And Du Bois, of course, had been a student of William James at Harvard.

As we saw in Chapter 1, Du Bois had been inspired by pragmatist ideas about the plurality of the self and the contingency of reality, history and morality in developing the theories in *The Souls of Black Folk* (1903). As Hutchinson points out, one result was the relevance of Dewey's emphasis on the 'aesthetic quality of experience' – the means whereby lived intellectual realities have aesthetic qualities – to the development of the literature and art of the Harlem Renaissance. Aesthetic experience, for the pragmatist, is the relationship between each moment and the previous one, the coalescence and overall unity of a chain of moments. The meaning of any given experience, therefore, is built on the accumulation of singular moments or perceptions into a composite whole. However, crucial to the aesthetic experience is its *transference*; it is only through exchange that cultural integration can begin. Dewey had used the metaphor of the artist painting brush strokes on a canvas to demonstrate his point about the layering of moments into an overall experience. But on another level, too, Dewey saw art as crucial to the exchange and integration of experience. Since it is designed for public consumption, he argued, it thereby creates a link between the perceiver and the creator. And this integration of moments, of minute instances of perception or experiences, into an overarching 'aesthetic experience' informed the wider political outlook of Locke and Du Bois, emphasising the importance of the specifically African American experience to the wider democratic American experience, corresponding to Waldo Frank's notion of ethnic American identity as part of a wider stream of American cultural identity. So the art form created in the mind of the painter or the writer becomes inextricably associated with the politics of the outside world, giving it a purpose beyond its intrinsic value – and indeed this kind of erasure of divisions between internal and external realities encapsulates Dewey's philosophical aims. In short, art has a social and, in most cases, a political purpose.[11]

The tension between the political message and the intrinsic quality of art would come to dominate many discussions about African American art and literature, as the editorial choices of

Johnson and Locke show. For the black artist, difficult decisions would have to be made: which should come first, politics or poetry? For Du Bois, the only literature worth reading was that dedicated to the cause of uplift; for a writer like Countee Cullen, however, the answer was less clear. The shape of Cullen's verse structures often seems to relegate the actual content of his poetry to the sideline – although for Cullen the very contrast between content and poetic form contributed to the poetry's political import. That so much of the writing of the Harlem Renaissance is given over to the unique experience of being an African American indicates a deliberate decision to impress that experience onto the wider canvas of American life. It also suggests the desire to forge an intellectual link between the black writer or artist and the white reader or viewer, a technique not dissimilar to the appeal to a common humanity we see in eighteenth- and nineteenth-century slave narratives.

The other obvious question was whether avant-garde literary experiment or traditional realistic verisimilitude was best suited to the black experience. Again, this had a political context: avant-garde structures were often associated with expatriates who had deliberately turned away from the United States (for instance, Eliot and Pound), thus presenting a problem for an artist who wanted to bridge the gap between black and white America. On the other hand, the more traditional forms of poetry and fictional realism were rarely associated with the black experience. For the likes of Cullen and McKay, therefore, the use of, say, the sonnet was a deliberately political act, designed to show how traditional structures could encompass the black experience – although their critics argued that by accepting traditionally white structures, they had effectively enslaved their art.

An associated concern for many Harlem Renaissance artists was the issue of racial inheritance and its relevance for the new black writing of the early twentieth century. Carl Van Vechten explored this idea in his depiction of Hester Albright and her mother in his controversial novel *Nigger Heaven* (1926). The Albrights refuse to visit an exhibition of 'awfully vulgar' African wood carvings and are horrified when Webb Leverett breaks into a passionate rendition of a spiritual.[12] Of course the folk tale and the slave narrative are typically black forms of literature in the American canon, yet intellectuals debated their relevance to the modern American experience. Similarly, spirituals, jazz, gospel and the blues are musical forms commonly associated with the black experience, and many writers integrated the rhythms of these forms into their work. For instance, Hughes's *Montage of a Dream Deferred* (1951) offers a marvellous medley of jazz, ragtime, blues, boogie-woogie, bebop, swing and poetry, while his second collection of poems, *Fine Clothes to the Jew* (1927), was predominantly influenced by the blues. Yet some critics argue that this was to 'racialise' art, effectively imprisoning it in a racial ghetto and achieving a kind of literary segregation, in which African American literature is perceived as separate and 'different' to canonical white literature. In terms of the shaping of American modernism, this issue of ghettoisation is especially pertinent. For much of the twentieth century, African American contributions to modernism were simply ignored by New Criticism, which instead privileged white innovators such as T. S. Eliot and Ezra Pound and the writers of the Lost Generation. What evolved was the notion of a separate black modernism, somehow divorced from the work of white writers, especially that of the so-called 'high modernists'.[13] Only relatively recently have critics such as Rachel Farebrother and George Hutchinson, amongst others, demonstrated the cultural relationships between black and white American modernists, and argued the case for an African American modernism, both influential upon and influenced by European modernist writing.[14]

When we think about the Harlem Renaissance, it is important to remember that this was not so much a 'School' as the collective work of a group of individual African American writers, drawn, like their white counterparts described in Chapter 2, to the metropolitan charisma of New York City. There was no single literary philosophy guiding them, nor even a uniform perception of what was taking place around them. They were linked, however, by a common black experience and the desire for self-definition and self-expression. Harlem, the nexus of black American energy, 'the Mecca of the Negro', was crucial to these aims. Situated, as it was, in one of the largest metropolises in the world, which was undergoing massive architectural, geographical and demographic development, Harlem pulsated with the energy of optimism. Locke called it 'a race capital',[15] and in 'The New Negro', he identified the city as a gateway to modernity for black Americans, the 'home of the Negro's "Zionism"' (p. 14) with 'the same role to play for the New Negro as Dublin had for the New Ireland or Prague for the New Czechoslovakia' (p. 7). Weldon Johnson, meanwhile, claimed in 'Harlem: The Culture Capital' that 'the Negro's advantages and opportunities are greater in Harlem than in any other place in the country, and that Harlem will become the intellectual, the cultural, and the financial center for Negroes of the United States'.[16] And Claude McKay's *Home to Harlem*, not unlike Van Vechten's *Nigger Heaven*, associated Harlem with an expansive, fertile and heady carnal energy:

> Harlem! Harlem! Little thicker, littler darker and noisier and smellier, but Harlem just the same. The niggers done plowed through Hundred and Thirtieth Street. Heading straight for One Hundred and Twenty-fifth. Spades beyond Eighth Avenue. Going, going, going Harlem! Going up! . . . Oh Lawdy. Harlem bigger, Harlem better . . . and sweeter.[17]

In short, for a generation of writers Harlem encapsulated the aspirations and potential of African American culture. It was not merely the intellectual and spiritual home for one of the more important strands of American modernism; it was nothing less than a crucible of musical, literary and visual forms, which would profoundly influence the nature of twentieth-century American cultural identity.

LANGSTON HUGHES

Often regarded as the unofficial poet laureate of Harlem, Langston Hughes was undoubtedly one of the most important figures in twentieth-century black American writing. Hughes wrote about Harlem more than any other poet of his generation and it is fascinating to follow the trajectory of his depictions, moving from unbridled joyousness at the potential of 'Jazzonia', the moniker he gave the city in his first collection, *The Weary Blues* (1926), to

Harlem as the site of thwarted hopes and dissatisfaction in *Montage of a Dream Deferred*, which was published in 1951. The intervening twenty-five years brought the Great Depression, which saw the closure of many of Harlem's famous clubs, the end of Prohibition, the 1935 race riot which effectively brought an end to the New Negro Movement and, of course, the Second World War. In the meantime, Hughes had changed greatly as a poet, moving from the role of favourite son of the Harlem Renaissance (due, at least partially, to his celebration and integration of African American dialect and the non-combative tone of his early poetry), to something of a literary outcast for his second, very poorly reviewed collection *Fine Clothes to the Jew* (1927), then a poetic representative of the black proletariat (he denied being a member of the Communist Party despite having travelled to the USSR in the 1930s) in collections such as *Shakespeare in Harlem* (1942), *Fields of Wonder* (1947) and *One Way Ticket* (1949). While the general tone of Hughes's poetry changed across his career, his commitment to the inspirational qualities of Harlem never waned. As he put it:

> I live in the heart of Harlem. I have also lived in the heart of Paris, Madrid, Shanghai and Mexico City. The people of Harlem seem not very different from others, except in language. I love the colour of their language: and, being a Harlemite myself, their problems and interests are my problems and interests.[18]

The emphasis here on colourful Harlem language was no doubt informed by his commitment to the rich, rude tang of African American dialect, with its musical inflections and rhythmical variations. It was also part of the legacy he inherited from his acknowledged influence, Paul Laurence Dunbar, a pioneer of conversational African American dialect poetry. Moreover, Hughes's interest in the language of Harlem exhibited a commitment to the representation of a specifically black voice, a commitment he underlined in his famous essay 'The Negro Artist and the Racial Mountain' (1926).

Also notable in Hughes's declaration of affection for Harlem is the poet's commitment to an affinity between the singular self and the wider community. The 'problems and interests' of the people become those of the poet. The poet, therefore, becomes a public figure, taking on the social, cultural and, in this instance, political role set out for the poet by Emerson and Whitman (see Chapter 1). What this suggests is his complex inheritance: his affinity on the one hand with a specifically black heritage and literary ancestry and, on the other, with the white literary past of the nineteenth-century canon. Hughes addresses this dual inheritance, a clear example of the 'twoness' of black Americans described by Du Bois in *The Souls of Black Folk*, in one of his most anthologised poems, 'I, Too'. First published in *The Weary Blues*, the poem is clearly a homage to Whitman's 'I Hear America Singing' (1865) and plays upon two themes: the idea of dispossession and the notion of the poet as a democratic hero, a representative of his culture. The use of the word 'too' twice (once at the beginning and once at the end of the poem), effectively encasing the poetic content, is a deliberate play on the notion of 'twoness', and underlines the doubly focused theme. In apparent contrast, the 'I' is immediately foregrounded, placing the subjective poetic consciousness at the centre of the dramatic action:

> I, too, sing America
> I am the darker brother.
> They send me to eat in the kitchen
> When company comes.

The vanquished 'I' is a Cain-like figure, banished from the table of plenty but growing strong as he prepares to return and claim his rightful inheritance. But rather than wanting revenge, the 'I' yearns only for recognition and acknowledgement of the injustice of his treatment:

> Besides,
> They'll see how beautiful I am
> And be ashamed—[19]

The emphasis here upon visual recognition is a quiet demand for visibility, a common trope in much African American literature, an appreciation of the black subject's rightful place at the table. But this corresponds with a desire to be heard. The 'I' draws attention to his 'song', which is where Hughes enters into a kind of poetic transaction with Whitman. In 'I Hear America Singing', Whitman lists the voices he hears: the carpenter, the mechanic, the mason, the boatman, the young wife at work, each of whom is committed to the great American democratic experiment. Hughes's subject intervenes to insert himself into this group; the poem is his 'strong melodious song' which allows him to assert his own identity.[20] No longer the dispossessed outsider, he declares 'I, too, am America'. Again, the final line presents an interesting juxtaposition. Both a declaration of independence and an affirmed identification with the collective, it situates the black subject as definitive of America, and in true Whitmanian style affirms the poet's position as democratic spokesman for his people.

Voice and song are also important in 'The Weary Blues', the title poem in Hughes's first collection, which features a black musician who plays the blues on Lenox Avenue. In terms of form and content, the poem draws upon the rhythm of the blues, and sets up a symbiotic relationship between the poet or observer and the musician, such that by the final line of the poem it is unclear to whom the pronoun 'he' refers. From the very beginning of his career, Hughes was keen to emphasise the importance of black music to his writing. Musical forms gave his poems their vernacular authenticity. As he explained in 'The Negro Artist and the Racial Mountain':

> Most of my poems are racial in theme and derived from the life I know. In many of them I try to grasp and hold some of the meanings and rhythms of jazz . . . Jazz to me is one of the inherent expressions of Negro life in America: the eternal tom-tom beating in the Negro soul – the tom-tom of revolt against weariness in a white world, a world of subway trains and work, work, work; the tom-tom of joy and laughter and pain swallowed in a smile.[21]

Hughes's enthusiasm for jazz extended to black musical culture more widely, including spirituals, work songs, field hollers, blues, gospel, ragtime and rock 'n' roll. The presence of jazz in his poetry is deliberately subversive, its improvisational quality a rebellious challenge to the closed structures of dominant white literary forms. In 'The Weary Blues' we can observe the tension between the musical rhythms as they compete with the measured verse patterns which struggle to contain them. The established AAB blues rhythm (with its 11:11:6 measured lines) in the first three lines of the poem is immediately disrupted with a repeated line and a fifth, unrhymed line:

> Drowning a drowsy syncopated tune,
> Rocking back and forth to a mellow croon,
>   I heard a Negro play.
> Down on Lenox Avenue the other night
> By the pale dull pallor of an old gas light
>   He did a lazy sway. . . .
>   He did a lazy sway. . . .
> To the tune o' those Weary Blues. (p. 33)

The overflowing lines suggest a kind of escape, which is precisely what the musician holds out to the observer. The musical interlude offers a welcome respite, a mesmerising dreaminess which washes over the wearying day. So entrancing is the music, in fact, that by the end of the evening 'he slept like a rock or a man that's dead' (p. 34). The hypnotic power of the blues musician lulls the observer into self-forgetfulness, evident in the absorption of the initial subjective 'I', locked within its measured lines, into the colloquial 'I's' and 'I got' of the musician in the middle section of the poem, culminating with the indeterminate 'he' in the final line.

Hughes's poetry is often regarded as an act of celebration, demonstrating a kind of racial pride in its vibrant images and throbbing rhythmical pulse. But as in 'The Weary Blues', there is often an underlying despair in the musical phrases, a sorrow which suggests a political message about the plight of the African American, 'the pain swallowed in a smile' as Hughes described it in the 'The Negro Artist and the Racial Mountain'. In an early poem such as 'Cabaret', for instance, he depicts the quiet sadness of the jazz band beneath the frippery and the movement of the dancers:

Does a jazz-band ever sob?
They say a jazz band's gay.
Yet as the vulgar dancers whirled
And the wan night wore away,
One said she heard the jazz-band sob
When the little dawn was grey. (p. 29)

And in 'Harlem Night Club' the reader feels the urgency of an impending ending, and the associated gloom that will come when the band finishes playing:

Sleek black boys in a cabaret,
Jazz-band, jazz-band, —
Play, plAY, PLAY!
Tomorrow . . . who knows?
Dance today!
. . .
Jazz-boys, jazz boys, —
Play, plAY, PLAY!
Tomorrow . . . is darkness.
Joy today! (p. 32)

The poem is tremendously evocative of the frenzied movement of the dancers in its exultant exclamations, the dexterity of the players in their hyphenated quick-time, and the passion of the participants imploring the band to 'Play, plAY, PLAY!' (the typography rising in an insistent urgency) before the coming of the dawn and the darkness of tomorrow. However, as in 'Cabaret', we are presented with a sense of impending doom, a feeling that the party will come to an end when the music is hushed and the night sky brightens to reveal, somewhat paradoxically, darkness. Thus the apparent formal freedom and ebullience of these early poems mask a deeper, darker meaning: an underlying anxiety that dreams may not be realised, that black musical rhythms may present nothing more than a different kind of enslavement, and a fear that the great Harlem show will come to an end.

The poems in Hughes's second collection, *Fine Clothes to the Jew*, return to this abiding sense of despair and place it at centre stage. Unlike *The Weary Blues*, the follow-up collection resists the celebratory mask of jazz and, in its fulsome embrace of the blues, presents realistic portrayals of urban African American life: poems of poverty, loneliness, empty sexual encounters and violence. Most of the poems are presented through a black voice, without the framing, standard English voice of the observer which we saw in 'The Weary Blues'. The critic Arnold Rampersad even describes the entire first collection as a 'mulatto-like text', an admixture of black and white dialects.[22] But *Fine Clothes to the Jew* breaks this mould and emphasises the slang, rhythm and modulations of a lower class black vernacular. As with *The Weary Blues*, there is an emphasis on the sound of the poetry, now even more pronounced. Indeed, as a whole, the collection is a composite structure following the motions of an extended piece of music, from overture to coda, with each movement shifting in focus to offer insights into the daily violence and social injustices in lower class African American lives, whether they be forsaken lovelorn women, menial labourers or the victims of physical abuse.

'Midwinter Blues', for instance, captures the despair of a deserted woman, whose lover has departed on 'the night befo' Christmas . . . when the coal was low' (p. 151). The entire poem is a direct and deliberate counterpoint to Clement Clarke's poem of yuletide expectation, 'Twas the Night Before Christmas' (1822). Hughes's blues verse, adapted from the musical form, offers a repetition of the first line in the third line, and the second within the fourth, before closing the stanza with a different pair of unrhymed lines which in each instance compound the woman's sense of misery:

> In the middle of the winter,
> Snow all over the ground.
> In the middle of the winter,
> Snow all over the ground—
> 'Twas the night befo' Christmas
> My good man turned me down.

The pathetic fallacy of the bleak midwinter scene indicates the pain of the loss but also the speaker's mental anguish. The repetition of 'don't know's' and 'mind' in the first and third lines of the second stanza suggests the effect of this desertion upon her psychological wellbeing, again a stock feature of blues music, and this recurs in the final stanza when she promises to plant a rose at the back door. The rose, a traditional symbol of love, takes the poem from midwinter to spring. In this instance, rather than signalling new life, the rose is the harbinger of death, planted in the ground for financial expediency: 'so when I'm dead they won't need / No flowers from the store' (p. 151).

These final lines return the poem to its original context, the night before Christmas, and emphasise the futility of expectation. The speaker may have anticipated a gift from her lover, but instead is left with an empty fire and a broken heart. As she anticipates her death, she realises that the hope for funeral flowers is foolhardy. Unable to rely on a lover, she will need to provide for herself even in death. The critic David Chinitz describes the woman's final resolution as an exhibitionistic 'pout [which] shows her thoughts turning back to a world she doesn't expect to be leaving', indicative that she will go on just as the blues always go on; 'the end of the song is not the end of the singer'.[23] And, indeed, this seems to be the thrust of the entire collection. Hughes's hard-bitten African Americans may be downtrodden but they, like the blues, will go on. Indeed, the collection offers a turning point in Hughes's career and more generally in the poetry of the Harlem Renaissance; it signals a shift to an assertive, direct and angry African American voice. As Howard Mumford Jones, one of the few contemporary critics who admired Hughes's collection, observed, *Fine Clothes to the Jew* had 'contributed a really new verse form to the English language'.[24]

CARL VAN VECHTEN

The raw emotive power of the blues was appreciated by Carl Van Vechten, a white writer, photographer and philanthropist who had been a flamboyant presence in Harlem since the beginning of the 1920s. Van Vechten, a great advocate of racial integration, was patron to a number of young African American artists, including

Hughes, Hurston and Nella Larsen. It was Van Vechten who suggested the titles of both Hughes's first and second collections of poetry and helped to secure his contracts with Knopf, and it was Van Vechten who encouraged Hughes to fully embrace the blues in his second volume of poetry. In essays published in 1925 and 1926 he described the blues as 'symbolic poetry . . . eloquent with rich idioms, metaphoric phrases and striking word combinations'.[25] Beyond their aesthetic value, he felt the blues offered insights into a racist society which had failed to recognise the psychological legacy of its past.

And just as *Fine Clothes to the Jew* was one of the most poorly received collections of the era for its supposedly negative portrayal of African American life, so one of the most controversial novels to emerge was undoubtedly Van Vechten's *Nigger Heaven* (1926). W. E. B. Du Bois described it as 'a blow in the face' and advised readers to 'drop the book gently into the grate';[26] and Van Vechten's good friend Countee Cullen apparently turned 'white with rage' and broke off their friendship when the author attempted to explain the irony of the title. Even Van Vechten's own father implored him to change the title: 'I have never myself spoken of a coloured man as a "nigger." If you are trying to help the race, as I am assured you are, I think every word you write should be a respectful one towards the blacks.'[27] Hughes, on the other hand, defended the novel, writing at the time that 'no book could possibly be as bad as *Nigger Heaven* has been painted'.[28] Later, in his autobiography, however, Hughes admitted that 'the word *nigger* to colored people of high and low degree is like a red rag to a bull . . .Negroes do not like it in any book or play whatsoever, be the book or play ever so sympathetic in its basic treatment of the race.'[29] Similarly, James Weldon Johnson, another Harlem resident who had benefitted from Van Vechten's close association with the up-and-coming publishing houses, advised that 'the book and not the title is the thing' and noted that 'the author pays colored people the rare tribute of writing about them as people rather than as puppets'.[30] But in his autobiography, he conceded that 'most of the Negroes who condemned *Nigger Heaven* did not read it; they were estopped by the title'.[31]

For the rest of his life, Van Vechten maintained that the title was ironic, deployed to evoke the history of oppression endured by African Americans and, as he pointed out in the novel, a direct reference to the balcony section of segregated theatres reserved for black patrons. Yet there was undoubtedly an element of opportunism in his choice. *Nigger Heaven* was the best-selling novel of the Harlem Renaissance, going through nine reprints in just thirteen months after its initial publication. As Kathleen Pfeiffer observes, Van Vechten even encouraged Ronald Firbank to change the title of his novel *Sorrow in Sunlight* (1924) to *Prancing Nigger*. Indeed, even his advice to Hughes to call his second collection *Fine Clothes to the Jew* was another example of his appetite for opportunistic sensationalism. However, the title was not the only source of contention within the novel, since Van Vechten's reproduction of blues lyrics without permission got him into legal trouble. Keen to return his patron's favours, Hughes stepped in and overnight produced a series of blues lyrics, which Van Vechten used in later editions to 'authenticate' his portrayal of Harlem culture. Again, we might see this as a clever marketing ploy; yet it also reveals something of the cachet Hughes carried at the time and Van Vechten's respect for him. It also offers an interesting inversion of the 'authenticating' documents, written by white supporters, which usually accompanied nineteenth-century slave narratives.

While Van Vechten's appreciation of the aesthetic quality of the blues is beyond doubt, there also is no doubt that he also recognised their commercial potential. In an article for *Vanity Fair* in 1926, he observed:

> It is a foregone conclusion that with the craving to hear these songs that is known to exist on the part of the public it will not be long before white singers have taken them enough their own so that the public will be surfeited sooner or later with opportunities to enjoy them . . . Thus [the reluctant artist] readily delivers his great gifts to the exploitation of the white man without – save in rare instances – making any attempt, an attempt foredoomed to meet with success, to capitalise them himself.[32]

The words clearly reflect those uttered by his H. L. Mencken-inspired character, Russett Durwood, to Byron Kasson, hinting at the white fascination with black culture which was at the root of the controversies surrounding the novel's title, its sexually-charged content and its depiction of African Americans. And yet for all his ruthless self-interest, the irony is that Van Vechten's novel offered a compelling illustration of the potential to *reverse* the exploitative aspects of the white middle-class love affair with modern African American culture.

The novel centres on the relationship between the not-so-subtly named Mary Love, an apparently repressed African American librarian, and Byron Kasson, a pale-skinned, down-at-heel, aspiring writer, running from the unfulfilled expectations of his family. Around this basic story, Van Vechten installs a cast of representative characters: the young intellectuals (Olive Hamilton, Howard Allison and Dick Sill); the established middle-class 'Brooklyn set'; the jaded entertainer and her sycophantic sidekicks (Adora Boniface, Arabia Scribner and Piqua St Paris); the sexually rapacious young black actress (Lasca Sartoris); the pimp (Scarlet Creeper); the whore (Ruby) and the shady, entrepreneurial politician (Randolph Pettijohn, the Bolito King). The intellectuals talk of uplift and racial pride; the entertainers swill champagne and dance through the night; and the politician and the pimp compete for women and territory. Meanwhile the serious-minded Mary, whose bookshelves groan under the weight of Johnson, Toomer, McKay, Du Bois and Fauset, struggles with her intellect, which she feels distances her from her fellow Harlemites:

> Savages! Savages at heart! . . . To be sure, she too felt this African beat – it completely aroused her emotionally – but she was conscious of feeling it. The love of drums, of exciting rhythms, the naïve delight in glowing colour – the colour that exists only in cloudless, tropical climes – this warm sexual emotion, all these were hers only through a mental understanding . . . We are all savages, she repeated to herself, all, apparently, but me! (pp. 89–90)

Despite her intelligence, Mary's thoughts reveal her attachment to stereotypes. The sexual passion she longs to experience is seen as part of her black racial ancestry, but the 'consciousness' and 'mental understanding' which she cannot shrug off are antithetical to her 'savage' impulses. She has, we are told, 'an instinctive horror of promiscuity . . . [which] might, she sometimes argued with herself, have something to do with her white inheritance' (p. 53).

We might well view Mary's thoughts as those of a rational thinking person within an irrational world. Certainly, the world she inhabits is licentious, raucous and diverse. But her views about her identity and those of her fellow Harlemites are merely part of the novel's wider associations between blackness and primitivism. On numerous occasions, Harlem is described as 'a jungle' (p. 209), a hellish 'pandemonium' (p. 38); its jazz bands 'perform wild music, music that moaned and lacerated one's breast with brazen claws of tone, tortured music from the depths of hell' (p. 254); its women are described as 'lovely animal[s] swathed [in] leopard fur' (p. 231). Indeed, Van Vechten seems intent on accentuating the anarchic and animalistic elements of Harlem life, deliberately neglecting the serious, intellectual qualities of his protagonists to focus on the excesses of the promiscuous night clubbers and the deeper passions of Byron and Mary. It would be easy to dismiss these kinds of descriptions as patronising and racist, and indeed many critics have done so; but in most cases the characters described in such colourful terms are in fact playing a particular role.[33] All are *performers*, from the queenly stage actress Adora to the self-made sausage-seller-cum-would-be politician. The fur-clad Lasca is a self-described maneater and tells the broken-hearted penniless writer: 'I use 'em until I tire of 'em and then I say, damn you and good-bye!' (p. 259). The self-promoting Dick Sill takes on a new role in passing as a white man. And from the very beginning of the book, the sense of performance is evident in the flamboyant strut of the Scarlet Creeper as he wanders through the streets of Harlem, taking in the women, the musicians and the Charleston dancers on the sidewalk. Even Mary, in denying her passions and focusing on her improving activities, consciously *plays the role* of the New Negro, the middle-class intellectual.

As part of this fascination with performance, the notion of the *gaze* is one of the novel's central themes. Each of these performers is aware of their audience, conscious that they are being watched, the quality of their performance weighed and measured. This dual theme of performance and the gaze is present in the very title, *Nigger Heaven*, which Van Vechten impresses upon the reader as a theatrical reference. This interpretation of the theme is further underlined when the narrator introduces the matter of Mary and Olive's trips to the theatre and their ability to pass and therefore avoid the segregated seats when unaccompanied by a dark-skinned companion. When we first meet Mary, she is a watchful presence at Adora Boniface's party, observing her majestic hostess and admiring her African stateliness, taking in the adulterous Sylvia Hawthorne carrying on 'under auspices which would not too completely compromise her either in the eyes of her husband or the eyes of the more formal Harlem world to which she belonged' (p. 20), and spotting the 'sullen mien' of Nellie, the servant ordered to supply more champagne (p. 28). She takes the time to gaze at her own 'rich golden-brown' skin reflected in Adora's mirror (p. 25), while her first encounter with Byron is yet another exercise in observation:

> She decided, with a kind of voluntary optimism, the view from this window is superb. [At] a pool below . . . several men were bathing. Two or three of them lay recumbent on the sand, their brown limbs gleaming like bronze in the sun. Others splashed about in the water. Now a youth was mounting the tower in preparation for a dive. He was, she noted, slightly lighter in colour than the others, almost the shade of coffee diluted with rich cream, her preferred tint. . . . Now, in a wide, parabolic curve, he dived, cut the water with his hands, and disappeared. Mary emitted an involuntary cry of pleasure: the action was so perfect; *thrilling*, she defined it. (p. 24)

The sensuous orgasmic pleasure Mary takes at the sight of Byron's body is part of her sexual awakening, his breaking the water a foreshadowing of his later rupture of Mary's purity. It also, perhaps, hints at her later psychological instability, caused by Byron's desertion of her.

From this point onwards Mary becomes less aloof and self-possessed, overtaken by desire and emotion as the relationship progresses. But her voyeurism, as well as the various instances of observation throughout the novel, reflects a deeper point, hinting at the scopophilic attraction of the black body for the white spectator – an attraction which the novel deliberately exploits. The novel self-consciously draws attention to its own strategies, its own fascination with the black body and the black community, but it does so knowingly in its depiction of a series of characters who exploit their bodies for largely material ends. Thus the stereotypical characteristics of black identity are deliberately and ostentatiously exaggerated to please the white visitors to the Harlem nightclubs and the white readers of Van Vechten's novel. Byron even touches on this in his tirade against the cult of Harlem:

> Nigger Heaven! Nigger Heaven! That's what Harlem is. We sit on our places in the gallery of this New York theatre and watch the white world sitting down below in the good seats in the orchestra. Occasionally they turn their faces up towards us, their hard cruel faces, to laugh or sneer, but they never beckon! (p. 149)

Through the character of Russett Durwood, Van Vechten advises capturing the attention of those upturned faces and maintaining it by means of a seductive, yet artificial, exhibitionism to achieve a greater end, whether that be literary, financial or political. Thus *Nigger Heaven* is a flamboyant performance, a carefully constructed artifice, luring the reader towards a deeper understanding of his black brethren by first exciting his scopophilic pleasure and then eliciting an empathetic response to the humanity of a given character. Sensation, exploitation and revelation mark the pages of *Nigger Heaven*, but they also serve as its modus operandi.

COUNTEE CULLEN AND CLAUDE MCKAY

In 'The Negro Artist and the Racial Mountain', Langston Hughes wrote of the black American poet who had told him he wished to be known as a poet rather than as a Negro poet. Hughes accused the writer of overthrowing his ancestry and effectively admitting that he wanted to be white, and doubted if, 'with his intense desire to run away from his race, this boy would ever be a great poet'.[34] Given the details of the offending poet's middle-class Baptist background and education, there is little doubt that the writer Hughes had in mind was Countee Cullen, one of the early stars of the Harlem Renaissance. And in some ways Hughes's rather gloomy prediction was quite right. For all his Harvard masters degree, his New York University Phi Beta Kappa membership and his Guggenheim fellowship, Cullen never achieved the potential his early poetry promised before his early death in 1946.

In 1924 Cullen had declared in an interview that 'if I am going to be a poet at all, I am going to be POET and not NEGRO POET', and throughout his career he was to remain faithful to that ideal.[35] In the foreword to an edited collection of the work of thirty-eight black poets, he reiterated his antipathy to the notion of a distinctly black art:

> Negro poetry, it seems to me, in the sense that we speak of Russian, French or Chinese poetry, must emanate from some country or other than this in some language other than our own. Moreover, the attempt to corral the outbursts of the ebony muse into some definite mold to which all poetry by Negroes will conform seems altogether futile and aside from the facts.[36]

This disavowal of a racialised poetic identity, needless to say, did not endear him to many of the Harlem Renaissance writers, who viewed the role of their art as the promotion and celebration of black identity and black culture. Yet some were more sympathetic. Zora Neale Hurston, for instance, appreciated and shared what she saw as his artistic sincerity:

> I have always shared your approach to art. That is, you have written from within rather than to catch the eye of those who were making the loudest noise for the moment. I know that hitch-hiking on bandwagons has become the rage amongst Negro artists for the last ten years at least, but I have never thumbed a ride and can feel no admiration for those that travel that way.[37]

Given the strong elements of folklore and African American dialect in her writing, Hurston's letter is, on the face it, quite surprising. But Cullen was not really objecting to the insertion of African American content; only to the means whereby others would control his art by setting formal limits, 'definite molds', upon it. Hurston faced exactly the same kind of struggle in her attempts to champion Haitian and Caribbean art and cultural practices as worthy topics for African American art. Though popular later, these forms were not initially welcomed by the black bourgeoisie.

Ironically, though, it was precisely this audience that most appreciated the poems in Cullen's first anthology *Color* (1925).[38] One of its most celebrated poems is undoubtedly his elegant sonnet 'Yet Do I Marvel', which contained what James Weldon Johnson described as 'the two most poignant lines in American literature' in its final rhyming couplet:

> Yet do I marvel at this curious thing:
> To make a poet black and bid him sing![39]

Certainly, the speaker's heartfelt admission that the ways of God are beyond his comprehension offers a deeply personal and plaintive cry for enlightenment: why would the benevolent God described in the opening line create a black poet, a poet burdened with an ancestry of oppression and pain, whose duty it is to sing? The word 'sing' evokes the lyrical ballads of William Wordsworth and William Blake, poets Cullen admired deeply, and takes us back to Whitman's 'Song of Myself' or 'I Hear America Singing', in which the poet celebrates his own powers and those of the heterogeneous nation. But the word 'sing' also draws attention to the formal composition of the sonnet, and its original derivation from the Italian 'sonetto', 'little song'. Carefully executed in its rhyme scheme and uniform iambic measurements, Cullen's sonnet moves from an easy acceptance of the ways of God in the octet to a more inflamed questioning in the sestet. Whereas the octet enumerates a series of interested questions, the sestet is marked by the severe, hard 'c' sounds of 'cares' and 'compels', the multisyllabic 'inscrutable', 'catechism' and 'curious', and the repetition of the ambiguous 'awful'. Indeed, the sestet enacts the difficulty of singing for the black poet. Unlike a Whitman who celebrates his own powers, Cullen's poet has more in common with the dejected speaker of Shakespeare's Sonnet 29, a poet who beweeps his outcast state, troubles deaf heaven with his bootless cries and looks upon himself and curses his fate. And by encasing his poignant racial – yet deeply personal – content in a typically Western poetic form, Cullen is also drawing attention to the act of creation as a wilfully complex, ambiguous and unknowable enterprise, subject only to the hand and whims of the creator.

Cullen returned to the theme of the dissonance between black and white cultural ancestry in his most famous poem, 'Heritage'. Although Cullen did not align himself with his people in the manner of, for example, Langston Hughes, the fact that the poem provides epigraphs to both Van Vechten's *Nigger Heaven* and Larsen's *Passing* is evidence of its wider relevance to the black American community. 'Heritage' offers a sustained meditation on the nature of personal and national identity, religious sensibilities and sexual inclinations, the disjuncture between the persona's sterile contemporary culture and his fertile heritage. The poem opens with a question about the relevance of an African inheritance to the speaker and offers a mythic landscape of an imagined Africa. The typographic change to italics indicates a wider shift from the mythic and objective to the immediate and personal, reiterating the question of relevance. The second stanza illuminates the difficulty in answering the question by revealing the speaker's pent-up sexual energy, bound by the social mores of his contemporary culture; an energy he attributes to the fertile African past:

> So I lie, whose fount of pride,
> Dear distress, and joy allied,
> In my somber flesh and skin,
> With the dark blood dammed within
> Like the great pulsing tides of wine
> That, I fear must burst the fine
> Channels of the chaffing net
> Where they surge and foam and fret.

The frenzied fricatives surge against the restrictive 'i' sounds, mimicking the throbbing 'dark blood' which pulsates within the

'I', the speaker's body, and beats against his thumb-stopped ears, seeking the release enjoyed by the 'young forest lovers' (p. 2062). The speaker's recumbent position places him in a kind of impotent limbo between cultures, unable either to indulge or to escape the fertile urges associated with his African past.

In the third stanza, the speaker returns to the present and attempts to underplay the significance of his ancestry, which is reduced to 'a book one thumbs / Listlessly, till slumber comes'. The heathen symbols of power which once intoxicated him are no more than faintly remembered decorative items. To preserve and protect himself he must make himself like the tree which 'budding yearly must forget / how its past arose or set' (p. 2063). Yet the difficulty of suppressing the past is underlined by the re-emergence of the 'jungle boys and girls in love', symbols of the speaker's carnal urges, in Stanza 4, treading up and down on their 'jungle track'. With their slick, wet bodies, they haunt the speaker, and like the rain 'work on [him] night and day', beckoning him to 'dance the Lover's Dance' (p. 2063). The predominance of the rain in this fourth stanza suggests a cleansing and revitalising power which the speaker attempts to resist; yet its insistent drip suggests that the tide, like the dammed black blood of Stanza 1, will break through the net and engulf him.[40]

The fifth stanza pitches the pagan African gods against Jesus Christ, the white deity to whom the speaker belongs. The use of the word 'belong' in this brief stanza suggests enslavement, which is underlined by the 'high-price' paid for his conversion. While the Africans fashion their gods in their own likeness, the speaker bears no resemblance to his Christ and again finds himself trapped between the pagan culture of his past and the Christianity of his present. Thus, in the sixth stanza, he admits attributing to his Christ the black features he desires in a deity. Here the dammed-up tension between sexual desire and religious propriety comes to bursting point, with the persona begging forgiveness for the needs which 'sometimes shape[s] a human creed'. The final, italicised section of the poem sees the speaker attempting to regain his 'civilized' composure 'lest [he] perish in the flood' (p. 2063). Again, we return to the notion of entrapment: caught between worlds, between the desiccated present and the fecund past, the speaker is engulfed by his fear that a 'hidden ember' may reignite his carnal passions. The strictly controlled couplets combined with the uniform rhyme scheme and seven-beat line reinforce this sense of enclosure, formally stemming the flood of emotion and desire which threaten to burst through the speaker's psychological dam. In this way, far from embracing a white poetic identity as Hughes and others had charged, Countee Cullen uses Western poetic forms to embody the cultural shackles which bind black subjectivity. His poetry, perhaps more than any other of his generation, formally and thematically demonstrates the difficulty of reconciling black and white worlds. But it simultaneously hints at the possibility of doing so.

The Jamaican-born Claude McKay had a similarly ambivalent relationship with the key figures of the Harlem Renaissance, and he admitted his distance from the 'Negro elite', whom he perceived as an educated bourgeois group who, in their focus on literature and culture as a means to achieve racial uplift, had forgotten about the plight of ordinary, working-class black Americans. In his autobiography, *A Long Way from Home*, he described the writings of Locke and others as dedicated only to the 'pace and progress of smart Negro society' and dismissed Locke's famous essay as 'a remarkable chocolate soufflé of art and politics, with not an ingredient of information inside it'.[41] While entertainingly harsh, McKay's estimation of Locke and many of the other contributors to *The New Negro* was remarkably prescient, anticipating the more politically driven work of the Black Arts Movement which would come to dominate the 1960s, and aligning him with some of the more radical figures of the era, including the Jewish socialist writer Mike Gold, the socialist writer, editor and dramatist Frank Harris, and the journalists Floyd Dell and John Reed. The poems McKay published in *The Seven Arts* in 1917 brought him to the attention of Max Eastman, editor of *The Liberator* magazine, where he served as an associate editor until 1922. However, his time at *The Liberator* and the circumstances of his departure from it reveal much about his views on art and politics. The magazine was dedicated to the principle of fusing art with political concerns. However, it gradually became more economic in its focus. This placed a strain on McKay's relationship with Gold, his co-editor, which was fraught with difficulty. McKay described the pugilistic Gold as a 'petty and spiteful . . . social revolutionary [whose] passion was electrified with personal feeling that was sometimes as acrid as lime-juice'.[42] When Gold challenged him to a fistfight, McKay resigned. But, as Daniel Aarons has observed, the clash between them reveals a 'free, undisciplined writer' without the zealousness of the 'disciplined responsible party member'.[43]

The notion of McKay as an 'undisciplined' writer is all the more curious given his dedication to the tightly controlled formal structures of the sonnet. Almost all of the poems in *Harlem Shadows*, including the famous 'If We Must Die', are composed in the sonnet form, deploying the same tight metrical and rhythmical measurements that Cullen had also used. The undisciplined aspect of McKay has perhaps less to do with the shape of his poetry itself, but his unwillingness to subject himself to any controlling force, be it capitalist, socialist or religious. When he first came to the United States in 1912, he travelled to South Carolina to study at Washington's Tuskegee Institute but quickly left for Kansas State University, citing Tuskegee's mechanised and militaristic approach to learning as the reason for his departure. After just two years in Kansas he left for New York and between 1919 and 1934 travelled to London, Belgium, Holland, the Soviet Union, France, Morocco and Spain. His peripatetic lifestyle reveals an agitated restlessness, which is also evident in the shifts from the dialectic lyrics of his very early *Songs of Jamaica* and *Constab Ballads*, to free verse and the carefully wrought sonnets which dominate *Harlem Shadows* – and later still from poetry to prose.

Agitation is what drew McKay to the sonnet form. Its tight structure offered an antidote to the chaotic and violent modernity he saw unravelling around him in Harlem, a city with which he always had a love–hate relationship. The Red Summer race riots inspired what became his manifesto sonnet, 'If We Must Die', which in its form and content juxtaposes deathly chaos with poetic order:

> If we must die, let it not be like hogs
> Hunted and penned in an inglorious spot,
> While round us bark the mad and hungry dogs,
> Making their mock at our accursèd lot.[44]

The speaker instructs the implied addressee to fight back against the violence inflicted upon him, to retaliate with brute force and bravery and, if necessary, to sacrifice his life. Notably, in syncopation with the tight formal structure of the poem, the speaker suggests a measured response to the violence inflicted upon his 'kinsmen', a noble defiance which moves progressively forward. The ten-beat iambic rhythm of the poem mimics this proposed advance. The overall thrust of the poem is also a kind of militaristic forward progression, moving from the indefinite 'if' at the beginning of the poem to the assertive and exhortative 'fighting back!' which closes the concluding rhyming couplet. While oppressed by their enemies' 'thousand blows', the defenders, by combining strength and discipline, can deal 'one deathblow' against the 'murderous, cowardly pack'. Throughout the poem the assailants are depicted as animals, a monstrous 'cowardly pack' of 'mad and hungry dogs', while the victims boldly refuse such associations. They will 'not be like hogs', nor will they be 'hunted and penned'; instead, they are the ever-questing noble kinsmen, who fight for honour to the death.

First published in *The Liberator*, the poem was reprinted in almost every black newspaper and magazine, and found its way into sermons, classrooms and political rallies. The enormous and immediate impact of the poem astonished McKay and gave him a deep sense of the political potential of his poetry:

> To thousands of Negroes who are not trained to appreciate poetry, 'If We Must Die' makes me a poet. I myself was amazed at the general sentiment for the poem. For I am so intensely subjective as a poet, that I was not aware, at the moment of writing, that I was transformed into a medium to express a mass sentiment.[45]

His apparent disbelief at having somehow spoken for the masses from his own subjective imagination seems somewhat disingenuous, given the moment of its composition and the company he was keeping at the time of writing. Frank Harris even claimed to have supplied him with the inspiration for what he called the 'fighting poem' in an angry exchange with McKay for allowing Eastman's magazine, rather than *Pearson's Magazine*, to publish the poem.[46] And Harris's belief that the poem somehow belonged to his magazine, contrasting with McKay's claim for the subjective nature of his poetry, points to an interesting tussle between the individual poet and the masses, raising the question which dogged many Harlem Renaissance writers: should art have a political end or is it purely a matter of aesthetics?

The answer remains ambiguous. On the one hand, McKay insisted that the poem must reflect the poetic imagination and poet's aesthetic impulses. And there is no doubt poetry designed purely for the purposes of propaganda simply did not interest him: hence his break from Harris, Eastman and Gold, and his renunciation of Locke, Du Bois and Walter White. On the other hand, we cannot ignore the sheer political power of a poem such as 'If We Must Die' or poems such as 'In Bondage' (1920), 'Enslaved' (1921) or 'To "Holy" Russia' (1920), to name but a few. Mark Helbling makes the case that McKay had not anticipated speaking for and reaching a mass audience.[47] But having produced a poem in the aftermath of a series of nationwide riots and published it in numerous socialist and race-related magazines, what on earth did he expect? What else could he have been trying to do? Furthermore, McKay's relationship with Harris (who had advised on changes to 'The Lynching') suggests that he had, at the very least, previously discussed the general purpose of poetry with him. That he discussed such a topic with a radical such as Harris suggests that he *did* hope to capture the sentiments of the masses, again pointing to McKay as a politically focused writer. Nonetheless, his ambiguity on the matter, combined with his ideological restlessness and diverse poetic influences, reveal a poet who, above all, strove for artistic liberty, released from the shackles of patronage, nationhood and colour consciousness.

ZORA NEALE HURSTON

At the 1925 *Opportunity* awards post-dinner party, one figure in particular stood out. Zora Neale Hurston made a dramatic entrance. Weaving through the crowd brandishing a brightly coloured scarf, she brought proceedings to a halt by loudly announcing the title of her prize winning play, 'Color Struck!' To produce such an effect was undoubtedly Hurston's intention. She was, throughout her life, a voluble and loquacious individual, encouraged at a young age to exert her voice and personal pride.[48] Her journey to the *Opportunity* dinner had been a tough one, including a spell working with a travelling dramatic company, a return to high school at the age of twenty-six, and a series of menial jobs. However, her impact upon the legacy of the Harlem Renaissance was enormous; without doubt, she was the most significant African American woman writer of her generation. At the 1925 awards, Hurston won the silver medal in two categories: the fiction prize for her short story, 'Spunk', which Locke chose for publication in *The New Negro*, and the dramatic prize for *Color Struck*. That she also received honourable mentions in two other categories merely reinforced her stunning success.

Hurston's achievements marked the beginning of a career which reached its literary apex in *Their Eyes Were Watching God* (1937), generally regarded as her most important novel, thanks to its emphasis on the black female experience, Hurston's integration of the black Southern vernacular with standard English, and her foregrounding of the black oral culture of storytelling. She had been honing these features of her writing since her first story 'John Redding Goes to Sea' (1921), which appeared in *The Stylus*, the literary magazine at Howard University, and instantly brought her talent to the attention of Alain Locke. Locke introduced her to Charles Johnson, editor of *Opportunity*, who published 'Drenched in Light' in the magazine's December 1924 issue. Indeed, her dramatic entrance at the *Opportunity* party is in many ways a symbol of her entrance to the Harlem scene. A loud, powerful and colourful presence, she breathed fresh life into the pages of Harlem's journals with her focus on the traditions, folklore and stories of ordinary, uneducated, Southern African Americans. She also insisted upon the importance of the female voice and the stories of women, their importance to the African American community and their impact upon successive generations. And, while her work does not lack evidence of racial and cultural pride, she brought an ambivalent and questioning perspective to the folk traditions integrated within her fiction.[49]

The issue of African American folklore had been a vexed and critical one for the founding fathers of the Harlem Renaissance. Du Bois felt that it could be used as a crucial tool in the promotion of the race, noting in *The Souls of Black Folk* that 'the Negro folk song [was] . . . the singular spiritual heritage of the nation and the greatest gift of the Negro people'.[50] Similarly, in 1931, James Weldon Johnson regarded 'folklore [as] "the touchstone . . . the magic thing . . . that by which the Negro can bridge all chasms"'.[51] However, for many contemporary thinkers, folklore also had the potential to recreate and entrench racial stereotypes; even Johnson himself, in his preface to the first edition of *The Book of Negro American Poetry* (1922), seemed to take a very dim view of it.[52] But as Hurston wrote in her unpublished essay, 'You Don't Know Us Negroes', there was a danger of 'margarinizing' black culture:

> The decade just past was the oleomargarine era in Negro writing. Oleomargarine is the fictionalized form of butter . . . it has everything butterish about it except butter. And so with the writings that made out they were holding a looking-glass to the Negro had everything in them except Negroness.[53]

As she saw it, the 'folklore' in the writing of the previous decade was not real African American folklore and had little to do with the customs and practices of real people. For her, real folklore, language and dialect was that which she collected from her Boasian-influenced anthropological studies, being the testimonies and tales of the people with whom she had interacted in the South, and she saw it as her duty to integrate these real stories and practices with the fictional stories she created. Moreover, she was committed to an appraisal of these traditions and she used her fiction as a vehicle to comment upon the merit or otherwise of the customs she observed, rather than falling into the modernist trap of romanticising folk and primitive cultures.

Hurston's ability to work with and critically examine community folk traditions testifies to her self-perception as something of a cultural outsider. This clearly owes much to her dual roles as fabulist and anthropologist, storyteller and cultural scientist. But, perhaps more pertinently, her isolation from her family and her

Eatonville origins solidified this sensibility. Certainly, her desire for financial and intellectual independence honed an individualistic streak which could seem adversarial to her peers. This outsider cast of mind is clearly evident in her compelling portrait of Janie Crawford, the central figure in *Their Eyes Were Watching God.* Fiercely independent and uncompromising in her pursuit of an ideal love, Janie tells her story much like Nick Buchanan tells his in *The Great Gatsby* (1925). Recalling her life story and journey for Pheoby to impart to the inquisitive and hostile community, to which she once belonged but from which she is now isolated, Janie is a kind of narratological framing device – both within her story but also separate from it. Hurston too occupies such a space. Filling the narrative with materials drawn from her own girlhood, her memories of Eatonville and the real inflections of Southern dialect (drawn from her anthropological work and her personal experience), she distances herself from them to offer a fictional portrait of one woman's quest for independence. This distance allows her to express ambivalence about the practices and values of the community, their tendency toward narrow-mindedness, their mean-spirited jealousy, inherent patriarchy and desire to know and control the women within it.

The reader's first taste of this tension between the community and the individual woman occurs in the opening pages, where a group gathered on a roadside porch observe Janie's return to town. The portrayal of the group is not negative. Indeed, in many ways it is quite sympathetic, drawing attention to the townspeople's mule-like daily toil and their custom of gathering at the stoop at the end of the day to exert their voice 'so the[ir] skins felt powerful and human. They became lords of sounds and lesser things. They passed nations through their mouths. They sat in judgement'.[54] The ascension of the sitters from 'tongueless, earless and eyeless conveniences' to 'lords' who sit in judgement corresponds with a loss of sensibility and human empathy. The men leer at Janie's breasts, buttocks and hair as she wanders past in her shirt and overalls, while the women make stinging remarks on her morality. As the narrator observes: 'They made burning statements with questions, and killing tools out of laughs. It was mass cruelty. A mood come alive. Words walking without masters; walking together like harmony in a song' (p. 10). While the portrayal of the group is not altogether positive, it does draw attention to the power of language and the voice, both of which are crucially important to the novel. Thus, the townspeoples' voices liberate them. When she passes, Janie shares a few words with her audience and the effect of her speaking disarms her detractors. Her words stun them into a silence where 'nobody moved, no body spoke' and 'Pearl Stone opened her mouth and laughed real hard because she didn't know what else to do' (p. 11). This brief opening scene encapsulates most of Hurston's thematic concerns – the importance and impact of the female voice, the individual female experience, storytelling, the role of the black community and the tension between the female self and community – and sets the scene for the emergence of a modern black folk heroine.

From the outset, Janie takes control of her narrative and tells her story on her own terms, making a bid for the self-assertion and self-empowerment denied her by her various husbands and by her own grandmother who 'ends [Janie's] childhood' by forcing the marriage to Logan Killicks (p. 26). True to his name, Killicks kills the blossoming sensuality in Janie and thwarts her dream of a marriage made out of love. Moreover, Logan attempts to kill her independent spirit and stifle her voice, accusing her of behaving like 'white folks' and insisting 'let's don't talk no mo' (p. 51) as well as asking her not to 'change too many words wid me' (p. 53). Her second husband, the smooth-talking Joe Starks, dazzles her with 'speeches' and 'rhymes' (p. 56) and brings her the economic security her grandmother had associated with the disastrous marriage to Killicks. Just as Starks is able to use his silver tongue to woo Janie, he charms the folk of Eatonville, talking himself into the role of mayor and convincing people to move to the new black town. Janie, however, is stopped short in her speechmaking. Enjoined to offer a few words on the election of her husband, she is curtailed:

> "Thank yuh fuh yo' compliments, but mah wife don't know nothin' 'bout no speech-makin'. Ah never married her for nothin' lak dat. She's uh woman and her place is in deh home".

> Janie made her face laugh after a short pause, but it wasn't too easy. She had never thought of making a speech and didn't know if she cared to make one at all. It must have been the way Joe spoke out without giving her a chance to say anything one way or another that took the bloom off of things. (pp. 69–70)

Joe's unwillingness to allow his wife to speak grows stronger throughout the years of their marriage but so too does her desire to exert her voice. When she teases him in front of his customers, one man describes her a 'born orator' and the entire town 'talked it for three days' (p. 92). Later still, thrusting herself into a conversation in which she belittles her husband, she is described as getting 'too moufy' (p. 117). Their competing voices culminate in his deathbed scene, in which Joe can only express a wordless 'sound of strife', while Janie is at last able to address the community.

Even the relationship with Vergible Tea Cake Woods, 'a bee to the blossom' (p. 161), the man who restores Janie's faith in love and rekindles the sexual passion she first tastes under the pear tree in the early scenes of the novel, is not without its spats and jealousies. And as in the marriages to Logan and Starks, the power and control of the female is at the heart of the relationship with Tea Cake. His ability to physically beat his wife 'relieved that awful fear inside him. Being able to whip her reassured him in possession' (p. 218). Their struggle culminates in a quasi-biblical flood scene wherein the male and female battle for survival. Saved by the sacrificial, life-giving cow, Janie turns a hunting rifle on her rabid husband and kills him in order to save her own life. Once again, she has survived and outlived her male companion.

By the end of the novel, Janie is back at the point of the novel's departure. She is restored to the fertility of her youthful days beneath the pear tree, by virtue of Tea Cake's seeds which she means to plant and in her nurturing of Pheoby:

> 'Lawd!' Pheoby breathed out heavily, 'Ah done growed ten feet higher from jus' listenin' tuh you, Janie. Ah ain't satisfied wid mahself no mo'. Ah means to make Sam take me fishin' wid him after this . . .' (p. 284)

Her words awaken within the younger woman a desire for marital and sexual equality, and she passes her story on to Pheoby so that it can be retold and disseminated within the community, just as she had told the story of Tea Cake's death to the courthouse and sent word of the funeral to Sop to be relayed to all the others. Like the orally transmitted folk tales Hurston collected during her expeditions to the South, Janie's story is told, passed on and retold. But unlike Hurston's accumulated tales, this is the story of a black woman's fight against – and her victory over – the patriarchy inherent in folk cultures and communities. Janie reaches the end of her narrative as a strong, feminist, African American voice, unashamed of her past and in control of her story. Much like Hurston's booming call at the *Opportunity* awards party, her voice commands attention, uncowed by embarrassment, shame, or the accepted social rules of polite decorum. Both Hurston and her heroine embody the individual voice. Both are rooted within the folk community but also distant from it, and both are inspired by its variety and harmony but also conscious of its limitations. In Janie Crawford, Zora Neale Hurston offers an eloquently vociferous survivor, a new modern model of black femininity – a figure not unlike herself.

JEAN TOOMER

This emphasis upon the black female experience and fascination with the folk tradition of the rural South are also at the heart of Jean Toomer's *Cane* (1923), a seminal work for the early the Harlem Renaissance. An admixture of styles, influences and genres, *Cane* is perhaps the most experimentally ambitious work of the Harlem Renaissance, deeply indebted to literary innovators such as Carl Sandburg, Sherwood Anderson, Frost and even Eliot, yet also rooted in the African American experience. Like Hurston, Toomer was intensely interested in cultural anthropology and came under the influence of one of the most important figures in the field, Waldo Frank. 'He has so many elements that I need,' wrote Toomer of his mentor, even dedicating the third and final section of *Cane* to him.[55] Toomer was attracted to Frank's cultural nationalism, his faith in the poet as a crucial national figure, and his Whitmanesque ideas about the centrality of sexuality to individual and collective identities.[56] Frank's proposals for a new 'ethnic federalism' which would displace Anglophilia and replace it with the 'buried cultures' of Native Americans, Mexicans and African Americans, appealed to Toomer's personal and wider cultural sensibilities, facilitating a cultural pluralism which was inherent in his sense of self but also evident in his writing. In an oft-quoted letter to *The Liberator*, Toomer explained:

> In my body were many bloods, some dark blood, all blended in the fire of six or more generations . . . I was then either a new type of man or the very oldest. In any case, I was inescapably myself . . . From my own point of view I am naturally and inevitably am American.[57]

For Toomer, this mixture of identities was supremely American, and he famously resisted the bifurcation of his own identity when his publishers at Boni and Liveright asked him to highlight his mixed ancestry in marketing the book. Taking exception to the request, he even threatened to withdraw his work. He later blamed the publishers for the book's limited sales, claiming that their insistence upon labelling him had alienated a wider audience.

Like Hurston, Toomer was strongly influenced by Boasian theories of anthropology, which he had picked up from Waldo Frank. As we saw in the analysis of Hurston, a central aim of this kind of study is to unearth the links between the lives of social groups and their physical and geographical environments. For Toomer, this principle became a key element of his methodology in *Cane*, whose three sections shift from the South to the North and back to the South again. Crucial to all of the sections, even those set in Chicago and Washington, is Georgia, where Toomer had worked at the all-black Sparta Agricultural and Industrial Institute:

> Here was red earth, here pine trees, and smoke or haze in the valley. Here was cane or cotton fields, here cabins. Here was the south, before cities. Here were Negroes, people of the earth, and their singing. Never before had I heard spirituals

> and work songs. Here I heard them in their native setting, and they were like a part of me. At times I identified with the whole scene so intensely that I lost my own identity.[58]

This sense of fusion with the Georgian landscape reiterates some of the ideas expressed in Toomer's letter to *The Liberator*, namely the poet's role as the spokesman for a people, for a place, for a culture. There is a Whitman-esque intensity in the poet's apparent identification with the soul of the South; indeed his intention is for his words to constitute the lived realities and histories of the region. According to Frank, who contributed a preface for the work, Toomer had pulled it off: *Cane* is the South. And the various portraits of Southerners, each striking in their individual pathos, coalesce into a wider panorama, which encapsulates the unique cultural experience of black Southerners, shaped by the history and physical contours of their landscape. The graphic arcs or crescents which precede the first and second sections of the work indicate that these sections are but partial portraits. The almost conjoined arcs at the beginning of the third section suggests a kind of completed, circular whole, a full circle enclosing the culture therein. This graphic image of the circle (and it is important to note that it is *not* fully closed) reflects Toomer's search for literary, spiritual, personal and cultural wholeness, which he saw as central to his enterprise: 'I had been, I suppose, unconsciously seeking – as man must ever seek – an intelligible scheme of things, a sort of whole into which everything must fit . . .'.[59] And this quest for wholeness links his project with that of the high moderns who, as we shall see in Chapter 6, sought to disinter an underlying coherent wholeness from beneath the fragmented rubble of modernity.

As in Eliot and Pound (and, indeed, Ransom and Tate), there is in Toomer a deep suspicion of industrial modernity. This is perhaps most evident in the middle section, set in the urban North, with its unhappy African Americans shackled by white cultural mores and technologies. As Toomer explained in his unpublished autobiography, the South remained a space 'before cities', marked by an organic earthiness, and by the spirituals and work songs which testified to the soul of a people. In *Cane*, therefore, the reader is presented with the repeated field holler of 'Eoho' from 'Cotton

Song' to 'Harvest Song' and from 'Calling Jesus' to the story of Ralph Kabnis. The image of the pine trees, drawn from Toomer's personal observations, recurs throughout the text, as does the reference to the Georgian 'purple dusk', 'cane', 'moon' and 'fire'.[60] Characters appear and reappear in different stories. The overall effect is to unify the individual poems and stories into a coherent piece of literature, which encapsulates both the history of a people ('Eoho' is suggestive of a history of slavery which infects the speech of even contemporary African Americans such those in 'Kabnis') and the geography of the place. However, the organic wholeness of this incandescent landscape is not idealised and its history of violence is never far from the surface of the text. That the black cultures of the South are so tied to the soil is partially due to the spilled black blood which has saturated the terrain, from the child which 'fell out of [Karintha's] womb onto a bed of pine needles in the forest' (p. 2) to the battered and burned Tom Burwell in 'Blood-Burning Moon' (pp. 34–5), from the white ashes of 'black flesh after flame' in 'Portrait in Georgia' (p. 27) to the baby ripped from Mame Lankins's belly and nailed to a tree in 'Kabnis' (p. 90). Thus, Toomer sets up a complex interplay of sensuality, fertility, bloodshed, death, celebration and ambivalence in his anthropologically inspired portrait of black Southern culture.

The experiences of women are crucially important to *Cane*. While the first section focuses on a series of stories about different Georgian women, the subjugation of the female features in all three sections of the book. Sexuality is an integral part of Toomer's female subject, and the first story is the tale of Karintha, a beautiful and much desired African American girl who 'ripens too soon', with her first sexual encounter coming at the age of twelve. Indeed, in all the stories, female sexuality is exploited. Karintha's innocent sensuality is emphasised by her oneness with the natural environment: 'her skin is like dusk on the eastern horizon' and 'her sudden darting past you was a bit of vivid color, like a blackbird that flashes in light' (p. 1). And as the pine trees are ground to dust by the mechanised forces of the sawmill, so the fruit of her womb is devoured by the sawdust and flames of the mill. The smoky wraith of Karintha's dead baby weaves its way through the entire book, embodied in the squealing field rat disembowelled by the black reapers in 'Reapers' and the 'dead birds . . . found / in wells a hundred feet below the ground' (p. 4) in 'November Cotton Flower', and culminating in the horrific story of Mame Lamkins in 'Kabnis'. The point, as mentioned, is to illustrate the indelible links between a people, their heritage and a landscape. But we are also presented with the centrality of these women's stories to an oral culture; their tales are told and retold, passed on and gathered up by the implied addressee. The oral quality of these narratives is accentuated by the mournful spiritual songs which flank many of the stories (see 'Karintha', 'Becky' and 'Carma') and add to the circularity, wholeness and endurance of black folk culture. And the rootedness of black culture is analagous to the 'deep-rooted cane' of the book's epigraph, the 'fermenting syrup' its blood and stories.

The second section of the book shifts northwards to Washington, DC, and opens with a heady portrait of 'Seventh Street', the 'whizzing, whizzing . . . bastard of Prohibition and the War' (p. 39), which in its composition and pace anticipates Dos Passos's *Manhattan Transfer* (1925). The immediate effect, of course, is to bamboozle, to demonstrate the alienating effect of white Northern culture upon the African American subject. Rhobert is described as 'sinking as a diver would sink in mud should the water be drawn off' (p. 40) and the college-educated, intellectual young man of 'Avey' is increasingly alienated from the eponymous female, who retains the sensuous impulses of her Southern inheritance. Unlike Avey, Muriel in 'Box Seat' is imprisoned in the 'bolted box' (p. 62) of Northern 'zoo restrictions and keeper-taboos' (p. 59) enforced by her landlady, Mrs Pribby. Entirely subordinated to white culture, she rejects the advances of her Southern suitor and goes off to watch a vaudeville boxing match between dwarves, blind to her own enslavement to the white values of a 'technical intellect' and 'machine-age designs' (p. 64). 'Bona and Paul', the final story in the second section, returns to the trope of the couple whose values are at odds, first in their tussle on the basketball court and later in their ill-fated courtship. Paul, dubbed 'Mr. Philosopher' (p. 77), is frequently likened to the moon in his waxing and waning understanding of Bona, a Southern white woman who shares with her African American counterparts a strong-willed sensuousness. His procrastinations and intellectual deliberations over their relationships are but 'matches thrown into a dark window' (p. 78) and in the end she rejects him as 'Coloured; cold. Wrong somewhere' (p. 74). In each instance, the anxiety of the young man represents that of the earnest racial protestor or black intellectual messiah. Each in some way tries to 'save' the woman in question. Yet in 'Avey' and 'Bona and Paul', Toomer clearly presents this as a debilitating and impotent exercise, as the young men ultimately fail to recognise the fact of their own enslavement and lost black souls.

The final section of the book, 'Kabnis', offers a portrait of a Northern mixed-race American intellectual who travels South in search of an authentic racial and spiritual identity, only to find himself at odds with the community, being at last interred underground in 'The Hole'. This story clearly anticipates Ralph Ellison's *Invisible Man* (1952) in which an intellectual young man travels from the South to the North in search of himself, only to lose his sense of selfhood and end his narrative buried in the underground basement of a tenement block. Kabnis is the embodiment of the Joycean modern artist, a self-exiled Dedalus figure, full of self-doubt and anxieties, searching for the truths which will enable him to understand both himself and his race.[61] Discomfited by his environment, Kabnis is sleepless and fearful, haunted by images of violence and torture and unable to connect with the landscape:

> Dear Jesus, do not chain me to myself and set these hills and valleys, heaving with folk-songs, so close to me that I cannot reach them . . . What's beautiful there? Hog pens and chicken yards. Dirty red mud. Stinking outhouse . . . This loneliness, dumbness, awful, intangible oppression is enough to drive a man insane. Miles from nowhere. A speck on a Georgia hillside. (p. 83)

Unable to unite with his people or the South, he is also aware of his own minuteness in the grand scheme of his race's history, and conscious of the impotence of his enterprise. Later, he confesses to Halsey and Layman his lack of appreciation for the spirituals, and is so overcome by the story of Mame Lamkins that he imbibes the prohibited 'corn licker', which loses him his job because of the harm such an act does to 'the progress of the Negro race' (p. 93).

Trapped within 'the Hole', which is Halsey's ironmongery workshop, Kabnis maintains his dialectic on the nature of black identity, unable to reconcile his black self with his American self, thereby exhibiting a Du Boisian double-consciousness which results in a kind of racial self-hatred. He continues to fulminate against the black community, their traditions and their faith until his final epiphany. Father John, an obvious John the Baptist figure, utters a hesitant indictment against the 'white folk' who 'made the Bible lie' (p. 115) in assigning the sins of Cain to their black brethren. This revelation engenders a new hope by the end of the novel. It hints at a transformation in Kabnis, as he ascends the stairs to the workshop while outside the sun, a 'gold-glowing child . . . steps into the sky and sends a birth-song slanting down gray dust streets and sleepy windows of the southern town'. The glowing disc of the rising sun (the living child) offers an antidote to the pale moons and dead children of the previous sections. And in the near-completion of the graphic arc that precedes Section 3, and the closing of the 'soft circle' (p. 116) that contains Carrie Kate and Father John, Toomer hints at the wholeness that was the ultimate aim of so many Harlem Renaissance writers.

NOTES

1. Langston Hughes, *The Big Sea: An Autobiography* (New York: Hill and Wang, [1940] 1993), p. 249. David Levering Lewis also uses the term as the title for his influential study. See David Levering Lewis, *When Harlem Was in Vogue* (New York: Knopf, 1981).
2. Ibid. p. 223.
3. See George Hutchinson, *The Harlem Renaissance in Black and White* (Cambridge: Belknap Press of Harvard University Press, 1995); Emily Bernard, 'The Renaissance and the Vogue', in George Hutchinson (ed.), *The Cambridge Companion to the Harlem Renaissance* (Cambridge: Cambridge University Press, 2007), pp. 28–40.
4. W. E. B. Du Bois, 'Returning Soldiers', *The Crisis*, 18 (May 1919), p. 13. Also available online from the Gilder Lehrman

Center for the Study of Slavery, Resistance, and Abolition; http://www.yale.edu/glc/archive/1127.htm (accessed 22 January 2012).

5. W. E. B. Du Bois, 'Criteria of Negro Art', *The Crisis*, 32 (October 1926), p. 296.
6. James Weldon Johnson (ed.), 'Preface' to *The Book of American Negro Poetry* (New York: Harcourt Brace, [1922] 1969), p. 9.
7. Alain Locke, 'The New Negro', in Alain Locke (ed.), *The New Negro: Voices of the Harlem Renaissance* (New York: Simon and Schuster, [1925] 1992), p. 4. Subsequent references will appear in the text.
8. A. Philip Randolph and Chandler Owen, *The Messenger* (November 1917). Cited in Jervis Anderson's *A. Philip Randolph: A Biographical Portrait* (Berkeley: University of California Press, 1972), p. 83.
9. Jonathan W. Gray, 'Harlem Modernisms', in Peter Brooker, Andrzej Gasiorek, Deborah Longworth and Andrew Thacker (eds), *The Oxford Handbook of Modernisms* (Oxford: Oxford University Press, 2010), p. 243.
10. See 'Niagara's Declaration of Principles' (1905). Available online from the Gilder Lehrman Center for the Study of Slavery, Resistance, and Abolition, http://www.yale.edu/glc/archive/1152.htm (accessed 23 January 2012).
11. See John Dewey, *Art as Experience* (New York: Perigee Books, [1934] 1995).
12. Carl Van Vechten, *Nigger Heaven* (Urbana: University of Illinois Press, [1926] 1954), p. 70. Subsequent references will appear in the text.
13. See Houston Baker, for instance, who makes the case that 'Africans and Afro-Americans . . . have little in common with Joycean or Eliotic projects' in *Modernism and the Harlem Renaissance* (Chicago: University of Chicago Press, 1987), pp. xv–vi. Similarly, Paul Lauter argues for a separate black modernism in 'Race and Gender in the Shaping of the American Literary Canon: A Case from the Twenties', in Judith Newton and Deborah Rosenfelt (eds), *Feminist Criticism and Social Change: Sex, Class and Race in Literature and Culture* (New York: Methuen, 1985), pp. 19–54.

14. See George Hutchinson, *The Harlem Renaissance in Black and White* and Hutchinson (ed.), *The Cambridge Companion to the Harlem Renaissance*; and Rachel Farebrother, *The Collage Aesthetic in the Harlem Renaissance* (Aldershot: Ashgate, 2009).
15. Cited in Nathan Huggins, *American Renaissance* (Oxford: Oxford University Press, 1971), p. 58.
16. James Weldon Johnson, 'Harlem: The Culture Capital', in Alain Locke (ed.), *The New Negro: Voices of the Harlem Renaissance*, pp. 310–11.
17. Claude McKay, *Home to Harlem* (New York: Cardinal, [1928] 1965), pp. 25–6.
18. Langston Hughes, *Simple Speaks His Mind* (Long Island: Aeonian Press, 1950), p. 232.
19. Langston Hughes, 'I, Too', in *Selected Poems* (New York: Serpent's Tail, [1959] 1999), p. 275. All subsequent references to Hughes's poetry will appear in the text and refer to this collection.
20. Walt Whitman, 'I Hear America Singing', in *Leaves of Grass*, ed. Jerome Loving (Oxford: Oxford University Press, [1891–2] 1990), p. 17.
21. Langston Hughes, 'The Negro Artist and the Racial Mountain', in Addison Gayle (ed.), *The Black Aesthetic* (New York: Doubleday, 1971), p. 171.
22. Arnold Rampersad, 'Langston Hughes's *Fine Clothes to the Jew*', *Callaloo*, 26 (Winter 1986), p. 149.
23. David Chinitz, 'Literacy and Authenticity: The Blues Poems of Langston Hughes', *Callaloo*, 19 (Winter 1996), p. 189.
24. Cited in Rampersad, 'Langston Hughes's *Fine Clothes to the Jew*', p. 155.
25. Carl Van Vechten, 'The Black Blues', in Cleveland Amory (ed.), *Vanity Fair: A Cavalcade of the 1920s and 1930s* (New York: Viking, 1960), pp. 95–6.
26. W. E. B. Du Bois, 'Review of *Nigger Heaven* by Carl Van Vechten', *The Crisis* (December 1926), p. 81.
27. Cited in Kathleen Pfeiffer's 'Introduction' to *Nigger Heaven* (Urbana: University of Illinois Press, [1926] 2000), p. xiv, p. vii.
28. Langston Hughes, 'Review of *Nigger Heaven* by Carl Van

Vechten', *Pittsburgh Courier* (1927), cited in Emily Bernard, 'The Renaissance and the Vogue', in Hutchinson (ed.), *The Cambridge Companion to the Harlem Renaissance*, p. 38.

29. Langston Hughes, *The Big Sea: An Autobiography*, p. 268.
30. Van Vechten rescued *The Autobiography of an Ex-Colored Man* from obscurity and secured its republication by Knopf in 1927. Cited in Kathleen Pfeiffer's 'Introduction' to *Nigger Heaven* (Urbana: University of Illinois Press, [1926] 2000), p. xxxiv.
31. James Weldon Johnson, *Along this Way* (New York: Penguin, [1933] 1990), p. 382.
32. Carl Van Vechten, 'Moanin' Wid a Sword in Mah Han'', *Vanity Fair* (1926), reprinted in *"Keep A-Inchin' Along": Selected Writings of Carl Van Vechten about Black Art and Letters*, ed. Bruce Kellner (Westport: Greenwood, 1979), p. 55.
33. David Levering Lewis views the book as a 'colossal fraud in which the depiction of the Talented Tenth in high baroque is barely muffled by the throb of the tom-tom'. See Lewis, *When Harlem Was in Vogue*, p. 188. Similarly, Robert O'Meally contends that Van Vechten's novel reveals that 'he never gave up the cliché image of blacks as a naturally arty and primitive people'. See Robert O'Meally, 'Harlem Renaissance Man', *Times Literary Supplement* (30 September 1988), p. 1066.
34. Langston Hughes, 'The Negro Artist and the Racial Mountain' (1926), in Addison Gayle (ed.), *The Black Aesthetic*, p. 167.
35. Margaret Sperry, 'Countee P. Cullen, Negro Boy Poet, Tells His Story', *Brooklyn Daily Eagle* (10 February 1924). Cited in James Smethurst, 'Lyric Stars: Countee Cullen and Langston Hughes', in Hutchinson (ed.), *The Cambridge Companion to the Harlem Renaissance*, p. 112.
36. Countee Cullen, 'Foreword' to Countee Cullen (ed.), *Caroling Dusk: An Anthology of Verse by Negro Poets* (New York: Harper and Brothers, 1927), p. xi.
37. Letter from Zora Neale Hurston to Countee Cullen, 5 March 1943. See *Callaloo*, 6 (May 1979), p. 90.
38. And it was this class which Hughes (although he does not mention Cullen by name in 'The Negro Artist and the Racial

Mountain') sees his errant young poet as belonging to: 'His family is of what I suppose one would call the Negro middle class: people who are by no means rich yet never comfortable nor hungry – smug contented respectable folk, members of the Baptist church', p. 167.

39. Countee Cullen, 'Yet Do I Marvel', in Mary Loeffelholz (ed.), *The Norton Anthology of American Literature, 1914–1945*, vol. D (New York: Norton, 2007), p. 2061. All subsequent references to Cullen's poetry will refer to this source and appear in the text.
40. For the similarities between Eliot's poem and 'Heritage' see David A. Kirby, 'Countee Cullen's "Heritage": A Black "Waste Land"', *South Atlantic Bulletin*, 36.4 (November 1971), pp. 14–20.
41. Claude McKay, *A Long Way from Home* (New York: Arno Press, 1969), pp. 321–2.
42. Ibid. p. 140.
43. Daniel Aaron, *Writers on the Left: Episodes in American Literary Communism* (New York: Columbia University Press, 1992), p. 95.
44. Claude McKay, 'If We Must Die', in *Complete Poems*, ed. William J. Maxwell (Urbana: University of Illinois Press, 2004), p. 177.
45. Claude McKay, *A Long Way from Home*, p. 228.
46. Ibid. pp. 32–3, p. 98.
47. Mark Helbling, 'Claude McKay: Art and Politics', *Negro American Literature Forum*, 7.2 (Summer 1973), p. 51.
48. For an authoritative account of Hurston's life, including her childhood and her relationship with her mother, see Robert E. Hemenway, *Zora Neale Hurston: A Literary Biography* (Urbana: University of Illinois Press, 1977).
49. A number of critics have emphasised Hurston's ambivalence toward black folk cultures. See, for instance, William M. Ramsay, 'The Compelling Ambivalence of Zora Neale Hurston's *Their Eyes Were Watching God*', *Southern Literary Journal*, 27.1 (Fall 1994), pp. 36–50, and Carla Kaplan, 'Zora Neale Hurston and the "Margarine Negro"', in Hutchinson (ed.), *The Cambridge Companion to the Harlem Renaissance*, pp. 213–35.

50. W. E. B. Du Bois, 'The Sorrow Songs', in *The Souls of Black Folk* (London: Penguin, [1903] 1996), p. 205.
51. James Weldon Johnson (ed.), 'Preface' to *The Book of American Negro Poetry*, p. 21. Reference to the 1931 preface.
52. See Alain Locke, 'The New Negro', in Alain Locke (ed.), *The New Negro: Voices of the Harlem Renaissance*, p. 5.
53. Zora Neale Hurston, 'You Don't Know Us Negroes', unpublished essay. Cited in Kaplan, 'Zora Neale Hurston and the "Margarine Negro"', p. 217.
54. Zora Neale Hurston, *Their Eyes Were Watching God* (London: Virago, [1937] 2006), p. 10. All subsequent references will appear in the text.
55. Jean Toomer, letter to Gorham Munson (31 October 1922). Cited in *The Letters of Jean Toomer, 1919–1924*, ed. Mark Whalan (Knoxville: University of Tennessee Press, 2006), p. 90.
56. For a thoughtful appraisal of Toomer's relationship with Frank and the often forgotten 'Young Americans' of the Chicago Renaissance, see Mark Whalan's excellent *Race, Manhood, and Modernism in America* (Knoxville: University of Tennessee Press, 2007).
57. Jean Toomer, letter to *The Liberator* (19 August 1922). Cited in *The Letters of Jean Toomer, 1919–1924*, ed. Whalan, pp. 70–1.
58. Jean Toomer, 'On Being American'. Cited in Mark Whalan, 'Jean Toomer and the Avant-Garde', in Hutchinson (ed.), *The Cambridge Companion to the Harlem Renaissance*, p. 73.
59. As Michael Krasny observes: 'The arcs represent the basic design of *Cane*, which, like a circle, moves from the simple forms of life in the South to the more complex forms in the North and back to the South in "Kabnis"'. See Michael Krasny, 'The Aesthetic Structure of Jean Toomer's *Cane*', *Negro American Forum*, 9.2 (Summer 1975), p. 42.
60. Jean Toomer, *Cane* (New York: Liveright, [1923] 1975). All subsequent references will appear in the text.
61. Many critics read Kabnis as the implied addressee of the book's first section and an extension of Paul, John and the young man in 'Avey'. For an extended and convincing reading

of Kabnis as a Dedalus-like figure, see William J. Goede, 'Jean Toomer's Ralph Kabnis: Portrait of the Negro Artist as a Young Man', *Phylon*, 30.1 (First Quarter 1969), pp. 73–85.

CHAPTER 6

'Make it New!' Experiments in Poetry and Drama

In 1911 the English poet and critic T. E. Hulme foretold in *Speculations* a period of 'dry, hard, classical verse'.[1] He predicted a new kind of poetry, which was to be the antithesis of Victorian romanticism and would be realised as Imagism (or *Imagisme* in its earliest incarnation). And although the origins of Imagism are contested, it is generally agreed that while Hulme himself anticipated the movement in some of his earlier poems, such as 'Autumn' and 'A City Sunset' (1909), it was the American poet Ezra Pound who promoted and brought it to wider public attention.[2] Indeed, the catalyst for the inception of Imagism was the famous meeting between Pound, his former fiancée Hilda Doolittle (H. D.) and Richard Aldington in the spring of 1912 in the tearoom of the British Museum, where Pound edited H. D.'s verse 'Hermes of the Ways' and applied the signature 'H. D. Imagiste'.

'Ezra was so much worked up by these poems of H. D.'s that he removed his pince-nez and informed us that we were Imagists', wrote Aldington later. 'Was this the first time I had heard this Pickwickian word?'[3] The following autumn, when *The Ripostes of Ezra Pound* was published, Pound added, as an appendix, 'The Complete Poetical Works of T. E. Hulme', as well as a preface which introduced the mysterious '*Imagistes*' to the world. The inclusion of Hulme's works was partly a joke between friends, given that the 'Complete Poetical Works' consisted of just five short poems. Yet it was also an act of appropriation, relegating Hulme to a mere appendix supporting Pound's writing. But of course Hulme's importance went well beyond this. He had developed his ideas about the need to find new expressive modes for poetic language at the Poets' Club, which he joined in 1908 (Pound himself becoming a member after his arrival in England) and later the Succession Club, also known as the School of Images, which he founded with F. S. Flint. For Hulme, whose ideas had been informed by his reading of Henri Bergson's theories of interpenetration, the modern French symbolists (Remy de Gourmont and the *vers librists*) and the reactionary group Action Française, figurative language had become tired, inefficient and inappropriate for representing modernity. And his repeated calls for a new 'attitude of the mind', the necessity of *vers libre*, a 'new technique, new convention' and 'new spirit' in poetry found their way into the manifestos of Flint and Pound for what was to be one of the most important and radical innovations in Anglo-American poetry: Imagism.[4]

Ezra Pound was a party to many of these early discussions about how contemporary poetry might be replaced by '*vers libre*, by the Japanese tanka and the haikai'. But even before his move to England he had expressed remarkably similar ideas in a letter of October 1908 to William Carlos Williams.[5] His 'ultimate attainments of poesy', he explained, were:

1. To paint the thing as I see it.
2. Beauty.
3. Freedom from didacticism.
4. It is only good manners if you repeat a few other men to at least do it better or more briefly. Utter originality is of course out of the question.[6]

Compared to his remarkably similar 'A Few Don'ts for an Imagist' (1913), these maxims show that Pound was already developing the foundational tenets of Imagism even before he moved to England and encountered Hulme, Flint and the other members of the Poets' Club. In this context, his angry reaction to Flint's 1915 article 'The History of Imagism' for *The Egoist* (which he called 'bullshit') is hardly surprising.

Furthermore, Pound's centrality to the movement is validated by his practical efforts to get examples of Imagist writing into print. Soon after the British Museum meeting, he set about promoting the work of Aldington and H. D., which he sent to Harriet Monroe at her recently founded *Poetry* magazine. Aldington's work appeared first, in November 1912, with a biographical note which described the *imagistes* as 'ardent Hellenists who are pursuing interesting experiments in *vers libre*; trying to attain in English certain subtleties of cadence of the kind which Mallarmé and his followers studied in French'.[7] H. D.'s poems appeared in the January 1913 edition of the magazine, followed in the March issue by Flint and Pound's celebrated manifestos. Flint outlined three precepts which have come to be regarded as the rules of Imagism:

1. Direct treatment of the 'thing' whether subjective or objective.
2. To use absolutely no word that does not contribute to the presentation.
3. As regarding rhythm: to compose in the sequence of the musical phrase not in the sequence of a metronome.[8]

Pound, meanwhile, stressed the necessity for linguistic brevity and defined the 'Image' as 'that which presents an intellectual and emotional complex in an instant of time', designed 'to record the precise instant when a thing outward and objective transforms itself, or darts into a thing inward and subjective'.[9]

A year later, Pound published an anthology, *Des Imagistes* (1914), which included the work of six Americans (Pound himself, Skipwith Cannell, H. D., William Carlos Williams, Amy Lowell and Allen Upward), four English poets (Aldington, Flint, Ford Madox Hueffer and John Cournos) and an Irishman (James Joyce). Strictly speaking, only the work of Pound, H. D. and Aldington conformed to the tenets of Imagism and, perhaps as a result, the volume was not well received on either side of the Atlantic. Indeed, by 1915 Pound had gravitated toward Vorticism, about which he had written an article for *Blast!* in September 1914. But his departure from Imagist circles was confirmed by the arrival of Amy Lowell, a wealthy Bostonian socialite who sought to establish a semblance of 'democracy' amongst the discontented Imagists. Her suggestion of an annual anthology entitled *Some Imagist Poets* did not go down well with Pound, who wrote in August 1914:

> I should like the name 'Imagisme' to retain some sort of meaning. It stands, or I should like it to stand, for hard light, clear edges. I cannot trust any democratized committee to maintain that standard. Some will be splay-footed and some sentimental.[10]

The 1915–17 volumes of *Some Imagist Poets* seemed to confirm Pound's fears, moving away from the original precepts of Imagism toward *vers libre*, with the hardness of the 'Image' replaced by a more generalised pictorial impression. Amy Lowell also brought in the American poet John Gould Fletcher, convinced D. H. Lawrence to contribute to the 1915 and 1916 anthologies and introduced 'polyphonic' prose, a rhythmical form of prose which deploys characteristics of verse other than strict metre.

For Pound, this 'Amygism' was simply intolerable, and he took every opportunity to parody and deride the editor. But already Imagism seemed to be approaching its natural end. In *Tendencies in Modern American Poetry* (1917), Lowell wrote:

> There will be no more volumes of *Some Imagist Poets*. The collection has done its work. These three little books are the germ, the nucleus of the school; its spreading out, its amplifications, must be sought in the unpublished work of the individual members of the group.[11]

Indeed, the movement remained dormant until 1930, when Aldington published the *Imagist Anthology 1930,* containing poems by everyone who had contributed to the earlier publications except 'poor Amy who was dead, Skipwith Cannell whom we couldn't trace, and Ezra who was sulky'.[12]

By excluding some of the early American contributors, Aldington gave the impression that Imagism was exclusively a British phenomenon, an impression strengthened by the fact that even most of the Americans were based in London. What is more, Pound's diatribes against the United States helped to widen the gulf between his literary projects and the influences of his homeland. But the importance of this short movement to modern American poetry should not be underestimated, for Pound's example had a tremendous influence on American Objectivist poets such as William Carlos Williams, George Oppen and Louis Zukofsky. Writing in the February 1931 Objectivist issue of *Poetry*, Zukofsky remarked that 'the poems of Ezra Pound alone possess objectivication to a most constant degree; his objects are musical shapes'. Indeed, with its commitment to precision and exactitude, Objectivism was, if anything, a distilled version of Imagism, albeit one placing more emphasis on the physical shape of the poetry and its aural, musical qualities. The connection between Objectivism and Imagism was perhaps best articulated by the American poet Jack Spicer in his *Letters to Lorca* (1957): 'I would like to make poems out of real objects . . . I would like to point to the real, disclose it, to make a poem that had no sound in it but the pointing of a finger'.[13] And certainly what we see in American poetry is a clear line of influence from the Imagists through the Objectivists to Charles Olson, Denise Levertov and Marianne Moore. Indeed, the tremendous impact of Imagism's economy and precision on twentieth-century American poetry can hardly be exaggerated. Even contemporary poets such as Robert Creely and John Hoffman essentially work in Imagism's shadow.

Perhaps the most immediate characteristic of Imagist poetry is its sheer brevity. Pound's 'direct treatment of the thing' encouraged short, hard poems such as 'In a Station of the Metro', distilling language to get at the essence of the object. Yet not all modernist poets were similarly brief; indeed, many tried to explore the sublime, transcendent imagination in much longer works. Wallace Stevens, for instance, uses the poetic 'I' in his 'rage for order' (a term made famous by his poem 'The Idea of Order at Key West') as a means of classifying the chaotic modern world. Similarly, William Carlos Williams, who contributed to many of the Imagist volumes, later created a five-book epic monument to one New Jersey city in *Paterson* (1964). And Pound himself spent much of his creative life working on a long epic sequence, *The Cantos* (1964), which examined the relationship between history, the self and the transcendental.

As early as 1908, the Anglo-Irish poet William Butler Yeats identified 'two ways before literature – upward into ever growing subtlety . . . when literature becomes religion . . . or downward, taking the soul with us until all is simplified and solidified again. That is the choice of choices – the way of the bird, until common eyes have lost us, or to the market carts'.[14] Traditionally, critics have seen Yeats as taking the road upward, and his protégé Pound as taking the downward trajectory to the 'market carts', focusing on the 'thingyness' of things while Yeats stared myopically into the world of allusive symbols. There is certainly some truth in this, but there is also a middle ground, in which modern poetry became both 'more subtle' and allusive, and yet more solid in its emphases. T. S. Eliot, one of the high priests of modernist poetry, offers a case in point in the modernist masterpiece *The Waste Land* (1922), which combines a highly wrought chain of allusions with hard images of a coarsened landscape and the living dead. He also depersonalises the poetic voice, a recurrent aspect of Imagism: 'The progress of the artist is continual self-sacrifice, a continual extinction of the personality'.[15] Eliot's work might reach for the sublime, but it is solidly rooted in the grubby details of the immediate, modern world. Indeed, his work offers a perfect example of how modernist poetry can evade Yeats's 'choice of choices', the poet not necessarily choosing between lofty (and lengthy) abstraction or hard, small objects, but finding a place somewhere between the two.

While the story of modern American poetry has been told, retold and endlessly contested, the story of modern American drama has been relatively neglected. Drama has undoubtedly been marginalised in twentieth-century criticism, losing out to the poetic concentration of the New Critics, the subsequent focus on prose, and the canon-busting theoretical studies with which the century closed. Writing in 1992, Christopher Bigsby wondered: 'Whatever happened to American drama? Why is it that literary critics, cultural historians, literary theorists, those interested in the evolution of the genre, in discourse and ideology, find so little to say about the theatre and the American theatre in particular?'[16] In the twenty years or so since Bigsby's observations the critical scene has evolved, not least due to his own co-edited multi-volume complete history of the American theatre. Younger scholars have also contributed to filling this gap in American literary studies, including Theresa Saxon, Gary Richardson, Stephen Watt and Sally Burke. Still, the critical chasm identified by Bigsby is perhaps attributable to the relatively late development of an indigenous American drama. While there was plenty of interest in the theatre throughout the eighteenth and early nineteenth centuries, with the likes of William Dunlap and Royall Taylor producing some fine work, it was not until the last part of the nineteenth century that genuinely American drama captured the public imagination.

Perhaps the foremost modern American play was James Herne's *Margaret Fleming* (1890), which raised the kind of moral questions typically associated with Ibsen or Shaw. The play focuses on a woman forced to confront the practical outcome (as well as the emotional implications) of her husband's infidelities. Merging melodrama with realism, *Margaret Fleming* paved the way for drama interested in exploring the psychological theories of Freud and Jung, such as Susan Glaspell's *Suppressed Desires* (1914) and Eugene O'Neill's *The Emperor Jones* (1924), *Desire Under the Elms* (1924) and *Mourning Becomes Electra* (1931). Herne's play also brought to the fore the issues of women's rights and the position of women within marriage and society. For instance, after confessing and apologising to his wife for his moral misdemeanours with Lena Schmidt, Philip Fleming is shocked at his wife's response:

> MARGARET: Suppose – I – had been unfaithful to you?
> PHILIP: (*With a cry of repugnance.*) Oh, Margaret!
> MARGARET: (*Brokenly.*) There! You see! You are a man, and you have your ideals of – the – the – sanctity – of – the thing you love. Well, I am a woman – and perhaps – I, too, have the same ideals.[17]

The suggestion that a wife might expect the same degree of loyalty, devotion and respect from a husband hints at the incarceration of women within the institution of marriage – an issue famously addressed by Charlotte Perkins Gilman in her short story 'The Yellow Wallpaper' (1892). Herne deliberately juxtaposes Margaret's inherent goodness (she adopts and nurses the illegitimate child born to her husband's mistress and stands by the errant Philip as he attempts to rebuild his reputation) with her husband's moral dissolution, bringing our attention to the misogyny engrained in the male psyche. But Margaret does not accept her compromised position unquestioningly, and by the end of the play the dynamics in the relationship have been radically altered.

Similar ideas were also at play in Susan Glaspell's *Trifles* (1916), based on the real-life story of an Iowan farm wife's alleged murder of her husband. In the play, the murder seems to have been carried out in apparent retaliation for the murder of a pet canary (not the most subtle image of domesticated femininity), Glaspell implying that the wife's voice, like that of the canary, has been stifled by a loveless image. Again the play focuses on the difference in attitudes between the sexes, in this instance between the men investigating the case and their wives who are called in to assist. The men rifle through the effects of the Wrights, rampaging across the crime scene, oblivious to the clues of emotional and psychological abuse. The women, on the other hand, are capable of reading the signs and recognise the real nature of the relationship. Nonetheless, their voices or opinions are not solicited by their husbands (just as Minnie's story is never heard) and their potential insights go unrecognised. Glaspell's play offers a stylistic departure from the work of Herne, as she deliberately works her political theme into the structure of the play. Minnie Wright, the alleged murderess, is the absent heart of the drama. Her story is reconstructed (both in the retelling of the real-life case by Glaspell and in the investigations of the men within the play), but she is never present or heard. In this way, Glaspell signals both the centrality and the invisibility of women in American life, a theme which was to feature in later works such as *Berenice* (1919), *Inheritors* (1921) and the Pulitzer Prize winning *Alison's House* (1930).

Glaspell's dramatic work with the Provincetown Players (where she championed the early plays of a young Eugene O'Neill) and her later involvement with the Federal Theater Project not only address feminist concerns, but reveal a deep interest in class and the effects of capitalism upon human consciousness and relationships. Indeed, this played a part in much dramatic work of the period, especially plays produced after the onset of the Great Depression. For instance, Clifford Odets's *Waiting for Lefty* (1935) for the

Group Theater in New York centres on the planning of a labour strike, while Sidney Kingsley's *Dead End* (1935) examines the gulf between the very wealthy and the very poor by exploring the juxtaposition of a luxury apartment house next to a tenement slum block in New York City. A much earlier work, Charles Klein's *The Lion and the Mouse* (1905), examines the power of corporate monopolies. And one of the most successful and experimental works of this kind was Elmer Rice's *The Adding Machine* (1923), in which a department store accountant finds himself displaced by the machine after more than two decades of service. As his boss explains: 'efficiency – economy – business – *business* – **Business**'.[18] Angered, Mr Zero murders his boss, a crime for which he is later tried and executed. After his death he awakes in the afterlife, only to find himself a mere cog in a much larger machine, in which souls are repaired, rebranded and returned to service. Shifting away from realism, the play deploys a range of expressionistic techniques to dramatise the interior consciousness of Zero, including a revolving floor space which moves to the sound of a merry-go-round, flashing lights, and various cacophonous offstage sounds. With the shift to the afterlife in the second half of the play, the viewer is presented with an entirely subjective scene, the expression of Zero's deepest fears and nightmares, as his spirit is broken. He chooses to spend his time working on the celestial adding machine, only to be displaced once again and returned to earth for reuse. Merging the representation of the psychological with the social and philosophical concerns of the time, the play represents a transition from the realist mode to the more experimental and overtly political agitprop drama of the late 1920s and 1930s.

Contemporary American dramatists, from David Mamet and Tony Kushner to Edward Albee and Wendy Wasserstein, owe much to these early formal experiments. From *Margaret Fleming* through to a play such as *Angels in America* (1993) we can trace a thread of social radicalism, or at least social conscience, with authors often frankly confronting issues such as poverty, prejudice, inequality and hypocrisy. Indeed, a deep concern with contemporary moral, social and political issues has been a mainstay of American drama ever since the dawn of the twentieth century, from plays about women's rights or gay liberation to fierce denunciations of the ills of capitalism. But alongside this has been a strong commitment to formal experimentation which began in the years of modernist experiment across the literary and visual arts. Not unlike American poets and novelists, modern American dramatists sought out ever more radical means with which to address an increasingly complex modernity. Their work is often unheralded; today, Fitzgerald and Hemingway are far better known than Glaspell or O'Neill. But it was no less compelling and successful, and if we want to understand the full breadth of the modernist moment, we need to look to the theatre as well as the printed page.

EZRA POUND

Despite his reputation as perhaps the most influential and genuinely innovative of all American modernists, Ezra Pound remains a very hard man to like. In later life in particular, he became notorious for his inexcusable anti-Semitism and enthusiasm for his native land's fascist adversaries. Between 1941 and 1943, for example, he made a series of shameful broadcasts for Rome Radio supporting the regimes of Benito Mussolini and Adolf Hitler, denigrating the United States and identifying the Jews as responsible for the economic ills of modernity. And in one particularly painful broadcast he turned his ire towards Britain:

> But you let in the Jew and the Jew rotted your Empire and you yourselves outjewed the Jew. Your allies in the victimized holdings are the *bunya*, that is the money lender. You stand for NOTHING but usury, and above metal usury you have built up bank usury . . .[19]

Since even some of his poetic works, including seven sections of *The Cantos* dealing with the topic of usury, contain anti-Semitic content, it is never easy to separate the poet from the pernicious politics.

All the same, there is no escaping Pound's enormous contribution to literary modernism. As we have seen, he encouraged and championed a range of young poets including William Carlos Williams,

H. D. and Louis Zukofsky. The final version of Eliot's *The Waste Land* is highly indebted to Pound's editorial eye, and Pound was a great help to James Joyce, including his poem 'I Hear an Army' in *Des Imagistes*, sending the first chapter of *A Portrait of the Artist as a Young Man* (1916) to *The Egoist*, and even helping to arrange the publication of early chapters from *Ulysses* (1922) in the *Little Review* in 1918. Even Yeats, with whom Pound spent three winters (1913–16) at Stone Cottage in Sussex, acting as his secretary, confessed his admiration. 'To talk over a poem with him', Yeats remarked, 'is like getting you to put a sentence into dialect. All becomes clear and natural'.[20] These are not, however, qualities readily associated with Pound's own poetry, which often strikes readers as almost dementedly difficult. Even at the level of basic comprehension, Pound's work can be almost unfathomable, blending Greek, Latin, French, Spanish, German and Chinese as well as a heady mixture of myths, diffuse histories and personal observations. And while the author himself insisted that his work was perfectly simple, instructing the reader to move smoothly through the work without recourse to notes, the sheer range of his references and allusions can be horribly daunting for even the most seasoned scholar.

One factor in Pound's sheer difficulty was his constant innovation, his continuous quest for poetic reinvention and inquiry. Once he had mastered each technique or become associated with each new trend, he immediately moved on, as though in some unending poetic quest. First an Imagist, then a Vorticist, he was determined to create an American epic of his own. Writing to his mother in 1908, he explained that he had found in the Portuguese poet Luis de Camões, the author of *Os Lusiades*, the kind of epic style which would be well received by the American academy.[21] From the late 1910s through to his death, Pound laboured at his most challenging of works, *The Cantos*. In the meantime, he honed his skills with a wide variety of verse styles, not least in his Imagist poem 'In a Station at the Metro', the most anthologised of all his works. Like so many contributions to *Des Imagistes*, the poem is startling in its brevity, with the title forming the first line:

> The apparition of these faces in the crowd;
> Petals on a wet, black bough.[22]

The supreme poetic expression of Pound's precepts of Imagism, this twenty-word (when including the title) haiku-like poem vividly presents a moment in time, in which the expunged poetic 'I' regards the faces of the underground commuters as like the petals on a gleaming branch. There is no simile, however, in Pound's short verse. The title line situates the poem in the Paris underground, the hellish site of transport machinery, from which the natural world is banished. Curiously, however, the faces coalesce and come to form the natural image of a cluster of petals on a wet branch, thereby juxtaposing two separate ideas (one of the central features of the Japanese haiku): the natural world of the petals and the Dante-esque world of ghosts, inherent in the word 'apparition'. The word 'station' within the title is also important, not merely in terms of situating the poem but its connotation of an end zone, a terminus, a stopping place. In its way this word encapsulates the point of the 'Image', which is to arrest, freeze and capture a moment in time, to render stationary both the observation and the impression it forms on the perceiving mind.

The reference to the underground evokes a classical world, calling forth the ghosts of Aeneas, Odysseus, Dante and Sir Orfeo, amongst others. Pound's engagement with the classical world is not unique among the modernists, many of whom turned to the classical past as a palliative for the lost radiance of modernity. Indeed, another of Pound's contributions to *Des Imagistes*, 'The Return' (1912), turns to the classical world and to the subject of poetry itself:

> See, they return; ah, see the tentative
> Movements, and the slow feet,
> The trouble in the pace and the uncertain
> Wavering!

The classical gods are brought back to life by modern poetry, but their movements are tentative, shaky and uncertain due to 'trouble in the pace' and the altered, unstable metrical feet of the poetry within which they are regenerated. Thus, in an exquisite merging of form and theme, the unstable rhythm is the key to the meaning of the poem: the ancient gods may return but they do so within the radical new structures of modern poetry. The dissonance between past and present is made manifest in the shift from present to past tense halfway through the poem:

> These were the 'Wing'd-with-Awe',
> Inviolable.
> Gods of the wingèd shoe!

Set at the approximate mid-point of the poem, the isolated 'inviolable' performs an act inverse to its meaning and breaks the poem in two. From this point onwards, line continuity is lost; in its place, we have a fragmented series of exclamatory statements which culminate in an image of the gods as 'slow on the leash / pallid . . . leash-men'.[23] Fragmentation ultimately gives way to stasis, with the word 'pallid' suggesting the white stone of a statue or the deathliness of a wan face. The gods may return, but their vitality is diminished by the structures of modernity.

The gods make a more assertive return in the first of Pound's cantos, which introduces an Odysseus-like figure as he prepares to embark on a journey.[24] Again, the ancient merges with the modern, as Odysseus's quest merges with that of the poet: each goes in search of a lost civilisation. Indeed, this opening canto introduces one of the overriding themes: the history of various global civilisations, from Confucian China to the rise and fall of the European empires, from the emergence of an independent United States to the resurgence of Mussolini's Italy. However, while composed chronologically, *The Cantos* do not work in a linear fashion. They jump forwards and backwards in time, as seen in the opening canto with the juxtaposition of the Greek hero and the modern poet, or as demonstrated by the references to Robert Browning and Picasso in Canto II and the subsequent shift to the story of Myo Cid (1043–1099) in Canto III.

Pound claimed that the shape of *The Cantos* was 'ideogrammic', which is a more complex and layered version of his theory of the 'Image':

> [The] Chinese ideogram does not try to be a picture of a sound, or to be a written sign recalling a sound, but it is still

> the picture of a thing; of a thing in a given position or relation, or of a combination of things. It *means* the thing or the action or the situation, or quality germane to several things that it pictures. . . .
>
> [The Chinese man] is to define red. How can he do it in a picture that isn't painted in red paint?
>
> He puts (or his ancestor put) together the abbreviated pictures of
>
> ROSE CHERRY
> IRON RUST FLAMINGO[25]

Pound evidently believed that an abstract concept could be constructed from a series of concrete images. (Thus the abstract colour red is constructed out of a series of markers, which everyone knows.) In the same way, each canto is composed of various ideograms, building to create a concrete image or event which contributes to the overall thematic concept. Each canto is layered (though not dependent) upon its predecessor to build toward Pound's ultimate theme. Indeed, the first thirty cantos form the bedrock of concrete images to which Pound returns as he works toward the completion of the poem.

One of the abiding features of the epic form is its beginning *in medias res* (in the middle of things), with the reader left to pick up the thread of a story whose origins lie in the distant past. Homer and Virgil, whose epic poems suffuse the atmosphere and rhythm of the first canto, both use this technique, and since Pound saw himself as their heir, it is no surprise that he followed suit. Thus Canto I opens with the conjunctive 'And', which suggests not a beginning but the ebb and flow of history as 'we [the poet and Odysseus] set up mast and sail on that swart ship'.[26] The men set off on a voyage for paradise, and for Odysseus this paradise is clearly his home, Ithaca, towards which he sails blindly, buffeted by the gods along the way. At this early stage of the poem, however, the nature of the *poet's* destination is not outlined, and so he travels with Odysseus to the Underworld of Pluto (Hades) and Prosperina (Persephone) in a purgative act of preparation for the journey ahead. Canto I ends with the emergence of the poet and Odysseus from the darkness of hell, revitalised for the quest of finding or founding a new heavenly civilisation. The concluding line of the canto, 'So that:', contributes to the impression of movement and process which the connective 'And' creates at the beginning, sweeping the reader through to the second canto.

Canto II resumes the seafaring theme, inspired by the ancient epicists but also by the old English poem 'The Seafarer'. Here the navigating sailor is Acöetes, who discovers on board Dionysus in the guise of 'a young boy loggy with vine-must' (p. 7). When the ship is attacked by Lydian criminals, eager to sell the boy into slavery, the god reveals his powers and in a series of metamorphoses transforms the men into disfigured man-beasts. The primary theme in Canto II is metamorphosis, which is evident not only in the shape-shifting Dionysus but also in the overall structure. The canto embodies the ideogrammic method, shifting from Robert Browning's notoriously difficult poem 'Sordello' (1840), based on the life of the idealised Lombardi troubadour Sordello da Gioto, to the Han Dynasty poet So-shu (Ssu-ma Hsiang-ju), to the old Irish sea god Lír, to the 'eyes of Picasso', and eventually returning to the classical scene at hand. The theme of metamorphosis is also evident in the verse itself, which becomes more rhythmical in the scenes outlining Dionysus's supernatural powers. Canto II also admits the introduction of a new theme, which comes to dominate later cantos: the disfiguring qualities of greed (later referred to as usury) which transmogrifies the Lydian pirates.

Canto III opens with a continuation of the lyric mode from Canto II and resumes the focus on greed, with the introduction of a new historical figure, Myo Cid, the hero of the oldest preserved Spanish epic poem, *El Cantar de Myo Çid*. Here, Myo Cid is celebrated for his skill at fooling the usurers to obtain money to pay the knights involved in the salvation of Christian European civilisation:

> And left his truck with Raquel and Vidas,
> That big box of sand, with the pawn-brokers,
> To get pay for his menie (p. 12).

A more modern version of European civilisation is also linked to the theme of usury and greed in the opening lines of Canto III, which refer to Pound's 1908 trip to Venice. The poetic 'I' which opens the canto sits 'on the Dogana's steps / For the gondolas cost too much, that year' (p. 11). Sitting before the Venetian waters, the poet falls into a reverie in which the Tuscan gods, minor gods, warrior gods and nymphs float about him and arise out of the canal before he summons the Spanish knight in the second section of the canto. The structural juxtaposition of the modern poet inspired by the gods with the medieval hero, Myo Cid, echoes the shape in Canto I and encapsulates Pound's intention for the entire cantos: to present the history of a civilisation in a single modernist epic poem, through an ideogrammic layering of concrete and subjective facts, events and stories. And the abiding, if sporadic, presence of the poet throughout *The Cantos* testifies to Pound's insistence on the civilising role of the poet as guardian of the nation and his faith in the restorative power of literature: for 'if a nation's literature declines', he wrote, 'the nation atrophies and decays'.[27]

H. D. (HILDA DOOLITTLE)

Often praised as the finest of the Imagist poets, H. D. published her first poems under the moniker 'H. D. Imagiste' in Harriet Monroe's *Poetry* in January 1913. Heralding the birth of Imagism, 'Hermes of the Way', 'Priapus' and 'Epigram' essentially conformed to the criteria of the new movement that were revealed in a subsequent issue of the magazine. Crucially, the poems also disclose H. D.'s commitment to Hellenism, which she maintained throughout her work, and which firmly rooted her in the modernist literary canon, as part of the new wave of classicism foreseen by T. E. Hulme. As T. S. Eliot had remarked in his celebrated review of Joyce's *Ulysses*, the evocation of the classical past through the 'mythical method' was 'a goal toward which all good literature strives, so far as it is good'.[28] Writing a year later on Hulme, Eliot added that 'classicism is in a sense reactionary, but it must be in a profounder sense revolutionary'.[29] No wonder, then, that H. D.'s interest in the classical world endeared her to the likes of Pound and Eliot and helped earn her the title of 'Imagiste'. Unfortunately, her early champions turned against her after the initial sweep of excitement about the new classicism had subsided. By the time of her publication of H. D.'s second volume of poems in 1921, both Pound and Eliot now dismissed her preoccupation with ancient Greece as narrow and decadent. She was a 'refined, charming and utterly narrow-minded she-bard', wrote Pound, who claimed she peddled 'Alexandrine Greek bunk'.[30]

As critics such as Susan Friedman have argued, the decline of H. D.'s literary reputation is due in part to the centrality of a female subjectivity within her poetry. In an age when poetry was cultivated as hard and classical by predominantly male poets, H. D.'s failure to abandon the feminine rendered her poetry soft and of 'dubious . . . authenticity', according to Douglas Bush, who repeatedly dismissed her work as 'female' romanticism.[31] 'H. D.'s myth is as elementary as the fortunate fall,' wrote the critic Joseph N. Riddel:

> The identity of the creative self as woman is threatened not only by the incompleteness of the female but by the insubstantiality of subjectivity which characterizes the feminine . . . In terms of the self-consciousness that forces her to contemplate her ambiguous role as woman poet, she seeks the completeness of the subject in the object. She must turn herself into a poem.[32]

Many readers will disagree with Riddel's assumptions about the 'incompleteness' and 'ambiguity' of the female poet, and Friedman in particular has taken issue with some of his judgements. But of course there are more positive ways of interpreting H. D.'s work, and in particular her classical enthusiasm; and indeed some critics see it as simultaneously engaging with and running counter to the more overtly aesthetics of Pound and Eliot. Sympathetic critics have often seen H. D.'s classically suffused lyrical world as a rejection of the epic imperative associated with militarism and masculinity.[33] Marianne Moore, for example, admired the work for precisely its feminine 'heroics which do not confuse transcendence with domination'.[34]

In H. D.'s first poem to appear in *Poetry*, 'Hermes of the Ways', Hermes, messenger to the gods, does not seem to offer the clear lines of communication associated with the Poundian 'Image':

I know him
Of the triple path-ways, Hermes,
Who awaiteth.
Dubious.
Facing three ways . . .
The boughs of the trees
Are twisted
By many bafflings.[35]

The use of the word 'dubious' is deliberately double-edged; Hermes is unsure about his own ability to convey his message adequately, but the word also suggests that Hermes may in fact be untrustworthy and duplicitous, 'facing three ways'. In some ways, then, this is a subtle refutation of Pound's claims about the clarity of the Imagist poem with its hard, crystalline lyricism – and makes for a telling contrast with the *opening* lines of H. D.'s poem:

The hard sand breaks,
And the grains of it
Are clear as wine (p. 64).

Without superfluous lyricism or figurative ornament, the poem begins: what we have here is an objective rendering of the space between land and sea, and a strong imagistic presentation of the sand. The ambiguous, in-between nature of this location is almost imperceptible, as the poem continues with a series of concrete, Poundian images. However, the ambiguity of the location is underlined by the inappropriateness of Hermes as a subject for the Imagist object. His uncertainty is inherent in his very role – interlocutor between the godly and human worlds and guardian of the borders between them – and is heralded in the very title of the poem with the indefinite word 'ways'.

A further complication arises with the introduction of the subjective 'I'. In fact, the presence of the speaker calling to Hermes seems another shift away from Imagist precepts. The 'I' recognises the 'triple path-ways', the multifaceted nature of the messenger. The poetic 'I', it seems, can distinguish the room for complication within the image, the difficulty of portraying 'the direct object of the "thing"'. Lashed by the dune wind which 'whips round [her] ankles' (p. 64), the 'I' is brought together in the in-between place with the dubious Hermes in the perfect Image, 'where sea-grass tangles with / shore-grass' (p. 65). And of course for H. D. Imagiste, the allusion to the classical myth is more than a mere technique to portray the inadequacies and sentimentality of modernity. It enables the poet to present the inherent complications of the myth, and subtly to undermine the masculinist assumptions of modern classicism.

Published in *Some Imagist Poets* (1915), 'Oread' is generally considered the Imagist poem *par excellence*. While nimbly capturing an instant of time, it summons the Oread, a mountain nymph often associated with Artemis, the Greek goddess of the hunt. The poem, a single unified image, is an invocation:

> Whirl up, sea –
> Whirl your pointed pines
> Splash your great pines
> On our rocks,
> Hurl your green over us,
> Cover us with your pools of fir (p. 62).

Again, H. D. gravitates away from the static Image – the brief moment of observation, impression and perception – towards a more dynamic depiction of the relationship and space between the land and the sea. The dynamism of the poem is underpinned by the series of imperative verbs, which constitute five words of the twenty-six word poem, and contribute to the energetic sense of motion which drives both the poem and the sea forward: 'whirl', 'whirl', 'splash', 'hurl' and 'cover'. The Oread, it seems, calls upon the sea to rise and cover the 'pointed pines', yet somewhere in the instruction the sea undergoes a kind of metamorphosis and *becomes* the pinewood trees, while the great pine trees take on the qualities of the sea. Meanwhile the wind, which in 'Hermes and the Ways' seemed to capture the subjective 'I', is implicitly presented as the elixir facilitating the transformation. So what we have here is a dynamic interplay of the elements of earth, wind and water, natural forces rising and fusing at the command of the invisible, unnamed Oread. Indeed, the very invisibility of the Oread contributes to the sense that she herself *embodies* all three animated elements; in a sense, therefore, the poem's title embodies its entire content. What we do not have, though, is a poem moving from the concrete to the abstract, as was often common in Imagist poems such as Pound's 'In a Station at the Metro'. Instead 'Oread' juxtaposes two concrete concepts, the earth and the sea, such that they merge in a whirlpool of green, without the aid of simile, metaphor or symbol, without metre or rhythm other than the organic rhythm of the invigorating wind.

H. D.'s fascination with ancient Greece reappears in 'Priapus', a poem based on the myth of the fertility god popularly known for his permanent and very pronounced erection. Perhaps none of her poems engages so subtly with images of female reproductive and regenerative power, and when we consider the poem's multiple, layered religious images, it is difficult not to see it as a quiet but brilliantly effective rebellion against the hardness of Pound's Imagism. What we have, in effect, is a prayer-like incantation to Priapus, the son of Dionysus and Aphrodite, cursed by the jealous Hera to a lifetime of impotence despite his engorged penis. Almost mad with frustration, Priapus begs to be spared the loveliness of the lush autumn harvest, which represents the fruits of a fertility he can never achieve:

> I saw the first pear
> As it fell.
> . . .
> And I fell prostrate,
> Crying.
> Thou hast flayed us with thy blossoms;
> Spare us the beauty
> Of fruit trees! (p. 61)

The feminine, uterine shape of the pear teases the unhappy god, and makes for a compelling contrast with his grotesque and exaggerated masculinity, but it also represents, in a single Image, both fertility and decay. In the moment of its fall the pear occupies an intermediary space between growth and death, teetering on the delicious precipice of possibility and peril.

The falling fruit also recalls the lapsarian moment in the Garden of Eden. Here, too, a male god guards the garden, as well as the feminine (and forbidden) fruit which he can never taste. And of course this layering of Greek and Christian myth contributes to the condensed, conflicting mood of the poem. For instance, the single word 'flayed' in the first stanza invokes mythological images from both traditions. Flaying features in both the myth of the hubristic satyr Marsyas, flayed alive as punishment for losing a musical contest with the god Apollo, and the story of Jesus Christ, flayed before the crucifixion. (Tellingly, Christ was frequently identified with Apollo in medieval Christianised readings of pagan mythology.) So we might see the speaker as both worthy and unworthy, punished and punisher. And indeed this ambiguity is evident from the outset, the identity of the speaker being difficult to distinguish from that of the god Priapus. We might see Priapus as the figure who falls to the ground, crying at the loveliness of the orchard. Yet in the second stanza the 'I' of the poem brings an offering to the 'rough hewn / God of the orchard'. The god of the orchard is clearly Priapus. So who then is the speaker? This unsettling sense of indeterminacy is compounded by the formal, high-register pronouns 'thou' and 'thee', which along with the refrains, bring to mind the words of the Christian liturgy. At the very heart of the poem, therefore, is an indefinite selfhood, a kind of vagueness, intensified by the parenthetical reference to the 'son of the god'. The god referred to in this instance is, of course, the shape-shifting god of the harvest, Dionysus. But the attentive reader will also recall the biblical and liturgical references to Christ as 'the son of God', symbol therefore being piled on symbol, myth on myth.

The final stanza presents a cornucopia of harvest produce in a riot of sexually suggestive images, from the 'fallen hazel-nuts' released from their 'green sheaths' to the 'dripping . . . red-purple' grapes, from the broken pomegranate spilling its seed to the 'shrunken fig' (p. 62). All are placed before the god 'as offering'. Yet in the final line there is once again an element of ambiguity: 'I bring thee *as* offering'. Here, 'I' may refer to the speaker, presenting the ripe fruit as an offering to the god. However, there is a subtle difference from the wording in the second stanza: 'I bring thee *an* offering'. Perhaps 'thee', Priapus, is the 'offering'. And what we have, then, is an offering to the reader himself: the fruit of the poet's labour, 'Priapus', the poem itself.

WILLIAM CARLOS WILLIAMS

The personal and literary friendship between Ezra Pound, H. D. and William Carlos Williams long predated their involvement with Imagism. As students at the University of Pennsylvania in the early 1900s, Pound and Williams struck up a friendship based on their mutual literary aspirations, and the two men continued their correspondence well into later life. Of their friendship, Williams once remarked that 'before meeting Ezra Pound is like B.C. and A.D.'. Pound, he recalled, 'was impressed with his own poetry; but then I was impressed by my own poetry, too, so we got along alright'.[36]

From the outset, the two men were often astonishingly frank about each other's work. Pound's famous response to Williams's *Poems* (1909), for example, was devastatingly critical:

> Individual, original it is not. Great art is it not. Poetic it is, but there are innumerable poetic volumes poured out here in Gomorrah. There is no town like London to make one feel the vanity of all art except the highest. To make one disbelieve in all but the most careful and conservative presentation of one's stuff . . . If you'll read Yeats and Browning and Francis Thompson and Swinburne and Rossetti you'll learn something of the progress of Eng. poetry in the last century.[37]

However, it seems that Williams had been equally frank about Pound's *A Lume Spento* (1908), for in October of that year, Pound told him: 'Of course you don't have to like the stuff I write . . . I am damn glad to get some sincere criticism anyhow.... I am doubly thankful for a friend who'll say what he thinks – and I hope I'm going to be blessed with your criticism for as long as may be'.[38]

Despite their close association, Williams and Pound were always moving in slightly different directions. Even in that letter of 1908, Pound made very clear his reverence for foreign literature and

English poetry in particular, and in the same letter he admitted borrowing from the rules of Spanish, Anglo-Saxon and Greek metrics. Williams's focus, however, was always on the local and specific, exploring the homely beauty of the American scene. And their divergent attitudes to the literature and culture of the United States were perhaps encapsulated by their responses to the father of modern American verse, Walt Whitman. For the young Williams, Whitman had been a poetic model; like the self-proclaimed 'rough bard', Williams had a deep enthusiasm for the American idiom and commitment to the poetic channelling of the cadences of the American voice. By contrast, Pound thought that Whitman's 'crudity is an exceeding great stench, but it *is* America. He is the hollow place in the rock that echoes with his time . . . He is disgusting.'[39]

For Pound, the nationalistic aspects of Whitman's poetic mission were clearly out of sympathy with his own international modern concerns; what was more, Whitman's cosmic vision appeared at odds with the precepts of Imagism. Pound pressed these views on Williams, often recommending writers and techniques that would, he thought, improve his friend's verse. Of course there is no need to deny Pound's influence, which is very strong in poems such as 'Metric Figure' and 'The Shadow' (both of which were included in *Des Imagistes*) as well as in Williams's later Objectivist verse. But for all Pound's efforts, Williams never fell out of love with Whitman. His poem 'The Wanderer' (1917), for example, consciously echoes 'Crossing Brooklyn Ferry':

> But one day, crossing the ferry
> With the great towers of Manhattan before me,
> Out at the prow with the sea wind blowing,
> I had been wearying many questions
> Which she had put on to try me:
> How shall I be a mirror to this modernity?

Like Whitman's poem, 'The Wanderer' is characterised by a poetic subjectivity that is itself embraced by the wider American landscape. In this instance, the poet's role is to reflect the modernity inherent in 'the great towers of Manhattan'. Throughout the poem, the speaker pursues an elusive female figure:

> Even in the time as yet
> I had no certain knowledge of her
>
> . . .
>
> Suddenly I saw her! And she waved me
> From the white wet in the midst of her playing!
> She cried me, "Haia! Here I am, son![40]

The figure takes him on a journey through space and time over the course of eight days, surveying the mountain tops and the grimy corners of the city, dazzling him with both the beauty and squalor of the United States, until the final day when the speaker abandons himself to 'the filthy Passaic' and the river 'enter[s] his heart' (p. 11). His union with the female figure engenders a rebirth in the form of a son who will continue the journey through 'new wandering'. Whitman's influence here is hard to miss, from the thematic thrust of the poem to the 'Broadway' section's clear reworking of key lines from 'Crossing Brooklyn Ferry'. The ultimate marriage of the landscape and the poet with the prospect of continual renewal is Whitman through and through, of course, as are the exclamatory declarations, the general exuberance of tone and the implicit belief in the messianic and expansive possibilities of the poet.

In his autobiography, Williams wrote that the 1913 Armory Show in New York had had a tremendous impact on his poetic approach, intensifying his faith in local virtue:

> Whether the Armory Show in painting did it or whether that also was no more than a facet – the poetic line, the way the image was to lie on the page was our immediate concern. For myself all that implied, in the materials, respecting the place I knew best, as finding a local assertion – to my everlasting relief. I had never in my life felt that way. I was tremendously stirred.[41]

What really excited Williams was an exhibition by the American Association of Painters and Sculptors, which seemed to herald the birth of an indigenous American modernism, alongside the Cubist and Futurist styles of European artists such as Picasso and Duchamp. His immersion in the visual arts led to his involvement with 'The Others', a group centred on Man Ray's artists' colony in Ridgefield, New Jersey. Along with Alfred Kreymborg, Wallace Stevens and Skipwith Cannell, Williams helped launch *Others: A Magazine of the New Verse* in 1915. The magazine was markedly different from other little magazines of the time, combining avant-garde experimentalism with a distinctively American sensibility. The poems published in *Others* were typically written in free verse, marked by everyday plain language and first-person voices in generally slim verse forms with some typographical experimentation. They were set out as individual expressions, subject only to their own internal metrical and rhythmical rules, thereby rejecting the established rules of English poetry.

This emphasis on individual expression often resulted in a personal and idiosyncratic idiom. Williams's most famous and most frequently parodied poem, 'This is Just to Say' (1934), offers a prime example:

> I have eaten
> the plums
> that were in
> the icebox
> and which
> you were probably
> saving
> for breakfast
> Forgive me
> they were delicious
> so sweet
> and so cold (p. 354)

Frequently described as an Imagist poem, 'This is Just to Say' owes more to Williams's Objectivist period, which of course developed out of Imagism, and certainly the poetic cadence and the simplicity of the voice suggests the influence of 'The Others'. Behind this apparently weightless, transient poetic moment, therefore, we can detect a number of influences.

The poem positions itself is a 'found object', not unlike Marcel Duchamp's 'Fountain', which was among the more avant-garde exhibitions at the Armory Show, in the form of a note stuck to the front of the fridge (or 'icebox') with an admission and a request for forgiveness. Immediately, the reader is confronted with the 'thingyness' of the poem as a whole. The poem does not enclose or show the note, but rather presents itself *as* that very object. The lack of metrical regularity and the lack of punctuation contribute to the sense that this is not a poem with its attendant rules and careful measurement, but a hastily scribbled note, a snatched moment of intimacy. For the critic Marjorie Perloff, this simply reflects Williams's failure to understand poetic metre, and she cites John Gerber's interview with the poet, in which Williams, mistaking sight for sound, seemed to misunderstand the nature of metric regularity – which explains why it is the poem's typography, not its metre, that offers direction for the voice or eye.[42]

There is no doubt that the typography contributes to the rhythm. But of course Williams had *deliberately* rejected the traditional rules of scansion, as part of his quest to create a new American form from ordinary, idiomatic language. Since the native, individual voice is what gives the poem its metrical structure, for Williams it *is* absolutely regular: 'the American language must shape the pattern . . . [as] it is a contortion of speech to conform to rigidity of line'. Traditional poetic metres, he believed, simply could not accommodate the syncopated rhythms of the American voice. Indeed, he even envisaged the complete abandonment of iambic English measurement:

> It is basic for us to know that the English prosody we imitate as a matter of course is not determined by the mere facts of the mechanical syllabic sequences but an accretion through the ages from English history and character. And that these are NOT *our* character.[43]

So, when Williams describes the poem as 'metrically absolutely regular' his model of regularity demands that we rethink the very nature of poetic metre. The regularity of 'This is Just to Say' is set by the natural voice of the speaker through normal speech rhythm and syntax, which will naturally vary from speaker to speaker. This metrical indeterminacy corresponds to the thematic ambiguity of the poem. For some critics, the poem captures the lapsarian moment of temptation, the consumption of forbidden fruit; others see the poem as a meditation on sexual betrayal; and still others see it as concerned only with the object at hand, the note on the icebox. But perhaps all readings are valid: the poem has been placed in the hands of the reader, who is free to construct his own meaning, set to an idiomatic and idiosyncratically determined metrical pace.

Like 'This is Just to Say', ' The Red Wheelbarrow' (1923) also 'offers a snatched moment, a discussion or a thought interrupted':

so much depends
upon
a red wheel
barrow
glazed with rain
water
beside the white
chickens. (p. 277)

The poem is not unlike Pound's 'In a Station at the Metro' and reveals Williams's interest in Imagism in terms of its brevity, the absence of a mediating poetic 'I', and the shift with each additional couplet from the abstract to successively more concrete observations, although often Imagist pieces move the other way, from the concrete to the abstract. No verb appears in the poem except for the introductory 'depends', but we are never told exactly what it *is* that depends upon the wet, red wheelbarrow. Attentive to colour and texture, which is unsurprising given Williams's artistic interests, the poem moves from rhetorical abstraction in the first couplet, to the title object in the second, to the qualities of the object, and to its relational attitude to another object (in this case, the 'white chickens') in the final couplet. And as the reader moves through the various couplets, he moves from an abstract position into a familiar organic world, perhaps suggesting that a shift from abstraction enables one to approach the 'real' textured world of physical objects: 'That is the universal I am seeking: to embody that in a work of art, a new world that is always "real"'.[44]

In its movement from couplet to couplet to the material 'white chickens' at the end, the poem enacts the perceptive shift from the world of abstractions through to vital, physical reality. Here the punctuation is crucial, beginning, without capitalisation, in an unclear position in the middle of a thought or conversation. There is no sense of an actual beginning; the reader feels that he is stumbling upon something, perhaps a private interaction or thought. But the culmination of the poem in the full stop brings the reader to a definite end point, rooted in the external world of the white chickens. Thus the poem thematically and formally embodies the means whereby the abstract world of perception 'depends upon' or is closely related to the actual material world. And it is precisely this relationship between the interior world of perception and the exterior world of physical realities that is the 'so much' referred to in the opening line of the poem. It is the embodiment of Williams's famous maxim, 'no ideas but in things'.[45] External realities fire the world of perception; it is the object that gives shape to the poem. For Williams, the life force of American poetry is the physical stuff of reality itself.

T. S. ELIOT

Few literary events caused William Carlos Williams greater indignation and disappointment than the enormous international success of T. S. Eliot's *The Waste Land* (1922), which Williams considered a 'great catastrophe'.[46] Until that point, Williams had been working towards a new formal freedom for American poetry; now, he thought, Eliot's English-influenced verse had undermined everything he was trying to accomplish. Indeed, Williams regarded Eliot's work, with its carefully wrought allusions, classicism and complex metrical sequences, as 'Puritan', 'dangerous' and 'conformist'. Eliot, he thought, had set American poetry back 'twenty years' and gave it 'back to the academics'.[47] No doubt much of this was rooted in genuine aesthetic disagreements. But there was also surely a personal element. Once Williams had been Ezra Pound's protégé. But now Pound had transferred his affections from his old college friend to a St Louis-born, London-based bank clerk. It is no wonder Williams was so angry.

As early as 1914, Pound had told Harriet Monroe at *Poetry* that Thomas Stearns Eliot was simply the most important new voice in English-language poetry. And although *The Waste Land* was not published until eight years later, its appearance triumphantly vindicated Pound's prediction. The poem combines a version of Pound's ideogrammic method with a disjunctive poetic narrative, elements of various mythic and religious traditions, and a dizzying array of different languages, presenting a devastatingly nihilistic perspective on contemporary Western civilisation in the aftermath of the First World War. Self-consciously and deliberately difficult, the poem, like the works of Pound and indeed Williams, forces the reader to enter into an intense intellectual negotiation with its words, images and meanings. Like Pound in *The Cantos*, Eliot rails against the perceived degeneration of civilisation, in this instance a civilisation decimated by the horrors of a war which had led to the fall of the German, Russian and Austro-Hungarian empires, the collapse of class cohesion, the rise of militant, atheist communism, and the transformation of the social position of women. Thus the poem presents itself as a series of fragments and dissonant voices, scattered debris in a sterile, exhausted cultural landscape.

From the start, the overriding impression is one of disorder and disintegration, heightened by a bewildering variety of references to mythical structures, and buttressed by the often opaque 'Notes' at the end, which refer the reader to Jessie L. Weston's *From Ritual to Romance* (1920) and James G. Frazer's *The Golden Bough* (1890) for insights into 'the title . . . the plan, and a good deal of the incidental symbolism'. In fact, Eliot had already begun working on the poem when he acquired Weston's book in 1920. By contrast, his interest in Frazer and other anthropological writers had developed at Harvard and clearly informed his interest in religious fertility myths. Central to Frazer's thesis was the notion of the wounded or dying king, who must submit to death in order to be resurrected and to see fertility return to the land. Building upon Frazer's ideas, Weston explored the legend of the Fisher King, which she believed, had become entangled with the Arthurian legend of the Holy Grail. Wounded in the thigh or groin, the King is rendered impotent. His kingdom suffers barrenness until an appointed knight comes to heal the king, enabling him to die at peace, and prompting the restoration of the land to bloom and blossom. Death, in other words, brings fertility; winter brings the spring. In *The Waste Land*, however, the regenerative potential of the Fisher King is never entirely certain:

> I sat upon the shore
> Fishing, with the arid plain behind me
> Shall I at least set my lands in order?
> London Bridge is falling down falling down falling down[48]

Here, in a juxtaposition maintained from the very beginning of the poem, the desert imagery ('arid plain') contrasts with the possible life-giving qualities of the water at the shore. Between the desert and the water the king must reside, dangling his line as the lands around him crumble into fragments.

The proximity of death is present from the very beginning of the poem, which opens with an epigraph from the *Satyricon*, in which the desiccated Cumaean Sibyl looks at the future and proclaims a desire for death. The poem, it seems, shares the Sibyl's predicament: surveying the cultural landscape, it sees only the decayed remnants of former glory. The first section of the poem takes up this theme. Taking its name from the Book of Common Prayer, the section juxtaposes a number of different voices, each offering a portrait of degeneration or lost innocence. The reader is confronted, in the first instance, with a dead land and the possibility of renewal with the spring rain. Yet potential new life is met with dismay: April, in stark contrast to its depiction in Chaucer's *Canterbury Tales*, is seen here as 'the cruellest month', a far cry from 'warm' winter and its 'forgetful snow' (p. 51). A series of scenes from the past are conjured in the lines which follow: coffee drinkers by the Starnbergersee caught out by the rain (in another oblique reference to the Fisher King legend, the lake was the drowning place of the mad King Ludwig II of Bavaria); the words of Marie recalling a childhood memory of 'staying at the arch duke's' (taken from a courtier's memoir of the Viennese court before the First World War); the disembodied words of a Lithuanian German. The sheer disorderliness of the various voices from the past, tumbling downwards like the frightened Marie on her sled, suggests both the familiar and the unfamiliar, hinting at a shared stable past, but at the same time suggesting the transience of memory and the ephemeral nature of happiness.

Amid the desert imagery of the second stanza we find religious phrases from the Books of Ezekiel and Ecclesiastes, which, again, suggest the imminence of death: 'I will show you fear in a handful of dust' (p. 52). The tension between life and death is evident in the desperate roots, which try to grow from the 'stony rubbish' and vainly seek succour from the 'dead tree' and the 'dry stone'. The prophetic voice which offers to 'show you something different' (p. 51) yields only a vision of fear in the form of the 'shadow' of death 'striding behind you' and 'rising to meet you'. Slipping into a further memory, after the lines from Wagner's opera *Tristran and Isolde*, a new voice is introduced: the 'hyacinth girl'. She presents a vision of abundant fertile renewal in her full arms and wet hair, a fertility which is shunned by the desolate 'I' figure who is afraid of the consequences of her embrace. Again, the 'I' is synonymous with the Fisher King, stricken by impotence but unwilling to take the leap into death which will accelerate renewal.

Like the other voices in 'The Burial of the Dead', the 'I' is 'neither / Living nor dead' (p. 52), doomed to a purgatorial existence between worlds. Compounding this sense of entrapment are the German lines from Wagner which encase the 'I' figure and his 'hyacinth girl'. The latter quotation pertains to the sea, but does not hold out the promise of renewal and rebirth: instead, it tells only of emptiness and further desolation. Even life-giving waters are rendered sinister. Certainly, the water is feared by the inhabitants of Eliot's desolate landscape: in the third stanza, too, the charlatan clairvoyant Madame Sosostris, who replaces the prophetic voices of the Sibyl, Ezekiel and Ecclesiastes, offers 'your card, the drowned Phoenician Sailor' and warns her client to 'fear death by water'. The pearly-eyed sailor presents another image of possible rebirth, evoking Ariel's song of the resurrected sailors from Shakespeare's *The Tempest*. Nonetheless, fear seeps through to the final stanza of the first section, in which the living dead flow over London Bridge in Baudelaire's 'Unreal City' (p. 53), culminating in the horrifying vision of a sprouting corpse in danger of premature disinterment by the scrabbling nails of a hungry dog.

This abiding sense of fear, seen first in the frightened Marie as she accelerates downwards, is carried through to the next sections of the poem. Indeed, it characterises the voices of the women in the second section, 'A Game of Chess'. The emphasis on beseeching women's voices finds its classical counterpart in the voiceless Philomel, raped and silenced by her brother-in-law, 'the barbarous king', who despite her mutilation fills 'all the desert with inviolable voice' (p. 54). The nervous middle-class woman implores her lover or husband to stay with her, fearful of the noises coming from under the door, terrified of 'pressing lidless eyes and waiting for the knock upon the door' (p. 56). Even Lil, the working-class woman who sits in a pub with an unsympathetic friend, is afraid that her husband will look elsewhere now that her beauty has passed and her fertility has been poisoned. She knows that Albert, recently returned from the war, will expect 'a good time' from his wife, who despite her relative youth ('only thirty-one'), looks 'antique' and is physically rotting away; even her friend reminds her that she is in need of 'some teeth' (p. 56).

At every turn, fear is associated with the nothingness of silence. The upper-class woman awaiting her lover in her chamber is 'troubled, confused / And drowned' (p. 54). Ultimately she is voiceless, 'framed by . . . stone'. Philomel, despite her nightingale song, is deprived of her human voice. The anxious woman's panicked questions are never answered and culminate in a series of 'nothings':

> Nothing again nothing.
>   'Do
> You know nothing? Do you see nothing? Do you remember
> Nothing?' (p. 55)

Lil's responses to her friend's admonitions are drowned out by the vigour of the woman's criticisms and cut off by the foreboding death-knell refrain of the publican: 'HURRY UP PLEASE ITS TIME / HURRY UP PLEASE ITS TIME' (p. 57). And finally, the repeated goodnights of Shakespeare's Ophelia foreshadow her madness and her death by drowning, as she slips into the abyss of silence. Each woman, therefore, presents a thwarted, fruitless fertility. As with the episode between the typist and the 'young man carbuncular' (p. 60), or indeed the sexual humiliation of the Thames daughters in the 'The Fire Sermon', sexual opportunity is apparently available but ultimately empty, offering nothing but the degraded hollow of 'O O O O' (p. 55) and 'Nothing / la la' (p. 62).

Madame Sosostris's tarot card comes up in the fourth section of the poem, 'Death by Water', when 'Phlebas the Phoenician, a fortnight dead' makes his entrance. The death of the Phoenician enables life to go on, for 'Gentile or Jew' to 'turn the wheel and look to windward' (p. 63). Phoenicia, an ancient civilisation in Canaan, refers to the so-called Fertile Crescent, the wet territory bordering the Mediterranean Sea, offering blessed relief after the deserts of the Middle East. In the Bible, of course, it is the Promised Land, the 'land of milk and honey', sought by the Israelites wandering in the desert (their 'waste land'). But the word also evokes the phoenix, the self-immolating bird which sacrifices itself to enable new life to rise from the ashes. And this suggestion of potential regeneration continues into the final section of the poem. In 'What the Thunder Said' we return to an arid landscape, a mountainous place of 'rock and no water' and 'dry sterile thunder without rain' (p. 64). Water remains elusive but, in contrast to 'The Burial of the Dead', is at least actively sought in 'empty cisterns and exhausted wells' (p. 66).

At last the thunder brings not just rain, but the single letter 'DA' repeated three times, which is further elaborated in three Sanskrit words: 'Datta. Dayadhvam. Damyata' (p. 67). The revelations of the thunder, drawn from Hindu fables, are the three principal virtues of charity, compassion and self-control, the precepts upon which to rebuild a dying civilisation. Each injunction is followed by a personal reflection on death, imprisonment and obedience, the last of which seems to approach an understanding of the self-sacrifice required:

> The sea was calm, your heart would have responded
> Gaily, when invited, beating obedient
> To controlling hands (p. 67)

But this understanding is only tentative. The Fisher King remains caught between the land and the shore, while London Bridge remains in the transitive phase of 'falling'. Regeneration is possible, as seen in the resurrected Christ on the road to Emmaus, but not guaranteed; the third figure on the road has not yet been recognised by his followers. The thrice-repeated 'Shantih', precariously unpunctuated, offers an unstable closure to the poem and hints at the possibility of a fragile peace.

EUGENE O'NEILL, SUSAN GLASPELL AND THE PROVINCETOWN PLAYERS

Regret at the lost spiritual harmony of modernity is as much a feature of modern American drama as it is of poetry. As we have seen, American dramatists have often been keen to address the predominant issues of the day. Throughout the twentieth century, their works eagerly embraced debates about psychoanalysis, socialism, the effects of war, social cohesion and the relationship between the sexes. And though not all dramatists conformed to this pattern, the two most influential American playwrights of the first half of the century – Eugene O'Neill and Susan Glaspell – certainly did. It makes sense to consider them side by side, not least because O'Neill began his career as a protégé of Glaspell and her husband George (Jig) Cram Cook when they were running the Provincetown Players. In time, O'Neill's reputation would eclipse theirs; nonetheless, the ethics and practices of their company had a tremendous impact on his entire dramatic output, and proved enormously influential on the development of modern American drama in the first half of the century. Indeed, Glaspell, who was also a successful novelist and short-story writer, remained an important figure in American theatre until her death in 1948. It is probably no exaggeration to say that without the influence of her socially-driven themes, her creative vision for the Provincetown Players and her work for the Little Theatre and the Federal Writers' Project, much subsequent American drama would be almost unrecognisable.

While staying in Provincetown in the summer of 1915, Glaspell, Cook and Neith Boyce hosted readings of their plays, *Suppressed Desires* (a Freudian-inspired comedy) and *Constancy* (a play about the difficulties of male–female intimacy), on the bayside veranda and in the sitting room of a rented vacation cottage. Friends and acquaintances who had missed the initial performances demanded a chance to see the plays and Lewis Wharf, which sat directly opposite Glaspell's Provincetown house, was turned into a makeshift theatrical space. On 28 August, the temporarily titled 'Provincetown Players at the Wharf' again presented *Constancy* and *Suppressed Desires*. But by early September two new plays were offered: *Change Your Style* by Cook and *Contemporaries* by Wilbur Daniel Steele. Again, the subject matter was highly topical. Cook's work parodied a debate within the local art community between the Moderns who championed the Cubist and Futurist work shown at the Armory Show, and the Conservatives who favoured more traditional painterly forms. Steele's play, meanwhile, was highly allegorical, inspired by the case of the Industrial Workers of the World agitator Frank Tannenbaum, who in 1914 had led unemployed workers into New York churches demanding food and shelter. *Contemporaries* sets Tannenbaum as a modern-day Christ figure, didactically likening the teachings and story of Christ to social radicalism.

Enthused by the success of their season, Cook and Glaspell consolidated their ideas for a new kind of theatre. Part of the reason for their early success was the theatre's sense of communal cooperation, as well as its reflection of the issues that mattered to the wider community. From the outset, therefore, they aimed to present locally inspired drama with a distinctly American voice. They sought to be free of the trappings of commercially driven theatre, and free to embrace experimental writing and stagecraft. Behind it all, though, was a fierce sense of social commitment. Glaspell had spent much of her early working life as a journalist on the *Des Moines Daily News* and had encountered at first hand the gruelling hardships faced by immigrants and workers, as well as the inequality faced by women of all social backgrounds, all of which informed her fictions and drama. Through their Greenwich Village lifestyle, Glaspell and Cook were also linked to other free-thinking radicals, whose ideas on art, politics and labour manifestly inspired the ethos of the Players. And their friendship with Robert Edmond Jones, one of the most successful practitioners of a new form of stagecraft that sought to integrate scenic detail with subject matter, helped pioneer a new kind of expressionism in the American theatre.

The summer of 1916 brought even more people to Provincetown, keen to see the triple bill, which comprised a revival of *Suppressed Desires* and two new plays: Boyce's melodrama *Winter's Night* and *Freedom*, a parody by Jack Reed. Among those who descended upon the holiday town was the young dramatist Eugene O'Neill who, according to Glaspell's recollection, turned up with a 'whole trunk full of plays' from which he selected *Bound East for Cardiff*:

> Gene took *Bound East for Cardiff* from his trunk, and Freddie Burt read it to us, Gene staying out in the dining-room while the reading went on.
>
> He was not left alone in the dining room when the reading had finished.
>
> Then we knew what we were for.[49]

Glaspell's memoir places O'Neill's work at the heart of the group. The first of many plays to draw on O'Neill's autobiographical experiences as a sailor, the play is essentially plotless, focusing on the death of a seaman and using the effects of fog as well as the repetitive sounds of the sea, the snoring crew and the steamship horn to portray a mood of supernatural eeriness. Opening at the Wharf in July 1916, it played again in August and topped the bill at the Playwrights' Theater in New York the following November. The success of *Bound East* solidified the relationship between O'Neill and the Players until the early 1920s when, finding his desire for financial success increasingly at odds with the foundational tenets of the group, O'Neill began producing work for Broadway, including *Beyond the Horizon* (1920) and *Anna Christie* (1921), which won him his second Pulitzer Prize.

Like so many of O'Neill's plays, *Anna Christie* is a story of the sea. It is the tale of Anna and Chris Christopherson, an estranged father and daughter who come to rebuild their relationship. The title character, Anna, is a prostitute who turns her back on the trade after reuniting with her father, finding herself cleansed and under the bewitching spell of 'dat ole davil, sea'.[50] Her emotional attachment to the shipwrecked Irishman, Mat Burke, forces Anna to confess her past, and leads initially to Burke's vituperative rejection of her before their reconciliation in the final act. Though some readers may recoil at its stereotypical portrayals of drunken Swedes and an unintentionally comic pugilistic Irishman, the play touches on a number of distinctly modern themes. In the first instance, the drama focuses on a kind of power struggle between the sexes. Anna, the fallen woman, is initially portrayed as a victim, given over by her father to cruel cousins (one of whom sexually assaults her) and later rejected by her suitor for her past. Throughout the play, she frequently laments her treatment at the hands of men:

> ANNA: It was all men's fault – the whole business. It was men on the farm, ordering and beating me – and giving me the wrong start. Then when I was a nurse, it was men again hanging around, bothering me, trying to see what they could get. And now it's men all the time. Gawd, I hate 'em all, every mother's son of 'em! (I, 50)

Nonetheless, Anna comes to control the men around her. In many ways she is a life-giving force, reigniting a gentle paternal love within her father and evoking a passionate ardour in Mat. Her transformative power over the opposite sex is demonstrated by her father's decision to change his drinking habits, and by her physical control of Mat:

> *He tries to kiss her. At first she turns away her head – then overcome by a fierce impulse of passionate love, she takes his head in both her hands and holds his face close to hers, staring into his eyes. Then she kisses him full on the lips.* (III, 77)

Anna derives her strength, both physical and emotional, from the sea and the fog (both of which are referred to as 'she'). Emaciated by life on the farm and in Minneapolis, she is reinvigorated, made 'healthy' and 'transformed' by the sea. Her lingering presence on the barge, contemplating the fog with 'awed wonder' (II, 57), precedes the shipwrecking of Mat, and in the penultimate act her presence on the foggy cobb foreshadows the physical fight between Christopherson and Burke and the shocking revelation of her prostitution. And just as Anna remains at the edge of the sea after her father and lover depart on the *Londonderry*, a thick fog envelops the barge prompting yet another verbal tirade from the older man:

> CHRIS: Fog, fog, fog, all bloody time. You can't see vhere you vas going, no. Only dat ole davil, sea – she knows! (p. 96)

Chris's attitude to the sea, a mingled antipathy and attraction, is not unlike his relationship with his daughter, who provokes in him both great affection and profound uneasiness. From her initial letter announcing her imminent arrival, he is emotionally buffeted by powers beyond his control. And, indeed, by the end of the play, both Mat and Chris are blind to what lies ahead on their voyage to Cape Town. Only Anna's future seems secure. Isolated from the men who seek to control her, she heralds their departure and raises a glass to the sea.

While thematically more than theatrically daring, *Anna Christie* nonetheless shows one of O'Neill's most distinctive characteristics: the deployment of regional dialect. While twenty-first-century sensibilities might be offended by the thick intonations of his Swedes and Irishmen, O'Neill's ability to capture the African American voice and his willingness to place it centre stage is surely one of his most significant contributions to modern American theatre. Indeed, in the casting of the black actors Charles Gilpin and Paul Robeson, his plays *The Emperor Jones* (1920) and *All God's Chillun Got Wings* (1924) were particularly groundbreaking. And despite his forays into Broadway, O'Neill continued to give his more experimental pieces to the Players and other smaller art-house groups in Greenwich Village.

The expressionistic *Emperor Jones*, which focuses upon an individual human consciousness afflicted by terror, melancholy and trauma, is perhaps the most obvious example. Loosely based on the American occupation of Haiti after 1915, the play was more overtly experimental than any of O'Neill's previous works. The Players built a cyclorama, a large wall, to portray a sense of infinity and the immensity of the Great Forest, which threatens to engulf Brutus Jones. Needless to say, the dark shadows of this background also suggest Jones's subjective consciousness, as he loses the trappings of his sequestered role and descends deeper into the chaos of his subconscious, primal self. Combined with the ceaseless and increasingly voluble thud of the tom-tom drums which mimic the sound of a stressed heartbeat, the effect is to subject the audience to Jones's hallucinations and memories, which range from his personal subjugation in the United States to the terror he inflicts upon his own African subjects. So Jones vividly recollects his days on a chain gang in the United States, and imagines small '*formless creatures . . . which squirm toward him in twisted attitudes*' (II, 17) emerging from the darkness of the forest to consume him. His eventual death by silver bullet coincides with the final hallucination of his imminent sacrifice to the Congo witch doctor. The entire effect is deeply hypnotic, deliberately evoking psychoanalytic notions of the primal nature of the individual, simmering beneath the veneer of rational consciousness.

O'Neill always denied the influence of Freud upon his early work. Still, there can be little doubt that the ideas of psychoanalysis, especially regarding sexuality, must have had a profound impact on the play cycle *Mourning Becomes Electra*, which enacts the Freudian notion of sexual attraction between parents and children. The trilogy (*Homecoming*, *The Hunted* and *The Haunted*) focuses on the Mannon family in the aftermath of the Civil War. Here O'Neill deploys a typically modernist technique – what Eliot called the 'mythical method' – to draw 'a parallel between antiquity and contemporaneity', using the *Oresteia*, the only surviving trilogy of Greek classical drama, as the model for his play.[51]

The first play of Aeschylus's trilogy, *Agamemnon*, tells of the warrior's return from the ten-year battle of the Trojan War and his murder by his wife Clytemnestra in revenge for the sacrifice of their daughter Iphigenia. The second play, *The Libation-Bearers*, sees the return of Agamemnon's son Orestes to avenge his father. Encouraged by his sister Electra, Orestes murders his mother and her lover, Aegisthus, but is haunted afterwards by the Furies. *The Eumenides*, the final part of the trilogy, sees Orestes's appeal to the gods, his absolution and the transformation of the Furies into the kindly Eumenides. And although O'Neill clearly simplifies his classical model, the basic structure remains intact. Following Euripides's *Electra* and Sophocles's *Oedipus The King*, O'Neill took out the details about Agamemnon's sacrifice of Iphigenia, reworked the entire final part of the trilogy and focused above all on the character of Electra (Lavinia Mannon), whom he regarded as the most interesting female character in all literature. The notions of the Electra and Oedipal complexes remain intact in the relationship between Lavinia and her brother Orin (Orestes), both of whom actively desire the parent of the opposite sex, and are the victims of socially repressive conventions as well as their own basic human instincts.

While O'Neill certainly sought to reflect twentieth-century American concerns, he never broke entirely with the conventions of classical theatre. A particular priority was to translate the classical sense of fate into modern psychological terms – for example, by using a Greek-inspired Chorus in the grounds-keeper Seth, as well as various townspeople at the beginning of each play. What is more, O'Neill's detailed stage directions pay great attention to the set. All but one of the trilogy's fourteen scenes take place before the Mannon family home, a 'white Grecian temple portico with its six tall columns' and, in keeping with the Greek tradition of masked performance, each member of the Mannon family is described as having a 'strange, life-like mask-like impression'.[52] The impassive, classical face of the Mannon house, which Christine Mannon (Clytemnestra) likens to a sepulchre, represents the Mannons themselves, with their pale, deathly visages and their fatal sense of ancestral purity. Indeed, the house becomes a kind of tomb, encasing the body of Ezra Mannon in the second play but also representing the death of the Mannon line, with the lonely, doomed spinster, Lavinia, the last of her family, locked within the house at the end of the cycle. According to Christine, the ancestral house is 'a temple for [Puritan] hatred' (*Homecoming*, I, 15) and, indeed, the nature of each child's desire for its parent can easily be read as a perverse yearning for familial purity, untouched by others. We learn from Seth that the family are exceptionally strict about trespassers on the property. Seth also tells the story of the ostracism of the French servant Marie Brantôme, mother of Christine's young lover, Adam Brant, while the ultimate transgressor, the New York-born Christine, is driven to death for her crimes against the purity of the family. Highly reminiscent of the themes of Edgar Allen

Poe, the thwarted fertility of sensuality and new love (embodied in the relationship between Christine and Adam and the potential marriages of Orin to Hazel Niles and Lavinia to Peter Niles) lies at the heart of the play. The repression of desire by a sterile demand for purity leads only to personal, familial and cultural stasis. To put it simply, it represents a rejection of life and a submission to death.

The repression of desire takes on an altogether lighter tone in 'the first American Freudian play', Susan Glaspell's ironic *Suppressed Desires: A Comedy in Two Episodes* (1914), a play she co-wrote and performed in with Cook, and which launched the Provincetown Players.[53] Five years earlier, Freud and Jung had visited the United States, and many avant-garde writers and artists embraced their ideas. Close friends of Glaspell and Cook, including Floyd Dell, Mabel Dodge and Max Eastman, did much to popularise psychoanalysis in lengthy newspaper and magazine features. Indeed, by 1915 psychoanalysis had become so popular in Greenwich Village that Glaspell complained it was impossible 'to go out and buy a bun without hearing of someone's complex'.[54] The topic and the scene seemed ripe for parody, and Glaspell duly provided one.

In a studio apartment in Washington Square South, Henrietta and Stephen Brewster discuss Steve's subconscious mind. A devotee and patient of Dr A. E. Russell, Henrietta believes her analyst can make sense of her husband's dreams. Meanwhile her sister Mabel relates a dream of her own, in which she is a hen made to move quickly through a crowd who shout 'Step, Hen!' as she passes by.[55] As her sister is ignorant of psychoanalysis, Henrietta quickly advises a session of therapy; she believes that Mabel's 'living Libido – the centre of the soul's energy – is in conflict with petrified moral codes' (ii, 17). In order to placate his wife, Steve agrees to see Dr Russell who quickly identifies marital dissatisfaction as the cause. Unfortunately, this news reduces Henrietta to tears over her paper on psychoanalysis for the Liberal Club. Worse still is her sister's revelation that her 'Step, Hen!' dream is actually a repressed desire for Stephen and a wish to supplant Henrietta in his affections. After a series of entertaining exchanges between the three, with Henrietta's patronising pseudo-analytical babble being repeated back to her, the distressed woman promises to burn all her copies of *The Journal of Morbid Psychology* and renounce psychology altogether, while her smug, satisfied husband advises Mabel to keep on suppressing her desire for him. And for all this slight piece's comic overtones, it also embraces one of Glaspell's chief themes: the battle between the sexes for power and control. In the first scene, Henrietta may seem in control of her husband and sister, but it is she who is controlled by her devotion to Dr Russell, as evidenced by her slavish reiteration of his ideas, as well as her befuddlement when those ideas are brought to bear on her own domestic situation. Mabel's dream, too, is one of control. Ordered by the crowd to 'Step, Hen!', which she initially interprets as a command to move along quickly, she feels anxious and agitated when asked to step aboard by overbearing tram conductors in Chicago. And while Henrietta attempts to exert some control over Stephen's dream, by the end of the play she submits entirely to his control, relinquishing her studies and promising to burn her books and papers. Even Mabel is subordinated to Stephen, who tells her to continue suppressing her desire.

This notion of a battle for control is also manifest in Glaspell's next play, *Trifles* (1916) – a work that, rather ironically, she had been told to write by her husband.[56] Based on the trial of Margaret Hossack, which Glaspell had covered as an investigative reporter, the play centres on the relationship between two women, Mrs Hale and Mrs Peters, who accompany their husbands to the home of Minnie and John Wright shortly after Mr Wright has allegedly been strangled his wife. Remarkable for its brevity, the play develops its dramatic intensity through what is unseen and unsaid. While the men speak at length about the possible motivation for the crime, the behaviour of the alleged perpetrator and the general state of the house, the women's voices are more stilted. Their understanding of the reality of the marriage is built on small observations, from Minnie's sewing to her ruined preserves and threadbare clothes. Through wordless gestures and glances they piece together a loveless, lonely and silent existence. Mrs Hale perceptively identifies the problem and the reason for the crime:

> I know how things can be – for women. I tell you it's queer, Mrs Peters. We live close together and we live far apart. We

> all go through the same things – it's just a different kind of the same thing.[57]

Meanwhile, their husbands and the district attorney can see no motivation for the murder. Ironically, the crime was discovered by Mr Hale, who was hoping to tempt the taciturn Mr Wright to join a telephone cooperative, a form of communication which might have freed Minnie from her isolation but which, inevitably, would have been rejected by her husband. Indeed, Glaspell places silence at the heart of the play, both as a theme and as a bold dramatic method. We learn that Minnie may have been driven to murder by the silencing of her pet canary songbird, which was probably strangled by her husband. Minnie is the silent heart of the play, absent and voiceless, unable to defend herself against the men's claims about her integrity, her sanity and the quality of her housewifery. We learn of her early life as a local choirgirl, her song silenced by the union with John. And Glaspell compellingly reveals her story through silences, hurried gestures, looks exchanged between the women in the kitchen, inferences and intonations. Dismissed by the men as the site of the women's 'trifles', the kitchen becomes a representation of Minnie Wright's psychic world. The unbaked bread, the soiled hand towel, the disturbed pans in the cupboard, the preserves oozing from the cracked jars and the hauntingly evocative rocking chair are all symbols of Minnie's troubled consciousness, while the dead canary buried in the sewing basket is a symbol of her thwarted capacity for joy.

Trifles may be a quiet play, even a slight one; yet few dramas so faithfully reflect the concerns of the modernist moment. In its emotional expressionism, its fidelity to regional dialect, its deft attention to psychological trauma, its depiction of the elasticity of morality, its concern with interior and exterior gender politics, its anticipation of feminism and, perhaps above all, its preoccupation with language and its limits, it deserves a place alongside Pound's *Cantos* and Eliot's *The Waste Land* as one of the outstanding monuments of literary modernism.

NOTES

1. T. E. Hulme, *Speculations*, ed. Herbert Read (London: Routledge and Kegan Paul, 1960), p. 133.
2. For more on the contested nature of the origins of Imagism see Robert Hampson and Will Montgomery, 'Innovations in Poetry', in Peter Brooker, Andrzej Gasiorek, Deborah Longworth and Andrew Thacker (eds), *The Oxford Handbook of Modernisms* (Oxford: Oxford University Press, 2010), pp. 63–6. See also, Patrick McGuinness, 'Imagism', in David Bradshaw and Kevin Dettmar (eds), *A Companion to Modernist Literature and Culture* (Oxford: Blackwell, 2006), pp. 181–8.
3. Richard Aldington, *Life for Life's Sake: A Book of Reminiscences* (London: Viking Press, 1968), p. 122.
4. T. E. Hulme, *Speculations*, p. 122.
5. F. S. Flint, 'The History of Imagism', *The Egoist*, 2.5 (1 May 1915), p. 71.
6. Ezra Pound, *Selected Letters 1907–1941 of Ezra Pound*, ed. D. D. Paige (New York: New Directions, 1950), p. 6.
7. 'Notes and Announcements', *Poetry: A Magazine of Verse*, 1.2 (November 1912), p. 65.
8. F. S. Flint, 'Imagisme', *Poetry: A Magazine of Verse*, 1.6 (March 1913), p. 199.
9. Ezra Pound, 'A Few Don'ts By an Imagiste', *A Magazine of Verse*, 1.6 (March 1913), p. 200.
10. *Selected Letters 1907–1941 of Ezra Pound*, ed. D. D. Paige, p. 38.
11. Amy Lowell, 'The Imagists: "H. D." and John Gould Fletcher', in *Tendencies in Modern American Poetry* (New York: Macmillan, 1917), p. 255.
12. Richard Aldington, *Life for Life's Sake*, pp. 130–1.
13. See *Poetry: A Magazine of Verse*, 37.5 (February 1931). Cited in Peter Jones's 'Introduction' to Peter Jones (ed.), *Imagist Poetry* (London: Penguin, 1972), p. 37.
14. W. B. Yeats, 'Discoveries', in *Essays and Introductions* (London: Macmillan, 1967), p. 267.
15. T. S. Eliot, 'Tradition and the Individual Talent' (1919), in

Selected Prose of T. S. Eliot, ed. Frank Kermode (London: Faber and Faber, 1975), p. 40.

16. Christopher W. E. Bigsby, *Modern American Drama, 1945–1990* (Cambridge: Cambridge University Press, 1992), p. 1.
17. James A. Herne, *Margaret Fleming* (New York: Appleton-Century-Crofts, [1890] 1957), p. 543. Available online: http://gateway.proquest.com.ezproxy.lib.le.ac.uk/openurl/openurl?ctx_ver=Z39.88-2003&xri:pqil:res_ver=0.2&r es_id=xri:lion&rft_id=xri:lion:ft:dr:Z000780783:0 (accessed 13 December 2011).
18. Elmer L. Rice, *The Adding Machine* (New York: Samuel French, 1956), p. 29.
19. Broadcast, 15 March 1942. Cited in *'Ezra Pound Speaking': Radio Speeches of World War II*, ed. Leonard W. Dobb (Westport: Greenwood Press, 1978), not paginated. Available online: http://www.vho.org/aaargh/fran/livres10/Pound Radiospeeches.pdf (accessed 23 January 2012).
20. Cited in Richard Ellmann, *Eminent Domain: Yeats Among Wilde, Joyce, Pound, Eliot and Auden* (New York: Oxford University Press, 1967), p. 66.
21. See Mary Ellis Gibson, *Epic Reinvented: Ezra Pound and the Victorians* (Ithaca: Cornell University, 1995), p. 84.
22. Ezra Pound, 'In a Station at the Metro', in *Personae*, ed. Lea Baechler and A. Walton Litz (New York: New Directions, 1991), p. 111.
23. Ezra Pound, 'The Return', in *Personae*, p. 69.
24. This section will focus on just the first three cantos.
25. Ezra Pound, *ABC of Reading* (New York: New Directions, [1934] 2010), pp. 21–2.
26. Ezra Pound, *The Cantos* (New York: New Directions, [1962] 1996), p. 3. All subsequent references will appear in the text.
27. Ezra Pound, *ABC of Reading*, p. 32.
28. T. S. Eliot, 'Ulysses, Order and Myth' (1923), in *Selected Prose of T. S. Eliot*, ed. Frank Kermode, p. 176.
29. T. S. Eliot, 'A Commentary', *Criterion*, 2 (April 1924), p. 232.
30. Ezra Pound, *Selected Letters 1907–1941 of Ezra Pound*, ed. D. D. Paige, p. 157.
31. Douglas Bush, *Mythology and the Romantic Tradition in*

English Poetry (Cambridge: Harvard University Press, 1969), p. 502.

32. Joseph N. Riddel, 'H. D. and the Poetics of "Spiritual Realism"', *Contemporary Literature*, 10.4 (Autumn 1969), p. 449.
33. See Cassandra Laity, 'H. D., Modernism and the Transgressive Sexualities of Decadent-Romantic Platonism', in Margaret Dickie and Thomas Traversano (eds), *Gendered Modernism: American Women Poets and Their Readers* (Philadelphia: University of Pennsylvania Press, 1996), pp. 45–67; Rachel DuPlessis, *H. D.: The Career of That Struggle* (Bloomington: Indiana University Press, 1986); Steven Matthews, *Modernism* (London: Arnold, 2004), pp. 108–9.
34. Marianne Moore, *Complete Prose*, ed. Patricia Willis (New York: Viking, 1986), p. 82.
35. H. D., 'Hermes and the Ways', in Peter Jones (ed.), *Imagist Poetry* (London: Penguin, 2001), pp. 64–5. All subsequent references to H. D.'s poems refer to this anthology and will appear in the text.
36. William Carlos Williams, *I Wanted to Write a Poem: The Autobiography of the Works of a Poet*, ed. Edith Bell (London: Jonathan Cape, 1958), p. 17.
37. Ezra Pound, *Selected Letters 1907–1941 of Ezra Pound*, ed. D. D. Paige, pp. 7–8.
38. Ibid. pp. 3–5.
39. Ezra Pound, 'What I Feel About Walt Whitman', in *Ezra Pound: Selected Prose, 1909–1965*, ed. William Cookson (London: Faber and Faber, 1973), p. 115.
40. William Carlos Williams, *The Collected Earlier Poems* (London: MacGibbon and Kee, 1938), p. 3. Subsequent references will appear in the text.
41. William Carlos Williams, *The Autobiography of William Carlos Williams* (New York: New Directions, 1967), p. 138.
42. See Marjorie Perloff, '"To Give a Design": Williams and the Visualization of Poetry', in *Dance of the Intellect: Studies in the Poetry of the Pound Tradition* (Evanston: Northwestern University Press, 1985), p. 90.
43. William Carlos Williams, *The Selected Letters of William*

Carlos Williams, ed. John C. Thirlwall (New York: McDowell, Obolensky, 1957), p. 269.

44. William Carlos Williams, *Selected Essays* (New York: New Directions, 1969), p. 196.
45. William Carlos Williams, *The Autobiography of William Carlos Williams*, p. 390.
46. Ibid. p. 146.
47. Ibid. p. 174, p. 146. Williams notes: 'Eliot had turned his back on the possibility of reviving my world . . . If with his skill he could have been kept here to be employed by our slowly shaping drive, what strides might we not have taken! We needed him in the scheme I was half-consciously forming. I needed him: he might have become our adviser, even our hero. By his walking out on us we were stopped, for the moment, cold' (p. 174).
48. T. S. Eliot, *The Waste Land*, in *Selected Poems* (London: Faber and Faber, [1922] 1954), p. 67. All subsequent references will appear in the text.
49. Susan Glaspell, *The Road to the Temple* (Jefferson: MacFarland, [1927] 2005), pp. 253–4.
50. Eugene O'Neill, *Anna Christie*, IV, in *Three Great Plays: The Emperor Jones, Anna Christie, and The Hairy Ape* (Mineola: Dover Thrift Editions, 2005), p. 96. All subsequent references will appear in the text and refer to this collection.
51. T. S. Eliot, '*Ulysses*, Order and Myth' (1923), in *Selected Prose of T. S. Eliot*, ed. Frank Kermode, p. 176.
52. Eugene O'Neill, *Mourning Becomes Electra* (London: Nick Hern, [1931] 2002), I, v and I, ix. All subsequent references will appear in the text and refer to this edition.
53. See W. David Sievers, *Freud on Broadway: A History of Psychoanalysis and the American Drama* (New York: Hermitage House, 1970), p. 4.
54. Susan Glaspell, *The Road to the Temple*, p. 250.
55. Susan Glaspell, *Suppressed Desires: A Comedy in Two Episodes* (Boston: Dodd, Mead, 1924), p. 9. Subsequent references will appear in the text and refer to this edition.
56. In various interviews and essays, Glaspell recalled that she came to write *Trifles* because her husband had 'forced' her to

do so. For a full description of the origins of *Trifles* see Mary Heaton Vorse, *Time and the Town: A Provincetown Chronicle* (Chapel Hill: Rutgers University Press, [1942] 1991), p. 103.

57. Susan Glaspell, *Trifles* (1916), in *Plays by Susan Glaspell* (Champaign: Book Jungle, 2011), p. 19.

Conclusion: New York, 1939

On Sunday, 30 April 1939, more than 200,000 people packed into Flushing Meadows for the grand opening of the New York World's Fair. Built on the remains of a vast ash dump in the borough of Queens, it was one of the biggest expositions in human history. Like so many before it, the Fair seemed to revel in the possibilities of technology. It was opened by President Franklin D. Roosevelt, whose address was carried across the nation not merely by radio but also – for the first time – by television. It boasted its own special subway line; it had an air-conditioned theatre where audiences watched a Chrysler Plymouth being assembled before their eyes; it showed off electric typewriters and rudimentary calculators, express trains and speech synthesisers, colour photographs and nylon fabrics. 'The eyes of the Fair are on the future', declared the official brochure, 'not in the sense of peering toward the unknown nor attempting to foretell the events of tomorrow and the shape of things to come, but in the sense of presenting a new and clearer view of today in preparation for tomorrow; a view of the forces and ideas that prevail as well as the machines'.[1] This was a vision of a new United States, clean and safe, sleek and streamlined, remodelled in the fires of the machine age. Tomorrow, it seemed, had come at last.

When Henry Adams had visited the World's Columbian Exposition in 1893, the spectacle had seemed to him to capture the experience of modernity itself, with its extraordinary industrial strength, technological expertise and exciting potential for change and rebirth. In 1939, however, the mood was very different. The weather was warm, the exhibits were breathtaking and the crowds were enormous, but it was hard to miss the looming shadow of war. When Germany invaded Poland in September, the exposition was still running, and when it opened for its second season in April 1940, the Polish and Czechoslovakian pavilions were closed. 'For Peace and Freedom' read the exposition's new motto, but events overseas were making a mockery of its lofty ideals. The New York police were called to defuse a bomb in the British pavilion, the Soviet pavilion was symbolically dismantled, and by the time the Fair closed in October 1940, many European exhibitors' homelands had been crushed by the Nazi war machine, leaving them to seek refuge in the United States. The Fair featured in many popular films and stories of the day, most famously Alfred Hitchcock's screwball comedy *Mr and Mrs Smith* (1941). Yet perhaps it is telling that when Gene Raymond and Carole Lombard visit the exposition in Hitchcock's film, their ride malfunctions and they are left dangling in the air in the pouring rain. With the world increasingly consumed by bloodshed, modernity itself seemed to have broken down. And even the Fair itself, despite the excitement of the huge crowds, was widely seen as a failure. Although it recouped almost $50 million in ticket sales, costs had been far higher. In the end, the Fair Corporation – which had been symbolically located on an upper floor of the Empire State Building – was forced to declare bankruptcy. And as the United States moved towards all-out war, nothing, it seemed, better captured the bankruptcy of the modernist experiment itself.[2]

On the face of it, therefore, the 1939 New York World's Fair seems to mark the end of the modernist era. Many of its most accomplished figures, such as Ezra Pound, Gertrude Stein and F. Scott Fitzgerald, were either long past their best or shuffling off the stage. As the nation turned its attention to the struggle against first the Axis powers and then Soviet Communism, the drive to experiment, to 'make it new', seemed to have lost some of its appeal. And although the likes of Ernest Hemingway and T. S. Eliot endured into the 1960s, they were no longer the young meteors of yesteryear; after years railing against the literary establishment, they had become an establishment in their own right. In an age of capitalist abundance, television advertising and mass consumerism, wrote the novelist John Barth in 1967, it was time for a younger generation to turn their backs on the legacy of the late Victorians and to break away from the 'literature of exhaustion'. It was time, he thought, to embrace 'postmodernism'. 'My ideal Postmodernist author neither merely repudiates nor merely imitates either his 20th-century Modernist parents or his 19th-century premodernist grandparents', he wrote a decade later. 'He has the first half of our century under his belt, but not on his back. Without lapsing into moral or artistic simplism, shoddy craftsmanship, Madison Avenue venality, or either false or real naiveté, he nevertheless aspires to a fiction more democratic in its appeal'.[3] For Barth, and for many of his contemporaries, the high modernist moment had passed.

But was that really true? Does it really make sense to think of a clean break between modernism and postmodernism? The answer, I think, is that it does not. Much of what we commonly think of as postmodern – playful narratives by the likes of Barth, Thomas Pynchon and Don DeLillo, for example – is so clearly indebted to modernism that it seems almost wilfully arbitrary to draw a stark line between the two.[4] Like modernists, postmodernists often saw themselves as an avant-garde; yet like many modernists, they deliberately blurred the lines between high and low culture. Fitzgerald and Hemingway did not see themselves as undemocratic writers; indeed, one of modernism's defining characteristics is surely that, despite the political arch-conservatism of Pound and Eliot, it opened the text to a distinctly democratic cacophony of competing voices. Modernists, like their postmodern heirs, were often torn between history and future, forever looking backwards to the classical past, but also looking forward, forging new identities for themselves and a new civilisation from the ruins of yesteryear. We think of postmodernism in terms of irony, pastiche, intertexuality and meta-fictions; one of the abiding traits of postmodern literature is the story within a story. But you have merely to open a copy of *The Waste Land* or *The Great Gatsby*, and you find yourself in a bewildering world of competing voices and contradictory stories, shot through with a black sense of humour, yet built on layer upon layer of literary allusions and classical references. If they were written today, critics would surely rush to hail them as monuments of postmodernism. The only thing that disbars them is the date of publication.

The truth is that we do not merely live in a world the modernists made; we live in the very same world they inhabited. As a purely chronological concept, American literary modernism is widely agreed to have petered out at the end of the 1930s. But its concerns remain as compelling as ever. The modernists lived in a world haunted by nightmares of war, decay, decadence, contagion, and economic and cultural disintegration. So do we; indeed, in an age of deep environmental anxiety, Eliot's image of the arid wasteland seems more apposite than ever. Our world, like theirs, is overshadowed by consumer capitalism, mass communications and shifting racial and gender identities; by fragmentation and fluidity; by chaos and confusion. Our lives are dominated by industry, science and technology; more than ever, we are shaped by the experience of the modern city. Like our predecessors in the 1910s and 1920s, we tell ourselves stories, hastily assembled from the relics of history; these fragments we have shored against our ruins. In purely canonical terms the modernist moment, the moment of Pound and Eliot, Fitzgerald and Hemingway, O'Neill and Glaspell, Faulkner and H. D. and Hughes and Toomer, may have long since passed. But in its ambitions and anxieties, its dreams and nightmares, it is with us still.

NOTES

1. Bill Cotter, *The 1939–1940 New York World's Fair* (Charleston: Arcadia Publishing, 2009), p. 9.
2. *New York Times*, 5 July 1940; and see Joseph Mauro's excellent book *Twilight at the World of Tomorrow: Genius, Madness, Murder, and the 1939 World's Fair on the Brink of War* (New York: Ballantine, 2010).
3. John Barth, *The Friday Book: Essays and Other Non-Fiction* (Baltimore: Johns Hopkins Press, 1984), pp. 62–76, 193–206.
4. For a sustained discussion of the links between DeLillo and

modernism (via Joyce) see Catherine Morley, *The Quest for Epic in Contemporary American Fiction: John Updike, Philip Roth and Don DeLillo* (New York: Routledge, 2009).

Student Resources

GLOSSARY OF KEY TERMS

Abstraction

An 'abstraction' is a concept or idea, rather than an object. In art or literature, therefore, 'abstract' work tries to evoke sensations or ideas, rather than merely depicting objective reality. Abstract art became increasingly popular in the early decades of the twentieth century, thanks largely to pioneers such as Matisse, Picasso and Kandinsky.

American Renaissance

In the arts generally, the period from roughly 1830 to 1870, marking a new self-confidence in the culture of a booming economic powerhouse. In literature specifically, the American Renaissance is often associated with New England and New York writers such as Ralph Waldo Emerson, Henry David Thoreau and Walt Whitman, driven by both the quasi-religious idealism of the transcendentalist movement and a new, self-consciously optimistic kind of American cultural nationalism.

Civil War

Perhaps the decisive moment in American history, the Civil War was precipitated by the election of the anti-slavery Republican Abraham Lincoln in November 1860. When eleven Southern slave states broke away to form the Confederacy, war broke out in April 1861. It took four years to defeat and conquer the Southern secessionists. The war kept the Union together and smashed the institution of slavery; it also confirmed the emergence of the North as the most progressive and dynamic part of the nation.

Constructivism

Emerging out of the chaos of the Russian Revolution in 1919, Constructivism developed out of Futurism, placing an emphasis on the social function of art. It was often deliberately utilitarian and mechanical, with a strong socialist or utopian element, and embraced all things industrial, urban and modern.

Conspicuous consumption

Coined by the social theorist Thorstein Veblen in his book *The Theory of the Leisure Class* (1899), conspicuous consumption refers to extravagant spending by an elite purely to buttress its status or to secure approval – for example, spending on fashionable clothes, elaborate architecture or expensive artworks. It provoked enormous criticism from social critics at the turn of the twentieth century; many of the characters in the novels of the day, from *The Portrait of a Lady* to *The Great Gatsby*, are devoted to conspicuous consumption.

Cubism

Pioneered in the 1900s and 1910s by Pablo Picasso and Georges Braque, Cubist artwork tried to break up objects into abstract surfaces and geometrical patterns, often reassembling them in unusual or surprising ways. Cubists often encouraged spectators to look at objects in different ways at once: in literature, meanwhile, writers such as William Faulkner used multiple viewpoints and different narrators to present several different ways of seeing the same event.

Dada

Born in Zurich in 1916, Dada was an artistic movement lasting about six years. It mocked bourgeois conventions and artistic standards, and deliberately provoked audiences and readers, often through techniques such as collages and montages. Its principal figures included Marcel Duchamp, Tristan Tzara and Hugo Ball; many later embraced surrealism or other modern art movements.

Expressionism

Originating above all in Germany and central Europe in the first years of the twentieth century, Expressionism placed a heavy emphasis on subjective viewpoints and emotional reactions, often presenting artworks heavy with suffering or angst. A typical proto-Expressionist artwork might be Munch's famous portrait *The Scream*: as in Expressionist literature, the content is highly influenced, even distorted, by the emotional effect.

Fascism

Fascism emerged in Europe as a reaction to the trauma of the First World War. Steeped in violence, fascism rejected the compromises of parliamentary democracy and argued that only national renewal, often based on the strong leadership of one party or one man, could banish degeneracy and decay. In its original form it was often deeply anti-capitalist, yet many fascists enthusiastically embraced urban modernism, regarding it as an antidote to the sentimentality and corruption of the past.

Fugitive Movement

The Fugitives were a group of Southern poets clustered around the magazine *The Fugitive*, published at Vanderbilt University from

1922 to 1925. Fascinated by the disappearing Old South, and often highly sceptical of the virtues of modernity, they overlapped with, and anticipated, the Southern Agrarians.

Futurism

Founded by the Italian writer Filippo Marinetti in 1909, Futurism enthusiastically embraced the car, the machine, speed, youth, technology and violence. Turning their backs on the past, Futurists threw themselves into the pursuit of modernity, rejecting artistic conventions and glorying in the chaos of the city. Their enterprise petered out in the First World War, but had a profound influence on movements such as Dada, Constructivism and Vorticism.

Imagism

Imagism was a British and American poetic movement in the first years of the twentieth century, associated above all with the likes of Richard Aldington, Ezra Pound and H. D. Experimenting with radical verse forms, they tried to eliminate all unnecessary words, believing that greater austerity would allow a more direct treatment of the object being described. For T. S. Eliot, 'the starting-point of modern poetry is the group denominated "imagists" in London about 1910'.

Impressionism

A nineteenth-century art movement based above all in France, which reacted to the development of photography by trying to capture on canvas the play of light, the effect of movement and the overall visual *impression*, rather than the objective reality, of a given scene. Key figures included Claude Monet, Pierre-Auguste Renoir and Edgar Degas; though enormously popular today, impressionist painters were often reviled at the time.

Jazz Age

The Jazz Age is a label often used to describe the 1920s (see also the 'Roaring Twenties'), evoking the glamour, excitement, excess and consumerism of the decade after the First World War. The rise of jazz is often seen as an indelible part of 1920s culture; since it was associated with African Americans, nightclubs and the booming American city, it became a symbol of cosmopolitanism and sophistication.

Modernism

Modernism is a notoriously slippery term; in very basic terms, though, it refers to Western culture, art and literature between roughly 1890 and 1940. In particular, it describes artists and writers who grappled with the issues of urbanisation, science, technology, social fragmentation and the opportunities and flaws of booming industrial capitalism. It can be seen as a reaction against Victorian realism, a response to the First World War, or even an enthusiasm for the possibilities of the future. But there were many different kinds of modernism, and elements can be found in almost all literary work of the period.

Mise en abyme

Literally, 'placed into the abyss': in literature, a technique in which there is a play of texts within a text, with one story framed by, and often reflecting, another. A good cinematic example would be the film *Inception* (a 'dream within a dream'); for a literary example, see Nella Larsen's *Passing*.

Modernity

The experience of being modern; in historical terms, the experience of the West after about 1700, marked by the emergence of big cities, the growth of industry, the expansion of literacy, the decline of organised religion and the rise of science and technology.

Nativism

Nativism in the United States has a long history, and essentially means anti-immigration sentiment. Throughout American history, nativists have argued that particular ethnic groups (originally the Germans, then the Irish, the Italians, eastern European Jews, and so on) were not 'true' Americans and were undermining the nation's integrity. It was particularly strong in periods of high immigration, such as the 1890s and the 1920s.

Naturalism

An ultra-realist literary movement from roughly the 1880s onwards, marked by a close attention to the details of ordinary working-class and middle-class life. Naturalist writers were highly influenced by Darwin's ideas of evolution, and often sought to show how heredity and environment shaped the lives of their characters. Their works were often deeply pessimistic and broke new ground in depicting sex, crime and poverty; the most famous example is the French novelist Emile Zola.

New Criticism

A school of literary criticism that developed during the 1930s and 1940s, inspired by the work of Allen Tate, Robert Penn Warren and John Crowe Ransom (the 'Southern Agrarians'). New Criticism tried to set aside the details of the author's life, his background, the historical context and questions of moral judgement, focusing narrowly on the text itself. Emphasising meticulous close reading, it dominated American scholarship until the early 1970s.

Pantheism

Pantheism is a belief that Nature and God are effectively the same thing; pantheists argue that God *is* creation. It became highly popular with Romantic poets like Wordsworth and Coleridge in Britain, before being taken up by American transcendentalists such as Emerson and Whitman.

Postmodernism

An even slipperier concept than modernism itself, the label 'postmodernism' describes the intellectual movement that dominated Western culture after about 1940. Postmodernism often tries to 'deconstruct' or undermine grand narratives and big ideas, arguing that there is no such thing as absolute truth, and that even reality itself is a social and linguistic 'construct'. Card-carrying postmodernists place a heavy emphasis on diversity, plurality and relativism; they reject empiricism and realism; they often reject earnest ideological or religious commitments; and their work is often dominated by a strong sense of contingency, irony and playfulness.

Pragmatism

Associated with American philosophers such as William James and John Dewey, pragmatism emphasised the importance of arguing from empirical reality, rather than from philosophical abstractions. Pragmatism is often seen as supremely sceptical in response to epistemological uncertainly, but it is also a philosophy of action.

Primitivism

A late-nineteenth-century artistic movement that tried to borrow ideas and motifs from outside the Western developed world, the most famous example being the painter Paul Gauguin's use of Tahitian imagery. Primitivism reflected a deep anxiety about technological modernity; while clearly informed by colonial imperialism, it was also an attempt to strip away urban capitalism and get 'back to basics'.

Progressivism

The progressive era refers to the last decade of the nineteenth century and first two decades of the twentieth, when American politics was largely dominated by the spirit of rational, optimistic, 'progressive' reform. Progressives tended to be urban, well educated, wealthy and middle-class; they believed in harnessing the power of science and the state to bring social improvement.

Realism

In fiction, the attempt to capture objective 'reality' as faithfully as possible, usually through detailed descriptions of everyday life. Realism is associated above all with the mid-to-late Victorian novel, from British and European authors such as Eliot, Balzac, Flaubert and Zola to Americans such as Stephen Crane and William Dean Howells.

Reconstruction

Reconstruction is the label usually given to the period immediately after the American Civil War, lasting from 1865 to roughly 1877. In particular, it refers to the attempt to 'reconstruct' the defeated Confederate South through federal legislation and military intervention – an enterprise that was eventually undermined by Northern exhaustion and the armed resistance of the Ku Klux Klan.

Southern Agrarians

A group of twelve Southern writers, historians and essayists, all with roots in the old Confederacy, who published the manifesto *I'll Take My Stand* in 1930, pleading for a return to the land and to traditional, old-fashioned moral and cultural values as an antidote to urban, capitalist materialism.

Surrealism

Developing from the Dada movement during the 1910s, surrealism aimed to shock and surprise the viewer or the reader, moving behind the limits of rationalism. 'Surrealism', wrote the movement's founder, André Breton, 'is based on the belief in the superior reality of certain forms of previously neglected associations, in the omnipotence of dream, in the disinterested play of thought.'

Symbolism

Symbolism was a largely late Victorian literary and artistic movement, inspired by the works of Edgar Allen Poe and Charles Baudelaire, reacting against the empirical, middle-class basis of realism, and trying to evoke sensory and sensual experiences through a succession of dream-like images. Nostalgic, mystical and often disturbing, it was conceived as a form of escape from the reality of Victorian urban capitalism.

Transcendentalism

Developing out of Unitarian Christianity in the 1830s and 1840s, and associated above all with Ralph Waldo Emerson, transcendentalism tried to move beyond the limits of organised religion, encouraging individuals to embrace the mysteries of the divine. The aim, Emerson wrote, was 'to look at the world with new eyes . . . As fast as you conform your life to the pure idea in your mind, that will unfold its great proportions'.

Transnationalism

Coined by the critic Randolph Bourne in 1916, 'transnationalism' calls for writers and scholars to break out from their national boundaries, developing a new kind of literary culture appropriate for a globalised age. Transnationalism emphasises the links between writers from across the world, and explicitly transnationalist scholars try to undermine the notion of 'national' literatures.

Vorticism

Developing from Cubism and Imagism in 1914, Vorticism was a largely British movement associated with Wyndham Lewis and his magazine *Blast!*, which only ran for two issues. Vorticists keenly embraced speed, movement and the machine age; impatient to break with the past, they celebrated motion and dynamism.

ELECTRONIC RESOURCES AND REFERENCE SOURCES

- African American Perspectives: Pamphlets from the Daniel A. P. Murray Collection, 1818–1907, http://memory.loc.gov/
Full text version of speeches and important documents relating to African American history
- British Association for American Studies: http://www.baas.ac.uk
Offers a number of links to publications from Edinburgh University Press, Cambridge University Press and Microform Academic Publishing. Carries an invaluable database of American newspaper resources in UK institutions.
- Eccles Centre, British Library: http://www.bl.uk/ecclescentre
Based at the British Library, which carries the foremost collection of books, manuscripts, journals and newspapers outside the United States.
- Henry James's prefaces: http://www.henryjames.org.uk/prefaces/text01.htm
All the prefaces available to download and search.
- Internet Archive: http://www.archive.org/
Repository of free online books, newspapers and magazines.
- MAPS / Modern American Poetry: http://www.english.illinois.edu/maps/
Excellent and thorough guide to American poetry with lots of critical essays and snippets from relevant books and articles.
- Modernist Magazines Project: http://www.cts.dmu.ac.uk/exist/mod_mag/index.htm
An invaluable resource, the Modernist Magazines Project offers free access to a wide range of modernist publications.
- New York City Timeline: http://www.gothamcenter.org/features/timeline/
Chronological, searchable, annotated timeline with photographic illustrations.
- Perspectives in American Literature: http://www.csustan.edu/english/reuben/pal/table.html
Essays and bibliographies on the history of American fiction and on a range of individual authors.
- Project Gutenberg: http://www.gutenberg.org/
Original repository of free online books.

- Provincetown Playhouse: http://www.provincetownplayhouse.com/history.html
  Links to short essays and bibliographies on a range of American dramatists.
- The Academy of American Poets: http://www.poets.org/
  Links to short essays and bibliographies on a range of American poets.
- The Library of America: http://www.loa.org/
  Online catalogue of Library of America holdings and publications.
- The Literary Encyclopaedia: http://www.litencyc.com/
  Online encyclopaedia with plenty of relevant entries for American modernism.
- The Modernist Journal Project: http://dl.lib.brown.edu/mjp/
  Excellent resources which offers free access to a wide range of modernist publications, including *Poetry* and *Others*.
- The Modernism Lab at Yale: http://modernism.research.yale.edu/
  Virtual space dedicated to collaborative research into the roots of literary modernism.
- The Poetry Foundation: http://www.poetryfoundation.org/
  Links to short essays and bibliographies on a range of American poets.
- Voices from the Gaps (Women Writers and Artists of Color): http://voices.cla.umn.edu/
  Essays and bibliographies on a variety of writers who are often omitted from literary canons.

QUESTIONS FOR DISCUSSION

Introduction

- What differentiates American literary modernism from other national modernisms?
- 'Modern, modernism, modernisms . . . so heterogeneous a category is of little use'. Is modernism a useful concept?

CHAPTER 1: The Making of American Modernism

- 'Though typically described as a twentieth-century movement, American modernism is actually a nineteenth-century phenomenon.' Is that really true?
- Why might Ralph Waldo Emerson be considered important to American modernism?
- Was Walt Whitman the father of modern American poetry?
- Consider Henry Adams's faith in the feminine as a modern antidote to the 'masculine' entrepreneurialism and scientific rationalism of the late nineteenth century.
- In what ways could Henry James be described as an experimental writer?
- How far can we apply W. E. B. Du Bois's notion of 'twoness' (expressed in *The Souls of Black Folk*) to all Americans?

CHAPTER 2: Tales of New York City: The Birth of the Modern Metropolis

- 'New York is both the emblem and site of modernism in its fullest manifestation.' Discuss with reference to at least two modernist texts.
- How is the architectural landscape of the city reflected in the immigrant characters in *Manhattan Transfer*? How does this compare with similar treatments in other texts of the era?
- To what extent does Anzia Yezierska's presentation of the city conform to or undermine the notion of the melting pot?
- Discuss the relationship between conspicuous consumption and the city in Nella Larsen's *Passing*.
- Why might Edith Wharton be described as a 'reluctant modernist'? Discuss with reference to *The House of Mirth*.
- Do you agree that Theodore Dreiser was 'a modern without the doctrine of modernism'?
- How does Hart Crane respond to the challenge of representing the ever-evolving nature of New York City in *The Bridge*?

CHAPTER 3: Regional American Modernism

- Do you agree that regionalism and modernism are polar opposites?
- In 1922 Willa Cather declared that 'the world [had] split in two'. What did she mean, and how is this sentiment expressed in the themes and formal composition of *The Professor's House* and *My Ántonia*?
- How do past and present intersect in the works of Ellen Glasgow?
- '*The Sound and the Fury* is above all a demonstration of the inadequacy of language.' Do you agree?
- To what extent is Allen Tate a nostalgic poet?
- How did John Crowe Ransom and Robert Penn Warren differ, if at all, in their poetic treatment of Southern history?

CHAPTER 4: Home Thoughts from Abroad: The Lost Generation

- 'Exile and displacement are recurring themes in modernist literature and recurrent features of modernist writers' lives.' Do you agree, and how does either Fitzgerald, or Hemingway, or Stein or Barnes thematically and formally treat the subject of exile?
- How far can F. Scott Fitzgerald be considered a distinctly and specifically American writer?
- To what extent can we see Ernest Hemingway's fiction as a response to the trauma of the First World War?
- Is it fair to consider Djuna Barnes a predominantly gay writer?
- 'A number of crazy men and women are writing stuff which remarkably passes for important composition among certain persons who should know better' (James Thurber). How important and influential were the works of Gertrude Stein?

CHAPTER 5: 'When Harlem Was in Vogue': African American Modernism

- Does the writing of the Harlem Renaissance constitute a distinct and separate strand of American modernism?

- How does the poetry of Langston Hughes depict both formally and thematically the realities of the Jazz Age?
- 'Harlem is where sex and race meet.' Discuss with reference to Carl Van Vechten's *Nigger Heaven*.
- 'In poem after poem, Cullen states or implies that the Negro in America is a perpetual alien.' Discuss with regard to any of Countee Cullen's poems.
- Discuss the issues of race, resistance and nationhood in the poetry of Claude McKay.
- To what extent do Zora Neale Hurston's works reflect her interest in African American folklore?
- How far does Jean Toomer's literary experimentalism reflect his attitude to the plight of African Americans?

CHAPTER 6: Make it New!: Experiments in Poetry and Drama

- 'It is in poetry that the most radical innovations in modern literature are to be found.' Do you agree?
- Ezra Pound – charlatan or genius?
- Discuss Hilda Doolittle's deployment of the 'mythical method' in relation to any of her poems.
- How might William Carlos Williams be described as the heir to Walt Whitman? Pay attention to form, language and dialect in your response.
- Does it make sense to consider T. S. Eliot as an American poet, a British poet, both, or neither?
- In what ways might Eugene O'Neill's plays be considered modern?
- How far might we consider Susan Glaspell a feminist playwright?

GUIDE TO FURTHER READING

General

Ardis, Ann L. and Leslie W. Lewis (eds), *Women's Experience of Modernity, 1875–1945* (Baltimore: Johns Hopkins University Press, 2003).

Beer, Janet and Bridget Bennett (eds), *Special Relationships: Anglo-American Affinities and Antagonisms, 1854–1936* (Manchester: Manchester University Press, 2002).

Berkowitz, Edward D., *Mass Appeal: The Formative Age of the Movies, Radio and T.V.* (Cambridge: Cambridge University Press, 2010).

Bradbury, Malcolm, *The Modern American Novel* (Oxford: Oxford University Press, 1983).

Bradbury, Malcolm and James McFarlane (eds), *Modernism: A Guide to European Literature, 1890-1930* (London: Penguin, 1976).

Bradbury, Malcolm and David Palmer (eds), *The American Novel and the Nineteen Twenties* (London: Edward Arnold, 1971).

Bradshaw, David (ed.), *A Concise Companion to Modernism* (Oxford: Blackwell, 2003).

Bradshaw, David and Kevin J. H. Dettmar (eds), *A Companion to Modernist Literature and Culture* (Oxford: Blackwell, 2006).

Brogan, Hugh, *Penguin History of the United States of America* (London: Penguin, 1985).

Brooker, Peter, Andrzej Gasiorek, Deborah Longworth and Andrew Thacker (eds), *The Oxford Handbook of Modernisms* (Oxford: Oxford University Press, 2010).

Brooker, Peter and Andrew Thacker (eds), *Geographies of Modernism* (New York: Routledge, 2005).

Crunden, Robert M., *Body and Soul: The Making of American Modernism* (New York: Basic Books, 2000).

Currell, Susan, *American Culture in the 1920s* (Edinburgh: Edinburgh University Press, 2009).

Diepeveen, Leonard, *The Difficulties of Modernism* (New York: Routledge, 2003).

Gray, Richard, *A History of American Literature* (Oxford: Blackwell, 2004).

Halliwell, Martin, *Transatlantic Modernism: Moral Dilemmas in Modernist Fiction* (Edinburgh: Edinburgh University Press, 2006).

Kalaidjian, Walter (ed.), *The Cambridge Companion to American Modernism* (Cambridge: Cambridge University Press, 2005).

Kolocotroni, Vassiliki, Jane Goldman and Olga Taxidou (eds),

Modernism: An Anthology of Sources and Documents (Edinburgh: Edinburgh University Press, 1998).
Levenson, Michael (ed.), *The Cambridge Companion to Modernism* (Cambridge: Cambridge University Press, 1999).
McKible, Adam, *The Space and Place of Modernism: The Little Magazine in New York* (New York: Routledge, 2002).
Matthews, Steven, *Modernism* (London: Arnold, 2004).
Matthews, Steven (ed.), *Modernism: A Sourcebook* (Basingstoke: Palgrave Macmillan, 2008).
Morley, Catherine and Alex Goody (eds), *American Modernism: Cultural Transactions* (Durham: Cambridge Scholar's Publishing, 2009).
Nicholls, Peter, *Modernisms* (London: Macmillan, 1995).
Reynolds, David, *America: Empire of Liberty* (London: Penguin, 2009).
Streissguth, Thomas, *The Roaring Twenties* (New York: Infobase Publishing, 2007).
Wilson, Sarah, *Melting-Pot Modernism* (Ithaca: Cornell University Press, 2010).

CHAPTER 1: The Making of American Modernism

The American Renaissance

Matthiessen, F. O., *American Renaissance: Art and Expression in the Age of Emerson and Whitman* (New York: Oxford University Press, 1941).
Wilson, Theodore, *Formalism, Experience and the Making of American Literature in the Nineteenth Century* (Cambridge: Cambridge University Press, 2007).

Ralph Waldo Emerson

Levin, Jonathan, *The Poetics of Transition: Emerson, Pragmatism and American Literary Modernism* (Durham, NC: Duke University Press, 1999).
Lysaker, John, *Emerson and Self-Culture* (Indianapolis: Indiana University Press, 2008).

Poirier, Richard, *The Renewal of Literature: Emersonian Reflections* (New York: Random House, 1987).

Porte, Joel and Sandra Morris (eds), *The Cambridge Companion to Ralph Waldo Emerson* (Cambridge: Cambridge University Press, 1999).

Walt Whitman

Lawson, Andrew, *Walt Whitman and the Class Struggle* (Iowa City: Iowa University Press, 2006).

Miller, James E., *The American Quest for a Supreme Fiction: Whitman's Legacy in the Personal Epic* (London: University of Chicago Press, 1979).

Price, Kenneth M., *Whitman and Tradition: The Poet in His Century* (New Haven: Yale University Press, 1990).

Henry Adams

Adams, Henry, *The Letters of Henry Adams*, ed. J. C. Levenson, Ernest Samuels, Charles Vandersee and Viola Hopkins Winner (Cambridge, MA: Harvard University Press, 1982–8).

Comley, Nancy R., 'Henry Adams' Feminine Fictions: The Economics of Maternity', *American Literary Realism*, 22.1 (Fall 1989), pp. 3–16.

Rowe, John Carlos, *Henry Adams and Henry James: The Emergence of a Modern Consciousness* (Ithaca: Cornell University Press, 1976).

Rowe, John Carlos (ed.), *New Essays on The Education of Henry Adams* (New York: Cambridge University Press, 1994).

Henry James

Edel, Leon (ed.), *The House of Fiction; Essays on the Novel by Henry James* (London: Rupert Hart Davis, 1957).

Freedman, Jonathan (ed.), *The Cambridge Companion to Henry James* (Cambridge: Cambridge University Press, 1998).

Haralson, Eric, *Henry James and Queer Modernity* (Cambridge: Cambridge University Press, 2003).

Perosa, Sergio, *Henry James and the Experimental Novel* (New York: New York University Press, 1983).

W. E. B. Du Bois

Campbell, James, 'Du Bois and James', *Transactions of the Charles S. Peirce Society*, 28.3 (Summer 1992), pp. 569–81.
Du Bois, W. E. B., *The Souls of Black Folk* (London: Penguin, [1903] 1989).
Du Bois, W. E. B., 'Criteria of Negro Art', *The Crisis*, 32 (October 1926), pp. 290–7.

CHAPTER 2: Tales of New York City: The Birth of the Modern Metropolis

Urban Modernisms

Brooker, Peter, *New York Fictions: Modernity, Postmodernism, The New Modern* (London: Pearson, 1996).
Burrows, Edwin G. and Mike Wallace, *Gotham: A History of New York City to 1898* (Oxford: Oxford University Press, 1998).
Goldsmith, Arnold L., *The Modern American Urban Novel: Nature as 'Interior Structure'* (Detroit: Wayne State University Press, 1991).
O'Connell, Shaun, *Remarkable, Unspeakable New York: A Literary History* (Boston: Beacon Press, 1995).
Stansell, Christine, *American Moderns: Bohemian New York and the Creation of a New Century* (New York: Metropolitan Books, 2000).

John Dos Passos

Ludington, Townsend, *John Dos Passos* (New York: Dutton, 1980).
Nanney, Lisa, *John Dos Passos Revisited* (London: Twayne, 1998).
Spencer Carr, Virginia, *Dos Passos: A Life* (Evanston: Northwestern University Press, 2004).
Wagner-Martin, Linda, *Dos Passos: Artist as American* (Austin: University of Texas Press, 1979).

Anzia Yezierska

Ebest, Ron, 'Anzia Yezierska and the Popular Debate over the Jews', *MELUS*, 25.1 (2000), pp. 105–27.

Gelfant, Blanche, *The American City Novel* (Norman: University of Oklahoma Press, 1954).

Yezierska, Anzia, 'America and I', in *The Open Cage: An Anzia Yezierska Collection*, ed. Alice Kessler-Harris (New York: Persea, 1979), pp. 20–33.

Nella Larsen

Cutter, Martha J., 'Sliding Significations: Passing as a Narrative and Textual Strategy in Nella Larsen's Fiction', in Elaine Ginsberg (ed.), *Passing and the Fictions of Identity* (Durham, NC: Duke University Press, 1996), pp. 75–100.

Davis, Thadious M., *Nella Larsen, Novelist of the Harlem Renaissance: A Woman's Life Unveiled* (Baton Rouge: Louisiana State University Press, 1995).

Larson, Charles R., *Invisible Darkness: Jean Toomer and Nella Larsen* (Iowa City: University of Iowa Press, 1993).

Edith Wharton

Lee, Hermione, *Edith Wharton* (London: Chatto and Windus, 2007).

Lewis Thompson, Stephanie, *Influencing America's Taste: Realism in the Worlds of Wharton, Cather and Hurst* (Gainesville: University of Florida Press, 2002).

Singley, Carol J., *Edith Wharton: Matters of Mind and Spirit* (Cambridge: Cambridge University Press, 1998).

Theodore Dreiser

Kazin, Alfred, *The Stature of Theodore Dreiser* (Evanston: Indiana University Press, 1955).

Matthiessen, F. O., *Theodore Dreiser* (London: Methuen, 1951).

Pizer, Donald, *The Novels of Theodore Dreiser: A Critical Study* (Minneapolis: University of Minnesota, 1976).

Shapiro, Charles, *Theodore Dreiser: Our Bitter Patriot* (Carbondale: Southern Illinois University Press, 1962).

Hart Crane

Butterfield, R. W., *The Broken Arc: A Study of Hart Crane* (Edinburgh: Oliver and Boyd, 1969).

Frank, Waldo, 'An Introduction by Waldo Frank', in Hart Crane, *The Bridge* (New York: Liveright, [1930] 1992), pp. xvii–xxxvi.

Leibowitz, Herbert A., *Hart Crane: An Introduction to the Poetry* (New York: Columbia University, 1968).

Sugg, Richard P., *Hart Crane's The Bridge: A Description of its Life* (Tuscaloosa: University of Alabama Press, 1976).

CHAPTER 3: Regional American Modernism

Regionalism

Cayton, Andrew R. L. and Susan E. Gray (eds), *The American Midwest: Essays on Regional History* (Bloomington: Indiana University Press, 2001).

Fetterley, Judith and Marjorie Pryse, *Writing Out of Place: Regionalism, Women, and American Literary Culture* (Champaign: University of California Press, 1993).

Fitzgerald, Michael W., *Splendid Failure: Postwar Reconstruction and the American South* (Chicago: Ivan R. Dee, 2007).

Foner, Eric, *Reconstruction: America's Unfinished Revolution: People and Politics After the Civil War, 1863–1877* (New York: Harper Perennial, 1990).

Gray, Richard and Owen Robinson (eds), *A Companion to the Literature and Culture of the American South* (Oxford: Blackwell, 2004).

Willa Cather

Bell, Ian, 'Re-writing America: Origin and Gender in *The Professor's House*', *Yearbook of English Studies*, 24 (1994), pp. 12–43.
Lee, Hermione, *Willa Cather: A Life Saved Up* (London: Virago, 1997).
Lindemann, Marilee (ed.), *The Cambridge Companion to Willa Cather* (Cambridge: Cambridge University Press, 2005).
Reynolds, Guy, *Willa Cather in Context* (London: Macmillan, 1996).

Ellen Glasgow

Bond, Tonette L., 'Pastoral Transformations in *Barren Ground*', *Mississippi Quarterly*, 32 (1979), pp. 34–48.
Caldwell, Ellen M., 'Ellen Glasgow and the Southern Agrarians', *American Literature*, 56.2 (Spring 1984), pp. 203–13.
Matthews, Pamela R., *Ellen Glasgow and a Woman's Tradition* (Charlottesville: University of Virginia Press, 1994).
Rouse, Blair, *Ellen Glasgow* (New Haven: Twayne, 1962).

William Faulkner

Godden, Richard, *William Faulkner: An Economy of Complex Words* (Princeton: Princeton University Press, 2007).
Gray, Richard, *The Life of William Faulkner* (Oxford: Blackwell, 1994).
Sensibar, Judith L., *The Origins of Faulkner's Art* (Austin: University of Texas Press, 1984).
Taylor, Walter, *Faulkner's Search for a South* (Urbana: University of Illinois Press, 1983).

Fugitives and Southern Agrarians: Allen Tate, John Crowe Ransom and Robert Penn Warren

Twelve Southerners, *I'll Take My Stand: The South and the Agrarian Tradition* (Baton Rouge: Louisiana State University Press, [1930] 2006).

Dupree, Robert S., *Allen Tate and the Augustinian Imagination: A Study of Poetry* (Baton Rouge: Louisiana State University Press, 1983).
Penn Warren, Robert, 'John Crowe Ransom: A Study in Irony', *Virginia Quarterly Review*, 11 (January 1935), pp. 93–112.
Rubin, Louis D., 'The Concept of Nature in Modern Southern Poetry', *American Quarterly*, 9.1 (Spring 1957), pp. 63–71.
Stewart, John L., 'Robert Penn Warren and the Knot of History', *ELH*, 26.1 (March 1959), pp. 102–36.
Stewart, John L., *John Crowe Ransom* (Minneapolis: University of Minnesota Press, 1962).
Strandberg, Victor H., *A Colder Fire: The Poetry of Robert Penn Warren* (Lexington: University of Kentucky Press, 1965).
Squires, Radcliffe (ed.), *Allen Tate and His Work: Critical Evaluations* (Minneapolis: University of Minnesota Press, 1972).
Tate, Allen 'Narcissus as Narcissus' (1938), in *Reason in Madness: Critical Essays* (New York: G. P. Putnam, 1941), pp. 132–51.

CHAPTER 4: Home Thoughts from Abroad: The Lost Generation

The Lost Generation and the Jazz Age

Baritz, Loren, *The Culture of the Twenties* (London: Macmillan, 1970).
Cowley, Malcolm, *A Second Flowering: Works and Days of the Lost Generation* (London: Andre Deutsch, 1973).
Katz, Daniel, *American Modernism's Expatriate Scene: The Labour of Translation* (Edinburgh: Edinburgh University Press, 2007).
Rhodes, Chip, *Structures of the Jazz Age: Mass Culture, Progressive Education and Racial Disclosures in American Modernism* (London: Verso, 1998).

Gertrude Stein

DeKoven, Marianne, *A Different Language: Gertrude Stein's Experimental Writing* (Madison: University of Wisconsin Press, 1983).

Hadas, Pamela, 'Spreading the Difference: One Way to Read Gertrude Stein's *Tender Buttons*', *Twentieth Century Literature*, 24.1 (Spring 1978), pp. 57–75.

Mitrano, G. F., *Gertrude Stein: Woman Without Qualities* (Aldershot: Ashgate, 2005).

Will, Barbara, *Gertrude Stein, Modernism and the Problem of 'Genius'* (Edinburgh: Edinburgh University Press, 2000).

Ernest Hemingway

Atkins, John, *The Art of Ernest Hemingway* (London: Spring Books, 1952).

Donaldson, Scott (ed.), *The Cambridge Companion to Ernest Hemingway* (Cambridge: Cambridge University Press, 1996).

Wagner-Martin, Linda (ed.), *New Essays on The Sun Also Rises* (New York: Cambridge University Press, 1990).

Wagner-Martin, Linda (ed.), *Ernest Hemingway's The Sun Also Rises: A Casebook* (New York: Oxford University Press, 2002).

F. Scott Fitzgerald

Bloom, Harold (ed.), *Modern Critical Interpretations of The Great Gatsby* (New York: Chelsea House, 1986).

Callahan, John F., *The Illusions of a Nation: Myth and History in the Novels of F. Scott Fitzgerald* (Urbana: University of Illinois Press, 1972).

Donaldson, Scott (ed.), *Critical Essays on Fitzgerald's The Great Gatsby* (Boston: G. K. Hall, 1984).

Prigozy, Ruth (ed.), *The Cambridge Companion to F. Scott Fitzgerald* (Cambridge: Cambridge University Press, 2002).

Djuna Barnes

Baxter, Charles, 'A Self-Consuming Light: *Nightwood* and the Crisis of Modernism', *Journal of Modern Literature*, 3.5 (July 1974), pp. 1175–87.

Broe, Mary Lynn (ed.), *Silence and Power: A Reevaluation of Djuna Barnes* (Carbondale: Southern Illinois University Press, 1991).

Goody, Alex, *Modernist Articulations: A Cultural Study of Djuna Barnes, Mina Loy and Gertrude Stein* (Basingstoke: Palgrave Macmillan, 2007).

Parsons, Deborah, *Djuna Barnes* (Tavistock: Northcote House, 2003).

CHAPTER 5: 'When Harlem Was in Vogue': African American Modernism

The Harlem Renaissance

Baker, Houston, *Modernism and the Harlem Renaissance* (Chicago: University of Chicago Press, 1987).

Early, Gerald, 'Three Notes Toward a Cultural Definition of the Harlem Renaissance', *Callaloo,* 14.1 (Winter 1991), pp. 136–49.

Hutchinson, George, *The Harlem Renaissance in Black and White* (Cambridge, MA: Belknap Press of Harvard University Press, 1995).

Hutchinson, George (ed.), *The Cambridge Companion to the Harlem Renaissance* (Cambridge: Cambridge University Press, 2007).

Levering Lewis, David, *When Harlem Was in Vogue* (New York: Knopf, 1981).

Langston Hughes

Bloom, Harold (ed.), *Modern Critical Views: Langston Hughes* (New York: Chelsea House, 1989).

Chinitz, David, 'Literacy and Authenticity: The Blues Poems of Langston Hughes', *Callaloo*, 19 (Winter 1996), pp. 177–92.

Davis, Arthur P., 'The Harlem of Langston Hughes' Poetry', *Phylon*, 13.4 (Fourth Quarter 1952), pp. 276–83.

Tracy, Steven C., *Langston Hughes and the Blues* (Urbana: University of Illinois Press, 1988).

Carl Van Vechten

Coleman, Leon, *Carl Van Vechten and the Harlem Renaissance: A Critical Assessment* (New York: Garland, 1998).

Kellner, Bruce, 'Carl Van Vechten's Black Renaissance', in Armijitt Singh, William S. Shriver and Stanley Brodwin (eds), *The Harlem Renaissance: Revaluations* (New York: Garland, 1989), pp. 23–33.

Van Vechten, Carl, *'Keep A-Inchin' Along': Selected Writings of Carl Van Vechten about Black Art and Letters*, ed. Bruce Kellner (Westport: Greenwood, 1979).

Countee Cullen

Braddock, Jeremy, 'The Poetics of Conjecture: Countee Cullen's Subversive Exemplarity', *Callaloo*, 25.4 (Autumn 2002), pp. 1250–71.

Kirby, David, 'Countee Cullen's "Heritage": A Black "Waste Land"', *South Atlantic Bulletin*, 36.4 (November 1971), pp. 14–20.

Schucard, Alan R., *Countee Cullen* (Boston: Twayne, 1984).

Smith, Robert A., 'The Poetry of Countee Cullen', *Phylon*, 11.3 (First Quarter 1950), pp. 216–21.

Claude McKay

Cooper, Wayne, 'Claude McKay and the New Negro of the 1920s', *Phylon*, 25.3 (Third Quarter 1964), pp. 297–306.

Helbling, Mark, 'Claude McKay: Art and Politics', *Negro American Literature Forum*, 7.2 (Summer 1973), pp. 49–52.

McKay, Claude, 'Boyhood in Jamaica', *Phylon*, 14.2 (Second Quarter 1953), pp. 134–45.

Wagner, Jean, *Black Poets of the United States* (Urbana: University of Illinois Press, 1973).

Zora Neale Hurston

Awkward, Michael (ed.), *New Essays on Their Eyes Were Watching God* (New York: Cambridge University Press, 1990).

Gunther Kodat, Catherine, 'Bite the Hand that Writes You: Southern African American Folk Narrative and the Place of Women in *Their Eyes Were Watching God*', in Anne Goodwyn

Jones and Susan V. Donaldson (eds), *Haunted Bodies: Gender and Southern Texts* (Charlottesville: University of Virginia, 1997), pp. 319–42.

Kalb, John D., 'The Anthropological Narrator of Hurston's *Their Eyes Were Watching God*', *American Fiction*, 16 (1988), pp. 169–80.

Lupton, Mary Jane, 'Zora Neale Hurston and the Survival of the Female', *Southern Literary Journal*, 15.1 (Fall 1982), pp. 45–54.

Jean Toomer

Caldeira, Maria Isabel, 'Jean Toomer's *Cane*: The Anxiety of the Modern Artist', *Callaloo*, 25 (Autumn 1985), pp. 544–50.

Fabre, Geneviève and Michael Feith (eds), *Jean Toomer and the Harlem Renaissance* (New Brunswick: Rutgers University Press, 2001).

Krasny, Michael, 'The Aesthetic Structure of Jean Toomer's *Cane*', *Negro American Forum*, 9.2 (Summer 1975), pp. 42–3.

Whalan, Mark, *Race, Manhood, and Modernism in America* (Knoxville: University of Tennessee Press, 2007).

CHAPTER 6: 'Make it New!': Experiments in Poetry and Drama

Modern Poetry

Altieri, Charles, *Painterly Abstraction in Modernist American Poetry: The Contemporaneity of Modernism* (Cambridge: Cambridge University Press, 1989).

Carr, Helen, *The Verse Revolutionaries: Ezra Pound, H. D. and the Imagists* (London: Jonathan Cape, 2009).

Jones, Peter (ed.), *Imagist Poetry* (London: Penguin, 2001).

Schwartz, Stanford, *The Matrix of Modernism: Pound, Eliot, and Twentieth-Century Thought* (Princeton: Princeton University Press, 1985).

Ezra Pound

Cookson, William, *A Guide to the Cantos of Ezra Pound* (London: Anvil Press, 2009).
Kenner, Hugh, *The Pound Era* (Berkeley: University of California Press, 1973).
Nadel, Ira (ed.), *The Cambridge Companion to Ezra Pound* (Cambridge: Cambridge University Press, 1999).
Stallard Flory, Wendy, *Ezra Pound and the Cantos: A Record of Struggle* (New Haven: Yale University Press, 1980).

H. D.

Collecott, Diana, *H. D. and Sapphic Modernism, 1910–1950* (Cambridge: Cambridge University Press, 1999).
Duncan, Robert, *The H. D. Book*, ed. Michael Boughn and Victor Coleman (Berkeley: University of California Press, 2011).
Laity, Cassandra, *H. D. and the Victorian Fin de Siècle* (Cambridge: Cambridge University Press, 1996).
Laity, Cassandra, 'H. D., Modernism and the Transgressive Sexualities of Decadent-Romantic Platonism', in Margaret Dickie and Thomas Traversano (eds), *Gendered Modernism: American Women Poets and Their Readers* (Philadelphia: University of Pennsylvania Press, 1996), pp. 45–67.

William Carlos Williams

Cushman, Stephen, *William Carlos Williams and the Meanings of Measure* (New Haven: Yale University Press, 1985).
Doyle, Charles (ed.), *William Carlos Williams: The Critical Heritage* (Boston: Routledge and Kegan Paul, 1980).
Fredman, Stephen, 'Williams, Eliot, and the American Tradition', *Twentieth Century Literature*, 35 (Fall 1989), pp. 235–53.
Tapscott, Stephen, *American Beauty: William Carlos Williams and Modernist Whitman* (New York: Columbia University Press, 1984).

T. S. Eliot

Ackroyd, Peter, *T. S. Eliot: A Life* (London: Penguin, [1984] 1998).

Chinitz, David E., *T. S. Eliot and the Cultural Divide* (Chicago: University of Chicago Press, 2003).

Kenner, Hugh, *The Invisible Poet: T. S. Eliot* (London: Methuen, 1966).

Rainey, Lawrence, *Revisiting The Waste Land* (New Haven: Yale University Press, 2005).

Modern Drama

Berkowitz, Gerald M., *American Drama of the Twentieth Century* (London: Longman, 1992).

Richardson, Gary, *American Drama from the Colonial Period Through World War I: A Cultural History* (New York: Twayne, 1993).

Saxon, Theresa, *American Theatre: History, Context, Form* (Edinburgh: Edinburgh University Press, 2011).

Sievers, W. David, *Freud on Broadway: A History of Psychoanalysis and the American Drama* (New York: Hermitage House, 1970).

Wilmeth, Don B. and Christopher Bigsby (eds), *The Cambridge History of American Theatre, 1870–1945*, vol. 2 (Cambridge: Cambridge University Press, 1999).

Eugene O'Neill

Black, Stephen A., *Eugene O'Neill: Beyond Mourning and Tragedy* (New Haven: Yale University Press, 1999).

Bogard, Travis, *Contour in Time: The Plays of Eugene O'Neill* (New York: Oxford University Press, 1972).

Manheim, Michael (ed.), *The Cambridge Companion to Eugene O'Neill* (Cambridge: Cambridge University Press, 1998), pp. 164–77.

Wainscott, Ronald H., *Staging O'Neill: The Experimental Years* (New Haven: Yale University Press, 1988).

Susan Glaspell

Ben-Zvi, Linda, *Susan Glaspell: Her Life and Times* (Oxford: Oxford University Press, 2005).

Burke, Sally, *American Feminist Playwrights: A Critical History* (New York: Twayne, 1997).

Murphy, Brenda, *The Provincetown Players and the Culture of Modernity* (New York: Cambridge University Press, 2005).

Index

EU Authorised Representative:
Easy Access System Europe Mustamäe tee 50, 10621 Tallinn, Estonia
gpsr.requests@easproject.com

Printed and bound by CPI Group (UK) Ltd, Croydon, CR0 4YY
22/08/2025
01941805-0004